Palimpsests

Buildings, Sites, Time

Architectural Crossroads
Studies in the History of Architecture

Vol. 4

Palimpsests

Buildings, Sites, Time

Edited by

Nadja Aksamija
Clark Maines
Phillip Wagoner

BREPOLS

D/2017/0095/244
ISBN 978-2-503-57023-5

Printed in the EU on acid-free paper

Table of Contents

IV Site Transformations

Acknowledgments

This volume originated in an international symposium organized by the Art History Program and held at Wesleyan University on 28 February and 1 March 2014. The lively and thoughtful discussion provoked by the papers convinced us that the topic under examination was timely and exceptionally rich, and that a volume dealing with architectural and site palimpsests would be a welcome conceptual and methodological tool for future scholarship in several related fields.

The editors are most grateful for the insightful contributions by the symposium participants and audience members, whose papers and comments have left a deep mark on our thinking about architectural and site palimpsests. Above all, we are indebted to our keynote speakers, Finbarr Barry Flood and Alina Payne, for providing the theoretical and historiographical parameters that helped situate the papers. We would also like to thank Francesco Ceccarelli, Katherine Kuenzli, and Véronique Plesch—who could not participate in the publication—for their important contributions. Other colleagues, including Azra Aksamija, Jonathan Best, Melissa Katz, Esther Moran, and Clare Rogan helped us with the logistics of the symposium, in addition to enriching the discussion with their perceptive observations.

In conceptualizing and realizing the volume with Brepols, we were assisted by the Architectural Crossroads series editor, Lex Bosman, and by Johan Van der Beke, who most competently oversaw the publication process. We gratefully acknowledge the anonymous peer-reviewer, whose astute comments helped improve the individual chapters. We also owe a great debt of gratitude to our artist colleagues at Wesleyan, Jeffrey Schiff and David Schorr, for their outstanding work on the cover. The team of editors and designers at Brepols helped make the book look as beautiful as possible.

Many departments and programs at Wesleyan University contributed to the financing of the symposium that has led to this volume. We gratefully acknowledge the generous support of the Art and Art History Department (in particular, the Samuel Silipo '85 Distinguished Visitor's Fund and the Virgil and Juwill Topazio Fund), as well as the following: Academic Affairs—Arts and Humanities; Anthropology Department; Archaeology Program; Center for the Humanities; Classical Studies Department; College of Letters; History Department; Medieval Studies Program; Religion Department; and Romance Languages & Literatures Department (in particular, the Thomas and Catherine McMahon Fund). We are grateful to the Kenan Foundation for supporting the publication.

Introduction
Palimpsests: Buildings, Sites, Time

Nadja Aksamija, Clark Maines, and Phillip Wagoner

The term "palimpsest" originally referred to a papyrus or parchment manuscript that had been inscribed, erased, and then reinscribed with a different text.[1] In recent years, the concept has been expanded and applied to architectural monuments and sites that likewise result from an accumulation of layered materiality and changing meanings.[2] This volume explores and develops the idea of the architectural and site palimpsest through a series of case studies drawn from different parts of the globe, from Europe and America to Africa and South Asia, and ranging in time from Roman Pompeii to Ground Zero in contemporary New York. The purpose behind such chronological and cultural breadth is to provide a multiplicity of examples from which a theoretical model of the three-dimensional palimpsest can be developed, and which would be applicable to monuments and sites from different historical periods and vastly diverse geographical contexts.

In the original sense of the word as a rewritten manuscript, the palimpsest possesses a distinct quality of temporal layering in that it embodies at least four successive chronological episodes. The first three episodes relate to the creation of the palimpsest *per se*. First is the initial inscription of the text on the parchment. After some amount of time—which varies considerably from case to case—this is followed by a second moment in which that first text is fully or partially erased, and then by a third (often in close succession) in which another, different text is overwritten on the erased parchment. Finally, there is a fourth temporal episode, unrelated to the making of the palimpsest, but rather pertaining to its recognition. These four moments are only the minimum required; in some cases, a manuscript that is a palimpsest can be erased and reinscribed more than once, yielding a longer sequence of temporal episodes.[3]

The use of the term "palimpsest" for buildings and sites is in some ways similar, but in others quite different. In applying the concept to architecture, it is the initial act of construction that corresponds to the writing of the original text of the manuscript.[4] A subsequent demolition or dismantling, either in whole or in part, of whatever is considered a building's "original" state corresponds to the act of erasure. The actual making of the architectural palimpsest—rebuilding in a new form either within the footprint of the original structure or expanding beyond it—corresponds to the act of reinscription. The fourth moment, one of recognition, remains a historically contingent cognitive act experienced by perceptive beholders at various points along the palimpsest's temporal arc.

In the architectural palimpsest, we may distinguish between two fundamentally different forms of erasure. The first involves a subtractive process, in which the building or some part of it is dismantled and removed to make way for the addition of a new part. The second process is additive, in that an existing surface may be masked by a new one, preserving it but effectively erasing it by making it no longer visible.[5] Architectural monuments may contain traces of one or both of these processes, the latter exemplified by the French abbey of Saint-Rémi de Reims, where an Early Gothic chevet replaced a smaller Romanesque one (subtractive; fig. 0.1), while late twelfth-century walls partially masked early eleventh-century ones in the basilica's nave (additive; fig. 0.2). We may also note that in the case of "additive erasure," the stages of erasure and reinscription coalesce together into a singular act.

0.1. Abbey of Saint-Rémi, Reims. Interior view toward the east showing in the foreground the eleventh-century nave walls with their Early Gothic layers and in the background the Early Gothic chevet that replaced the Romanesque sanctuary.

Erasures and reinscriptions by subtraction or addition notwithstanding, the abbey church of Saint-Rémi remains the abbey church of Saint-Rémi. It has been re-presented—that is, made present again—as a palimpsest, so that at least part of the original is seen through the experience of what is inscribed upon or within it.[6] In re-presenting the earlier stage as embedded within the later one, the palimpsested structure links at least two temporally distinct stages of making. The resulting old/new "cumulative" monument, therefore, simultaneously is and is not of its own time. It remains both embedded in the past and unfolding in the present. As Alfred Gell suggests in a related context, each subsequent act of reinscription represents a new act of creation, making each new stage of the palimpsest a new work, a re-presentation that is linked to—but also different from—the pre-palimpsestual original.[7]

Sites, too, can be considered productively as palimpsests. The concept of "site" is an elusive one, since the word is used in so many different senses. We are accustomed to speaking of habi-

0.2. Abbey of Saint-Rémi, Reims. Detail of the north wall of the nave showing the relationship between the eleventh-century nave wall and its late twelfth-century "layer."

tation sites, building sites, archaeological sites, and heritage sites, to name only a few. Nonetheless, all of these different types of sites appear to share two qualities in common: on the most basic level, they are particular locations in geographical space; in addition, they are defined in terms of some kind of meaningful human activity or experience. While sites can also be understood in the more abstract sense as Cartesian coordinates, it is their status as meaningful *places*, differentiated from their broader spatial surroundings, that best captures their particular ontology.[8] Depending on their scale, physical complexity, and the kinds of questions asked of them as cumulative entities, sites can be approached on an elastic scale that ranges from the micro to the macro, from a small sacred temple area, for example, to an entire city containing multiple discrete, as well as interconnected, monumental palimpsests.[9]

Although they are defined primarily in spatial and experiential terms, sites also exist in a temporal dimension and can thus become palimpsests as they develop and transform over time. Indeed, given the human propensity for continuing to occupy the same sites over long periods of time—be they the multi-religious epicenters such as the Temple Mount in Jerusalem, or the less symbolically charged places such as the Indian village of Kadwaha discussed by Tamara Sears in this volume—it may well be that the vast majority of sites are in fact palimpsestic, as Geoff Bailey has suggested.[10] One paradigmatic type of site—the archaeological—discloses this quality through its various occupational strata—the material and structural remains of later phases of occupation being deposited as new strata on top of older ones. This may be thought of as both an "additive" and "subtractive" mode of erasure, in that the older layers are covered over and often only partially preserved beneath the newer deposits. Unlike in the case of the architectural palimpsest, however, this process is in many cases non-intentional; the layers simply continue to accumulate as a byproduct of the ongoing activity on the site.

While the model of stratigraphic accumulation and orderly succession of discrete layers has guided much earlier archaeological thought and practice, it is now widely recognized that certain features perdure beyond a single set of stratigraphic boundaries to exhibit a quality of multi-temporality.[11] Here the temporal concept shifts from one of a sequence of distinct moments or phases to one of durations. An irrigation canal, for example, may have been initially constructed in one stratigraphic phase, but it may also have been maintained through several subsequent phases to continue its existence even while new strata were accumulating around it in adjacent parts of the site. It is in this context that the notion of the site palimpsest has most profitably been invoked by archaeological theorists;[12] these vestiges of an earlier time continue to be visible and relevant to later periods of occupation, in a manner somewhat reminiscent of the traces of an earlier erased text in a literal palimpsest showing through the newer text inscribed over it. It also opens up the possibility for shifting meanings and understandings of those vestiges on the part of later communities who perceived and used them.

One special type of palimpsestual site that figures in this volume is what we may loosely term the "site of memory," invoking Pierre Nora's *lieux de mémoire*.[13] These sites, including the Presidential Palace Museum in Kigali discussed by Annalisa Bolin, and the Ground Zero complex in Manhattan addressed by Joseph Siry, share in common their status as sites that have been transformed by traumatic events that have erased their original significance and demanded their reinscription as memorials and witnesses to human suffering. In responding to this imperative, both sites make effective use of relics, that is physical objects that are tangible remnants from the past being memorialized, including human remains, furnishings, and architectural fragments.[14] As such, these sites become powerful channels capable of symbolically collapsing time and making the past present again—which accounts for their political significance and their tendency to become contested between groups and interests with differing visions of past and future.

While there have been many studies of buildings and sites investigating specific, synchronic episodes in their biographies (with the majority privileging their moments of origination), very few have approached them from the diachronic perspective of the palimpsest, that is, recognizing that the fourth dimension—that of duration—is essential to understanding them as both historic and contemporary entities. As a hermeneutic tool, the concept of the palimpsest embraces the totality of time "compressed" in a given monument or site, while extracting a series of legible and meaningful episodes that Finbarr Barry Flood describes as the "highs and lows … that constitute the real stuff of interest rather than the mundane connective tissue."[15] This diachronic, or more precisely, multi-synchronic approach calls for a close reading of the fabric of the monument or site (combined, of course, with multi-pronged contextual research based on the available textual and other evidence), not merely in order to identify the significant layers of the palimpsest and the physical processes through which they were created, but just as importantly, to gauge the effects of past viewers' ability to see each of these layers and to understand the relationships between them. Indeed, the successful "reading" of the palimpsest—a re-presented monument or site—demands a sort of cognitive bifurcation that considers the original and the palimpsest both separately and simultaneously in their physical and semiotic dimensions.

In some of the buildings and sites discussed in this volume, it was not the intention of those intervening in the history of a given monument to call attention to the changes they were introducing, or to suggest the importance of a chronological succession. But in others, the evidence suggests that those who rebuilt or "reinscribed" older buildings fully intended their contemporaries to view them as palimpsests communicating clear messages about their changing (or purposefully unchanging) histories and significance. *Palimpsests: Buildings, Sites, Time* thus places its emphasis not on the moment of a building's or site's creation but, rather, on their larger "biographies."[16] As a corollary, it also moves beyond the notion of a singular, idealized viewer, in recognition of the need to understand changes not only in the life of the building or site, but also in the interests and perceptions of the successive communities of viewers who beheld and used them. This concept of the cultural biography of the monument or site brings us back to the original notion of the palimpsest, one that embodies writing, erasure, and rewriting over time. It allows us to see both the monumental and the site palimpsest as a narrative of historical processes, whether that narrative is one of deliberate revision, or one of unintended effect.

To be sure, cultural biography-oriented scholarship on monuments and sites has been well served by several key critical concepts—in particular, those of *spolia*, adaptive reuse, and appropriation. Given the well-developed literature that employs these concepts, we may reasonably ask whether the palimpsest provides any theoretical and methodological leverage that these other closely related critical tools do not. In order to do so, however, we must first consider each of them briefly.

Spolia may be defined as materials, works of art, or architectural components that are used or reused in a context for which they were not originally intended.[17] Spoliation originally carried negative, destructive connotations, and called to mind the spoils exacted from a defeated enemy.[18] More recently, the concept has been understood in a more positive light, and the creative, meaningful dimensions of spoliation are emphasized;[19] for instance, scholars now also recognize that not all *spolia* were stolen or reappropriated, but may have been received as diplomatic gifts. The concept is often called into play where symbolic assertions of a connection between earlier and later moments are being made by the incorporation of antique *spolia* within the architectural framework of a newer building.[20] A *locus classicus* is provided by the reuse of architectural elements from pagan Roman monuments in churches of the Early Christian and medieval periods, as in the reuse of Ionic columns in the arcade of Santa Maria Maggiore in Rome under the papal patronage of the fifth century.[21] Comparable instances can also be found in medieval South Asia, where, for example, sixteenth-century royal patrons in peninsular India went to great lengths to acquire antique building components from eleventh-century monuments associated with the Chalukya empire, so they could present themselves as successors to the former imperium (figs. 0.3 and 0.4).[22] Similar examples could no doubt be adduced from other parts of the world as well. Finally, a distinction is often drawn between what Tim Eaton has termed "practical reuse," in which locally available architectural members are reused for strictly utilitarian, functional purposes, and "meaningful reuse," in which the reused *spolia* are deployed in prominent, visible locations and are intended to function iconically and make a deliberate statement.[23] In most cases, *spolia* are related to the larger building or site as parts to a whole, which is one aspect that distinguishes them from the palimpsest, a higher order phenomenon that implicates entire monuments or sites and accounts for their layered temporality. *Spolia* can contribute to the palimpsestic nature of a building or a site, but in so doing they remain only a part, a discrete temporal "slice" of that larger entity, as Erik Gustafson shows in his study of a crusader portal reused in an Islamic *madrasa* in Cairo.

Turning to "adaptive reuse," this is a venerable practice as, for example, the conversion and redecoration of the Parthenon as a Byzantine church makes clear.[24] Although the notion was first articulated by Eugène-Emmanuel Viollet-le-Duc (1814–79) in the mid-nineteenth century,[25] and discussed again meaningfully by Alois Riegl (1858–1905) as "use-value" at the turn of the twentieth,[26] its currency as a modern architectural concept came into being during the 1960s when it was applied to the conservation and modification of buildings in American cities.[27] In contemporary adaptive reuse in the United States and Europe, emphasis has been placed on retaining part of the original building, frequently the façade, while transforming the interior to serve new programmatic functions and to meet contemporary building codes and standards of comfort. In the numerous cases when only the exterior "shell" of a historic structure is preserved, the palimpsest is thus inverted, as the old facade is retained and left

0.3. Two-storeyed pavilion at end of Virupaksha bazaar, Vijayanagara, fifteenth and sixteenth centuries. Showing reuse of eleventh-century Chalukya columns in ground storey.

visible, while the newer part of the structure is masked by it. Ghirardelli Square in San Francisco, which opened in 1964, is a case in point.[28] For the purposes of this volume, literature on adaptive reuse can be usefully divided into two types: works on adaptive reuse of architecture and sites carried out in the past; and works on adaptive reuse in the contemporary period, usually discussed in relation to preservation and heritage.[29] Monumental and site palimpsests almost always involve an element of adaptive reuse, but the two concepts are not identical, since "adaptive reuse" refers to a practice or a process, while "palimpsest" refers to the physical product of that process. An architectural palimpsest can, in fact, encompass several different synchronic episodes of adaptive reuse. For example, the thirteenth-century Venetian palace on the Grand Canal that later became the Fondaco dei Tedeschi (trading post for German merchants), was converted into a customs house under Napoleon, a post office under Mussolini, and most recently "a modern temple of consumption"[30] following a controversial redevelopment project by the architectural firm OMA (figs. 0.5-0.7).

This brings us to the notion of appropriation. If adaptive reuse is a process, then appropriation may be considered as one of the motivating forces behind that process.[31] In the adaptive reuse of a monument or site, one or more elements or aspects of the past embodied by the monument or site are appropriated by those carrying out the reuse. In certain cases, this process is driven primarily by symbolic or ideological motives, making that particular instance of appropriation "active, subjective and motivated," to borrow Robert Nelson's definition.[32] One particularly memorable example of this model was provided by Oleg Grabar, who argued that the Dome of the Rock in Jerusalem is best understood as a monument designed to bring about "the symbolic appropriation of the land" of Palestine by the new cultural force of Islam.[33] In other cases, the appropriation of a monument or site may be inadvertent or ideologically neutral, as when there simply is no other available "real estate."[34]

The term thus oscillates along the dialectical vector between the appropriator and the appropriated. Appropriations, like palimpsests, are

0.4. Close-up of reused Chalukya column in two-storeyed pavilion at end of Virupaksha bazaar, Vijayanagara.

not fixed or final. While the monuments or sites themselves may endure, these temporal episodes often survive only as residue. The meanings associated with the act of appropriation, or the creation of a palimpsest, may fade or be lost entirely over time because those acts are themselves historically contingent.

Neither adaptive reuse nor *spolia*, nor even appropriation, can be strictly equated with the notion of the monument or site as a palimpsest. Nor is the concept's critical potential exhausted by a combination of all three. *Spolia* may be present as parts of a given palimpsest; adaptive reuse may describe a key process at work in shaping the palimpsest; and a desire to appropriate a site and its past may serve as the ultimate impetus for creating the palimpsest. Moreover, given that the concept accounts for the total sum of significant temporal episodes—both positive and negative ones—present in a given building or site (thus moving us beyond the narrow obsession with their initial creation), it provides an alternative approach to the persistently thorny question of authenticity that often emerges in the literature on *spolia*, adaptive reuse, and appropriation. While the issue of authenticity has, in fact, been effectively addressed and articulated in the most recent conventions governing the preservation of the world's cultural heritage,[35] it still poses both methodological and philosophical stumbling blocks in certain areas of architectural history and philosophy.[36] In her essay, Nadja Aksamija discusses how the restoration and reconstruction of certain iconic buildings from the Italian Renaissance has been treated in the existing scholarship. She argues that part of the problem in that field appears to be the unwillingness to acknowledge and foreground the palimpsestual nature of some of the period's most esteemed monuments, as doing so could potentially destabilize their perceived authenticity.

As a conceptual metaphor and a methodological trajectory, the palimpsest provides still more in the way of interpretive resources, most of which stem from the term's original application to designate a certain type of manuscript produced through the processes of writing and erasure. Here we may briefly consider three specific components of the idea of the palimpsest that are not present in any of its relatives.

First, the palimpsest implies a distinction between a text and a support or carrier on which it is written—the prepared parchment folios, bound into a codex or some other format. This structure can be profitably adapted to the architectural palimpsest, though the latter's three-dimensional/spatial character complicates and expands the definition far beyond its traditional parameters. There are at least two distinct ways in which architecture can be read as a palimpsest. First, we may think of the site on which a building is constructed as the support and the building itself as the three-dimensional text written on top of it. This model accords equal importance to the invisible (e.g. foundations, and in later architecture, its mechanical infrastructure) and visible parts of architecture, acknowledging the building's total materiality and taking into account its spatial qualities. Alternatively (and depending on the kind of architectural palimpsest at hand), we may differentiate between the hidden structure and the legible "skin" of a building, that is, the inner structure corresponding to the support, and the visible forms and surfaces to the text "inscribed" onto it. The first model breaks wide open the very notion of what constitutes an architectural "text" and may be particularly useful for thinking about historic monuments that may appear not to have changed significantly since their initial construction but that may, in fact, hide new structural elements (e.g. steel beams, concrete, etc.) under the surface that help keep them "alive" after many centuries. It may also provide ways to read the layered materiality of architectural monuments in relation to the shifting semiotic signals encoded in their masses, voids, and surfaces that communicate the appropriate and/or possible movements and actions through the space to its users.

In the second model, the status of the visible forms and surfaces as "text" underscores the building's capacity to carry and convey meaning, whether at the level of architectural iconography (e.g. meanings associated with the different orders in classical architecture), or of the applied decorative program, including sculpture, painting, and textual inscriptions. Two of the essays in this volume examine cases in which written messages were added to buildings long after their original construction, addressing viewers directly and guiding both their understanding of the monument and their interactions with it. In some cases these texts were ephemeral and not intended to last, as with the Pompeiian political "posters" considered by Christopher Parslow. In others, they were meant to serve as a lasting record of public events, as with the monumental painted declarations of the new cults of Reason and the Supreme Being, which as Clark Maines shows, were added during the period of the Revolution to the façades and portals of many French churches, replacing their religious imagery and transforming them—if only very briefly—into temples of a new secular religion. Of course, in these and in all such cases, this type of visible

0.5. Façade of the Fondaco dei Tedeschi, Venice. First constructed in 1228, rebuilt between 1505 and 1508, with later changes. Documented in 2013, before the most recent restoration.

0.6. View of the interior of the Fondaco dei Tedeschi shopping center, Venice. Redesign by OMA, 2016.

0.7. View of the new escalator at the Fondaco dei Tedeschi shopping center, Venice. Redesign by OMA, 2016.

"text" is inextricably tied to the functioning and meaning of the "meta-text" of the architectural body as a whole, thus closely linking the two models of the architectural palimpsest.

Second, the palimpsest is based on the archetypal acts of erasure and rewriting, an alternation between destructive and creative practices that makes possible the generation of new meanings. We have just considered how architectural construction can be considered an act of inscribing a "text;" perhaps even more powerful as a critical tool is the notion of the creative power of erasure. Although the dismantling of a building's original "text"—whether it be the entire structure above the foundations or only select portions—is a destructive act, it is one that enables a new round of creation, as Sheila Bonde explores in her analysis of the Porta Nigra's transformation from Roman city gate to medieval monastic church and back again. Contributing still further to the creative power of erasure is that when selective, it can leave behind visible traces of the original text that can enter into a productive dialogue with the new one. Sometimes these traces are unintentional, but in other cases they are an integral component of the new text, like the brief and fragmentary quotations from a canonical source within the textual space of its commentary. Phillip Wagoner's essay on the conversion of the Bodhan temple into a mosque provides a compelling example of how such deliberately preserved traces of the original monument could "doubly charge" the meaning of the new structure. But even when it is essentially absolute, erasure—followed by rewriting—does not necessarily obliterate the memory of what was there before. As Sarah Newman discusses, the process of architectural reuse and rebuilding among the ancient Maya often involved a careful encasing of old structures inside the new ones. Though made practically invisible through this process of nesting, earlier buildings were not forgotten; instead, they symbolically infused the later strata, on which they were sometimes also commemorated in glyphic texts.

Third, the idea of the palimpsest invites us to think in terms of layers and layering, following the lead of the manuscript model, in which new text overlays the remnants of an earlier one. As we have discussed above, sometimes the layering in an architectural palimpsest is as planar as that in a manuscript palimpsest, as when writing has been inscribed on either the vertical or horizontal surfaces of a building. More often than not, however, this layering is actually three-dimensional. In this sense, we extend the notion of layering in the manuscript palimpsest, from which we have appropriated it, in order to talk about a much more complex spatial layering. One suspects that our propensity for thinking of spaces in terms of layers may be at least partly explained by technology, and the importance of the layer concept within familiar types of computer software, such as Computer Assisted Design (CAD) and Geographic Information Systems (GIS). But the initial point of departure for this conceptual move comes from the original manuscript palimpsest, and from the imaging technologies used to enhance and virtually separate their superimposed layers.

To be sure, any meaningful future study of complex architectural and site palimpsests will be immensely helped by the new technological possibilities, which are already enabling the creation of comprehensive digital archives for the collection, dissemination, cross-referencing, and visualization of multi-dimensional (spatial, temporal, material, etc.) data. The first step, however, requires that different kinds of questions be asked of the three-dimensional palimpsests, as exemplified by the essays collected in this volume. *Palimpsests: Buildings, Sites, Time* has no close antecedents. It builds out from literature on adaptive reuse, heritage conservation, *spolia*, and appropriation to develop a perspective on architectural monuments and sites that emphasizes reading the structure, or the place, as an evolved set of actions and conditions. It avoids privileging the moment of creation and emphasizes changing appearances linked to changing historical circumstances. The goal of the volume as a collection of chronologically and geographically diverse case studies is to present a range of methodological possibilities comfortably nestled under a single conceptual umbrella. It is our hope that the notion of the palimpsest can indeed become a paradigm-shifting framework for future research in architectural and landscape history, encouraging collaborative research among scholars from different fields and calling for a much more open and inclusive study of the buildings' and sites' "temporal density"[37] in order to extract and begin to understand the precious data contained in and between their layers.

Notes

1 The English term "palimpsest" is derived, through Latin, from the Greek *palin* "again" + *psestos* "scraped" or "rubbed," referring to the erasing of a written text. This etymology alludes to the method of preparing ancient writing materials by scraping or rubbing to make the surface smooth enough to be written upon. The earliest such writing materials in the Mediterranean basin were papyrus rolls, which were gradually replaced in the Early Middle Ages by parchment rolls and eventually codices (Dillon 2013, 13). The reference to "scraping *again*" implies the erasure of whatever text had been written on the page (or roll) after the initial preparatory scraping, so as to make it possible to re-inscribe it with a new text. In English, the first recorded use of the word "palimpsest" in this literal, paleographic sense occurs in the early nineteenth century, but very soon thereafter—starting with Thomas de Quincey in 1845—it also came to be used metaphorically to refer to analogous processes of erasure and re-inscription (such as "the palimpsest of the mind;" see McDonagh 1987). OED Online. http://www.oed.com/view/Entry/136319?rskey = U5hIcc&result = 1 (accessed 9 June 2016).

2 Application of the idea of the palimpsest to architecture can be traced back to the heyday of Post-Modernism in the 1980s, when influential architects including Peter Eisenman and Bernard Tschumi proved themselves careful readers of post-structuralist theorists such as Roland Barthes, Jacques Derrida, Gerard Genette, Umberto Eco, and others. From architecture as language or code and building as text it was but a short step to being able to think of buildings as palimpsests. In 1988, Eisenman memorably said of his Wexner Center for the Visual Arts at Ohio State University that "we used the site as a palimpsest: a place to write, erase, and rewrite" (quoted in Jencks 1988, 29). Architectural historians have been slow to pick up and extend the model; the first to do so explicitly appears to have been Finbarr Barry Flood (Flood 2003), followed by Gülru Necipoğlu, in her magisterial study of the Dome of the Rock (Necipoğlu 2008). A recent discussion of the concept of the architectural palimpsest as exemplified by the New Museum in Berlin can be found in Capdevila-Werning 2015. Concurrently, the concept was profitably developed by archaeologists concerned with the archaeology of time (Bailey [2006] 2007). Although the idea of the palimpsest is often invoked, the concept is rarely developed systematically as a critical tool; the present volume is intended as a contribution in that direction.

3 The reference here to series or sequences of temporal episodes may call to mind the theoretical work of George Kubler (see Kubler 1962), but the conception of temporality offered in *The Shape of Time* is fundamentally different from the one being developed here. Whereas Kubler's sequences are acts of making that result in a series of distinct products, our palimpsestual sequences are serial acts directed to the modification of a single entity after its initial creation.

4 Of course, with historic buildings this first step was in itself frequently palimpsestual, as many monumental structures took decades, or even centuries, to complete and often involved multiple architects. Examples are numerous, especially in the context of great ecclesiastical projects, such as the Milan Cathedral, which was finally completed in 1965 after close to six centuries of construction supervised by some 76 consecutive architects. Marvin Trachtenberg discusses this practice of "Building-in-Time" in his study of temporal modalities and architecture in Renaissance Florence. See Trachtenberg 2010.

5 In some instances, the original structure was enveloped by a later one, while remaining mostly intact and visible within it. In the case of the well-known Islamic citadel at Busra, Syria, built around an earlier Roman theatre, the original layer was mostly protected, rather than erased, by the later one. The relationship between the two monuments could be described as symbiotic: the bastions of the citadel could be reached by climbing the theatre's *cavea*. For a brief history and images of this extraordinary architectural palimpsest, see http://islamic-arts.org/2011/islamic-citadel-in-busra-basra/.

6 The concept of "representation" is a complex one, with a long biography in art history and philosophy. Commonly used in relation to painting and sculpture, it is less often applied to architecture or sites. It has at least two senses that are different, though not entirely separate. A representation may take the place of that which it represents, i.e. the latter being not present. A representation may also constitute a presenting again, a notion that is sometimes indicated as "re-presentation." In both cases, representation has a temporal dimension, but in neither case is it identical to that which it represents. Taken in the sense of re-presentation, the concept can be usefully discussed in relation to the recognition of monumental and site palimpsests. Summers 1996, 3–16, discusses the historical development of the concept from Plato to the present. For a recent collection of studies on representation, see Bonde and Houston 2013.

7 Gell 1998, 62–65, as highlighted by Flood 2014, 8. As Flood points out, though Gell's discussion here concerns iconoclasm, his argument is very relevant to the notion of the palimpsest as well.

8 For the relationship between space and place, see Tuan 1977. Although we here equate "site" with "place," some scholars, such as Edward Casey, draw a distinction between the two terms, taking "site" in the sense of a Cartesian location and "place" as an experientially defined one. See Casey 2000, 184–85.

9 Urban history is, of course, predicated on the study and understanding of entire cities as palimpsests, and it has produced a rich literature that cannot be examined here. In this volume, we have limited ourselves to the study of smaller sites, though in the case of Ground Zero, for instance, that smaller site could also be approached through the wider lens of the urban palimpsest of New York City.

10 Bailey (2006) 2007, 209.

11 Lucas 2005, 37–41. See also Holdaway and Wandsnider 2008, 1–12.

12 Bailey (2006) 2007, 198–223. See also Bailey 2008, 13–30; and Sullivan 2008, 31–45.

13 See Nora 1989.

14 For the use of the term "relics" in this sense, see Lowenthal 1985, 238–49.

15 Flood 2014, 6.

16 For the use of the term, see Kopytof 1986, 64–91.

17 On the concept of *spolia*, see Kinney 2006, who traces work since the groundbreaking study by Esch 1969. For a recent collection of essays dealing with *spolia* in different periods and geographical contexts, see Brilliant and Kinney 2011. It should be noted that our understanding of *spolia* is broader than some others, in that it does not necessarily imply despoliation or destruction, nor does it insist on ideological motivation.

18 Kinney 1995, 58. Kinney writes that "*spolia* are indices of destruction. They are the residues of violence inflicted by man…"

19 Among the creative applications of *spolia* are also the so-called "pseudo-*spolia*," such as those found on the treasury wall of the basilica of St Mark in Venice, which include "mediated copies of Byzantine artifacts or outright fakes" that imitated the "*spolia* style" of Byzantine churches. See Barry 2010, 26.

20 A telling example can be found at St Peter's in Rome, where thirty-eight of the original hundred columns from the fourth-century Constantinian basilica were strategically incorporated into the later, sixteenth- and seventeenth-century parts of the fully rebuilt church. See Bosman 2004.

21 On Santa Maria Maggiore, see Krautheimer 1961, reprinted with a postscript by the author in Krautheimer 1969, 181–96, and 414–20. For a more nuanced interpretation of reuse in Santa Maria Maggiore, and other fourth- and fifth-century monuments, see Brandenburg 2011. Brandenburg asserts that older elements reused in these buildings come from public warehouses and workshops and that this practice forms part of a long-standing building tradition. For him, the reused elements are not *spolia* narrowly defined, nor do they result from acts of appropriation carrying ideological significance. On stockpiling, see Greenhalgh 2009, 111-19.

22 Wagoner 2007.

23 Eaton 2000, 134–36. Eaton's work builds on David Stocker's seminal article, which defined three categories of cut stone reuse: casual (when "the original function of the stone is disregarded in its new use"); functional (when the old pieces were reused "for the purposes for which they were originally cut"); and iconic (when the stones reused also carried specific symbolic associations). See Stocker 1990, 84, 90, 93.

24 Kaldellis 2009.

25 Viollet-le-Duc writes: "The fact is that the best of all ways of preserving a building is to find a use for it, and then to satisfy so well the needs dictated by that use that there will never be any further need to make any further changes in the building." Viollet-le-Duc (1854) 1990, 222. He also states: "It would be understandable if an architect refused to install gas pipes in a church in order to avoid mutilation as well as to preclude possible accidents arising out of any attempt to install them; it would be understandable because the building can always be lighted by other means. If the same architect objected to a central heating installation on the grounds that this type of heating was not in use in the churches of the Middle Ages, however, then the whole thing would be merely ridiculous. There can be no reason to oblige the faithful to catch cold merely on account of archaeology!" Viollet-le-Duc (1854) 1990, 223.

26 Riegl (1903) 1982, 39–42.

27 For a recent discussion of historical adaptive reuse, see Brilliant and Kinney 2011. For a recent overview of the literature on contemporary adaptive reuse in relation to heritage, see Plevoets and Van Cleempoel 2011, 155–64. See also Cutler 1999, vol. 2, 1055–83.

28 The first major adaptive re-use project in the United States, Ghirardelli Square was transformed into a retail, dining, and entertainment hub by the landscape architect Lawrence Halprin. For a contemporary evaluation of the project, see Leefe 1965. For a recent study of Halprin's work in the context of American urban renewal, see Hirsch 2014.

29 Important works on adaptive reuse in contemporary architectural practice that employ the concept of a palimpsest include Machado 1976, 46–9; and Robert 1989.

30 http://www.frameweb.com/news/oma-transforms-venice-s-fondaco-dei-tedeschi-into-a-modern-temple-of-consumption (accessed 11 June 2016). This article reports that OMA's response to the critics of the project concerned that the changes to the building would damage its historic identity was that "the building has been intensively restored several times during its lifespan" and that, as "a bricolage of different times and materials, the structure objectively lacks authenticity." What was identified as the building's palimpsestual nature was therefore used as an argument in favor of dramatic erasure and rewriting of its existing, temporally layered interior. The new

Fondaco dei Tedeschi shopping center opened to the public in early June 2016, coinciding with the start of the architectural biennial in Venice.

31 See Schneider 2003, 215–29.
32 Nelson 1996, 118.
33 Grabar 1987, 43–71.
34 Bonde 1999, 64.
35 The conference on authenticity held in Nara in 1994 produced the most recent and inclusive document on the subject: the Nara Document on Authenticity. Article 11 of the Nara Document moved beyond some of the traditional definitions rooted in the Western views and practices of restoration—chiefly the 1964 Venice Charter for the Conservation and Restoration of Monuments and Sites—to recognize that the concept of authenticity is culturally specific and as such could only be evaluated within a particular cultural context. For a discussion of the Nara Document and its implications for the question of authenticity, see Labadi 2013, 47–48, and 113–26.
36 For a recent discussion, see Wicks 1994.
37 Flood 2014.

Bibliography

Bailey, Geoff. (2006) 2007. "Time perspectives, palimpsests and the archaeology of time," *Journal of Anthropological Archaeology* 26, 198–223.

Bailey, Geoff. 2008. "Time Perspectivism: Origins and Consequences," in *Time in Archaeology: Time Perspectivism Revisited*, ed. Simon Holdaway and LuAnn Wandsnider. Salt Lake City: University of Utah Press, 13–30.

Barry, Fabio. 2010. "*Disiecta membra*: Ranieri Zeno, the Imitation of Constantinople, the *Spolia* Style, and Justice at San Marco," in *San Marco, Byzantium, and the Myths of Venice*, ed. Henry Maguire and Robert S. Nelson. Washington D.C.: Dumbarton Oaks Research Library and Collection, 7–62.

Bonde, Sheila. 1999. "Renaissance and Real Estate: the Medieval Afterlife of the Temple of Diana at Nîmes," in *Antiquity and its Interpreters*, ed. Alina Payne, Ann Kuttner, and Rebekah Smick. Cambridge: Cambridge University Press, 57–69.

Bonde, Sheila, and Stephen Houston. 2013. "Introduction," in *Re-Presenting the Past: Archaeology Through Text and Image*, ed. Sheila Bonde and Stephen Houston. Joukowsky Institute Publication 2. Oxford and Oakville: Oxbow Books and The David Brown Book Company, 1–7.

Bosman, Lex. 2004. *The Power of Tradition: Spolia in the Architecture of St. Peter's in the Vatican*. Hilversum: Uitgeverij Verloren BV.

Brandenburg, Hugo. 2011. "The Use of Older Elements in the Architecture of Fourth- and Fifth-Century Rome: A Contribution to the Evaluation of Spolia," in *Reuse Value, Spolia and Appropriation in Art and Architecture from Constantine to Sherrie Levine*, ed. Richard Brilliant and Dale Kinney. Farnham and Burlington: Ashgate, 53–74.

—. 2005. *Ancient Churches of Rome from the Fourth to the Seventh Century: The Dawn of Christian Architecture in the West*. Turnhout: Brepols.

Brilliant, Richard, and Dale Kinney, eds. 2011. *Reuse Value, Spolia and Appropriation in Art and Architecture from Constantine to Sherrie Levine*. Farnham and Burlington: Ashgate.

Capdevila-Werning, Remei. 2015. "Palimpseste in der Architektur. Ein symboltheoretischer Zugang," in *Architektur und Philosophie: Grundlagen, Standpunkte, Perspektiven*, ed. Jörg H. Gleiter and Ludger Schwarte. Bielefeld: Transcript Verlag, 207–17.

Casey, Edward S. 2000. *Remembering: A Phenomenological Study*. 2nd ed. Bloomington: Indiana University Press.

Cutler, Anthony. 1999. "Reuse or Use? Theoretical and Practical Attitudes Toward Objects in the Early Middle Ages," in *Ideologie e pratiche del reimpiego nell'alto medioevo*, vol. 2. (Settimane di Studio del Centro Italiano di Studi sull'alto Medioevo, 46.) Spoleto: Centro italiano di studi sull'alto Medioevo, 1055–83.

De Quincey, Thomas. 1998. *Suspiria de Profundis* (1845), in *Thomas De Quincey: Confessions of an English Opium Eater and other writings*, ed. Grevel Lindop. Oxford: Oxford University Press, 87–181.

Dillon, Sarah. 2013. *The Palimpsest: Literature, Criticism, Theory*. London: Bloomsbury.

Eaton, Tim. 2000. *Plundering the Past: Roman Stonework in Medieval Britain*. Stroud: Tempus.

Esch, Arnold. 1969. "Spolien. Zur Wiederverwendung antiker Baustücke und Skulpturen im mittelalterlichen Italien," *Archiv für Kulturgeschichte* 52, 1–64.

Flood, Finbarr Barry. 2014. "Seeing Palimpsests: Materiality and the Visibility of Temporal Density," paper presented at the Art History Symposium *Monuments as Palimpsests*, Wesleyan University, February 28-March 1, 1–20.

—. 2003. "Pillars, Palimpsests, and Princely Practices: Translating the Past in Sultanate Delhi," *RES: Anthropology and Aesthetics* 43, 95–116.

Gell, Alfred. 1998. *Art and Agency: An Anthropological Theory*. Oxford: Clarendon Press.

Genette, Gérard. 1997. *Palimpsests: Literature in the Second Degree*. Trans. Channa Newman and Claude Doubinsky. Lincoln and London: University of Nebraska Press.

Grabar, Oleg. 1987. *The Formation of Islamic Art*. New Haven and London: Yale University Press.

Greenhalgh, Michael. 2009. *Marble Past, Monumental Present: Building with Antiquities in the Medieval Mediterranean*. Leiden: Brill.

Hirsch, Alison Bick. 2014. *City Choreographer: Lawrence Halprin in Urban Renewal America*. Minneapolis and London: University of Minnesota Press.

Hodder, Ian. 1986. *Reading the Past: Current Approaches to Interpretation in Archaeology*. Cambridge: Cambridge University Press.

Holdaway, Simon, and LuAnn Wandsnider, eds. 2008. *Time in Archaeology: Time Perspectivism Revisited*. Salt Lake City: University of Utah Press.

Holdaway, Simon, and LuAnn Wandsnider, eds. 2008. "Time in Archaeology: an Introduction," in *Time in Archaeology: Time Perspectivism Revisited,* ed. Simon Holdaway and LuAnn Wandsnider. Salt Lake City: University of Utah Press, 1–12.

Huyssen, Andreas. 2003. *Present Pasts: Urban Palimpsests and the Politics of Memory.* Stanford: Stanford University Press.

Jencks, Charles. 1988. "Deconstruction: The Pleasures of Absence," *Architectural Design* 58, no. 3/4, 17–31.

Kaldellis, Anthony. 2009. *The Christian Parthenon: Classicism and Pilgrimage in Byzantine Athens.* Cambridge: Cambridge University Press.

Kinney, Dale. 1995. "Rape or Restitution of the Past? Interpreting *Spolia,*" in *The Art of Interpreting,* ed. Susan C. Scott. Papers in Art History from The Pennsylvania State University, vol. 9. University Park: Pennsylvania State University Press, 53–67.

Kinney, Dale. 2006. "The Concept of *Spolia,*" in *A Companion to Medieval Art: Romanesque & Gothic in Northern Europe,* ed. Conrad Rudolph. Oxford: Oxford University Press, 233–52.

Koo, Young-Min. 2009. "An Analogy of Palimpsest as a Strategy Transforming Urban Structure into Architectural Discourse - Focused on Dominique Perrault's Architecture of Strata," in *Proceedings of the 4th International Conference of the International Forum of Urbanism (IFoU), the New Urban Question—Urbanism Beyond Neo-Liberalism.* Amsterdam and Delft. http://newurbanquestion.ifou.org/proceedings/index.html (accessed 13 June 2016).

Kopytof, Igor. 1986. "The cultural biography of things: Commoditization as process," in *The Social Life of Things: Commodities in Social Perspective,* ed. Arujun Appadurai. Cambridge: Cambridge University Press, 64–91.

Krautheimer, Richard. 1969. *Studies in Early Christian, Medieval, and Renaissance Art.* New York: New York University Press.

—. 1961. "The Architecture of Sixtus III: a Fifth-Century Renascence?" in *De Artibus Opuscula XL, Essays in Honor of Erwin Panofsky,* ed. Millard Meiss. New York: New York University Press, 291–302.

Kubler, George. 1962. *The Shape of Time: Remarks on the History of Things.* New Haven: Yale University Press.

Labadi, Sophia. 2013. *UNESCO, Cultural Heritage, and Outstanding Universal Value: Value-based Analyses of the World Heritage and Intangible Cultural Heritage Conventions.* Lanham: AltaMira Press.

Leefe, James M. 1965. "Ghirardelli Square: a critique," *Contract interiors* 125, no. 3, 98–109.

Lowenthal, David. 1985. *The Past is a Foreign Country.* Cambridge: Cambridge University Press.

Lucas, Gavin. 2005. *The Archaeology of Time.* London and New York: Routledge.

Machado, Rodolfo. 1976. "Old buildings as palimpsest: Towards a theory of remodeling," *Progressive Architecture* 11, 46–49.

McDonagh, Josephine. 1987. "Writings on the mind: Thomas de Quincey and the importance of the palimpsest in nineteenth-century thought," *Prose Studies* 10, no. 1, 207–24.

Necipoğlu, Gülru. 2008. "The Dome of the Rock as Palimpsest: 'Abd al-Malik's Grand Narrative and Sultan Suleyman's Glosses," *Muqarnas* 25, 17–105.

Nelson, Robert S. 1996. "Appropriation," in *Critical Terms for Art History,* ed. Robert S. Nelson and Richard Schiff. Chicago: University of Chicago Press, 116–28.

Nora, Pierre. 1989. "Between Memory and History: *Les Lieux de Mémoire,*" *Representations* 26, 7–24.

Plevoets, Bie, and Koenraad Van Cleempoel. 2011. "Adaptive reuse as a strategy towards conservation of cultural heritage: a literature review," in *Structural Studies, Repairs and Maintenance of Heritage Architecture XII,* ed. Carlos Brebbia and Luigia Binda. Chianciano Terme: WIT Press, 155–64.

Riegl, Alois. (1903) 1982. "The Modern Cult of Monuments: Its Character and Its Origin," trans. Kurt W. Forster and Diane Ghirardo, *Oppositions* 25, 21–51.

Robert, Philippe. 1989. *Adaptations, New Uses for Old Buildings.* Paris: Éditions du Moniteur.

Schneider, Arnd. 2003. "On Appropriation: a Critical Reappraisal of the Concept and its Application in Global Art Practices," *Social Anthropology* 11, no. 2, 215–29.

Stocker, David. 1990. "Rubbish Recycled: A Study of the Re-Use of Stone in Lincolnshire," in *Stone: Quarrying and Building in England AD 43–1525,* ed. David Parsons. Shoppwyke Hall: Phillimore & Co., 83–101.

Sullivan III, Alan P. 2008. "Time Perspectivism and the Interpretive Potential of Palimpsests: Theoretical and Methodological Considerations of Assemblage Formation History and Contemporaneity," in *Time in Archaeology: Time Perspectivism Revisited,* ed. Simon Holdaway and LuAnn Wandsnider. Salt Lake City: University of Utah Press, 31–45.

Summers, David. 1996, "Representation," in *Critical Terms for Art History,* ed. Robert S. Nelson and Richard Schiff. Chicago: University of Chicago Press, 3–16.

Trachtenberg, Marvin. 2010. *Building-in-Time: From Giotto to Alberti and Modern Oblivion.* New Haven and London: Yale University Press.

Tuan, Yi-Fu. 1977. *Space and Place: The Perspective of Experience.* Minneapolis: University of Minnesota Press.

Viollet-le-Duc, Eugène. (1854) 1990. *The Foundations of Architecture: Selections from the Dictionnaire Raisonné.* New York: George Braziller.

Wagoner, Phillip. 2007. "Retrieving the Chalukyan Past: The Politics of Architectural Reuse in the Sixteenth-Century Deccan," *South Asian Studies* 23, 1–29.

Wicks, Robert. 1994. "Architectural Restoration: Resurrection or Replication?" *British Journal of Aesthetics* 34, no. 2, 163–69.

Yoffee, Norman. 2007. "Perspectives into the Palimpsest: an Introduction to the Volume," in *Negotiating the Past in the Past: Identity, Memory, and Landscape in Archaeological Research,* ed. Norman Yoffee. Tucson: University of Arizona Press, 1–9.

I

Building Transformations

Chapter 1
Traces of Erasure and Questions of Intention in an Indian Mosque: The Deval Masjid at Bodhan

Phillip Wagoner

If works of architecture are in some sense "texts," then the palimpsest—with its attendant notions of erasure and re-inscription—offers a promising paradigm for understanding many monuments. That said, however, buildings and manuscripts are quite different orders of phenomena, and accordingly, there are bound to be certain problems of "fit" when one takes interpretive models deriving from the study of one and applies them to the analysis of the other. One such problem area relates to the shadowy traces that are often left behind in a palimpsest after erasing the original text. In the case of the celebrated Archimedes Palimpsest, for example, in some portions of certain pages one can barely make out the faint lines of a tenth century manuscript running vertically behind the far more visible horizontal lines of a thirteenth-century Byzantine prayer book (fig. 4.8).[1] When the older, infrequently read manuscript was scraped clean to produce recycled parchment for the copying of a newer and more relevant text, nearly invisible chemical residues were left behind in the parchment, and with the passage of time, chemical reactions have made them faintly visible. These traces were not left deliberately nor were they intended to signify anything; indeed, at the time of the re-inscription of the parchment, they would have been all but invisible to the naked eye. In buildings, on the other hand, there are many instances where analogous traces of an "erasing" process can be seen, and would have been perfectly legible even immediately after the remodeling of the original structure. These residual traces can only have been left deliberately, and must have been intended to contribute in some way to the meaning of the new structure. This difference between literal palimpsest manuscripts and monuments seen as "palimpsests" has important consequences for how we should approach the latter. In this essay, I will attempt to sketch out some of these implications through consideration of a single building from early fourteenth-century India, a mosque located in the town of Bodhan on the Deccan plateau (figs. 1.1 and 1.2).[2] Hopefully, consideration of this previously undocumented monument will provide some useful data permitting us to further clarify and refine the model of the palimpsest as it applies to architectural monuments.[3]

The mosque in question is known today by Bodhan's inhabitants as the "Deval Masjid"—literally, the mosque that was once a temple. The name itself suggests the building's status as a palimpsest, and visual inspection of the partially collapsed structure quickly confirms what the name suggests. One enters the building on the east, through an open pillared hall that is immediately recognized as the fore-hall (*mandapa*) of a Hindu temple built in the local architectural style of about 1200 CE (fig. 1.2).[4] In almost all respects, this hall preserves its original aspect, based on a nine-bay plan arranged in a three-by-three grid, with projecting porch extensions on the south, east, and north, and a trabeate system of construction using pillars, beams, and triangular ceiling slabs. The one striking departure from this original scheme is seen in the prominent hemispherical domes that were added when the building was transformed into a mosque, one atop each square bay, replacing the flat square ceiling slabs of the original temple (fig. 1.1). Moving through the hall toward the west, one comes to a more expansive hypostyle space of 45 bays arranged in a nine-by-five grid, readily identifiable as the prayer hall of the mosque (fig. 1.3). Since the mosque replaced a temple that had its entrance on the east, this means that the building was already

1.1. Deval Masjid, Bodhan, Nizamabad District, Telangana State, India, originally built around 1200, reconstructed in 1323. View from the northeast corner.

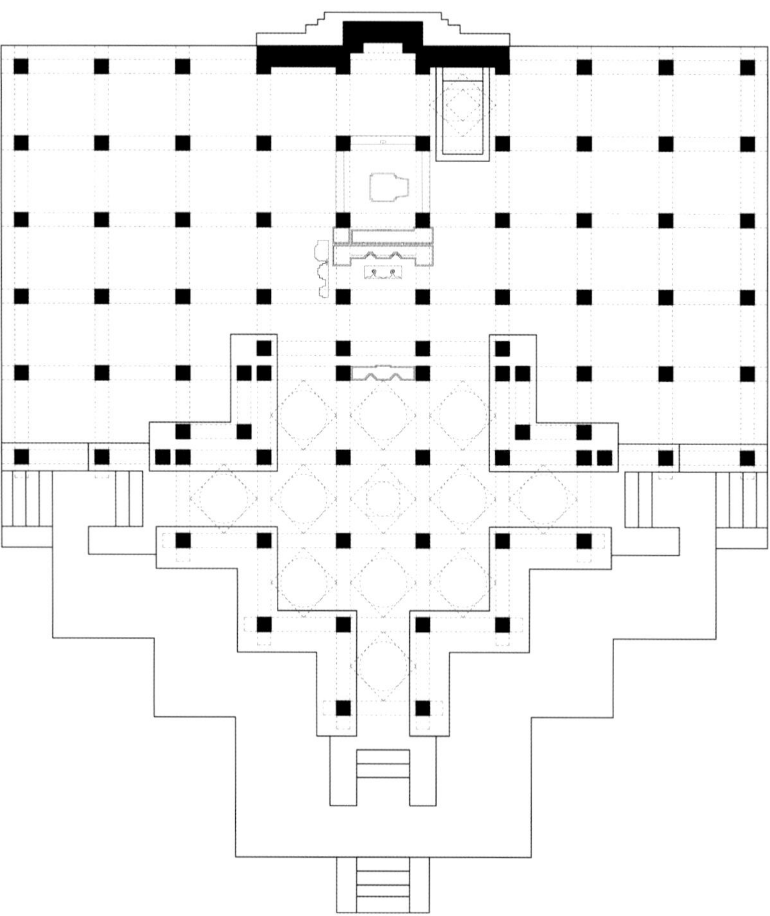

1.2. Plan of the monument as reconstructed around 1323. North is to the right.

1.3. View from the recycled temple *mandapa* to the *qibla* wall, showing the *mihrab* at the center of the wall.

oriented toward the west, which was fortuitously the approximate direction of Mecca in this part of India, and the direction (*qibla*) one was to face when performing ritual prayer. The arched niche (*mihrab*) in the center of the *qibla* wall can be seen, marking the space taken by the leader of prayer, and to the right of the *mihrab*, one can see the base of the now ruined pulpit (*minbar*) from which special prayers were delivered in the name of the ruling sultan (*khutba*) on the occasion of the Friday noon prayer (fig. 1.4).

Although the mosque's foundation is not dated epigraphically, its construction can be assigned to about 1323 CE on the basis of circumstantial evidence provided in a contemporary Persian historical text by 'Abd al-Malik 'Isami.[5] In this year, the chronicler notes that the Hindu chieftain or "Rai" of Bodhan was defeated in battle by an army of the Delhi Sultanate—that is, the Islamic, Persianate empire that had ruled over northern India since the early thirteenth century and had begun conquering the Hindu states of the Deccan in 1296 CE. The Rai surrendered his territory and his wealth, and "when he was given amnesty," according to 'Isami, "he embraced Islam, not alone but with all the members of his family and other dependents."[6] These circumstances suggest that the temple's conversion into a mosque would likely have been under the patronage of the unnamed Rai himself—guided, no doubt, by his Sultanate advisors—so as to provide himself, his family, and his dependents with the necessary architectural setting for Islamic ritual observance.

Much of the study of palimpsest manuscripts revolves around procedures used to make the ghostly traces of the older text more readily legible, and conversely, to lessen the visibility of the later text written across it. Of course, this is not done directly to the manuscript itself, but virtually, through computerized manipulation of digital images produced through the technique of multispectral imaging.[7] In this method, images taken at a variety of different wavelengths, from ultraviolet through the visible portion of the spectrum and into the infrared region, are

1.4. View of the ruined pulpit in the bay north of the *mihrab* bay, seen from northeast.

1.5. Column from the front of the temple vestibule now marking the central entrance to the prayer hall, showing the roughly dressed side of the shaft which in the temple would have been engaged in the fabric of the wall.

1.6. Floor of the former temple vestibule, showing the ornamental stepping stone, the floor moldings marking the threshold of the doorway to the sanctum, and the base of the *linga* pedestal on the floor of the sanctum.

1.7. Base of the *linga* pedestal on the sanctum floor.

combined to strengthen and enhance the visibility of features that are not ordinarily visible—much in the same way that remote sensing by satellite can reveal buried structures that are generally not visible in ordinary photographs. Although far more straightforward and low-tech, studying the monumental palimpsest calls for an analogous operation that similarly depends on detecting and clarifying the physical traces still remaining from the earlier building. These traces are often like the scattered pieces of a jigsaw puzzle, but just as a few widely separated pieces can begin to suggest the contours of a puzzle's image, so too will a few isolated traces begin to suggest the nature of the original monument.

In the case of the Bodhan mosque, there are several places where traces of the erased temple remain especially clear, providing the keys necessary for recovering its original design. First and foremost, there is the pillared hall at the entrance to the monument, which is not so much a "trace" in any strict sense, as an entire unerased portion of the original building that is still almost completely intact.[8] But its presence and form strongly imply that a temple proper, or *vimana*, consisting of a sanctum topped by a tower, would once have adjoined it on the western side. Indeed, examining the westernmost pair of columns of the pillared hall, which additionally mark the central entrance to the prayer hall, we see that there is a raised floor moulding running between them, with alternating recesses and projections (fig. 1.3). We also see from their roughly dressed lateral faces that these columns were not originally intended to be freestanding, but would have been engaged within a solid masonry wall that would have abutted their roughly dressed portions (fig. 1.5), and that the space between them would have been fitted with a doorframe. This floor molding, then, represents the raised threshold of the doorway that once led from the pillared hall into the temple proper. Other floor moldings from the original temple have been preserved as traces in the floor of the mosque, and enable us to reconstruct the sequence and nature of spaces in the original monument (figs. 1.2 and 1.3). The first doorway would have led the worshipper into a rectangular vestibule (*antarala*), leading at its western end through a second doorway providing access to the sanctum itself (*garbha-griha*, fig. 1.6). This is where the consecrated stone icon of the deity would have resided, standing on a raised altar pedestal in the middle of the chamber (fig. 1.7).[9]

Yet other traces permit us to reconstruct the design of the exterior of the temple. Thus, the moulded, elevated platform beneath the three central bays of the outer *qibla* wall (fig. 1.8) bears the same sequence of moldings and is at the same height as the elevated platform beneath the pillared hall on the east, indicating that this terrace for circumambulation (*jagati*) would have extended on all four sides of the temple. Moreover, the articulation of the exposed edge of this terrace on the *qibla* side suggests that each side of the sanctum's outer wall would have been articulated with a five-part rhythm of projections.[10] This inference is confirmed by the testimony of two single stones from the plinth marking the position of this outer wall on the southeast side (fig. 1.9). Putting all these indicators together—much as one deciphers the palimpsest's ghostly writing by recognizing a handful of clear letters and words and intuiting the contents of the intervening, illegible ones—it becomes possible to reconstruct the disposition of the original temple as seen here, and to do so in a way that clearly reveals the spatial and structural relationships between the monument's two phases (fig. 1.10).

Why were these various traces of the temple's original structure retained even after the building was redefined as a mosque? Clearly, they were not intended as clues for reconstructing the earlier building's design, although they certainly do help in that task. Rather, the purpose of these traces must have been more immediately located in the fourteenth century, and aimed more directly at the community that would be using the redefined building. The Persian chronicler's narrative about the Rai of Bodhan would appear to be relevant in this connection. As we have seen, the Rai was given amnesty after his defeat by the Sultanate's army, and as a result he embraced Islam together with his family and his followers. Conversion to Islam involved not only committing to the different religious practices of a new faith, but

1.8. View from the south of the exterior of the *qibla* wall showing the *mihrab* projection, and the uppermost moldings of the circumambulatory terrace at the base.

1.9. Bay immediately south of the *mihrab* aisle, showing two stones from the top of the temple plinth.

also renouncing the Hindu practices of his past, which from an Islamic perspective constituted idolatry, one of the gravest forms of sin. Instead of decommissioning the temple and building a mosque on a separate site, the Rai and his associates seized on a different option that would not only be more economical, but also quicker and potentially more effective in ensuring the thoroughness of their conversion. Desecrating the idol and dismantling the temple proper, the Rai's builders proceeded to erect a new structure that would serve the need for congregational, Islamic prayer. But they also retained the floor moldings of the original temple, as well as the base of the pedestal that had once carried the idol. It thus became possible for the Rai of Bodhan to enact ritually his rejection of idolatry by walking over these traces, walking right on through the most sacred space of the erstwhile sanctum and stepping across the idol's pedestal, each time he entered the prayer hall and approached the *mihrab* for prayer.[11]

This interpretation—that the deliberately reserved traces of the temple's floor served as a perennial reminder of the Rai's conversion and rejection of idolatry—is given further support by another set of traces remaining from a different mode of erasure that is also seen within the building. In this case, the act of erasure did not take the form of a structural dismantling, but instead involved the effacement of the decorative surface of otherwise unaltered structural members—namely, the four columns marking the central bay of the pillared entrance hall (fig. 1.11). As was typical in the thirteenth-century temple architecture of this region, these columns were once ornamented with relief sculptures of deities, mythic scenes, and other forms of figurative imagery prominently placed on the four faces of the square-sectioned blocks of the

1.10. Plan of temple as constructed around 1200, here conjecturally restored.

column's shaft. When the hall was converted to serve as the entrance to a mosque, these figural sculptures were chiseled off, in accordance with many centuries of customary usage that had avoided the use of figural imagery within the sacred space of the mosque. These images could just as well have been fully chiseled away, and the resulting surface polished smooth to remove all traces of them, but this is not what was done at Bodhan.[12] Instead, the outer, finished surface of each figure was removed, leaving a rough, irregular surface that still projects in slight relief, calling attention to itself through the contrast between its rough surface and the smoother pol-

1.11. Interior view of the temple *mandapa*, showing two columns at the north side of the central bay, seen from east.

1.12. Detail of one of the columns of the *mandapa*'s central bay, showing remnants of effaced mythological scene of "Churning of the Milky Ocean."

ish of the adjacent portions of the column. Some of the sculptures have been effaced in such a perfunctory manner that their outlines can still be read, and their original subject matter easily recognized, as in the case of one sculpture of an ascetic figure seated in yogic meditation, or another iconic presentation of the gods and demons churning the ocean for the nectar of immortality, using as their churning rod the uprooted mountain Mandara supported on the back of the cosmic tortoise (fig. 1.12). Especially in these cases, but arguably in the other less legible ones as well, leaving the roughed matrix of the stone would have served as a powerful index of the sculptures that were once there but had been removed, by extension reminding the Rai and his fellow converts of the decisive move they had made away from idolatry and toward the straight path of Islam.[13]

Let us now step back and underscore several key points that emerge from this consideration of the Bodhan mosque within the framework of the palimpsest paradigm. I am particularly interested in signaling two ways in which palimpsest monuments appear to differ from their manuscript counterparts.

The first has to do with the mode of relationship between the two "texts" that are conjoined in a palimpsest. In the palimpsest manuscript, the two texts are almost always semantically insulated and self-contained, despite the fact that they are physically linked on the same parchment. Thus, returning to the Archimedes Palimpsest with which this essay began, the texts originally inscribed on that parchment consisted of a selection of Archimedes' mathematical and scientific works, while the later superimposed text was a Byzantine prayer book. There is no give and take between the two at the semantic level, only at the physical by virtue of their sharing the same parchment ground. This situation is possible in manuscript palimpsests because the first text is generally erased to the point where it is no longer legible, the purpose after all being to appropriate scarce and valuable parchment by erasing a manuscript whose text has fallen out of use, so that a newer and more relevant text can be inscribed in its place.[14] Such manuscripts would not have been viewed in their own time as palimpsests as we use the term; that recognition can arise only from the perspective of a third point in time, distant enough from the times of both texts for the residual traces of the erased one to start to darken through chemical change.

In a palimpsest monument, on the other hand, there is almost always a semantic interweaving of the two "texts"—that is, the constellation of meanings and uses inhering in each successive phase or incarnation of the building. This is possible because much of the erasure is deliberately incomplete, intentionally leaving traces of the earlier phase behind, so they can enter into dialogue with the later phase. This is true not just from our third-point perspective as historians, but even from the perspective of the users of the building in the second phase. Thus, the meaning of the second phase monument cannot be self-contained, but is at least partially dependent on the presence and legibility of remnants of the earlier phase. At Bodhan, for example, the sculptures are chiseled away from the columns, but their outlines remain, calling attention to their one-time presence and current absence. Similarly, by retaining the floor moldings of the original temple within the prayer hall of the mosque, it becomes possible for the Rai of Bodhan to ritually enact his rejection of idolatry by walking over the traces of the deity's dismantled altar, each time he enters the prayer hall and approaches the *mihrab* for prayer.

The second point I would like to make relates to differences in scholarly orientation between those who study palimpsest manuscripts and those who study palimpsest monuments. At the risk of over-generalizing, it would appear that with manuscript palimpsests, the focus of analysis is overwhelmingly on recovering the original text, while the later overwritten text is taken to be of lesser importance. Again, a case in point is provided by the Archimedes Palimpsest. It is quite telling that this manuscript is referred to not by the name of the second text inscribed on its parchment—a Byzantine prayer book or *euchologion* copied in Jerusalem in 1229 CE—but is instead called by the name of Archimedes, the classical Greek mathematician who composed the seven treatises that had originally been inscribed on its parchment in the latter half of the tenth century. The great importance of this celebrated manuscript is that three of the treatises contained within its erased text were not previously known in any other copies, which has led to an impressive international and interdisciplinary research project to recover the erased text. On the website of the Archimedes Palimpsest Project, the authors admit that

> [w]hile it contains no less than seven treatises by Archimedes, calling it the Archimedes Palimpsest is a little confusing. As it is now, the manuscript is a Byzantine prayer book, written in Greek, and technically called a *euchologion*.[15]

They go on to state that "[t]he prayer book … is itself of some interest, and further information on its contents can be discovered in this website."[16] But they leave the visitor with no doubt that the abiding interest of this palimpsest is its nearly vanished text of previously unknown works by the great mathematician.

In the architectural palimpsest, on the other hand, I would suggest that it is the dynamic relationship between the two "layers" of the building that is generally of the greatest interest. At Bodhan, we can succeed in recovering the design of the earlier temple, but in and of itself, that is of little moment. Instead, what is of real interest is the spatial and structural relationship between the two successive phases of the building, and the way in which the mosque intentionally gestured back to the traces of the temple to determine its full range of meanings.

Notes

This essay is based on field documentation carried out in 2005 in collaboration with Richard M. Eaton, with funding from the Getty Foundation. Due to time pressures during our six-week 2005 field season, we could allot only one and a half days to Bodhan's Deval Masjid, which did not provide sufficient time to prepare on-site measured drawings of this previously undocumented monument. Accordingly, we carried out intensive photographic documentation and made detailed field notes as we discussed and interpreted the monument.

The plans of the building's two phases reproduced here were prepared after the fact through a second collaboration, with Julia Drachman, a Wesleyan Architecture major from the class of 2014. Although the drawings are not to scale and were not prepared in the field, they are the result of a time-consuming synthesis of the data of the 75 field photographs, and we believe they are a reasonably accurate representation of the building's structure and spatial organization. The final drawings were prepared in AutoCAD by Julia Drachman. The plan of the original temple is, of course, a conjectural restoration, based on its visible traces as explained in the text.

I am grateful to both of my collaborators for the opportunity to work with them, and for the proof they give to the adage that two heads are better than one.

1 Wilson 2004; Netz et al. 2011. See also the website of the Archimedes Palimpsest Project http://archimedespalimpsest.org/ (accessed 5 March 2016).

2 "The Deccan" refers to the upland plateau of peninsular India. Bodhan is located in the Nizamabad District of Telangana state (formerly Andhra Pradesh). The mosque has been briefly discussed in Eaton and Wagoner 2014, 48–52. It has been still more briefly mentioned by Radhakrishna Sarma 1972, 64, who recognized its status as a converted temple.

3 My thinking on monuments as palimpsests has been sharpened by a number of recent discussions of reuse, *spolia*, and appropriation in the South Asian context. Those that I have found particularly helpful include Meister 1972; Williams 1973; Davis 1993; Davis 1997; Patel 2004a; Patel 2004b; Patel 2009; Kasdorf 2009; Sears 2009; Flood 2003; Flood 2009; and Flood 2011. See also Wagoner and Rice 2001; Wagoner 2007; and Eaton and Wagoner 2014.

4 A date of the ninth or tenth century has been suggested (Radhakrishna Sarma 1972, 64), but this is certainly too early. Stylistically, the Bodhan temple compares closely with temples in the Sabbi-nadu region, just to the east of the site in the neighboring Karimnagar District, including the Siva Temple at Kothapalli (late twelfth and early thirteenth century), and the Trikuta temple at Nagunur (early thirteenth century). See Dhaky 1996, 485–89, and plates 1442–47. Some of the more archaic style columns in the added hypostyle prayer hall of the Bodhan mosque have evidently been taken from a different structure, most likely also a temple, dating to the early twelfth century.

5 Mahdi Husain 1967, vol. 2, 607.

6 Mahdi Husain 1967, vol. 2, 607.

7 Netz et al. 2011, 175–76. In the nineteenth and early twentieth centuries, enhancing the legibility of the erased text was often accomplished with chemical reagents. For an accessible overview of the history of changing techniques for recovering the palimpsested text, see Dillon 2013, 16–21.

8 This is by no means the only example in the Deccan of a palimpsest mosque that appropriates an earlier *mandapa* to serve as its entrance. Other examples include the mosque of Karim al-Din at Bijapur (founded 1320 CE), where an eleventh or twelfth-century *mandapa* at another site was dismantled and reconstructed at the entrance to the mosque's enclosure, perhaps at some point in the late fifteenth century (Kasdorf 2009, 59, and fig. 7; Eaton and Wagoner 2014, 44–48, where however the entrance is not discussed); and the congregational mosque at Warangal/Sultanpur, constructed on the site of the Svayambhusiva temple in 1323, in which the well-preserved plinth of the Nandi-mandapa on the east of the site suggests that it was retained to function as the foundation for the entrance of the new mosque (Wagoner and Rice 2001, figs. 24 and 29).

9 This icon would have been a *linga*—the cylindrical, aniconic representation of the god Siva who presides over the cosmic processes of creation and destruction. This can be inferred from the morphology of the pedestal, which would have been free-standing in the middle of the sanctum chamber. In the case of images of deities in anthropomorphic form, such as Vishnu or Surya, the pedestal generally abuts the rear wall of the sanctum, and a projecting tenon supports the back of the image's upper portion, as at the "Thousand-Pillared Temple" (Veyyistambhala Gudi) at Hanumakonda, where the western shrine (housing a Siva-*linga*) is free-standing, while the northern (Vishnu) and eastern (Surya) shrines abut the wall. See the plan in Dhaky 1996, fig. 237.

10 In the technical terms of Sanskrit architectural treatises, the *vimana* would have been "three-limbed" (*tryanga*). In other words, each face is resolvable into a pair of corner projections (*karnas*), flanked by a pair of intermediate projections (*pratibhadras*), all symmetrically arranged around a central projection (*bhadra*). In almost every documented case in this style, this "limb" articulation is the same in the terrace as it is in the *vimana*; this is how we know that the *vimana* at Bodhan would have been "three-limbed." For an idea of what this would have looked like, see the plan of the closely related Siva temple at Kothapalli in Dhaky 1996, fig. 248.

11 There is a long history of antecedents for this type of ritualized rejection of idols in South Asia, which may ultimately be traced back to early Islamic attitudes to pre-Islamic idol worship. Most famously, Mahmud of Ghazni is said to have taken the Siva-*linga* from Somnath to his capital, where he set it at the threshold of the city's Congregational Mosque so it could be trampled underfoot by all those entering. The discovery, during excavation of Mahmud's palace, of an image of the god Brahma with its face worn almost entirely smooth, led the excavator to suggest it had been set in a pavement in similar fashion. Perhaps the earliest evidence for this sort of practice in South Asia is the ninth-century mosque at Banbhore in Pakistan, which had a Siva-*linga* set in the pavement right at the entrance of the mosque's eastern doorway, on axis with the *qibla*. See Flood 2009, 32, and fig. 15.

12 Nor was this done in the construction of the Warangal-Sultanpur mosque later in the same year. Here, however, the figures were fully chiseled away, leaving a flat surface on each face of the columns' blocks, but the cut surface was not polished to the same lustrous finish as the matrix of the stone, leaving still a ghostly shadow-like image of the sculptures that had been removed.

13 For an analogous case from Revolutionary France, see Maines in this volume, esp. fig. 7.9 and its corresponding text.

14 In those palimpsests where faint traces of the erased text are still visible when the new text is inscribed, the traces would rarely be more noticeable or demanding of attention than the text showing through from a recto to a verso page.

15 *The Archimedes Palimpsest*.

16 *The Archimedes Palimpsest*.

Bibliography

The Archimedes Palimpsest, http://archimedespalimpsest.org/digital/google-book.php (accessed 5 March 2016).

Davis, Richard. 1997. *Lives of Indian Images*. Princeton: Princeton University Press.

—. 1993. "Indian Art Objects as Loot," *Journal of Asian Studies* 52, no. 1, 22–48.

Dhaky, M. A. 1996. *Encyclopaedia of Indian Temple Architecture. South India, Upper Dravidadesa, Later Phase, AD 973–1326*. New Delhi: American Institute of Indian Studies and Indira Gandhi National Centre for the Arts.

Dillon, Sarah. 2013. *The Palimpsest: Literature, Criticism, Theory*. London: Bloomsbury.

Eaton, Richard M., and Phillip B. Wagoner. 2014. *Power, Memory, Architecture: Contested Sites on India's Deccan Plateau*. New Delhi: Oxford University Press.

Flood, Finbarr Barry. 2011. "Appropriation as Inscription: Making History in the First Friday Mosque of Delhi," in *Reuse Value:* Spolia *and Appropriation in Art and Architecture from Constantine to Sherrie Levine*, ed. Richard Brilliant and Dale Kinney. Burlington: Ashgate, 121–47.

—. 2009. *Objects of Translation: Material Culture and Medieval "Hindu-Muslim" Encounter*. Princeton: Princeton University Press.

—. 2003. "Pillars, Palimpsests, and Princely Practices: Translating the Past in Sultanate Delhi," *RES: Anthropology and Aesthetics* 43, 95–116.

Kasdorf, Katherine. 2009. "Translating Sacred Space in Bijapur: The Mosques of Karim al-Din and Khwaja Jahan," *Archives of Asian Art* 59, 57–80.

Mahdi Husain, Agha, ed. and trans. 1967. *Futuhus-Salatin of 'Abd al-Malik 'Isami*, 3 vols. London: Asia Publishing House.

Meister, Michael W. 1972. "The 'Two-and-a-Half-Day' Mosque," *Oriental Art* 18, no. 1, 57–63.

Netz, Reviel, William Noel, Natalie Tchernetska, and Nigel Wilson. 2011. *The Archimedes Palimpsest*, 2 vols. Cambridge: Cambridge University Press.

Patel, Alka. 2009. "Expanding the Ghurid Architectural Corpus East of the Indus: The Jagesvara Temple at Sadadi, Rajasthan," *Archives of Asian Art* 59, 33–36.

—. 2004a. "Architectural Histories Entwined: The Rudra-Mahalaya/Congregational Mosque of Siddhpur, Gujarat," *The Journal of the Society of Architectural Historians* 63, no. 2, 144–63.

—. 2004b. *Building Communities in Gujarat: Architecture and Society during the Twelfth through Fourteenth Centuries*. Leiden: Brill.

Radhakrishna Sarma, M. 1972. *Temples of Telingana: The Architecture, Iconography and Sculpture of the Calukya and Kakatiya Temples*. Hyderabad: Osmania University.

Sears, Tamara I. 2009. "Fortified Mathas and Fortress Mosques: The Transformation and Reuse of Hindu Monastic Sites in the Thirteenth and Fourteenth Centuries," *Archives of Asian Art* 59, 7–31.

Wagoner, Phillip B. 2007. "Retrieving the Chalukyan Past: The Politics of Architectural Reuse in the Sixteenth-Century Deccan," *South Asian Studies* 23, 1–29.

Wagoner, Phillip B., and John Henry Rice. 2001. "From Delhi to the Deccan: Newly Discovered Tughluq Monuments at Delhi-Sultanpur and the Beginnings of Indo-Islamic Architecture in Southern India," *Artibus Asiae* 61, no. 1, 77–117.

Williams, Joanna. 1973. "A Recut Asokan Capital and the Gupta Attitude toward the Past," *Artibus Asiae* 33, no. 3, 225–40.

Wilson, Nigel. 2004. "The Archimedes Palimpsest: A Progress Report," in *A Catalogue of Greek Manuscripts at the Walters Art Museum and Essays in Honor of Gary Vikan, Bulletin of the Walters Art Museum* 62, 61–68.

Chapter 2
The Porta Nigra, Trier: Palimpsest, Cultural Biography, and Heterotopia

Sheila Bonde

The related strategies of the palimpsest, cultural biography, and heterotopia can be harnessed as a triple lens for viewing Trier's Roman north gate, the Porta Nigra (fig. 2.1). The gate was built in the second or early third century CE, as part of the fortification of the Roman capital. The gate lapsed into ruin in the late antique period, but housed a chapel to Saint Michael in its upper storeys. In the eleventh century, its religious purpose was expanded when part of the gate was converted for eremetic use by Saint Simeon, who lived for five years as a recluse in a cell within it. After Simeon's death, the structure was quickly converted to a double-storied collegiate church, with Simeon's body as the foundational relic. The church, dedicated to Saint Simeon, as well as its adjoining collegiate claustral buildings, remained in service through the eighteenth century. Napoleon Bonaparte ordered its de-consecration and de-restoration in 1804. Throughout the transformative biography of the Porta Nigra, the surfaces and spaces of the gate were sometimes literally scraped away, while at other times they were recovered and re-inscribed in an additive fashion, much like the palimpsest pages invoked in this volume.

The palimpsest is an apt metaphor for the successive changes wrought in architectural spaces. In 1998, researchers discovered mathematical proofs by Archimedes overwritten by biblical texts within a Byzantine *euchologion* (prayer-book) dating to *c.* 1229 (fig. 4.8). Ongoing work with the manuscript continues to reveal further ancient texts underneath the Byzantine overwriting.[1] Palimpsests such as this, with previous erasures still visible beneath the secondary text, are common in the medieval period, when parchment and vellum were costly materials. Architecture can also be a palimpsest: as cities and buildings—also expensive commodities—are modified and re-purposed, traces of their previous lives remain visible.

Several scholars have pointed to the utility of the palimpsest metaphor for architectural design, archaeological theory, and interactive display. As early as 1976, Rodolfo Machado examined critically the various metaphors used to describe the process of remodeling a building. He argued that the palimpsest forms both an interpretative and theoretical basis for architects "re-writing" buildings from the past, with the building serving as a cultural repository of function and meaning.[2] Geoff Bailey insists that the palimpsest should guide our thinking about the time dimensions of human experience.[3] Bailey sees palimpsests as a universal phenomenon in the material world, forming a set of overlapping categories of varying geographical scale and temporal resolution. Two recent dissertations employ the palimpsest as a frame for viewing Chinese urban development, and the architectural designs of Rafael Moneo and David Chipperfield, among others.[4] Developers at the interactive architecture lab at University College, London, have created a digital urban palimpsest. Using 3D scanning and virtual reality, their project records personal stories and local histories, layering them over the city at a 1:1 scale to construct a palimpsested collective memory for residents of areas undergoing dramatic urban redevelopment. The project aims to make planning practices more inclusive by using new technologies to put communities, government agencies, and developers in conversation.[5] These models demonstrate the ways in which the palimpsest can be a productive frame for examining a building or urban space with successive functions and appearances throughout time.

While the palimpsest is an important metaphor for interpretation of the Porta Nigra, I will

2.1. Porta Nigra, Trier. View from north.

also argue that the nature of architectural adaptation leads us to two further perspectives. The first stems from the temporal aspect of reuse, that is, the successive nature of conversion and adaptation. This diachronic aspect encourages us to adopt what Igor Kopytof has called the "cultural biography" of the structure.[6] Kopytoff sees the object as an economic and cultural commodity, with a life cycle like people:

> In doing the biography of a thing, one would ask questions similar to those one asks of people: … Where does the thing come from…? What has been its career so far…? … Biographies of things can make salient what might otherwise remain obscure. For example, in cases of culture contact, they can show what anthropologists have so often stressed: that what is significant about the adoption of alien objects is not the fact that they are adopted but the way that they are culturally redefined and put to use … A culturally informed economic biography of an object would look at it as a culturally-constructed entity, endowed with culturally specific meanings, and classified and reclassified into culturally constituted categories.[7]

Rather than focus upon the single moment of its creation, as is normative in art history, the changing functions and "culturally constituted categories" of the gate necessitate that we examine the *longue durée* of its existence, and the changing cultural circumstances of those biographic moments. The spoliate reuse of decorative and sculptural elements has been recognized as an important feature of medieval architecture, but far less attention has been accorded the wholesale re-occupation of sites and buildings from the past. My paper privileges the ongoing reuse of the entire Porta Nigra (as well as its larger architectural ensemble) across the eighteen centuries of its existence.

At the Porta Nigra, moreover, the past and present were at strategic moments made to coexist, turning the gate into what Michel Foucault would call a "heterotopia," or a space that maintains relationships to multiple times and places.[8] A utopia, of course, is an ideal social construction—an idea or an image that is not real but represents a perfected version of society. A heterotopia, on the other hand, is a real space with multiple relationships to other times and places. Foucault sketched the idea of heterotopia on three occasions: in the preface to his book, *Les mots et les choses*, published in 1966, where he focused upon the notion of heterotopia in language; in a radio broadcast on utopias and literature in the same year; and in a lecture presented to an architectural conference in 1967.[9] In this latter source, Foucault details a spatial rather than a linguistic approach to the concept:

> Utopias ... present society in a perfected form ... There are also in every culture ... places that do exist, which are something like countersites ... The mirror is after all a utopia, since it is a placeless place. In the mirror, I see myself where I am not ... but it is also a heterotopia in so far as the mirror does exist in reality, where it exerts a sort of counteraction on the position that I occupy.[10]

Foucault used the term heterotopia to describe spaces that have more layers of meaning or relationships to other places than might immediately be evident. Though his writing on heterotopias was more provocation than exegesis, Foucault developed several categories of heterotopic spaces, and three of those concepts will be useful for our examination of the Porta Nigra. First of all, a heterotopia can be a single real place that juxtaposes several spaces. A garden can be a heterotopia, if it is a real space meant to be a microcosm of different environments, with, for example, plants from around the world. Foucault's "heterotopias of time" (archives or museums that enclose in one place objects from many time periods) and "heterotopias of ritual" (places of worship that are accessible only to devotees) are both relevant. The Porta Nigra was, as we will see, a single real place that juxtaposed several temporal realities.

Monastic reuse

The adoption of inherited monuments by monastic communities was a dominant feature of the late antique and medieval landscape. Many of these exist as deliberate "countersites" to the pagan structures they occupy. According to Gregory the Great's *Life of Benedict of Nursia* (593–94), the sixth-century monastery of Monte Cassino was deliberately placed within the precinct of the temple of Apollo that crowned the hill, and the altar and grove that surrounded it. Benedict established the monastery there in *c.* 529.[11] Gregory reports that Benedict's first act was to smash the idol of Apollo and then to destroy the altar:

> Now the citadel called Casinum is located on the side of a high mountain. The mountain shelters this citadel on a broad bench. Then it rises three miles above it as if its peak tended toward heaven. There was an ancient temple there in which Apollo used to be worshipped according to the old pagan rite by the foolish local farmers. Around it had grown up a grove dedicated to demon worship, where even at that time a wild crowd still devoted themselves to unholy sacrifices. When [Benedict] the man of God arrived, he smashed the idol, overturned the altar and cut down the grove of trees. He built a chapel dedicated to St Martin in the temple of Apollo and another to St John where the altar of Apollo had stood. And he summoned the people of the district to the faith by his unceasing preaching.[12]

Whatever the truth-value of Gregory's narrative, it reveals monasticism's recognition of, and engagement with, monuments from the past. Gregory's *Life of Benedict* was among the most frequently copied manuscripts of the Middle Ages, giving continued cultural valence to the relationship between the Roman past and the monastic conversion of its former spaces.

While Gregory's aim at Monte Cassino was ostensibly to drive out idols from pagan sites, many of the popes in Rome focused more fully on the authority and allure of the Roman forum, establishing churches in most of its ancient monuments.[13] The former aula of the Templum Urbis Romae was converted into the (ultimately

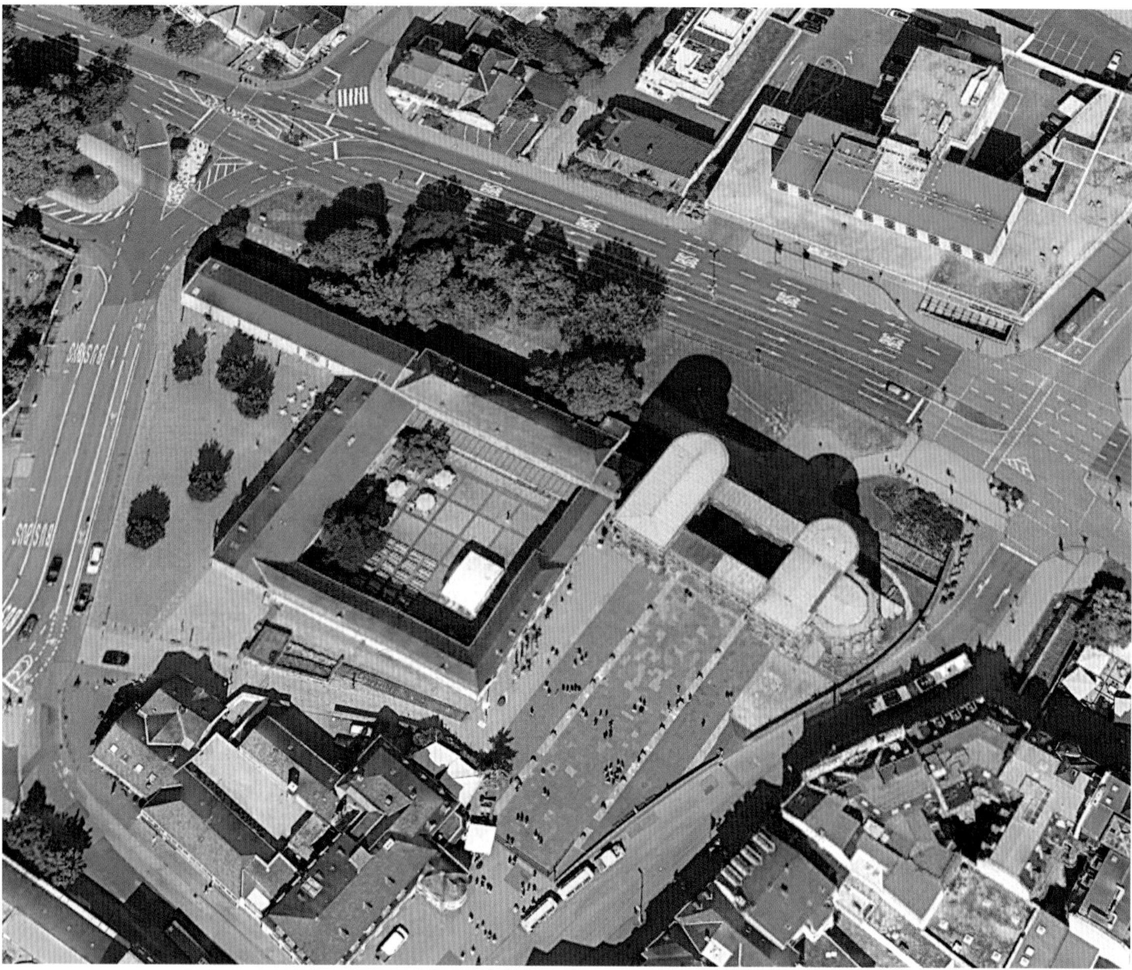

2.2. Aerial view of the Porta Nigra and Simeonstift.

monastic) church of Santi Cosma e Damiano, consecrated in 527 by Felix IV.[14] The former Curia Senatus was rededicated to Sant'Adriano by pope Honorius I (r. 625–38). After being given to pope Boniface IV (r. 608–15) by the Byzantine emperor Phocas in 609, the Pantheon became the earliest and best-known example of a Roman temple to undergo official conversion, when it was dedicated to Santa Maria ad Omnes Martyres.[15] It was not only popes, however, who converted ancient buildings to new religious purposes: a group of aristocratic women devoted themselves to strict asceticism and benevolent service. The leader of the group was Marcella (325–410), an ardent student of the Bible to whom Jerome referred questions from bishops and presbyters after he left the city. In the early fifth century, Marcella converted her Aventine hill palace to a monastery, the first convent for women in Rome.[16]

Textual and archaeological evidence demonstrates that monasteries occupied a variety of Roman sites, often within ancient temples, but also remodeling the more "neutral" building types of fortifications, granaries and warehouses, villas, baths—or city gates.[17] For example, a monastery was established on the site of the Roman fort of Reculver (Kent, England) in about 669, when King Ecgbert of Kent granted land for the foundation dedicated to Saint Mary.[18] Similarly, the monastery of São Cucufate (Alentejo, Portugal) was established on the site of a Roman agricultural villa in the ninth century, dedicated to the martyred Saint Cucuphas.[19] The monastery survived into the thirteenth century when a parish was established within it, and when its administration passed to Sao Vicente de Fora. The so-called "Temple of Diana" in Nîmes (Gard, France) was originally more likely a Roman archive building than a temple. The structure was given to a community of Benedictine nuns by the bishop in the late tenth century. The community adapted the library as their church and used its portico as their cloister until the eighteenth century.[20] The second-century amphitheater of Tarragona was the site of the martyrdom of the town's first bishop, Fructuarius, and two deacons. A Visigothic commemorative chapel was expanded in the twelfth century into the monastic church of Santa María del Miracle.[21] In the mid-eleventh century, the collegiate house of canons of Saint-Georges-de-Boscherville (Normandy, France) reoccupied the site of a succession of Gallo-Roman *fana* (shrines), the last of which had been converted into an early medieval funerary chapel before being abandoned.[22] These sites—and many others—demonstrate the coexistence of pragmatic reuse with a conscious awareness of the Roman past among medieval ecclesiastical and monastic patrons.

The Porta Nigra

The Porta Nigra was most likely built sometime between the last third of the second century CE, and the mid-third century CE.[23] The gate formed part of the fortification of Roman *Augusta Treverorum*, later the capital of Gallia Belgica and Roman prefecture of Gaul.[24] It served as the city's north gate (fig. 2.2). The gate was left unfinished, and was evidently built in a hurry, possibly by the military. The rushed and unfinished state is visible even today, with many blocks still with rough faces from the quarries, doorways unfitted, and decorative details roughed out but not completed.[25]

The exterior face of the Porta Nigra originally had two four-storey towers to either side of the two central arched gates (fig. 2.1). The Porta Nigra is a massive construction, built of large blocks of limestone held together without mortar but with iron clamps.[26] Although linked to the city walls, the gate was in essence a separate fortified building with an inner courtyard, 21.5 meters (71 feet) deep, with sentry walks on the second storey (fig. 2.3a). The entries were protected by portcullises so that anyone entering could be examined from the sentry passages—and then trapped by a planned second gate if they failed to pass inspection. The gate was first successfully tested in the late second century when insurgents threatened the town.[27] By the fifth century, however, Trier's fortifications ceased to be maintained, and habitation was reduced within the town.

With the change in function and context in the fifth century, we can invoke the metaphor of the palimpsest. The first instance of "erasure" at the Porta Nigra occurred at this time, when the structure became valued more for its constituent parts than its integral function. The iron and lead of the construction clamps was particularly attractive, and in many places the stone was gouged away to recuperate the clamps.[28] At about the same period, entire blocks of the upper storey of the east tower were quarried and carried away for construction of other buildings.

Saint Simeon and the Porta Nigra

The quarrying of the Porta Nigra might have continued but for the arrival of Saint Simeon of Trier (*c.* late 10th century–1035), also known as Symeon of Antioch.[29] Simeon spent the last five years of his life "enclosed" in a cell within the Porta Nigra. This religious conversion of the gate was preceded by a chapel dedicated to Saint Michael, which was inserted into the structure at some time prior to Simeon's arrival.[30]

Simeon came to Trier by a circuitous—and largely accidental—route. According to his *vita*, Simeon was born in the late tenth century in Sicily during Arab rule. His remarkable travels reveal him to have been one of the earliest global citizens. Simeon's father, a former Byzantine soldier, sent him to school in Constantinople when he was a child in order that he might acquire written Greek. Simeon developed a desire to lead a religious life, so he left Constantinople for Jerusalem. During the next seven years, he worked as a religious tour guide, leading pilgrims to the sacred sites of the Holy Land, until he decided to seek a new life as a recluse. Having heard of a hermit who lived on the banks of the Jordan River, Simeon requested to live as

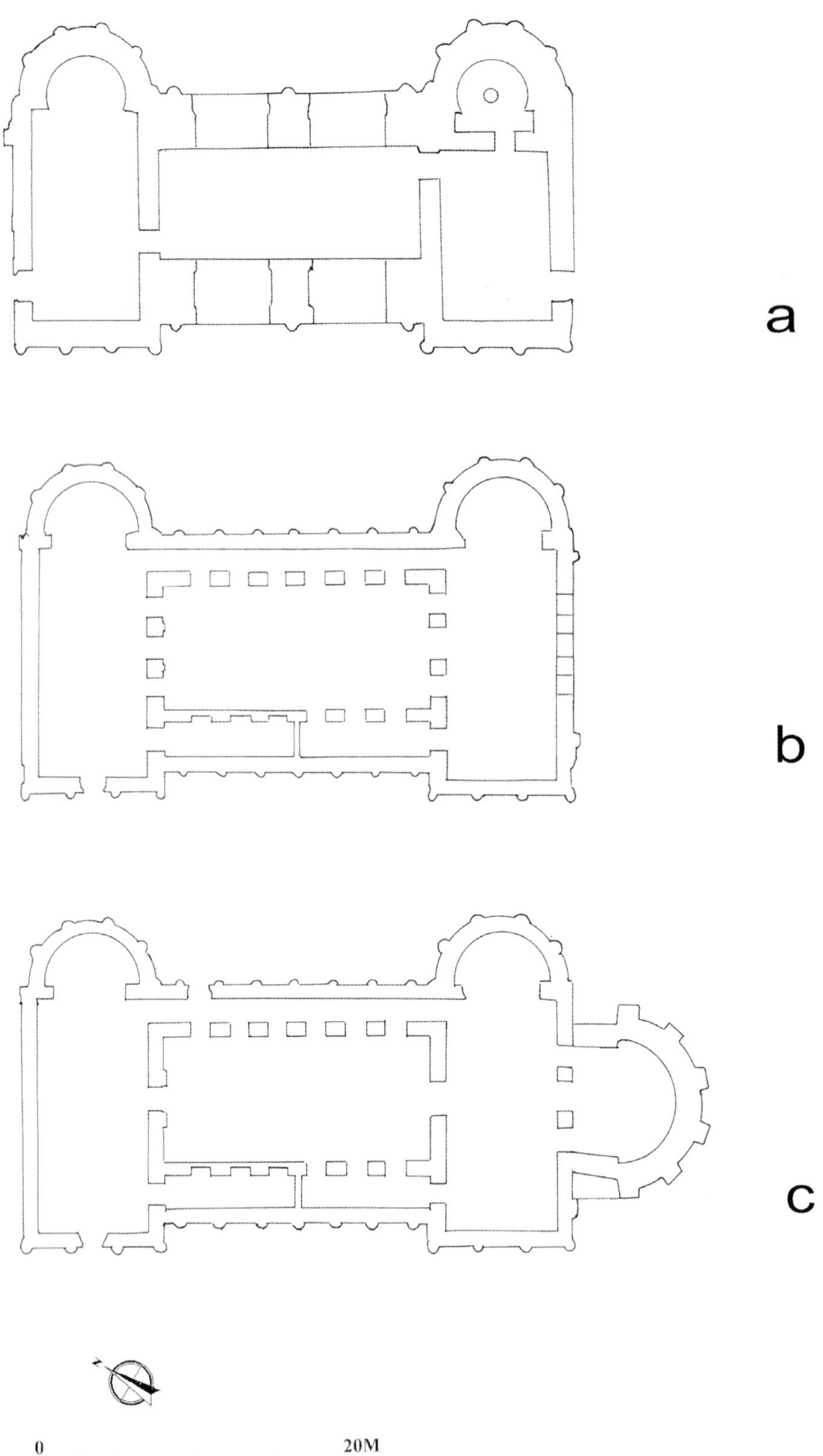

2.3. Plans of the Porta Nigra: a) Porta Nigra as Roman gate, second or early third century CE; b) plan of the church installed in the Porta Nigra, *c.* 1035–50; c) plan of the church, 1150–1700, with the apse added by Albero of Montreuil.

his servant and apprentice, living in the lower room of the hermit's tower residence. When Simeon's master suddenly disappeared, he decided to seek further training in a monastic setting. As the first phase of this monastic existence, he entered the Monastery of the Virgin in Bethlehem. Two years later, he sought admittance to the Monastery of Saint Catherine's on Mount Sinai in Egypt but he was torn between the eremetic and coenobitic lifestyles. With the abbot's permission, Simeon spent time as a hermit in a small cave on the banks of the Red Sea. A monk from the monastery brought him food once a week, but Simeon worried about the fatigue of the monk charged with his care, and was further disturbed by the traffic of passing sailors on the Red Sea. He decided to return to the monastery, but struggled with communal life. At one point, the abbot sent him to the top of Mount Sinai, but Simeon returned.

A turning point was reached in 1026. Richard II, Duke of Rouen, had pledged an annuity to the monastery that the community was obliged to collect. The abbot dispatched Simeon to present documents and collect the annuity from Richard. The trip turned out to be longer and more arduous than Simeon or the abbot could have expected. Travelling on the Nile to get there, Simeon's boat was attacked by pirates, and the crew was killed. Simeon was the lone survivor, escaping by diving into the sea. When he swam ashore, however, he found himself unable to communicate with the villagers. Simeon's biographer describes Simeon's astonishment when he—fluent in Egyptian, Aramaic, Arabic, Greek, and Latin—could not understand a word spoken to him. Eventually, Simeon made his way to Antioch where he quickly won fame as a scholar. There, he met Richard, abbot of the monastery of Saint-Vanne, and a German cleric, Eberwin, abbot of the monastery of Tholey (and Simeon's biographer-to-be). Both were on their way to the Holy Land on a remarkable pilgrimage that went overland via Belgrade, Hungary, and Constantinople to Antioch and beyond. Simeon joined the group on its return journey, though he was blocked from passing through Belgrade, lacking the necessary documents. Simeon finally succeeded in arriving in France, travelling via Italy. He reached Rouen (about a decade late for his appointment with Richard II), only to discover that Richard had died in the interim, and that no one could recall an annuity owed Saint Catherine's. Disconsolate, Simeon went to visit his new friends, Richard of Saint Vanne and Abbot Eberwin, and travelled to Trier in 1027. There he met Archbishop Poppo von Babenburg (1016–47), who was planning a pilgrimage to Jerusalem. After meeting Simeon, Poppo invited him to accompany him on the journey.

After the pilgrimage was complete, Simeon chose not to return to his own monastery in Egypt, instead accompanying Poppo back to Trier, a trip that lasted from 1028 to 1030. After their return, Simeon asked Poppo if he might—finally—realize his life's aim to live as a recluse, and the former Roman gate of the city, the Porta Nigra, was chosen as the locus of his hermitage. Poppo conducted a ceremony on 29 November 1030, before all the clergy and people. The day chosen was the feast of Saint Andrew, an important feast for the city of Trier. Simeon was enclosed in a cell, high in the east gate tower (fig. 2.3a).

Simeon lived as a hermit within the Porta Nigra for five years. He died in his cell on 1 June 1035. Very quickly, his *vita* attests, miracles began to occur, and pilgrims were attracted to the site.[31] A ladder was installed so that pilgrims might see into the holy cell. In the same year, Abbot Eberwin wrote an account of his life and miracles, and Bishop Poppo immediately sent that *vita* to Pope Benedict IX.[32] Within that same year, the pope issued a bull of canonization—one of the first such bulls—and Trier was thus quickly provided with a miracle-working saint.[33]

Reuse and relics at the Porta Nigra

Competition for saints' relics was one of the features of eleventh-century religious life in Trier. Simeon's enclosure had been celebrated on the feast of Saint Andrew, a saint whose relics were found in the cathedral church of Trier. Held within a decorated foot reliquary and portable altar, Saint Andrew's sandal is one of the important relics, along with the Seamless Robe of

2.4. Caspar Merian, *St Simeon in Porta Nigra in Trier*, engraving, 1670.

Jesus, the robe said to have been worn by Jesus during or shortly before his crucifixion. The cathedral also possessed one of the nails from the Crucifixion, as well as the skull of Saint Helena, mother of the emperor Constantine. Much effort had recently been devoted to the recovery and reburial of Saint Maximinus at his eponymous abbey outside the walls to the north of the Porta Nigra. By 952, behind the main apse of Saint Maximinus, a two-storied outer crypt was constructed around the three-celled core of the former Merovingian-Carolingian crypt, destroyed by the Norman invasions.[34] Sigehard's tenth-century account of Saint Maximinus' miracles celebrated the efficacy of his relics.[35] Thus, the canonization of Simeon turned the new church within the Porta Nigra into a pilgrimage destination and allowed it to participate in the cult of relics in the city. In fact, Simeon himself had requested that he be buried within the Porta Nigra, and not in the cathedral or another monastic church as Poppo had initially suggested.[36] The Life of Simeon written by Eberwin enjoyed remarkable popularity, surviving in more than fifty manuscripts. The widespread appeal of the *vita* also served to spread the fame of the saint and his relics at the new church. The rewriting of this *vita* echoed the palimpsestual nature of the building.

When Poppo died in 1047, he instructed that his own body should be added to the church, interred in Simeon's cell next to the saint. The physical "addition" of holy bodies was thus one of the strategies of conversion taken at the Porta Nigra. First, Poppo incorporated Saint Simeon's living body into the ruined Roman building,

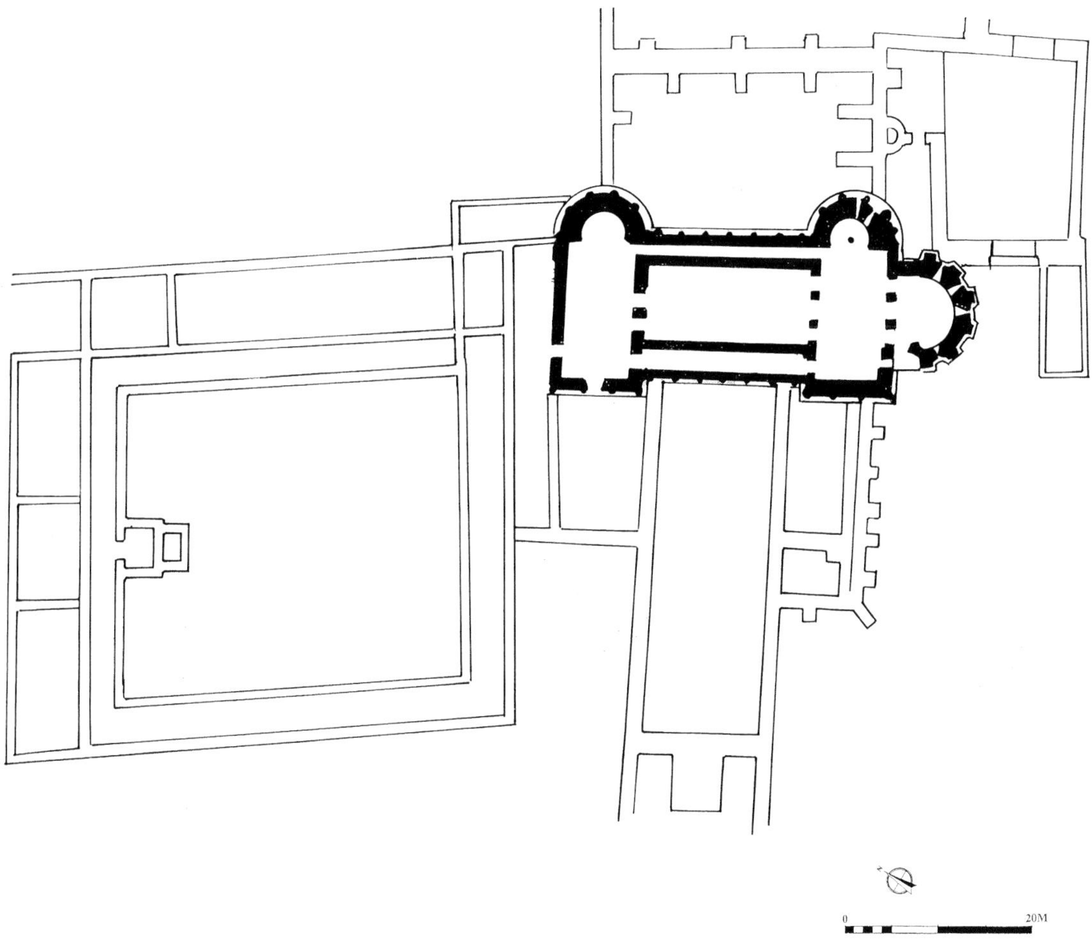

2.5. Reconstruction plan of the church of Saint Simeon (converting the Porta Nigra) and the Simeonstift in *c.* 1150, recording the platform and terracing shown in the Caspar Merian engraving (fig. 2.4) and discovered in excavations in the 1930s.

making Simeon's enclosure a sort of burial and his body that of a living relic. In fact, Eberwin likened his enclosure to "a sepulcher."[37] Soon after his death, Simeon's tomb became the foundational relic for the new church that converted the ancient structure (fig. 2.3b). The bishop's own body was added twelve years later. These burials constitute an embodied palimpsest for the Porta Nigra.

The Porta Nigra: conversion as palimpsest and heterotopia

An examination of the plan and elevation of the structure will help us "recover" the ways in which the Porta Nigra was converted into the church of Saint Simeon in the eleventh century—and the ways in which the building can be read as both palimpsest and heterotopia. Older views of the building before de-restoration of the nineteenth century preserve a record of the ecclesiastical aspects of the building. Caspar Merians' 1670 engraved view of the church is particularly rich in its detailed observation of the south elevation of the building (fig. 2.4). In the Merian view, we can appreciate the ways in which the Roman gate dictated the plan and guided the elevation of Poppo's new double church, with the monastic church in the uppermost storey and a parish church at the lower level (the second storey of the gate). Significantly, the Roman gate was still visible beneath its

2.6. View of the apse from southeast.

2.7. View of the Simeonstift *quadrum*.

palimpsested accretions, rendering it heterotopic—neither fully Roman nor fully medieval, but with past and present coexisting.

The very circulation level of the building was shifted for its new purpose. In order to manage access and entry to the "revised" building, the courtyard and gateways at the ground storey were "erased" by being filled with rubble. Significantly, it was this level that had held Simeon's cell. The sanctified level of the hermit's existence was buried, like the saint himself.

On the north (exterior) side a broad terrace was created with massive retaining walls. To the south, a new massive stairway beginning about 30 meters (100 feet) away from the church led to a spacious podium. From there, an angled stair led directly to the monastic church on the upper level (figs. 2.4 and 2.5). On the east tower of the gate was the "transept" crossing of the churches. Over the west tower rose a belfry.

The entire structure measured almost 50 meters (165 feet) to the top of the tower, and on its elevated platform, it dominated the north entrance to the town. From the twelfth century, the town walls began to be repaired. A new Simeon's gate for traffic was relocated adjoining the east end. With its elevated position, massive retaining walls, and incorporation into the town fortifications, the Simeonskirche became in effect a fortified church—a fortress of God—protecting the newly revived town through the intercession of its adopted saint.[38]

The twelfth century saw renewed additions and expansion to the "double" church. In *c.* 1150, after Poppo's death, Archbishop Albero of Montreuil (1131–52) reframed the east end of the building.[39] Albero had formerly been provost of the monastery of Saint Simeon, and thus knew the building well. He added an elaborately decorated apse with exterior gallery to the church (figs. 2.3c and 2.6). At this time, too, the separation between the floors of the two churches, originally accomplished by the addition of a simple wooden floor, was replaced by vaulting.[40]

The chancel of the collegiate church originally stood atop the new apse, as we can see in Merian's engraving (fig. 2.4). The new apse was the only addition to break the plan of the original building, but it did so with a form that echoed and repeated the shape and dimensions of the semicircular projections of the original towers. Those towers were now fitted with spiral staircases to accommodate movement within the "double" church.

The lower level of the Porta Nigra was now occupied, as we have seen, by the parish church (fig. 2.3c). The former Roman sentry walks were used as side-aisles, converting military elements to recognizably medieval religious ones, but without obscuring their Roman origin. The parish church space was entered from a door in the south aisle.

The top storey of the Porta Nigra was used for the collegiate church (fig. 2.4). It was arranged similarly, but with an additional upper level of clerestorey windows (only the lower section of this upper church, roofed in timber, now remains). The relic of Saint Simeon's body was located in the "crypt" of the double church, at the ground level of the east tower, directly beneath the parish church.

The transformation of the Porta Nigra into a church was not simply accomplished by the conversion of its interior to new religious functions. The ruined gate was very cleverly adapted (in fact, both inhabited as well as wrapped) and given a new identity, but without compromising its former plan or appearance. In this aspect, the Porta Nigra is visibly a palimpsest, erased and rewritten from gate into church, but without full erasure of its former appearance.

The Porta Nigra can also productively be seen as a heterotopia. The converted gate/church became at once an archive for Saint Simeon's relics, as well as a ritual space. Simeon's past occupation of the Porta Nigra as a hermit co-existed in the medieval communities' experience of the building. At times, the entire town might participate. For example, the calendar of feasts celebrated at Saint-Simeon makes clear that the death date for Saint Simeon, 1 June, as well as the death date for Poppo, 16 June, were celebrated as "stational feasts," with the chapters of both the cathedral and Saint-Paulin coming in procession to Saint Simeon.[41] On the day of the station, the faithful would gather in Saint-Simeon, singing the Litany of the Saints. In this way, the converted Porta Nigra would gather the community of Trier in a collective remembrance of Simeon's past life in the Roman gate. The Roman past, Simeon's life, and the present moment would be deliberately fused in heterotopic fashion for the faithful.

Simeonstift

It was not only the gate of the Porta Nigra that was reused in the medieval palimpsest. It is important to recognize that the adaptive reuse of the Porta Nigra included both the gate as well as the adjoining fortified precinct immediately to the west (fig. 2.3b). After Simeon's death in 1035, Poppo also set about the establishment of an adjoining community of canons dedicated to Saint Simeon, the Simeonstift, which was underway by 1042.[42]

The portion of the Roman city walls adjacent to the Porta Nigra were reused as the enclosure for the precinct (fig. 2.2). The double-storied claustral buildings of the Simeonstift formed a rough square, called the *quadrum*, around the garden (figs. 2.5 and 2.7). The dormitory lay on the upper storey to the north, with the refectory and fountain house to the west. The community's chapter room was situated in the northeast corner of the *quadrum*, next to the former west tower of the Porta Nigra.

The community continued to attract donations and support from a high level of secular and ecclesiastical society from the eleventh and twelfth centuries. Bishops continued to support the collegiate foundation, and emperors gave rich gifts. In 1098, for example, the emperor Henry VI confirmed all his possessions to the Simeonstift and granted more than sixty properties and privileges to it.[43] In this sense, the foundation was palimpsested with increasing properties.

2.8. View of the Rococo panels in the west tower.

In the thirteenth century, Simeon's and Poppo's tombs were transferred to the monastic church. Their tombs were thus made newly visible as indicators of the religious foundation of the church and monastic community. Again, the church was called to function as a heterotopia, with the moments of Roman past, eleventh-century foundation, and thirteenth-century present coexisting. Other burials were drawn to the site across time, and many were signaled by commemorative plaques placed on the walls of the narthex, nave, or aisles. The canons Heinrich von Rommersheim (d. 1474) and Nikolas von Strassburg (d. 1524), for example, are commemorated by inscriptions in the nave, while their tombs lay under the stone floor of the parish church (that is, in the rubble fill of the ground storey of the gate). The presence of tombs and burial inscriptions in the church signal the ways in which burial became a continuous palimpsestual activity from the thirteenth through the sixteenth centuries, with canons of the monastery incorporating their own bodies to the physical site of Simeon's past hermitage and burial, and their funerary inscriptions added to the surfaces of the Roman walls. While the presence of burials is normative within medieval churches, its performance within Saint-Simeon was heightened by the activity of pilgrims and devotional practices at the church.

The post-medieval Porta Nigra

The church was again "palimpsested" with Rococo decoration between 1746 and 1760. In 1755, the narthexes of both churches were covered with images of saints important to Trier (fig. 2.8). These panels were first cut into the stone, carving back the existing surfaces, recalling the scraping of the palimpsest. The panels

2.9. Hitler's banner hanging on the front of the Porta Nigra in April 1938.

were then coated with stucco, paint, and gilding, effectively rewriting the surfaces of the palimpsest. In the lower church, for example, Saint Martin of Tours, Saint Bernard of Clairvaux, Pope Leo IX, Theodore of Marseilles, and Paul of Constantinople were carved into panels on the west wall, and on the east, Athanasius, Augustine, Jerome, and Ambrose. Nearly all of the represented figures had visited Trier, accentuating the heterotopic fusion of past and present.[44] The *style* of the rococo decoration brought the church up to date with current fashion, while the *iconography* signaled the ongoing connection with a variety of past moments, further underscoring the heterotopic nature of the site.

The modern period was not kind to the claustral buildings adjacent to the church of Saint-Simeon. In the eighteenth century, the dormitory was divided into rooms. The northern third of the east wing was demolished in the nineteenth century. In 1802 Napoleon Bonaparte dissolved the church in the Porta Nigra and the monastery beside it, along with the vast majority of Trier's numerous churches and monasteries. At this time, the claustral area of the Simeonstift was converted into private residences and commercial spaces. In 1804, Napoleon visited Trier and ordered the accretions of the church removed from the gate, thus signaling a desire to return the monument to its Roman identity. That work of removing the infilling of the ground storey—with its burials—and the altars and fittings of the two churches, was not completed until the middle of the nineteenth century, but it began a significant shift in attitude in which the Roman past began to eclipse the medieval.[45] The process of "reinventing" Roman Trier was, in fact, begun by Napoleon. Starting in 1804, the connection between the gate and its monastic buildings was also severed, making the heterotopic nature of the site even clearer. Significantly, Karl Marx was born in 1818 and lived in a house down the street (now called Karl Marx Strasse) from the Porta Nigra. Marx may have been influenced by the revival of the Roman past at just this moment.[46]

The disconnection between the Porta Nigra and the collegiate cloister was further accentuated in the middle of the twentieth century when the former claustral buildings began to be used to display some of the city's collections. The conversion of the Simeonstift to a museum recalls Foucault's category of museums as heterotopias, where the past is collected in a single

2.10. Centurion guide at the Porta Nigra.

moment. The definition of that past, however, became as contested as that of the Porta Nigra.

A museum planned to unite all antiquities and museum collections of Trier was put on hold by the events of the Second World War. The museum collections were not spared Nazi propaganda. From 1937 to 1938 the Trier city council purged pieces of "non-German" art in order to enable cultural institutions to be harnessed for propaganda. Dutch and Italian masters were sold, and from the proceeds, contemporary German art was acquired, accentuating a nationalist identity for the museum. As the Porta Nigra became more Roman, the museum collections grew increasingly German.[47]

The war was disastrous for the city. Especially from 1944 onward, the city was on the front line. In December of 1944, Trier saw heavy bombing. Over 1600 houses were destroyed, and many of the ancient and medieval monuments were damaged. The Porta Nigra was spared by the bombing, but the Porta Nigra Plaz was renamed the Adolf Hitler Plaz in 1933. As an ephemeral palimpsest, flags bearing Hitler's image were hung from the Porta Nigra as he marched through the city in April 1938 (fig. 2.9).[48]

During the 1960s and '70s, the Porta Nigra and its former claustral buildings were restored. The gate was named a World Heritage site in 1986. Remarkably, the World Heritage designation recognizes the complicated cultural biography of the Porta Nigra:

> Of the buildings preserved from classical times, at least two of those described are unparalleled. The Porta Nigra, with its state of preservation and its architectural layout … is a unique construction that is unlike any of the other preserved Roman gates. Its development during the Middle Ages into a (likewise very unusual) double church also makes it a symbol of Western history.[49]

2.11. Karl Marx statues in front of the Porta Nigra, as part of an installation by the artist Ottmar Hörl, May 2013.

The claustral spaces were not included in the World Heritage recognition. The museum was reinstalled in those spaces in 2007. In these restorations, however, Trier's past was focused almost exclusively upon the Roman moment. A visitor to the Porta Nigra today is greeted by a gladiator clad in Roman cuirass and helmet (fig. 2.10). The Porta Nigra's identity is now firmly singular and Roman, while the adjacent museum is a separate enterprise—requiring a separate admission ticket for all visitors. While the museum is now dedicated to showing the entirety of Trier's local history, it highlights the life of Karl Marx who has eclipsed Saint Simeon as the city's favored personage. Within the context of a 2013 installation by the artist Ottmar Hörl, 500 one-meter tall statues in bright red were placed on the Karl Marx Strasse in front of the Porta Nigra (fig. 2.11), making the dominance of Marx in the cultural landscape of Trier palpable.

Conclusion

When I began working on this project (in the prehistoric era of the slide and photograph study room), I used to complain that images like this one were filed in the wrong drawer—stuck in Roman Trier under the heading of "city gate." For my research purposes, the Porta Nigra should instead have been filed in the medieval drawer—under "church." The digital age has at least allowed me to have a duplicate heading, but our scholarly practice in art history is just beginning to confront the multiple identities and the complicated cultural biographies of our objects and buildings. We continue, too often, to recognize only the single, originary phase of production or construction as legitimate. Refocusing our attention on cultural biography, successive palimpsests, and heterotopias allows us to recognize the complicated ways in which the ancient surfaces of the Porta Nigra were scraped, scrubbed, filled in, re-covered, and uncovered again to serve a changing and sometime competing list of new functions, recognizing all the while that the past often continued to co-exist with the present in the cultural experience of those spaces.

Notes

1 Netz and Noel 2007; *Archimedes Palimpsest*.
2 Machado 1976.
3 Bailey 2007.
4 Tran 2013; and Verheij 2015.
5 See Beaumont, Torisu, and Tveito 2016.
6 On the notion of cultural biography, see Kopytof 1986, 64–91; and Gosden and Marshall 1999.
7 Kopytof 1986, 66–68.
8 Foucault 1966a; Foucault 1966b; Foucault 1970; and Foucault 1984. See also Halbwachs 1992; and Connerton 1989.
9 See Foucault 1966a; Foucault 1966b; and Foucault 1967. On the history of Foucault's ideas on heterotopia, see Johnson 2006. *Les mots et les choses* was published in English in 1970 as *The Order of Things* (see Foucault 1970.) Foucault only gave his permission to publish the text of the 1967 radio broadcast in 1984 as "Des espaces autres" (see Foucault 1984).
10 Foucault 1984, 3–4.
11 On Monte Cassino, see esp. Bloch 1986.
12 Gregory the Great, in Kardong 2009, 49.
13 Jacks 2008.
14 Tucci 2004.

15 On the reuse of the Pantheon, see Krautheimer 1980, 72–75; and Christie 2006, 129.
16 Much of what we know about Marcella is found in the letters of Jerome, her associate. See Cain 2009, 68–98.
17 On the reuse of ancient structure as churches and monasteries, see Ward-Perkins 1984, 85–91; Greenhalgh 1989, 86–118; Leone 2007, esp. 185–211; Jacks, 2008; and Coomans 2012, esp. 222–25.
18 On Reculver, see Fletcher 1965; and Wilmott 2012.
19 On Sao Cucufate, see Alarcão (1979) 1980; *IGESPAR* 2011; and Mareco 2007, 128–37.
20 On the reuse of the "temple of Diana" at Nîmes, see Bonde 1999; and Bonde 1999–2000.
21 On the successive churches in the amphitheater in Tarragona, see Alföldy 1990; Alföldy 1991; *TED'A* 1990; Keay 1996, 22; and Bonde 2018 (forthcoming).
22 Le Maho 1986.
23 The date is controversial. See Dessau 1892–1916, vol. 1, 2287, 2616–17; Gose 1969, vol. 1, 34–38; and Wightman 1971, 95–96.
24 On the fortifications, see Wightman 1971, 92–94. On the Porta Nigra's Roman phase, see Gose 1969; Wightman 1971, 94–98; Parlaska 1973; Cüppers 1973a; Cüppers 1973b; Zahn 1974; Schwinden 2001; and Sturm 2002.
25 Wightman 1971, 96.
26 The completed west tower measured 30 meters (1000 feet) in height. The gate stretches 36 meters (119 feet) in width and is 21.5 meters (71 feet) deep.
27 The town was rescued by the legion at nearby Mainz. An inscription in Mainz attests to the gratitude of the citizens of Trier. See Sturm 2002, 2.
28 This is visible in the surviving fabric of the walls.
29 On Simeon, see AAAS 1695, Jun. 1, 87–107; and esp. Eberwin's *vita* of Simeon, AAAS 1695, Jun. 1, 89–95; Coens 1950; and Heinz 1967.
30 The chapel of Saint Michael is mentioned in AAAS 1695, Jun. 1, 87.
31 AAAS 1695, Jun. 1, 93–94.
32 AAAS 1695, Jun. 1, 98.
33 On the disputed chronology of Simeon's date of canonization, see Coens 1950, 184–87. Coens makes clear that the date must be in 1035. See also AAAS 1695, Jun. 1, 96–97; and for the papal bulls: Beyer 1860, vol. 1, 370–72; and Jaffé 1885, nos 4112 and 4113.
34 Sanderson 1965.
35 Nightingale 2001, 174–84.
36 AAAS 1695, Jun. 1, 93.
37 "… ut verius dicam sepulchrum." AAAS 1695, Jun. 1, 2.
38 On the importance of fortified churches in the medieval period, see Bonde 1994.
39 On Albero, see Pavlac 2008.
40 Traces of the vaulting are still visible.
41 Heyen 2002, 576–94.
42 For the act of foundation, see Beyer 1860, vol. 1, 372, doc. 318. On the medieval church and monastery of Saint Simeon, see Bunjes and Kutzbach 1938; Irsch and Bunjes 1938; Wisplinghoff 1956; Heinz 1967; Kubach 1974; Zahn 1974; Zahn 1977; Sturm 2002; and Heyen 2002, esp. 32–187.
43 Beyer 1860, vol. 1, 452, doc. 397.
44 Among the represented personages, only Augustine had not been present in Trier, although the city played a role in his conversion.
45 Müller 1998.
46 Hall 2011.
47 Leuchtenberg 2012.
48 Welter 1998.
49 World Heritage: http://whc.unesco.org/en/list/367 (accessed 30 August 2017)

Bibliography

AAAS (*Acta sanctorum quotquot toto orbe celebrantur quae ex Latin et Graecis, aliariumque gentium antiquis monumentis collegit, digessit, Notis illustravit Jannes Bollandus*). 1643–1940. Antwerp: Joannes Meursius; Brussels: Culture et Civilisation.

Alarcão, Jorge. [1979] 1980. "Escavações na villa luso-romana de S. Cucufate," *Humanitas* 31–32, 272–75.

Alföldy, Géza. 1991. *Tarraco* (ser. Temes d'història i d'arqueologia tarragonines, 8). Tarragona: Museu Nacional Arqueològic de Tarragona.

—. 1990. "Dues inscripcions monumentals de l'Amfiteatre de tarraco." In TED'A (Taller Escola d'Arqueologia), *Memòries d'excavacio* 3, 130–37.

The Archimedes Palimpsest, http://archimedespalimpsest.org/digital/google-book.php (accessed 30 August 2017).

Bailey, Geoff. 2007. "Time Perspectives, Palimpsests and the Archaeology of Time," *Journal of Anthropological Archaeology* 26, no. 2, 198–223.

Beaumont, J. Russell, Takashi Torisu, and Haavard Tveito. 2016. "The Palimpsest: A project by the Interactive Architecture Lab." https://www.designboom.com/architecture/the-palimpsest-interactive-architecture-lab-ucl-virtual-reality-11-21-2016/ (accessed 30 August 2017)

Beyer, Heinrich, with Leopold Elsester and Adam Goerz. 1860. *Mittelrheinische Urkundendenbuch: (Urkundenbuch zur Geschichte der mittelrheinischen Territorien: Von den älsten Zeiten bis zum Jahre 1169)*. Koblenz: J. Hölscher.

Bloch, Herbert. 1986. *Monte Cassino in the Middle Ages*. Cambridge: Harvard University Press.

Bonde, Sheila. 2018 (forthcoming). "The Afterlife of the Amphitheater: Cultural Biography and Social Memory at Tarragona," in *Reuse and Renovation in Roman Material Culture: Functions, Aesthetics, Interpretations*, ed. Molly Swetnam-Burland and Diana Y. Ng. Cambridge: Cambridge University Press.

—. 1999–2000. "L'effacement de Saint-Sauveur-de-la-Font: approches à la survivance de l'antiquitè durant le moyen âge," *Bulletin de l'Ecole Antique de Nîmes* 25, 57–76.

—. 1999. "Renaissance and Real Estate: the Medieval Afterlife of the Temple of Diana at Nîmes," in *Antiquity and its Interpreters*, ed. Alina Payne, Ann Kuttner, and Rebekah Smick. Cambridge: Cambridge University Press, 57–69.

—. 1994. *Fortress Churches of Languedoc: Architecture, Religion and Conflict in the High Middle Ages*. Cambridge: Cambridge University Press.

Bunjes, Hermann, and Baurat F. Kutzbach. 1938. *Die Wiederherstellung des Simeonsstiftes in Trier* (rep. from *Deutsche Kunst und Denkmalpflege* 4, 81–94). Berlin: n.p.

Cain, Andrew. 2009. *Letters of Jerome: Asceticism, Biblical Exegesis, and the Construction of Christian Authority in Late Antiquity*. Oxford: Oxford University Press.

Christie, Neil. 2006. *From Constantine to Charlemagne: An Archaeology of Italy,* AD *300–800*. Franham: Ashgate.

Coens, Maurice. 1950. "Un document inédit sur le culte de S. Syméon, moine d'orient et reclus a Trèves," *Analecta Bollandiana* 68, 181–96.

Connerton, Paul. 1989. *How Societies Remember*. Cambridge: Cambridge University Press.

Coomans, Thomas, ed. 2012. *Loci Sacri: Understanding Sacred Places*. Leuven: University of Leuven Press.

Cüppers, Heinz. 1979. *Trier: Porta Nigra*. Mainz: Landesamt für Denkmalpflege Rheinland-Pflaz, Verwaltung der Staatlichen Schlösser.

—. 1973. "Die Stadtmauer des römischen Trier und das Gräberfeld an der Porta Nigra," *Trierer Zeitschrift für Geschichte und Kunst des Trierer Landes und seiner Nachbargebiete* 36, 133–222.

Dessau, Hermann. *1892–1916*. *Inscriptiones Latinae Selectae*, 3 vols. Berolini: Weidmann.

Eberwin, "De sancto Symeone, recluso in porta Trevirensi," in AAAS 1695, Jun. 1, 89–95.

Ferrari, Michele C. 2002. "From Pilgrims's Guide to Living Relic: Symeon of Trier and his Biographer Eberwin," in *Latin culture in the eleventh century: Proceedings of the third international conference on Medieval Latin Studies*. Turnhout: Brepols, 324–44.

Fletcher, Eric. 1965. "Early Kentish churches," *Medieval Archaeology* 9, 16–31.

Foucault, Michel. 1986. "Of Other Spaces: Utopias and Heterotopias," trans. Jay Miskowiec, *Diacritics* 16, no. 1, 22–27.

—. 1984. "Des Espaces Autres," *Architecture /Mouvement/ Continuité* 5, 46–49.

—. 1970. *The Order of Things: An Archaeology of the Human Sciences*. London: Tavistock Publications.

—. 1966a. *Les mots et les choses*. Paris: Éditions Gallimard.

—. 1966b. "Utopie et littérature," recorded copy of a radio broadcast, 7 December. Centre Michel Foucault, Bibliothèque du Saulchoir, C116.

Gosden, Chris, and Yvonne Marshall. 1999. "The cultural biography of objects," *World Archaeology* 31, no. 2, 169–78.

Gose, Erich, ed. 1969. *Die Porta Nigra in Trier*, 2 vols. (ser. Trierer Grabungen und Forschungen, 4). Berlin: Gebr. Mann Verlag.

Greenhalgh, Michael. 1989. *The Survival of Roman Antiquities in the Middle Ages*. London: Duckworth.

Halbwachs, Maurice. 1992. *On Collective Memory*. Ed. and trans. Lewis A. Coser. Chicago: University of Chicago Press, 1992.

—. 1968. *La mémoire collective*. 2nd ed. Paris: Presses universitaires de France.

Hall, Edith. 2011. "Beneath the shadow of the Porta Nigra: Karl Marx and the ruins of Trier," in *Antiquity and the Ruin*, ed. Ahuvia Kahane, special issue of *European Review of History/ Revue européene d'histoire* 18, no. 5–6, 783–97.

Heinz, Albert. 1967. "Der heilingen Simeon von Trier: seine Kanonisation und seine Reliquien," in *Festschrift für Alois Thomas: Archäologische, kirchen- und kunsthistorische Beiträge. Zur Vollendung des 70. Lebensjahres am 18. Januar 1966*. Trier: Selbstvlg. d. Bistumsarchivs, 163–73.

Heyen, Franz-Josef. 2002. *Das Stift St Simeon in Trier* (ser. Germania Sacra, Das Erzbistum Trier, n.s., 41, no. 9). Berlin and New York: Walter de Gruyter.

IGESPAR (Instituto Gestão do Patrimonio Arquitectónico e Arqueológico). 2011. "Ruínas do antigo Convento de São Cucufate, também conhecidas por ruínas de Santiago." http://www.patrimoniocultural.gov.pt/pt/patrimonio/patrimonio-imovel/pesquisa-do-patrimonio/classificado-ou-em-vias-de-classificacao/geral/view/70270/ (accessed 30 August 2017)

Irsch, Nikolaus, and Hermann Bunjes. 1938. "Ehemalige Stiftskirche St Simeon," in *Die kirchlichen Denkmäler der Stadt Trier. Die Kunstdenmäler des Rheinprovinz* 13, no. 3, 463–97.

Jacks, Philip. 2008. "Restauratio and Reuse: The Afterlife of Roman Ruins," *Places* 20, no. 1, 10–20.

Jaffé, Philipp. 1885, *Regesta Pontificum Romanorum ab Condiata ad annum post Christum Natum*, vol. 1. Leipzig: Veit and Co.

Johnson, Peter. 2006. "Unravelling Foucault's 'different spaces'," *History of the Human Sciences* 19, no. 4, 75–90.

Kardong, Terrence G. 2009. *The Life of Saint Benedict by Gregory the Great: Translation and Commentary*. Collegeville: Liturgical Press.

Keay, Simon. 1996. "Tarraco in Late Antiquity," in *Towns in Transition: Urban Evolution in Late Antiquity and the early Middle Ages*, ed. Neil Christie and Simon Keay. Aldershot: Scolar Press, 18–44.

Kopytof, Igor. 1986. "The cultural biography of things: commoditization as process," in *The Social Life of Things: Commodities in Social Perspective*, ed. Arun Appadurai. Cambridge: Cambridge University Press.

Krautheimer, Richard. 1980. *Rome: Profile of a City, 312-1308*. Princeton: Princeton University Press.

Kubach, Hans Erich. 1974. "Zur romanische Simeonkirche in Trier," in *Festschrift für Franz Graf Wolff Metternich*. Neuss: Josef Ruland, 122–30.

Lefebvre, Henri. 1991. *The Production of Space*. Trans. Donald Nicholson-Smith. Oxford: Blackwell.

Le Maho, Jacques. 1986. *Boscherville: du temple païen à l'abbaye bénédictine*. Rouen: Musée départemental des Antiquités.

Leone, Anna. 2007. *Changing Townscapes in North Africa from Late Antiquity to the Arab Conquest* (ser. Studi storici sulla tarda antichità, 28). Bari: Edipuglia.

Leuchtenberg, Bettina. 2012. "Das Städtische Museum Trier in der NS-Zeit 1933–1945: Eine Institutionsgeschichte," *Kurtrierischen Jahrbuch hrsg. von der Stadtbibliothek Trier und dem Verein Kurtrierisches Jahrbuch* 52, 303–51. http://www.museum-trier.de/museum/geschichte-des-museums/das-trierer-staedtische-museum-in-der-ns-zeit/ (accessed 30 August 2017)

Machado, Rodolfo. 1976. "Old buildings as palimpsest: Towards a theory of remodeling," *Progressive Architecture* 11, 46–49.

Mareco, Patrícia Sofia Rasgado. 2007. "Sítios Arquelógicos e Centros de Intepretação, em Portugal-Alentejo e Algarve," Master's thesis, Universidade do Minho. http://repositorium.sdum.uminho.pt/handle/1822/7252 (accessed 30 August 2017)

Müller, Michael. 1988. "Trier von der Zeit des franzosischen Besatzung bis zum Wiederraufbau nach Zweiten Weltkrieg," in *Trier in die Neuzeit*, ed. Kurt Düwell and Franz Irsigler. Trier: Spee-Verlag.

Netz, Reviel, and William Noel. 2007. *The Archimedes Codex: How a Medieval Prayer Book is Revealing the True Genius of Antiquity's Greatest Scientist*. London: Weidenfeld and Nicholson Press.

Nightingale, John. 2001. *Monasteries and Patrons in the Gorze Reform: Lotharingia c. 850–1000* (ser. Oxford Historical Monographs). Oxford: Clarendon Press.

Parlasca, Klaus. 1973. "Die neue Veröffentlichung der Porta Nigra in Trier, Germania," *Germania* 51, 176–81.

Pavlac, Brian A. 2008. *Warrior Bishop of the Twelfth Century: The Deeds of Albero of Trier, by Balderich*. Toronto: Pontifical Institute Publications.

Sanderson, Warren. 1965. "The Early Mediaeval Crypts of Saint Maximin at Trier," *Journal of the Society of Architectural Historians* 24, no. 4, 303–10.

Schwinden, Lothar. 2001. "Die Porta Nigra," *Das Römische Trier. Führer zu den archäologischen Denkmälern in Deutschland* 40, 143–57.

Sturm, Conradin. 2002. *Porta Nigra, Trier*. Koblenz: Landesmedienzentrum Rheinland-Pfalz.

TED'A (Taller Escola d'Arqueologia). 1990. *L'Amfiteatre Romà de Tarragona, la Basílica Visigòtica I. l'Esglesia Románica* (ser. Mémoires d'Excavacío, 3). Tarragona: Taller Escola d'Arqueologia.

Tran, Ke Leng. 2013. "Architecture as Palimpsest: A Strategy of Immediacy," Ph.D. dissertation, Reyerson University.

Tucci, Pier Luigi. 2004. "The Revival of Antiquity in Medieval Rome: The Restoration of the Basilica of SS. Cosma e Damiano in the Twelfth Century," *Memoirs of the American Academy in Rome* 49, 99–126.

Urbach, Henry. 1998. "Writing Architectural Heterotopia," *The Journal of Architecture* 3, no. 4, 347–54.

Verheij, Robbert. 2015. "Palimpsest in Architecture: Six Personal Observations." Ph.D. dissertation, Faculty of Architecture, Delft University School of Technology.

Ward-Perkins, Bryan. 1984. *From Classical to the Middle Ages: Urban Public Building in Northern and Central Italy AD 300–850*. Oxford: Oxford University Press.

Welter, Adolf. 1998. *Trier 1939–1945. Neue Forschungsergebnisse zur Stadtgeschichte*. Trier: Petermännchen-Verl. der Trierer Münzfreunde.

Wightman, Edith Mary. 1971. *Roman Trier and the Treverii*. New York and Washington, D.C.: Praeger Publishers.

Wilmott, Tony. 2012. *Richborough and Reculver*. London: English Heritage.

Wisplinghoff, Erich. 1956. "Untersuchungen zur ältesten Geschichte des Stiftes St Simeon in Trier," *Archiv für mittelrheinische Kirchengeschichte* 8, 76–93.

Zahn, Eberhard. 1977. "Porta Nigra und Simeonstift," In *Trier. Führer zu den vor- und frühgeschichtlichen Denkmälern* 32, 61–74.

—. 1974. *Trier: Die Porta Nigra, die Simeonskirche, das Simeonstift*. Cologne: Rheinischer Verein für Denkmalpflege und Landschaftsschutz.

Chapter 3
A Crusader Portal on a Cairene *Madrasa*

Erik Gustafson

The funerary *madrasa* (1295–1303) of Sultan al-Nasir Muhammad Ibn Qalawun (1285–1341) is a multi-phase structure with a complex site history. Literary sources and inscriptions tell us that the Sultan al-'Adil Kitbugha (1245–97) appropriated a residence and began constructing a *madrasa* on the site in 1296 and that Sultan al-Nasir Muhammad took over and expanded the *madrasa* in 1299, finishing it in 1303.[1] The monument is unique in the Mamluk architecture of Cairo in that it incorporates a marble portal in the French Gothic style, dating to *c.* 1250 (fig. 3.1).[2] This portal is the visual anchor at the center of the façade, forcing any interpretation of the façade, and indeed the building as a whole, to hinge on and around the doorway.

Many other buildings in medieval Cairo reuse architectural elements from various sources; none has elicited the response to al-Nasir's monument, which has emphasized the portal as a war trophy marking the victory of Islam over Christianity. The fact that the portal was taken purportedly from a church in Acre has isolated its perceived meaning within the modern politics of the Crusades.[3] This essay turns from a reading of the façade through the portal alone to an interpretation of how the building deploys the portal and other elements to make an assertive statement for its Mamluk patron, that is to say, to use Geoff Bailey's words, how the monument accumulates and transforms "successive and partially preserved activities, in such a way that the resulting totality is different from and greater than the sum of the individual constituents."[4]

The building and its phases

The funerary *madrasa* of al-Nasir Muhammad sits disaxially within an irregular site located on the Bayn al-Qasrayn in old Cairo (fig. 3.2, no. 5). One enters the complex from the street, passing through the Gothic portal into a thick-walled passage that supports a minaret above. The *madrasa* itself is a cruciform structure with four *iwans* of varying size arranged around an open court with an ablution pool in the center (fig. 3.3). The mausoleum stands on the street side of the complex between the entrance passage and the later, adjacent *madrasa* of Sultan Barquq. The *qibla* wall of both the mausoleum and the prayer *iwan* are thus both next to the street. Multi-storeyed residential structures occupied the angles between the *iwans*.

Written sources shed some light on the phases and chronology of the complex. Writing in 1424, the Islamic historian al-Maqrizi (1364–1442) tells us Sultan Kitbugha appropriated the residence of an emir to build his *madrasa* in 1296 and that he also took the Gothic portal from the heirs of a second emir to use as a doorway for it.[5] Al-Maqrizi also tells us that Kitbugha erected the façade up to the top of the inscription band that runs across it, a fact confirmed by the inclusion of the date of 695 (1296) in the inscription. Writing in the early fourteenth century, al-Nuwayri (1279–1333), the Mamluk historian and close associate of al-Nasir, claimed that Kitbugha built the prayer *iwan* and the mausoleum, where additional *spolia* appear, and that al-Nasir completed the building and added the minaret.[6]

The written evidence thus suggests that the *madrasa* was begun on the street side and that Kitbugha was responsible for the mausoleum, the prayer *iwan*, and the entry passage with its Gothic portal. It is as yet unclear as to whether the pre-existing residence (presumably palatial) conditioned the alignment of any walls of the *madrasa* or whether any of walls of the residence were reused in elevation. It is also uncertain as to whether the Gothic portal was appropriated early enough in the building process to have

3.1. *Madrasa* and mausoleum of Sultan al-Nasir Muhammad ibn Qalawun, Cairo, 1295–1303. View of the façade. Documented in 2010.

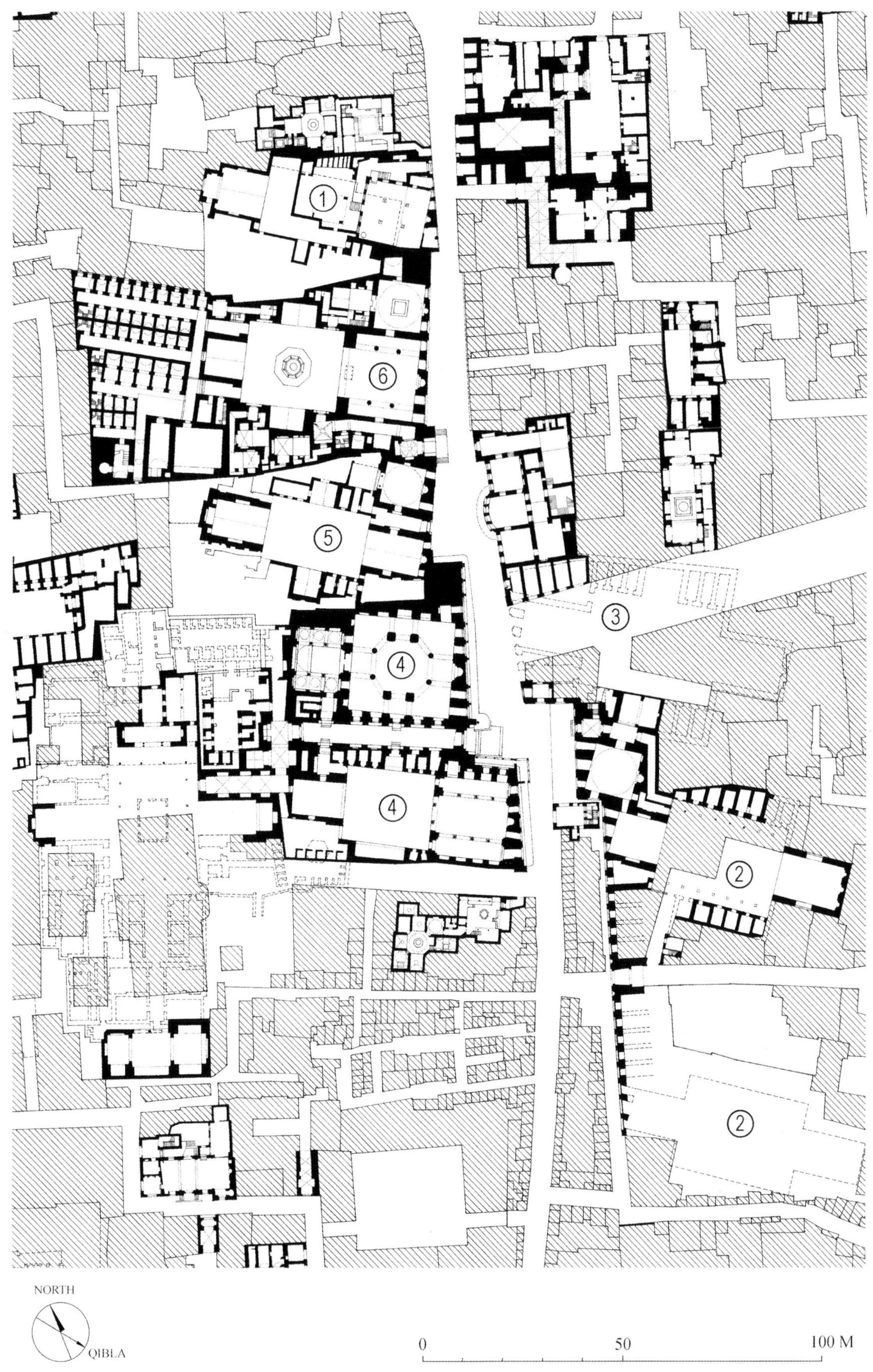

3.2. Area plan of the Bayn al-Qasrayn neighborhood of Cairo: (1) *madrasa* of Sultan al-Malik al-Kamil (1225); (2) mausoleum and *madrasa* of Sultan al-Salih (1243); (3) *madrasa* of Sultan al-Zahir Baybars (1263); (4) Sultan Qalawun mausoleum, *madrasa*, and hospital (1284–85); (5) Sultan al-Nasir mausoleum and *madrasa* (1295–1303); and (6) mausoleum and *madrasa* of Sultan al-Zahir Barquq (1384–68).

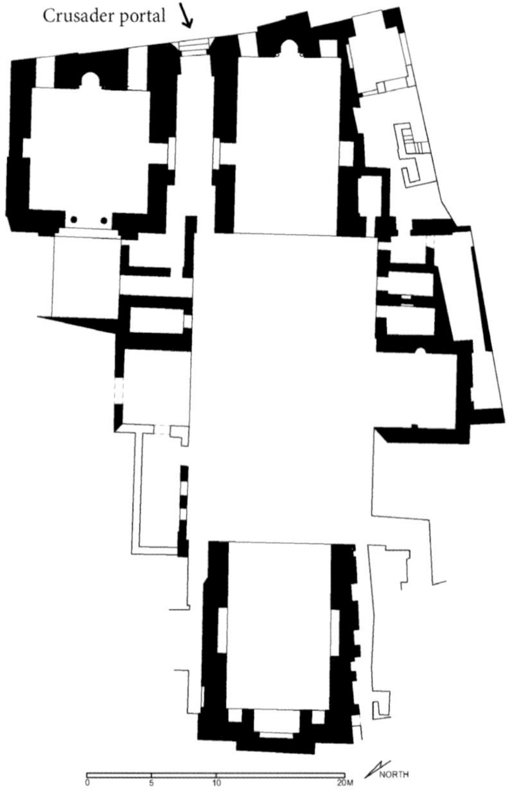

3.3. Plan of the funerary complex of al-Nasir, Cairo.

been part of the original design of the façade, or whether it was inserted later and replaced an earlier one, either materially or conceptually.

This essay considers the palimpsest as a cultural practice, one intentionally using the density of time and layering of memory as the means for communicating identity through architecture. Building from the premise of observing "a superimposition of successive activities,"[7] the varieties of layering encountered in the Crusader portal on a Cairene *madrasa* provide three avenues for inquiry. Concerning the fabric of building, the Gothic portal requires a careful examination of how the architectural composition is assembled. It specifically analyzes how the Crusader portal was fitted into the façade. A second avenue of inquiry looks at context, considering elite Mamluk viewers' socio-cultural priorities. These priorities functioned through a variety of spheres—aesthetic, political, religious, or social—often layering over one another in a palimpsest of ideas. A final avenue adopts the palimpsest as a metaphor offering a way to understand architecture in Mamluk Egypt. It is based on seeing architectural *spolia* and formal citations as metaphorical palimpsests that allude to spoliated or cited monuments. In this sense, the monumental *spolia* and formal citations function like Brilliant's *spolia in se* and *in re*.[8] Such metaphorical palimpsests are deployed together with new construction to form an architectural composition that emphasizes the density of time and space conceptually condensed into the new structure. In the *madrasa* of al-Nasir, all of these aspects combine to present a wide range of temporal and geographic elements within a visual discourse that required the memory and knowledge of the elite Mamluk viewer to become fully engaging.

The problem of the war trophy trope and spolia

The portal of the *madrasa* of al-Nasir has most often been examined and interpreted to illustrate the appropriation of Crusader materials as war trophies, architectural *spolia* celebrating Muslim victories over Christians. For example, Hillenbrand's caption for a photo of the portal reads, "Madrasa-Mausoleum of Sultan al-Nasir Muhammad, Gothic doorway from Acre reused as a trophy."[9] For Jacoby, "the re-use in a Muslim religious building of a portal that originally had adorned a Christian ecclesiastical structure amounted to a conscious and deliberate affirmation of the superiority of Islam over Christianity."[10] Mathews has recently emphasized the prominence of the portal in the center of Cairo, noting that "al-Nasir Muhammad's appropriated trophy of war received maximum visibility in the city."[11] Behrens-Abouseif is more equivocal on how to interpret the portal, indicating that it "is not without symbolic significance" as a trophy brought from Acre, one of two military victories establishing Mamluk legitimacy, but she also wonders whether its reuse was "due to its symbolic significance or its exotic character."[12] Finally, Folda is neutral on the portal's meaning, asserting that "in neither case do we really have a clear idea as yet of the extent to which generic materials and symbolic parts of important buildings were relocated from their

3.4. Funerary complex of al-Nasir, Cairo. Detail of the portal.

3.5. Funerary complex of al-Nasir, Cairo. Analysis of material sources in the al-Nasir complex portal: red = Crusader; blue = Mamluk; yellow = possibly Byzantine.

3.6. Funerary complex of al-Nasir, Cairo. Detail of portal colonnettes and capitals.

Crusader sites to Mamluk cities."[13] Yet thirty years ago, Sherif had already challenged the victory monument label.[14] In spite of her work, the Crusader portal in Cairo has become so completely associated with the concept of war trophies, that the association predisposes us to assumptions of triumph and booty over other interpretations of *spolia*.[15] The present essay looks to build on Sherif's prescient consideration of multiple systems of meaning underlying an elite Mamluk viewer's reception of the Crusader portal, considering several different ways through which the artifact was deployed.

As discussed in the introduction to this volume, the concept of *spolia* has been broadened by scholars to address a wide range of instances when a chronologically older object is used to emphasize a visual connection between earlier and contemporary moments.[16] The portal as *spolia* is one component of a nuanced architectural composition that allowed the Mamluk elites to assert their place on both the local and international stages.[17] When considering the building as one that employs metaphorical palimpsests, the portal as *spolia* becomes one supporting element in a complex composite whole. That is to say, though the Crusader portal in Cairo is unquestionably a spoliated object in the literal sense, its deployment on this building is part of a broader cultural articulation of Mamluk rulership and identity through the building as a single, unified statement.

Physical palimpsests: elisions and erasures

Emphasized by the minaret towering above, the Gothic portal is the central visual element on the *madrasa* façade, mediating the gaze of the passersby, as well as facilitating access for those wishing to enter (figs. 3.1, 3.4, and 3.6). The portal is set within the façade: it is flush with the surface of the latter, rising almost to the full height of the ground storey and balanced between two vertical blind panels. Above the socle courses on each side, splayed embrasures step back to receive four colonnettes corresponding to archivolts that enframe a trilobed tympanum. These colonnettes are in turn flanked by thinner, more delicate ones whose capitals make that zone into a frieze. The tympanum is opened with an oculus beneath its apex and is supported from below by double lintels carried on simple vertical jambs. The upper lintel has an Arabic inscription set in a recessed panel. The entire composition is framed by a thin moulding composed of two tori flanking a narrow fillet. This

3.7. Funerary complex of al-Nasir, Cairo. Detail showing the gap between the façade wall and the right embrasure of the portal.

moulding cuts into a fifth capital on each side of the portal before continuing to the top of the first storey on each side of the spandrel, where it turns inward to close the ensemble. The outermost capitals support the foliate archivolt that frames the tympanum and its simple moulded archivolts. That these capitals are partially cut away to fit in pieces of the moulding and that they are the same size as the Gothic capitals within the embrasures suggests that they too are Frankish *spolia*. The capitals are, however, completely different in style and composition, displaying none of the three-dimensionality of the inner capitals. This suggests that, while they may be Frankish, they may have been taken from another monument in Crusader territory or another opening on the same church as the rest of the Gothic portal. Inside the frame and above the portal proper is a blue-black and white foliate band that is similar to the lower lintel. Such two-color bands are common in Mamluk portal decoration, as Abdel-Naby has shown.[18] Set within the spandrel field, and framed by a simple rounded moulding, are two small tympana with foliate drill-work decoration that flank a smaller central roundel with an inscription "Allah."

For a casual observer, the portal is most likely simply that: an ornate door on a massive building (fig. 3.4). For the expectant eye of a Western art historian, the disparate stylistic vocabularies immediately stand out, bifurcating the portal into Crusader and non-Crusader parts (fig. 3.5). To the eyes of the Mamluk elite, looking to read the variety of formal elements within it, the portal must have offered a complicated rhetoric of what Humphreys has broadly called the "expressive intent" of Mamluk architecture.[19] Before addressing such questions of meaning and visual culture, the physical fabric of the portal requires attention. How did the builders of the *madrasa* reuse older Gothic masonry in their new, monumental doorway?

The portal as it is composed today is a mixture of Mamluk, Frankish, and possibly Byzantine elements, as well as some modern restoration work to replace eroded or lost masonry (fig. 3.5).[20] The French masonry includes the four pointed arches framed by the vegetal archivolt that is alone set in front of the plane of the façade; the trilobed tympanum with oculus; four foliate capitals on either side of the portal; and the thin colonnettes, supporting smaller capitals, set between the larger ones. Plagnieux has proposed that the Frankish portal was carved around 1250, possibly while Saint Louis was in Acre, by sculptors trained in Paris in the workshops of the Sainte Chapelle or the north transept of Notre Dame.[21] The thin band of stone (located just above the upper lintel) forms the base of the tympanum and matches the height of the impost block of the capitals. That a Crusader inscription or decoration was replaced by the Arabic one on the upper lintel, as suggested by Enlart, seems improbable, though a lintel of some greater thickness would seem to have been structurally necessary.[22]

Clearly not the entire original Gothic portal survives in the *madrasa* façade. The double lintels—the upper one with its Arabic inscription, the lower one with a black and white marble arabesque—are certainly Mamluk additions. Further, all the bases of the embrasure colonnettes are missing and the colonnette shafts are likely replacements. Three of the four colonnette shafts on each side of the portal are octagonal, while the fourth is cylindrical, but smaller than the circumference of the base of the capital above. The very thin colonnette shafts carved into the projecting angles of the embrasures are also round (fig. 3.6). It is unclear whether the octagonal colonnettes are original Crusader *spolia* or Mamluk replacements for lost shafts. On the outermost of the four colonnettes, a circular astragal marks the bottom of the capital and indicates that the corresponding shaft should also be round. Three of the remaining six capitals retain the space for an astragal, and have facetted surfaces behind the bell of the capital, indicating that the original, presumably round astragals have been cut back. The cutting back of the bottom of the capitals is most likely Mamluk work that aimed to match the capitals better to their octagonal shafts. In addition, it is unclear whether the marble of the shafts matches the marble of the arches above, taking into account the modern repairs at the top of the shafts. While the octagonal colonnettes can be identified as Mamluk insertions, they too may be *spolia*. On the other hand, octagonal columns are more common in Mamluk architecture and are rare in French Gothic buildings.

The spandrel field above the Gothic archivolts is also Mamluk work. The two small, round-arched tympana are filled with foliate reliefs that appear to bear traces of paint. The drill-work technique and style of these two inserted panels seems more Byzantine than Crusader; they are certainly not Mamluk. The inscription, "Allah," worked into the loop above the apex of the arch at the intersection of the spandrels, conceptually unifies the complete portal ensemble into one whole rather than into disparate Mamluk and Crusader elements. Indeed, the upper and lower sections are further united by a nearly continuous thin moulding, which runs up both sides and across the top, broken only by the slight projection of the Frankish console capitals, themselves partially cut by it. The Mamluk masonry continues the bright white marble of the original portal, not exactly the same kind of marble but a close match. The joggled blue-black and white bands that decorate the upper section, as well as the lintel, set off and balance the tympanum and arches, incorporating the Crusader fabric by visually framing it.

Examination of the Gothic portal fabric in relation to the façade reveals some interesting insights (fig. 3.4). No correspondence exists between the masonry courses of the façade proper or those of the door jambs and the coursing of the portal embrasures, to the extent these are visible. On the left side of the portal, the façade coursing alternates regularly between blocks with the long side facing outward and those with the short end facing outward, a standard masonry technique for making a right-angled wall. On the right side, this pattern occurs only in two or three courses. There are no extremely shortened blocks in the façade coursing on either side of the Gothic portal that might suggest a reworking of the size of the opening to accommodate it. The masonry surrounding the portal differs from the neat courses of the rest of the façade. There exist narrow gaps, greater on the right side, between the moulding, the portal, and the masonry of the façade (fig. 3.7). This allows us to suggest that the façade was erected first, leaving a gap for the portal to be fitted in. This gap evidently turned out to be slightly too large for the portal. It also suggests that the portal was intended to be reused in the façade from the beginning of construction. The relation of this same moulding to the masonry of the façade in the spandrel zone is also revealing. In the area above the moulding and especially along the right side, there are smaller, "filler" blocks and excessively thick mortar joints that suggest the same sort of patchwork adjustments to fit the upper part of the portal into the façade proper. With the proviso that it has not been possible to measure the coursing of the façade and the portal, it appears that wall courses on either side of the portal are the same size, at least up to two courses above the inscription. This is, of course, the point at which al-Maqrizi tells us that Kitbugha's construction stopped and al-Nasir's began. It may mean that while Kitbugha intended to reuse the Gothic portal in the *madrasa*, it was al-Nasir who actually had it built into the façade.

To summarize, no archaeological evidence can be presented to argue compellingly that the Gothic portal in the *madrasa* of al-Nasir is a *spolium* that was intended as the entry to the *madrasa* from the beginning of construction or that it is a spoliate palimpsest replacing a Mamluk portal originally designed for, or built into, the façade. The physical evidence of the *madrasa* of al-Nasir suggests that there was a simple rectangular opening built to accommodate the insertion of a portal, essentially independent of the façade proper, and this, in final analysis, tells us nothing certain regarding the question of *spolium* or palimpsest.

The moulded rectangular frame, the blue-black and white decorative bands, and the Arabic inscription on the upper lintel unite the Gothic portal and its Mamluk additions into a single statement of entry. Only careful observation reveals the gaps between portal and façade, the altered capitals, and filler blocks and larger mortar joints. That bases are missing from the colonnettes is potentially suggestive to a Western eye, but columns reused without bases could actually be found in medieval Cairo.[23] Without any pronounced structural markers, an elite Mamluk viewer had to recognize the stylistic and material values to parse the differences between the portal's components. The previous life of half the masonry of a church portal in Acre, or some other Crusader site, is erased and elided by its integration into the *madrasa*.[24] Such uncertainties add weight to thinking about this portal as a metaphorical palimpsest: a partially erased text identified through careful observation. But rather than providing fodder for a conclusion rooted in the easy trope of war trophy, a broader anthropology of metaphorical palimpsests prompts us to interrogate what issues these elisions and erasures might actually raise.[25]

Palimpsest of meaning: texts and lacunae

To investigate how the patrons and public Mamluk audience might have understood this portal, we first turn to the handful of texts associated with the complex. Two inscriptions decorate the façade of the *madrasa*, one across the width of the building on either side of the portal and the other across the lintel of the portal itself. These texts evidence different meanings and values related to both the portal and the *madrasa* as a monument, reflecting different layers of meaning in aesthetic, political, or religious terms depending on the priorities of the viewer. Which of those layers merits preeminence for any given viewer is impossible to say; they all function together in an aggregate, cumulative palimpsest of meanings,[26] which may vary depending on time and circumstance.

The funerary *madrasa* of Sultan al-Nasir Muhammad ibn Qalawun is a complex building, both chronologically and architecturally. The earliest written reference to the building is found in al-Nuwayri's *The Ultimate Ambition in the Arts of Erudition*. Al-Nuwayri, an official in the court of al-Nasir who actually lived in the *madrasa* for a time and who certainly knew its history, wrote:

> This madrasa and mausoleum were built by al-'Adil Zayn al-Din Kitbugha al-Mansuri during the period of his sultanate. He purchased the land, which was at that time occupied by

> a property known as al-Rashidi and consisted of a hammam and some residences. He bought it and demolished it, and built the mausoleum and madrasa. The mausoleum was completed along with the madrasa's prayer iwan and some adjoining areas before Kitbugha was deposed. Then the madrasa was shuttered and the construction ended.[27]

The building was thus well underway when construction paused until al-Nasir took over this site in 1299, expanding and completing it a few years later.

As mentioned earlier, Sherif was the first to challenge the victory monument label in her dissertation, demonstrating the complicated Mamluk history of the monument and its reception.[28] In this, she relied heavily on the Mamluk historian al-Maqrizi's description of the portal and its provenance, as described in his *Khitat* of 1424:

> It is one of the most splendid buildings in Cairo; its doorway is one of the most marvelous things made by man, for it is of white marble of wonderful shape and of the highest quality of workmanship. It was moved to Cairo from the town of 'Akka, for al-Malik al-Ashraf Khalil, son of Qala'un, when he took 'Akka on 17 Gumada I, 690 (18th May 1291), appointed the Emir 'Alam ad-Din Sangar ash-Shuga'i to demolish its walls and devastate its churches, and the latter found this doorway at the entrance to one of those churches of Akka. It was of marble, the bases, capitals, and shafts being all of one piece, and the whole was transported to Cairo and remained in his house until al-Malik al-Ashraf was killed, and also during the first reign of al-Malik an-Nasir. When he was deposed and Ketbugha [Kitbugha] became Sultan he took the house of the Emir Sayf ad-Din Balban ar-Rashidi to make it into a madrasa. His attention was then called to the doorway, and he took it from the heirs of the Emir Baidara to whom it had passed. Ketbugha [Kitbugha] used it as a doorway for his madrasa.[29]

Of primary importance to al-Maqrizi is the aesthetic significance of the portal. Indeed, the primary motive implied for Sanjar al-Shuja'i in taking the portal from Acre was not as a talisman of victory over the Christians, but for its material worth.[30] While the Mamluk author asserts that the portal came from a church, its value lay instead in the kind of stone used and the quality of its workmanship. Written over a century after the *madrasa* was built, the text nonetheless preserves the memory of how the portal came to Cairo, and the internal Mamluk politics leading to its eventual erection in public. By telling the story of the portal's removal from Acre, the text has been a useful source for treating the doorway as a war trophy, even though it begins with aesthetics and ends with politics, mentioning conquest only in passing. This is a text of memory and association, a narrative in which several layers have been melded into an accumulation of themes that are all key, but do not allow us to parse primacy of intent.

Al-Maqrizi's discussion also demonstrates that the complex provenance of the portal between its removal from Acre in 1291 and its installation on the *madrasa* in Cairo around 1295 must also be understood in terms of Mamluk politics. The occupying emir during the Sack of Acre was Sanjar al-Shuja'i, who originally collected the portal. Many churches have been suggested as the source for the portal by modern scholars, but it is impossible to know which was the parent building.[31] The components of the portal were brought back to Cairo, and sometime thereafter entered the possession of the viceroy Baidara. Baidara assassinated Sultan Khalil (1260s–93) in 1293, declaring himself sultan before being killed a few days later. Following Khalil's death, his young brother al-Nasir was elected sultan at the age of nine. Sanjar al-Shuja'i became vizier and co-regent, and was deeply embroiled in various intrigues, leading to his death in 1294 during fighting between his own faction and that of his main rival, his co-regent al-'Adil Kitbugha.[32] It was at the end of 1294 that Kitbugha deposed al-Nasir and became sultan, and soon in the following year began construction on the funerary *madrasa*.[33] Throughout all this political factionalism, the Acre portal had been kept in private homes as a collector's item. When and why exactly Baidara acquired the portal is unclear; al-Maqrizi mentioned only that it had passed to him.[34] However, Sanjar al-Shuja'i had married Baidara's mother, so following the deaths of both men in quick succession, the portal passed to Baidara's heirs.[35] Al-Maqrizi reports that Kitbugha's attention was drawn to the portal in the home of these heirs, whence he took it. Whether it was under Kitbugha, or under Sultan al-Nasir, that the Crusader portal was inserted into the façade of what had been begun as the former's funerary *madrasa*, remains unclear.

The two Arabic inscriptions, one on the façade proper and the other on the upper lintel of the portal are also essential to the understanding of the monument. The monumental inscription which spans the width of the facade reads:

> The foundation of this noble [dome] and blessed school was ordained by our lord the Sultan al-Malik al-Nasir Nasir al-dunya wa'l-din Abu'l Ma'ali Muhammad, that God glorifies his victories and doubles his power by Mohammad and his pure family! This [has been completed] in the months of the year 695 [1295–1296].[36]

Al-Nasir is named as the sultan who built the complex while maintaining the date of 695 (1296) when al-Nasir was in exile at Karak in Syria, suggesting that the names were changed after Kitbugha fell from power.[37] Such changes to replace or erase previous rulers were precedented in Islamic monumental inscriptions[38] and represent a clear case of a paleographic palimpsest. Al-Nasir purchased the property from Kitbugha in 1299 after regaining the throne, which is recorded in the inscription on the lintel of the portal, and construction seems to have been completed by 1303. The background to the portal's use on a building is therefore enmeshed in political factionalism, a layer of meaning indelibly attached to the Mamluk reuse and perception of the portal.

The inscribed reference to victories should not be read as a simple and straightforward allusion to the Crusader portal that it frames. Instead, we should understand that it relates primarily to the sultan's titles and role as leader of Muslims and Defender of the Faith and only secondarily to the Crusader portal that stands partially within it.[39] As military leaders newly arrived on the scene in the Near East, as well as new converts to Islam, waging war against infidels or heretics provided the Mamluks with both a *raison d'être*, as well as justification for their usurpation of power.[40] The larger inscription on al-Nasir's father's monument next door, the mausoleum and *madrasa* of Qalawun, includes "Victorious" as one of Qalawun's epithets and further asks that God glorify his victories.[41]

The inscription on the lintel of the Gothic portal forms a second textual palimpsest, insofar as it replaces a presumed Crusader lintel necessary to support the tympanum structurally. This inscription further emphasizes the religious role claimed by that sultan as patron:

> The foundation of this noble dome and blessed school was ordained by the most illustrious Sultan al-Malik al-Nasir Nasir al-dunya wa'l-din Muhammad, son of the Sultan al-Malik al-Mansur Saif al-din Qalawun al-Salihi, that God sanctifies his soul and illuminates his tomb! This [has been completed] in the months of the year 698 [1298–1299].[42]

Here on the portal itself, where modern scholarship would expect an assertion of Islamic victory over Christianity, we find only a dynastic and religious text. Such a declaration could be interpreted as an attempt to paper over the political reality that al-Nasir's second reign (1299–1309) served as a figurehead for the duumvirate of Emir Sanjar al-Jawli and Emir (later Sultan) al-Muzaffar Baybars al-Jashnakir.[43] That al-Nasir celebrated the inauguration of his *madrasa* in 1303, before adding the minaret in 1304, attests to the potential public role the building could play. Whether the monument argued for al-Nasir's rightful place as ruling sultan, or whether it was a screen legitimating the duumvirate through the teenage puppet, the architecture was at the forefront of Mamluk identity politics. Reading the portal simply in terms of its Crusader origin elides the complex context of Mamluk architectural patronage. Textually, the portal was simultaneously an aesthetic collector's item, a marker of political power through ownership, and an emblem of the *madrasa* architectural complex expressing politico-religious legitimacy, as well as a symbol of Mamluk military victories. These layers of meaning are intertwined from our temporal vantage point, bound together without any clear indicators about the dominant cause.

Such a layered view does reflect how the "men of the pen" would have perceived the portal on the *madrasa* of al-Nasir. As Behrens-Abouseif has noted, "the Turkic Mamluk culture at court coexisted with the dominant Arabic culture of the Egyptian population."[44] The literature and costumes of the court were rooted in Mongol and Turkic traditions, but such movements had no relation to the tremendous wave of Arabic literary, artistic, and religious learning spurred by the Mamluk patronage of pious foundations.[45] This learned elite emphasized their identity through written works and architectural inscriptions. Within that tradition, architecture was defined by its religious and social role, as well as its aesthetic and symbolic values, precisely the categories applied by Maqrizi and mentioned in the texts inscribed directly on the *madrasa* of al-Nasir. What for contemporary observers might have been clearly delineated meanings generated by the portal and façade are for modern observers a palimpsest of overlapping associations. While the texts tell us much about the values and status conveyed by the portal, the lacunae created by the passage of time restrict us to speaking of these layers together as a group.

Behrens-Abouseif argues that the ethnic Mamluk elites were themselves far more knowledgeable about architecture than the Arab intelligentsia, often spending extensive amounts of time visiting building sites and giving highly specific guidance.[46] Thus, while aesthetics, political power, and religious legitimacy were the frames of reference for the "men of the pen," architecture itself provided a distinct realm of discourse for the Mamluk elite.[47] In terms of the palimpsest notion underlying this essay, those layers of aggregated meanings were cultural responses to the façade as a traditional Mamluk monument. That palimpsest of meaning was a historical artifact framing the reused portal within the larger façade. By shifting from socio-religious contexts to the architecture itself, a different kind of palimpsest becomes operative: one driven by the *spolia* and the building itself, interpreted through the viewer's memory of the sources of the *spolia*.

Architecture: selection, removal, reinscription, memory

The traditional architectural-historical reading of a building typically takes architecture at face value. It betrays a modern epistemology of architecture, still generally the underlying narrative structure of architectural history.[48] The building represents one moment in time, an idealized auctorial statement that has authority and timelessness. A singular, underlying design should be identified, an overriding logic should dictate the relationship between the parts, and when a citation is made from other monuments, whether *in se* or *in re*, it should function as a footnote to make a visual allusion, mark a workshop connection, or denote a life-of-forms filial lineage. The building should be an objective, ontological entity, observable and describable within its hermetic bubble.

The epistemology of architecture can, however, be very much the opposite. While an axonometric drawing of a building would epitomize the encapsulated view of traditional architectural epistemology, an exploded view diagram would be a more appropriate graphic representation for a different view of architecture. Rather than simply articulating the individual constitutive elements of the building, however, such a diagram would need to explode into the architectural fields of visual reference for each element through the four dimensions of time and space. That is to say, the building would stand at the center of a temporal and geographic web of visual layers, both highlighting and masking visual markers in the same moment of perception. Each compositional choice made by a builder, architect, or patron exists in relation to some formal or geographic tradition, carrying in turn a range of associative meanings. With each architectural reference made, one element of the source-monument is adapted. Further, every additional compositional choice can amend, elide, erase, mask, or magnify any associative meaning already included in the design. Architecture as the biography of a building is

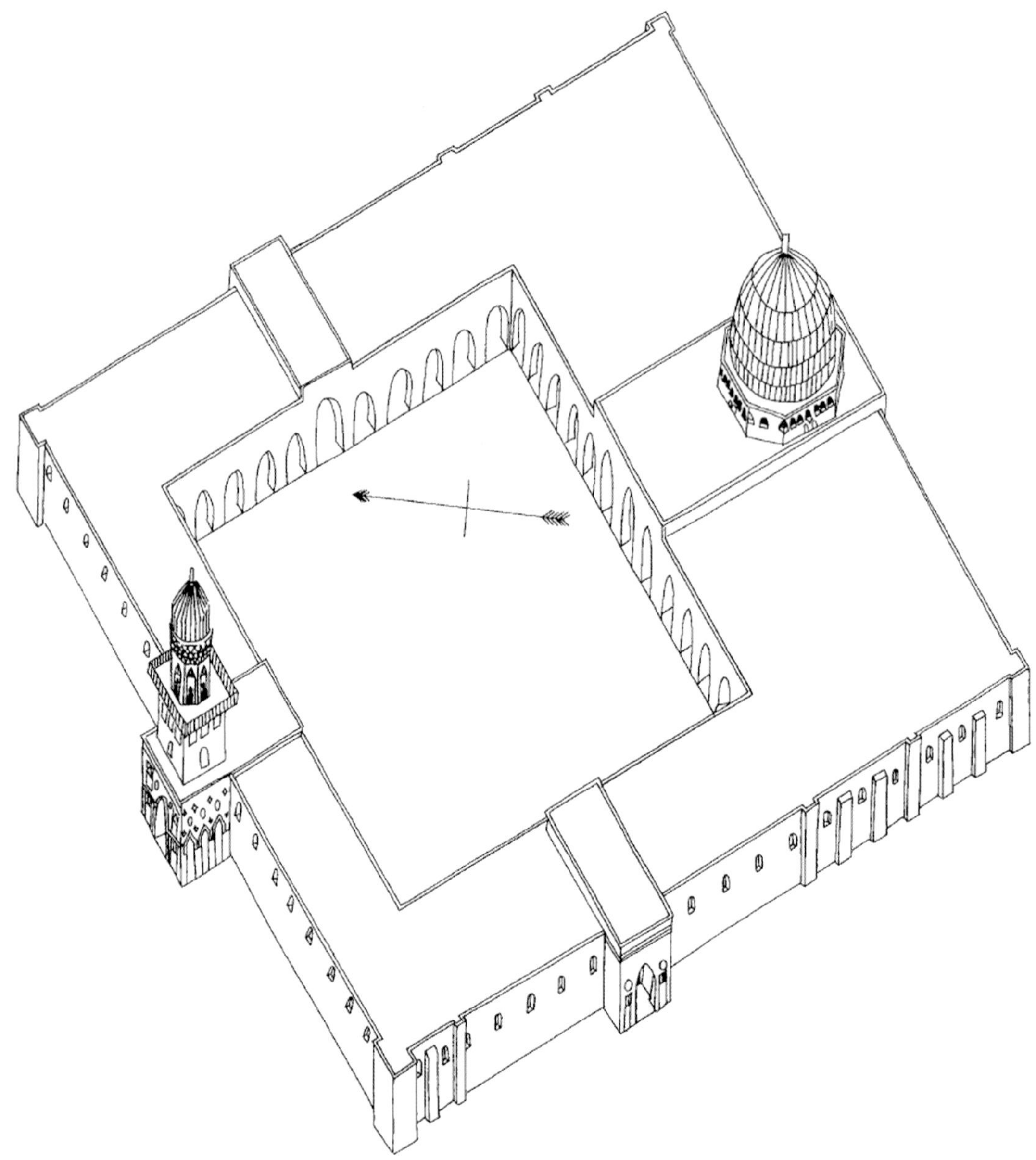

3.8. Axonometric reconstruction of the Great Mosque of al-Zahir Baybars, Cairo, 1267–69.

not simply that which is captured in a photograph, but rather a conceptual compilation of chosen new and older formal elements, as well as references, citations, and/or quotations (*spolia*). These older chosen elements, either *in se* or *in re*, make their antecedents visually present by recalling from memory the full physical reality of their source monuments.

Two functions of the author are at play within the paradigm of architecture as a more geographically and temporally aware narrative of buildings: authorship and authority. The design of a new building today, and we think in the Middle Ages as well, results from a dynamic interplay between patron, designer (or the medieval equivalent), and builder. Together they constitute authorship, the act of incorporating both their own ideas and material as well as those of others, which are "annexed for the purpose of confirming [their] own" work.[49]

3.9. Mausoleum of al-Mansur Qalawun, Cairo, 1284–85. View of the façade. Documented in 2010.

This highest level of authorship in the medieval European tradition chooses which outside sources they wish to use and which to exclude, so as to best argue the idea they wish to put forward. Also at play is authority, a source expected to be respected and believed. A skillful author deploys the most powerful authorities to legitimate and prove his own work of authorship. The reader of such a work relies on their memory to recognize the status of the authorities, to comprehend the nature of the arguments being made, and to judge the resulting authorial statement. Switching from literary to architectural practice, sources in this authorial analogy historically ground the practice of architectural biographies as a complex phenomenon. Authors choose the passages from the sources they require, effectively driving the larger context, purpose, and intent of that source material into memory. Building on such selective compilation and redeployment, authors write the first chapter of a building's biography by combining contemporary and reused elements in a new, cohesive composition. For the textual author the material is books; for the architectural designer the material is formal elements. While the ultimate focus of analysis is the biography of the building in its final form, the process resulting in what is often a monumental palimpsest is one of selection, erasure and/or removal, and reinscription.

The façade of al-Nasir's Cairene *madrasa* can productively be read through medieval Mediterranean and Near Eastern shared systems of formal signification that draw upon traditions of identity construction that are iconographic, as well as formal. These traditions function historically both on the level of immediate intellectual context and in a broader discourse of the visual culture of architecture. Because architecture is not normally portable like tapestries or domestic objects, recognition of *spolia* or formal citations results in the recollection of physically and/or temporally distant prototypes. Such distances require a body of knowledge to recognize and interpret the associative mean-

3.10. Remains of the *madrasa* of al-Salih Najm al-Din Ayyub (Salihiyya), Cairo, 1243. View of the central portal and one lateral bay. Documented in 2010.

ings of individual *spolia* or cited forms. When the buildings themselves form a consistent tradition, it is logical to consider that a relatively widespread discourse existed alongside them for such a visual language to be received as valuable.

The Crusader portal on the al-Nasir *madrasa* was not the first instance of this discourse in Mamluk architecture. Indeed, the incorporation of forms and styles from across the Muslim world was historically a common practice, not only for Islamic art in general, but also for Cairene architecture more specifically.[50] Earlier dynasties in Egypt such as the Tulunids, the Fatimids, and the Ayyubids had used *spolia* and formal citations to articulate their identities and legitimize their rules.[51]

The first major Mamluk architectural statement carried on this discourse, but also added to it. The Mamluk sultan who consolidated the new regime's power in both Egypt and Syria was al-Zahir Baybars I al-Bunduqdari, who ruled from 1260 to 1277.[52] Baybars' Great Mosque of 1267–69 is noteworthy for being built in what can accurately be described as the middle of nowhere, just north of the Fatimid city walls in a neighborhood that would remain empty of residences for several centuries (fig. 3.8).[53] The building is a novel combination of several traditions: old Abbasid rectangular pier forms and pointed arches are used to surround the courtyard; columns filled the *riwaqs* and prayer hall in the historic Damascene manner; and projecting portals on the northern, southern, and western facades are borrowed from the Fatimid tradition. To these tropes, already largely fused at the Fatimid mosques of al-Hakim (990–1003) and to a lesser extent al-Azhar (970–71, 1131–49) in Cairo, Baybars added a massive dome over the *mihrab*. Though small domes over the *mihrab* had been common since their Umayyad introduction, a large dome of this scale was new to Islamic Mediterranean architecture, having been introduced from Seljuk mosques in Iran.[54] In addition to employing a plethora of formal references throughout the new mosque, Baybars also sent wood and marble building materials from the sack of Jaffa in 1268. The wood was practically reused in constructing the dome and the marble was intentionally reused to decorate the *mihrab*.[55] Although now in a sadly ruined state, the mosque was a compelling palimpsest of multiple architectural references, including Crusader material for the first time. The decoration of the domed area is completely lost, making it impossible to determine whether the Crusader marble elements were incorporated in as synthetic a manner as on al-Nasir's façade. If this was indeed so (which seems likely given that is how most reused elements were deployed in Mamluk architecture),[56] the Crusader material would have been both a *spolium* and a formal referent. While the Fatimids and Ayyubids had built within the traditional discourse of Egyptian architecture, Baybars not only expanded the field of reference within Islamic architecture, but he also began to expand beyond the Islamic paradigms by incorporating Crusader materials. How those were displayed is unclear, but a powerful precedent had been set. By integrating these external elements, the palimpsest of associations not only served for internal legitimization, but also made a claim against Baybars' Ayyubid rivals about Mamluk aspirations in Syria.[57]

Sultan al-Mansur Qalawun pushed this architectural discourse even further when he built a massive funerary complex in 1284–85, comprising not only a large mausoleum but also a *madrasa* and a giant hospital (fig. 3.9). Flood has demonstrated the relationship between certain decorative motifs from the Great Mosque of Damascus and the interior decoration of Qalawun's mausoleum, linking the revival of a marble relief vine band, *mihrab* decoration, and mosaic work with a calculated attempt at legitimization by the Mamluk sultanate.[58] The plan of the mausoleum has also been linked to the Dome of the Rock, further aligning Qalawun with the major sites of Islam.[59]

The Qalawun complex has also long been noted for introducing non-Islamic forms into Mamluk architecture.[60] The treatment of the mausoleum facade with recessed panels surmounted by pointed arches framing three levels

3.11. Funerary complex of al-Nasir, Cairo. Detail of the mausoleum *mihrab* wall.

of windows is significantly different from the blind recessed panels on traditional Cairene architecture, such as the Ayyubid Salihiyya façade (fig. 3.10). There is an extensive scholarly tradition of pointing to Gothic structures in mainland Europe or Norman monuments in Sicily for the formal source of the biforate windows surmounted by an oculus.[61] Frankish slave labor in Cairo at Mamluk building sites has also been suggested as influential in some capacity.[62] I would further suggest Byzantium as a possible source for the motif of tiered windows framed by arched recesses, a repeated trope in Middle Byzantine architecture and taken up again during the Paleologan restoration (1261–1453) at sites such as the second church added to the monastery of Constantine Lips (now the Fenari Isa Camii) between 1282 and 1303 by the Empress Theodora;[63] the Parigoritissa church in Arta, Greece built for the royal house of Epirus between 1283 and 1296;[64] and the slightly later palace of the Porphyrogenitus (now the Tekfur Saray) probably built after 1350.[65] All three are royal sites, and both the monastery of Constantine Lips and the Parigoritissa in Arta served as dynastic mausolea. The range of formal elements in the façade of Qalawun's monument are drawn from across the eastern Mediterranean, combined and synthesized to articulate a uniquely Mamluk architectural/palimpsestual discourse.

The Qalawun funerary *madrasa* and hospital can be read as a highly complex palimpsest of associations with older Islamic monuments such as the Great Mosque of Damascus and the Dome of the Rock; traditional Cairene monuments including the *madrasas* of the Ayyubid al-Salih and the Mamluk Baybars (both across the street from the Qalawun complex); and international features such as the Crusader windows and the Byzantine blind arcading and dynastic mausoleum iconography.[66] The combination of these formal elements was not an assemblage of spoliate artifacts reused from all of the sources. Instead, it required the memory of the viewer to reconstitute the links and assess their significance. The intention was not to collect a variety of unique formal curiosities, but to amalgamate and fuse the collected associations into a new statement of identity. The palimpsest of architectural associations was used by the Mamluk sultan as a cultural tool to legitimate himself within the Islamic world, as well as assert his growing authority as a Mediterranean power, both through the visual power of architecture.

By comparison, the architectural associations created by Qalawun's son al-Nasir at his *madrasa* refined the solutions of his predecessors. As at the mosque of Baybars, al-Nasir integrated not only Islamic formal motifs, but also architectural elements from contemporary international powers. The *spolia* that constitute the façade portal have already been examined. Within the *madrasa*, reused objects were also deployed inside the mausoleum chamber. There, reused columns and Crusader capitals are paired around the *mihrab* and entryway of the space (fig. 3.11).[67] The columns are Romanizing, suggesting either an ancient, Byzantine, or Umayyad provenance. As with the Crusader portal, there is no textual or visual indication whatsoever that these objects are foreign. Rather, they are normalized within the design of the architecture. Columns support capitals, which in turn support one wooden frieze band decorated with a vine band motif beneath a now blank wood frieze whose inscription is lost. Whether these columns and capitals should be considered primarily as a practical reuse of building material or primarily as an intentional reuse in which the audience was meant to identify the sources and associated signification of the objects is unclear today.[68] While these reuses recall the temporal layers of their architectural sources, they also all contribute to the larger palimpsest of associations created by the builders of the *madrasa*.

Like the mosque of Baybars and complex of Qalawun, most of the features of al-Nasir's *madrasa* are generally in keeping with Cairene prototypes, such as the niches flanking the portal, which relate to the Salihiyya *madrasa* (1242–43) (fig. 3.10). The placement of the minaret above the portal recalls an identical placement at the Salihiyya, which is otherwise exceptional in Cairo where minarets are generally placed at the corners of buildings.[69] Further, the decoration of the first, square tier of the minaret also recalls Fatimid and Ayyubid patterns, although at al-Nasir's monument the work has been done in stucco rather than stone. The drum of the mausoleum, to the right of the portal, is closely based on the Ayyubid mausoleum of al-Salih (1250), built alongside his earlier *madrasa* (figs. 3.12–3.13). Inside the mausoleum, the vine relief on the frieze directly recalls Damascus (as was also the case in the mausoleum of Qalawun) and the squinches of the now-lost dome again recall the Ayyubid mausoleum of al-Salih. In the *madrasa* proper, the elaborate stucco decoration of the *mihrab* recalls the Iranian Tabriz style. The dating of this stucco work is problematic within the chronology of the *madrasa*, as the arrival of Persian artists following the establishment of diplomatic relations with the Ilkhanid court occurred ten years after the completion of the building.[70] The layout of four *iwans* around a courtyard adopted the standard Cairene *madrasa* model.

All of these formal elements contributed to the complicated narrative that is the *madrasa* of al-Nasir. The complex incorporates *spolia* in

3.12. Funerary complex of al-Nasir, Cairo. Detail of the mausoleum's lost dome and squinches.

3.13. Mausoleum of al-Salih Najm al-Din Ayyub, Cairo, 1250. Detail of the dome and squinches.

the portal and columns in the mausoleum, as well as formal elements cited from other monuments such as the Salihiyya façade features, historic minaret design traditions, a Damascene vine relief frieze, Ayyubid mausoleum architectural features, Iranian stucco decoration in the main *iwan* of the *madrasa*, and the four *iwans* that reference both Cairene tradition and Iranian Seljuk architecture. Taken together, this remarkably diverse range of reuses and formal citations works in concert to link conceptually Sultan al-Nasir with a broad temporal and geographic range of authority sources, placing those authorities at his disposal in articulating his own even greater power. These are not simply visual allusions in a *tromp l'oeil* presentation of cultural sophistication, but rather the physical representations of the building's temporal and geographic web binding al-Nasir to the larger world. Through this visual discourse, the young al-Nasir asserted his legitimacy and authority, tying the *madrasa* to the most important markers of Islamic law and proper Islamic rule. Unlike Qalawun, whose mausoleum drew from Syrian and Byzantine precedents, the mausoleum of al-Nasir's complex was rooted entirely in Cairene sources. Such a seemingly local emphasis, however, was balanced by the Iranian stuccowork of the *madrasa*, the Crusader capitals in the mausoleum, and most strikingly the Crusader portal reused on the façade. The Crusader portal, in particular, both represented and embodied an engagement with the larger Mediterranean world. Today, the portal functions as the most potent visual reference to our modern, Western eyes, as it links to many contemporary issues. The rest of the *madrasa*-mausoleum complex adds much more nuance and diversity to that one object, however, drawing on the highly potent visual discourse of Cairene medieval architecture to proclaim articulately and concretely al-Nasir's dominion over the dense world of time and memory that he ruled.

Conclusion

This essay has departed from the historiographic tradition of reading the al-Nasir façade and building through the portal alone, turning instead to an interpretation of how the patrons, designers, and builders of the complex deployed the portal and other visual elements to make an assertive statement of the sultan's power in the Mediterranean world. The notion of the biography of a building has brought to light the complexities and nuances of how this was accomplished, providing analytical leverage for the physical, socio-cultural, and visual layering of meaning at the al-Nasir *madrasa* complex. The palimpsest of associations—of *spolia* and formal citations—is a cultural practice, in which the "thickness" of time and the layering of memory produce a conceptual matrix for architecture to communicate and signify. Architecture in this view is epistemologically defined by the visual discourse that produced it and the culturally embedded statements it makes, rather than by an anachronistic, objective scale of aesthetic or formal judgment. The Crusader portal and larger al-Nasir *madrasa* complex together are made significant by writing the biography of the building, enriched as it is by the wealth of formal articulations, associative meanings, and markers of traditions that are visually selected, removed and/or erased, and reinscribed within the architecture. The building's full extent is not just what is captured in a photograph (fig. 3.1); rather, it is the entire conceptual range of cultural and physical elements discussed above. That the building hides nearly all of these from view, requiring the attentive and receptive viewers to tease out the full picture for themselves, is the greatest success of the architecture as an active, engaged cultural phenomenon.

Notes

1 The sources report the dates according to the Islamic calendar; for the reader's convenience, they are provided here according to the Gregorian calendar.

2 The most pertinent bibliography on the portal includes: Creswell 1959, vol. 2, 234–40; Jacoby 1982; Sherif 1988, 82–111; Behrens-Abouseif 1989, 100–01; Speiser, 1994; Hunt 1996; Harding and Micklewright 1997, 58–60; Mayer, Nogara and Speiser, 2001; Warner 2005, 97; Plagnieux 2006; Behrens-Abouseif 2007, 152–56; Speiser 2008; and Behrens-Abouseif 2012, 301–18.

3 As the text recording that the portal was taken from a church (1424) postdates the moment of removal

(1291) by nearly 150 years, the original site of the portal can only be conjecture. See Pringle 1993–2009, vol. 4, 24–25; Pringle 2007, 111–32. An earlier attribution of the portal to the church of Saint Andrew began with Enlart 1925, vol. 2, 15–23. Briggs thought the portal was taken from the church of Saint John; see Briggs 1924, 102. Similar portals, however, were also used in castles, such as Marqab and the Crac des Chevaliers. Whether the portal was indeed taken from a church or from some other non-religious but still Frankish site is impossible to say. My thanks to Clark Maines for this observation.

4 Bailey 2007, 203.

5 Creswell 1959, vol. 2, 234.

6 This information is taken from Behrens-Abouseif 2007, 152. The recent translation of al-Nuwayri's compendium contains a portion of his discussion of the funerary *madrasa*, but does not include discussion of the building's construction history. See al-Nuwayri 2016, 271–76. The Arabic edition, al-Nuwayri 2003, has not been available to the author. According to al-Nuwayri himself, the author actually lived at one time in al-Nasir's *madrasa*. See al-Nuwayri 2016, 276.

7 Bailey 2007, 203.

8 Brilliant 1982, 2-17.

9 Hillenbrand 2009, 386.

10 Jacoby 1982, 126.

11 Mathews 2012, 193.

12 Behrens-Abouseif 2007, 153–54. Behrens-Abouseif 2012, 310, points out that "the symbolic significance of such spoils was based evidently on the common knowledge of their Crusader provenance."

13 Folda 2005, 491.

14 Sherif 1988, 82–111. On Islamic war monuments, see Leisten 1996, 7–26. Interestingly, Leisten does not mention the *madrasa* of al-Nasir in his discussion.

15 For the historiography of *spolia* in the Islamic world, see Meinecke-Berg 1985, 131–42; Flood 2001b, 41–72; Flood 2006, 143–66; Flood 2009, 202–15; Gonnella 2010, 103–20; and Flood 2011, 121–47.

16 The most useful summary representation of several decades of work on *spolia* and reuse can be found in Brilliant and Kinney 2011. On *spolia* and appropriation, see Kinney's comments in the introduction, 7–9.

17 Mathews 2012, 197–200.

18 Abdel-Naby 2014, 82–93.

19 Humphreys 1972, 69–119. For more recent work on Mamluk patronage, see Fernandes 1997, 107–20; and al-Harithy 2001, 219–44. For the concept of a period eye, see Baxandall 1988, 29–108.

20 On the restoration of the complex, see Speiser, 1994; Speiser 2008. For the restoration history of the portal itself, see Mayer, Nogara, and Speiser 2001, 232–38; Mayer 2007.

21 Plagnieux 2006, 63–64.

22 Enlart 1925, vol. 1, 20.

23 To give one example, inside the Mosque of Amr ibn al-As in Fustat (Old Cairo) reused, baseless columns supporting a dome inside the northeastern corner of the prayer hall may date from al-Walid's 713 campaign. However, the mosque of Amr was doubled in size to the south by order of the Abbasid Caliph al Ma'mun around 830, with later near-total renovations in 1179, 1796, and 1875, making any reconstruction of the interior very difficult. See Behrens-Abouseif 1989, 47–50. Spoliated columns without bases were used under the dome over the *mihrab* and in the four corners of the courtyard in the mosque of al-Nasir at the Citadel (1318–35), under the dome over the *mihrab* and in the four corners of the courtyard in the mosque of Altinbugha al-Maridani (1339–40), and the *mihrab iwan* of the funerary *madrasa* of Sultan Barquq (1384–86) next to the funerary complex of al-Nasir. I am not aware of any Fatimid baseless columns.

24 Behrens-Abouseif 2014a, 402–25.

25 Behrens-Abouseif 2012, 310.

26 The notion of a "palimpsest of meaning" is borrowed from Bailey 2007.

27 al-Nuwayri 2003, vol. 32, 42. I am profoundly grateful to Elias Muhanna for translating this passage for me and for providing the citation.

28 Sherif 1988, 103–06. For Sherif, if symbolic value is to be found in the portal, it lies in linking the building's patron to Mamluks as the Defenders of the Faith. As such, it would not be a victory monument, but a sort of military monument; but see also Behrens-Abouseif 2012, 310, where the author suggests that time had shifted the portal's meaning for al-Maqrizi. Ultimately, Sherif argues for the fluidity of meaning, depending on the viewer.

29 Translation by Creswell 1959, vol. 2, 234, where he gives a full translation of al-Maqrizi's text.

30 Greenhalgh 2009, 447–82, discusses the widespread reuse of ancient marble in Egypt, Syria, and Turkey, though he does not mention the Crusader portal in discussing marble in Mamluk Cairo.

31 See Pringle 1993–2009, vol. 4, 24–25; Pringle 2007.

32 Irwin 1986, 85; Sherif 1988, 85–88. There seem to have been two contemporary emirs named 'Alam al-Din Sanjar, who are often confused by contemporary historians, as noted by Sherif 1988, 154, and Folda 2005, 673, note 63. See also Little 1986, 177–78. Burgoyne possibly conflated the two emirs in his discussion of the al-Dawadariyya in Jerusalem, at least as regards the emir's role at Acre, in Burgoyne 1987, 154, although perhaps his biography is also correct and Shuja'i was not killed in 1294.

33 Al-Nasir's first reign lasted for one year, from December of 1293 to December of 1294. Kitbugha replaced al-Nasir, ruling until December 1296. Kitbugha stepped down and Sultan al-Mansur Husam al-Din Lajin was elected, ruling until January of 1299, when al-Nasir returned to become sultan again. Al-Nasir's second reign lasted until 1309,

when al-Muzaffar Baybars al-Jashankir usurped the throne for one year. Al-Nasir returned for his final reign in 1310, and ruled for 31 years until 1341. See Irwin 1986, 85–104; Bosworth 1996, 76–80; Behrens-Abouseif 2007, 317–18.

34 Creswell 1959, vol. 2, 234.

35 Irwin 1986, 80.

36 "La fondation de cette noble [coupole] et du collège béni a été ordonnée par notre maître le sultan al-Malik al-Nasir Nasir al-dunya wal-din Abul Ma'ali Muhammad, que Dieu glorifie ses victoires et double sa puissance par Mahomet et sa pure famille! Cela [a été achevé] dans les mois de l'année 695 [1295–1296]." The translation from the French is mine. The translation into French from the Arabic is from Combe, Sauvaget, and Wiet, vol. 13, 144.

37 van Berchem 1894, 152–55, entries 100–03; Behrens-Aboussseif 2007, 152.

38 The Dome of the Rock is perhaps the earliest instances of the practice, when al-Ma'mun replaced Abd al-Malik's name with his own in the early ninth century; see Blair 1998, 29–42. Bloom has pioneered the question of erasure and replacement in Islamic inscriptions, identifying a variety of erased inscriptions on Aghlabid and Fatimid monuments in Tunisia; see Bloom 2015. He further suggested such practices were likely by Ayyubid rulers on Fatimid sites in Cairo (Bloom 2015, 71). For Bloom, such erasure served to emphasize the legitimization of current rulers, rather than a *damnatio memoriae* of previous ones. For Islamic inscriptions in general, see Blair 1998.

39 See, for example, Tabbaa 1986, 223–40.

40 Broadbridge 2001, 91–118; Broadbridge 2008, 6–26.

41 The full text of Qalawun's inscription reads: "This noble dome, this magnificent college, and blessed hospital was ordered by our Lord and Master, the August Sultan al-Malik al-Mansur, the Wise, Just, God-assisted, Victorious, Champion of the Faith, Conqueror, Sword of the World and True Religion... Lord of Kings and of Sultans, the Sultan of the Length and Breadth of the Earth... King of the Two Continents and the Two Seas, King of Kings of Arabs and Non-Arabs, the Guardian of the Two Qiblas, the Servant of the Two Sanctuaries, Qala'un al-Salihi, the Associate of the Commander of the Believers—may God prolong his glory, glorify his victories, elevate his beacon, and double his power—the incomparable among contemporary kings, the treasure of those destitute of resources, he who renders justice to the oppressed against the oppressor... The beginning of all this took place in 1284 and its ending in 1285." Translation from Williams 2008, 188–89.

42 "La fondation de cette noble coupole et du collège béni a été ordonée par le sultan très illustre al-Malik al-Nasir Nasir al-dunya wal-din Muhammad, fils du sultan al-Malik al-Mansur Saif al-din Kalawun al-Salihi, que Dieu sanctifie son âme et illumine son tombeau! Cela [a été achevé] dans le mois de l'année 698 [1298–1299]." The translation from the French is mine; the translation into French from the Arabic is from Combe, Sauvaget, and Wiet 1944, vol. 13, 183.

43 Holt 1986, 110.

44 Behrens-Abouseif 2007, 4–5.

45 Behrens-Abouseif 2007, 152, points out that al-Nasir's *madrasa*, like those of Qalawun and Khalil, taught all four of the *madhhabs* (schools of thought) of Islamic law.

46 Behrens-Abouseif 2007, 16–17.

47 Humphreys 1972, 69–119; Mathews 2012, 200. For more work on Mamluk patronage, see Fernandes 1997, 107–20; and al-Harithy 2001, 219–44.

48 Trachtenberg 2010, 1–24.

49 I use here a medieval European definition of authorship by Saint Bonaventure, taken from Minnis 2010, 94–103, esp. 94.

50 See Allen 1988; Bloom 1993, 21–28; Meinecke 1996; and Korn 2003, 237–60.

51 For the Tulunids, see Swelim 2015, 89–135. For the Fatimids, see Bloom 2008, 59–81, 117–55. For the Ayyubids, see Behrens-Abouseif 1989, 78–93; Korn 2004, vol. 2, 11–41; Korn 2004, vol. 1, 148–57, 159–77; and O'Kane 2009, 423–34.

52 Irwin 1986, 37–61; Thorau 1992.

53 Creswell 1959, vol. 2, 155–73; Bloom 1982, 45–78; Meinecke 1992, vol. 2, 26; Meinecke 1992, vol. 1, 31–36; Behrens-Abouseif 2007, 121–26.

54 See Bloom 1982, 68–71. For Iranian mosques, see Hillenbrand 1994, 100–14.

55 Much of the vast discussion regarding Late Antique *spolia* hinges on the discussion between practical and intentional reuse. See Alchermes 1994; Kinney 1995; Kinney 1997; Ward-Perkins 1999; Cutler 1999; Elsner 2000; and Liverani 2004.

56 Meinecke-Berg 1985, 131–42; Barrucand 2002, 37–75; Barrucand 2005, 23–44.

57 Taragan 2006, 54–66.

58 Flood 1997, 57–79.

59 Humphreys 1972, 69–119.

60 Creswell 1959, vol. 2, 198–203; Meinecke 1992, vol. 2, 61; Meinecke 1992, vol. 1, 44–46; Warner 2005, 96–97; Behrens-Abouseif 2007, 132–42.

61 Behrens-Abouseif 1995, 285–312.

62 Loiseau 2011. Loiseau does not explain why or how slave masons would be allowed to dictate questions of design, resulting in an argument implicitly based on the superiority of Western forms.

63 Macridy 1964, 279–98; Müller-Wiener 1977, 126–31; Kidonopoulos 1994, 86–87; Talbot 2001, 329–43; Marinis 2004.

64 Velenis 1988, 279–85.

65 Ousterhout 1991, 79.

66 Byzantine and European references were not *a priori* negative associations for the Mamluks. Following the re-establishment of the Byzantine Empire in 1261, Sultan Baybars and the Byzantine Emperor Michael VIII

Paleologus (1223–82) immediately developed strategic ties (see Canard 1937, 197–224; Holt 1986, 155–66; Thorau 1992, 120–33; Holt 1995). Byzantium served both as an ally against the Ilkhanid Mongols and their European allies. Early Mamluk rule was deeply dependent on alliances around the eastern Mediterranean and with the Golden Horde (the Kipchak Khanate); see Behrens-Abouseif 2014b; and Conermann 2014. Constantinople served as the slave trade hub to replenish the Mamluk military ranks, conducted by Genoese merchants from the Kipchak Khanate steppe through the Black Sea (see Jenkins 1988, 29; Amitai-Preiss 1995; and Amitai 2013). Genoese naval support was also involved in the Mamluk capture of Acre (see Ehrenkreutz 1981, 335–45). Further, since the Fourth Crusade (1204) there had been significant importation of looted goods from Constantinople into Egypt, mostly in precious metals and textiles (see Garcin 1974, 109–16; and Ciggar 2006, 663–81). The revival of mosaic work under Qalawun may also have been accomplished with Byzantine assistance (see Meinecke 1970, 295–96; and Meinecke 1971, 47–80).

67 Behrens-Abouseif 2007, 154.

68 Of course, both types of reuse can coexist in the same monument, varying in importance according to historical circumstances, as has been recently shown by Bonde and Maines 2017.

69 Behrens-Abouseif 2007, 153; Behrens-Abouseif 2010, 144–49.

70 Behrens-Abouseif 2007, 154–55.

Bibliography

Abdel-Naby, Heba Mahmoud Saad. 2014. "The Treatment of the Architectural Unit above Openings of the Mamluk and Ottoman Façades in Cairo," *Journal of Islamic Architecture* 3, no. 2, 83-92.

al-Nuwayri, Shihab al-Din Ahmad ibn ʿAbd al-Wahhab. 2016. *The Ultimate Ambition in the Arts of Erudition: A Compendium of Knowledge from the Classical Islamic World*. Ed. and trans. Elias Muhanna. New York: Penguin.

—. 2003. *Nihayat al-arab fi funun al-adab*. Beirut: Dar al-Kutub al-ʿIlmiyya.

Alchermes, Joseph. 1994. "*Spolia* in Roman Cities of the Late Empire: Legislative Rationales and Architectural Reuse," *Dumbarton Oaks Papers* 48, 167–78.

al-Harithy, Howayda. 2001. "The Patronage of al-Nasir Muhammad ibn Qalawun, 1310–1341," *Mamluk Studies Review* 4, 219–44.

Allen, Terry. 1988. *Five Essays in Islamic Art*. Sebastopol: Solipsist Press.

Amitai, Reuven. 2013. *Holy War and Rapprochement: Studies in the Relations between the Mamluk Sultanate and the Mongol Ilkhanate (1260–1335)*. Turnhout: Brepols.

Amitai-Preiss, Reuven. 1995. *Mongols and Mamluks: The Mamluk-Ilkhanid War, 1260–1281*. Cambridge: Cambridge University Press.

Bailey, Geoff. 2007. "Time Perspectives, Palimpsests and the Archaeology of Time," *Journal of Anthropological Archaeology* 26, 198–223.

Barrucand, Marianne. 2005. "Remarks on the Iconography of the Medieval Capitals of Cairo: Form and Emplacement," in *The Iconography of Islamic Art: Studies in Honour of Robert Hillenbrand*, ed. Bernard O'Kane. Edinburgh: Edinburgh University Press, 23–44.

—. 2002. "Les chapiteaux de remploi de la mosquée al-Azhar et l'émergence d'un type de chapiteau médiéval en Égypte," *Annales Islamologiques* 36, 37–75.

Baxandall, Michael. 1988. *Painting & Experience in Fifteenth-Century Italy: A Primer in the Social History of Pictorial Style*. Oxford: Oxford University Press.

Behrens-Abouseif, Doris. 2014a. "Between Quarry and Magic: The Selective Approach to Spolia in the Islamic Monuments of Egypt," in *Dalmatia and the Mediterranean: Portable Archaeology and the Poetics of Influence*, ed. Alina Payne. Leiden: Brill, 402–25.

—. 2014b. *Practising Diplomacy in the Mamluk Sultanate: Gifts and Material Culture in the Mamluk Islamic World*. London and New York: I.B. Tauris.

—. 2012. "Mamluk Perceptions of Foreign Arts," in *The Arts of the Mamluks in Egypt and Syria: Evolution and Impact*, ed. Doris Behrens-Abouseif, 301–18. Bonn: Bonn University Press.

—. 2010. *The Minarets of Cairo: Islamic Architecture from the Arab Conquest to the End of the Ottoman Empire*. London and New York: I.B. Tauris.

—. 2007. *Cairo of the Mamluks: A History of the Architecture and its Culture*. London and New York: I.B. Tauris.

—. 1995. "Sicily, the Missing Link in the Evolution of Cairene Architecture," in *Egypt and Syria in the Fatimid, Ayyubid and Mamluk Eras I* (Orientalia Lovaniensia Analecta 73), ed. Urbain Vermeulen and D. de Smet. Leuven: Peeters, 285–312.

—. 1989. *Islamic Architecture in Cairo: An Introduction*. Leiden: Brill.

Blair, Sheila. 1998. *Islamic Inscriptions*. New York: New York University Press.

Bloom, Jonathan. 2015. "Erasure and Memory: Aghlabid and Fatimid Inscriptions in North Africa," in *Viewing Inscriptions in the Late Antique and Medieval World*, ed. Antony Eastmond. Cambridge: Cambridge University Press, 61–75.

—. 2008. *Arts of the City Victorious: Islamic Art and Architecture in Fatimid North Africa and Egypt*. New Haven: Yale University Press.

—. 1993. "On the Transmission of Designs in Early Islamic Architecture," *Muqarnas* 10, 21–28.

—. 1983. "The Mosque of al-Hakim in Cairo," *Muqarnas* 1, 15–36.

—. 1982. "The Mosque of Baybars al-Bunduqdari in Cairo," *Annales Islamologiques* 18, 45–78.

Bonde, Sheila, and Clark Maines. 2017. "Reuses of the Past: Making and Reaffirming Monastic Identity at Saint-Jean-des-Vignes," paper presented at the symposium *Reuse Reconsidered*, Brown University, 15-17 September.

Bosworth, Clifford Edmund. 1996. *The New Islamic Dynasties: A Chronological and Genealogical Manual*. Edinburgh: Edinburgh University Press.

Briggs, Martin. 1924. *Muhammadan Architecture in Egypt and Palestine*. Oxford: Clarendon Press.

Brilliant, Richard. 1982. "I piedistalli del giardino di Boboli: Spolia in se, spolia in re," *Prospettiva* 31, 2–17.

Brilliant, Richard, and Dale Kinney, eds. 2011. *Reuse Value: Spolia and Appropriation in Art and Architecture from Constantine to Sherrie Levine*. Farnham: Ashgate.

Broadbridge, Anne. 2008. *Kingship and Ideology in the Islamic and Mongol Worlds*. Cambridge: Cambridge University Press.

—. 2001. "Mamluk Legitimacy and the Mongols: The Reigns of Baybars and Qalawun," *Mamluk Studies Review* 5, 91–118.

Burgoyne, Michael. 1987. *Mamluk Jerusalem: an Architectural Study*. Jerusalem: World of Islam Festival Trust.

Canard, Marius. 1937. "Une lettre du Sultan Malik Nasir Hasan à Jean Cantacuzène (750/1349)," *Annales de l'Institut d'Etudes Orientales* 3, 27–52.

Ciggar, Krijnie. 2006. "Byzantine *Spolia* in Egypt: Sultan Malik al-Adil and Byzantium's Cultural Heritage," in *Quarta Crociata: Venezia - Bisanzio - Impero Latino*, ed. Gherardo Ortalli, Giorgio Ravegnani, and Peter Schreiner. Venice: Istituto veneto di scienze, lettere ed arti, 663–81.

Combe, Étienne, Jean Sauvaget, and Gaston Wiet. 1944. *Répertoire chronologique d'épigraphie arabe*, vol. 13. Cairo: Institut français d'archéologie orientale.

Conermann, Stephan. 2014. *Everything is on the Move: The Mamluk Empire as a Node in the (Trans)-Regional Networks*. Goettingen: V & R Unipress.

Creswell, K. A. C. 1959. *The Muslim Architecture of Egypt*, 2 vols. Oxford: Clarendon Press.

Cutler, Anthony. 1999. "Reuse or Use: Theoretical and Practical Attitudes Toward Objects in the Early Middle Ages," in *Ideologie e pratiche del reimpiego nell'alto medioevo*. Spoleto: Centro italiano di studi sull'alto Medioevo, 1055–79.

Ehrenkreutz, Andrew. 1981. "Strategic Implications of the Slave Trade between Genoa and Egypt in the Second Half of the Thirteenth Century," in *The Islamic Middle East 700–1900*, ed. Abraham Udovitch. Princeton: Darwin Press, 335–45.

Elsner, Jas. 2000. "From the Culture of Spolia to the Cult of Relics: The Arch of Constantine and the Genesis of Late Antique Forms," *Papers of the British School at Rome* 68, 149–84.

Enlart, Camille. 1925. *Les monuments des Croisés dans le Royaume de Jérusalem*, 2 vols. Paris: P. Geuthner.

Fernandes, Leonor. 1997. "Mamluk Architecture and the Question of Patronage," *Mamluk Studies Review* 1, 107–20.

Flood, Finbarr Barry. 2011. "Appropriation as Inscription: Making History in the First Friday Mosque of Delhi," in *Reuse Value: Spolia and Appropriation in Art and Architecture from Constantine to Sherrie Levine*, ed. Richard Brilliant and Dale Kinney. Farnham: Ashgate, 121–47.

—. 2009. "An Ambiguous Aesthetic: Crusader spolia in Ayyubid Jerusalem," in *Ayyubid Jerusalem*, ed. Robert Hillenbrand and Sylvia Auld. London: Altajir Trust, 202–15.

—. 2006. "Image Against Nature: Spolia as Apotropaia in Byzantium and the dar al-Islam," *Medieval History Journal* 9, no. 1, 143–66.

—. 2001a. *The Great Mosque of Damascus: Studies on the Makings of an Umayyad Visual Culture*. Leiden: Brill.

—. 2001b. "The Medieval Trophy as an Art Historical Trope: Coptic and Byzantine Altars in Islamic Contexts," *Muqarnas* 18, 41–72.

—. 1997. "Umayyad Survivals and Mamluk Revivals: Qalawunid Architecture and the Great Mosque of Damascus," *Muqarnas* 14, 57–79.

Folda, Jaroslav. 2005. *Crusader Art in the Holy Land, From the Third Crusade to the Fall of Acre, 1187–1291*. Cambridge: Cambridge University Press.

Garcin, Jean-Claude. 1974. "La 'Méditerranéisation' de l'empire mamelouk sous les sultans bahrides," *Rivista degli studi orientali* 48, 109–16.

Gonnella, Julia. 2010. "Columns and Hieroglyphs: Magic Spolia in Medieval Islamic Architecture of Northern Syria," *Muqarnas* 27, 103–20.

Greenhalgh, Michael. 2009. *Marble Past, Monumental Present: Building with Antiquities in the Medieval Mediterranean*. Leiden: Brill.

Harding, Catherine, and Nancy Micklewright. 1997. "Mamluks and Venetians: An Intercultural Perspective on Fourteenth-Century Material Culture in the Mediterranean," *Revue d'art canadienne* 24, no. 2, 47–66.

Hillenbrand, Carole. 2009. *The Crusades: Islamic Perspectives*. Edinburgh: Edinburgh University Press.

Hillenbrand, Robert. 1994. *Islamic Architecture: Form, Function, Meaning*. New York: Columbia University Press.

Holt, Peter. 1995. *Early Mamluk Diplomacy, 1260–1290: Treaties of Baybars & Qalawun with Christian Rulers*. Leiden: Brill.

—. 1986. *The Age of the Crusades: The Near East from the Eleventh Century to 1517*. London: Longman.

Humphreys, R. Stephen. 1972. "The Expressive Intent of the Mamluk Architecture of Cairo: A Preliminary Essay," *Studia Islamica* 35, 69–119.

Hunt, Lucy-Anne. 1996. "Churches of Old Cairo and Mosques of al-Qahira: A Case of Christian-Muslim Interchange," *Medieval Encounters* 2, no. 1, 43–66.

Irwin, Robert. 1986. *The Middle East in the Middle Ages: The Early Mamluk Sultanate, 1250–1382*. London: Croom Helm.

Jacoby, Zehava. 1982. "Crusader Sculpture in Cairo: Additional Evidence on the Temple Area Workshop of Jerusalem," in *Crusader Art in the Twelfth Century*, ed. Jaroslav Folda. Oxford: British School of Archaeology in Jerusalem.

Jenkins, Marilyn. 1988. "Mamluk Jewelry: Influences and Echoes," *Muqarnas* 5, 29–42.

Kidonopoulos, Vassilios. 1994. *Bauten in Konstantinopel: Verfall und Verstörung, Restaurierung, Umbau und Neubau von Profan- und Sakralbauten*. Wiesbaden: O. Harrasowitz.

Kinney, Dale. 1997. "Spolia, Damnatio and Renovatio Memoriae," *Memoirs of the American Academy in Rome* 42, 117–48.

—. 1995. "Rape or Restitution of the Past: Interpreting *Spolia*," in *The Art of Interpreting*, ed. Susan Scott. University Park: Pennsylvania State University Press, 52–67.

Kopytoff, Igor. 1986. "The Cultural Biography of Things: Commoditization as Process," in *The Social Life of Things, Commodities in Cultural Perspective*, ed. Arjun Appadurai. Cambridge: Cambridge University Press.

Korn, Lorenz. 2004. *Ayyubidische Architektur in Ägypten und Syrien: Bautätigkeit im Kontext von Politik und Gesellschaft 564–658/1169–1260*. Wiesbaden: Reichert.

—. 2003. "Iranian Style 'Out of Place'? Some Egyptian and Syrian Stuccos of the 5–6th/11–12th Centuries," *Annales Islamologiques* 37, 237–60.

Leisten, Thomas. 1996. "Mashhad al-Nasr: Monuments of War and Victory in Medieval Islamic Art," *Muqarnas* 13, 7–26.

Lézine, Alexandre. 1965. *Mahdiya: Recherches d'archéologie islamique*. Paris: Libraire Klincksieck.

Little, Donald. 1986. "The Fall of 'Akka in 690/1291: The Muslim Version," in *Studies in Islamic History and Civilization in Honour of Professor David Ayalon*, ed. Moshe Sharon. Leiden: Brill, 159–81.

Liverani, Paolo. 2004. "Reimpiego senza ideologia: La lettura antica degli spolia dall'arco di Costantino all'età carolingia," *Mitteilungen des Deutschen Archäologischen Instituts, Römische Abteilung* 111, 383–434.

Loiseau, Julien. 2011. "Frankish Captives in Mamluk Cairo," *Al-Masaq* 23, no. 1, 37–52.

Macridy, Theodore. 1964. "The Monastery of Lips and the Burials of the Paleologi," *Dumbarton Oaks Papers* 18, 279–98.

Marinis, Vasileios. 2004. "The Monastery *tou Libos*: Architecture, Sculpture, and Liturgical Planning in Middle and Late Byzantine Constantinople," Ph.D. dissertation, University of Illinois at Urbana-Champaign.

Mathews, Karen Rose. 2012. "Mamluks and Crusaders: Architectural Appropriation and Cultural Encounter in Mamluk Monuments," in *Languages of Love and Hate: Conflict, Communication and Identity in the Medieval Mediterranean*, ed. Sarah Lambert and Helen Nicholson. Turnhout: Brepols, 177–200.

Mayer, Wolfgang. 2007. "Die Madrasa des Sultan al-Nasir Mohammed. Das Portal," in *Der Vergangenheit eine Zukunft: Denkmalpflege in der islamischen Altstadt von Kairo 1973–2004*, ed. Wolfgang Mayer and Philipp Speiser. Mainz am Rhein: Verlag Philipp von Zabern, 95–105.

Mayer, Wolfgang, Giorgio Nogara, and Philipp Speiser. 2001. "Archäologische Untersuchungen und Restaurierungsarbeiten an der Madrasa des Sultan an-Nasir Muhummad in Kairo," *Mitteilungen des Deutschen Archäologischen Instituts, Abteilung Kairo* 57, 219–38.

Meinecke, Michael. 1996. *Patterns of Stylistic Change in Islamic Architecture: Local Traditions versus Migrating Artists*. New York: New York University Press.

—. 1992. *Die mamlukische Architektur in Ägypten und Syrien (648/1250 bis 923/1517)*, 2 vols. Glückstadt: Verlag J. J. Augustin.

—. 1971. "Das Mausoleum des Qala'un in Kairo: Untersuchungen zur Genese der mamlukischen Architekturdekoration," *Mitteilungen des Deutschen Archäologischen Instituts, Abteilung Kairo* 27, 47–80.

—. 1970. "Byzantinische Elemente in der mamlukischen Architektur," *Kunstchronik* 23, 295–96.

Meinecke-Berg, Viktoria. 1985. "Spolien in der mittelalterlichen Architektur von Kairo," in *Ägypten: Dauer und Wandel*. Mainz: Philipp von Zabern, 131–42.

Minnis, Alastair. 2010. *Medieval Theory of Authorship: Scholastic Literary Attitudes in the Later Middle Ages*. 2nd edition. Philadelphia: University of Pennsylvania Press.

Müller-Wiener, Wolfgang. 1977. *Bildlexicon zur Topographie Istanbuls*. Tübingen: Ernst Wasmuth.

O'Kane, Bernard. 2009. "Ayyubid Architecture in Cairo," in *Ayyubid Jerusalem: The Holy City in Context 1187–1250*, ed. Robert Hillenbrand and Sylvia Auld. London: Altajir Trust, 423–34.

Ousterhout, Robert. 2002. "Byzantine Funerary Architecture of the Twelfth Century," in *Drevnerusskoe iskusstvo: Rus' i strany vizantiiskogo mira XII vek*, 9–17. St Petersburg: Dmitrii Bulanin.

—. 1991. "Constantinople, Bithynia, and Regional Developments in Later Paleologan Architecture," in *The Twilight of Byzantium: Aspects of Cultural and Religious History in the Late Byzantine Empire*, ed. Slobodan Ćurčić and Doula Mouriki. Princeton: Princeton University Press, 75–110.

—. 1987. *The Architecture of the Kariye Camii in Istanbul*. Washington, D.C.: Dumbarton Oaks.

Plagnieux, Philippe. 2006. "Le portail d'Acre transporté au Cairo: sources et diffusion des modèles rayonnantes en Terre Sainte au milieu du XIIIe siècle," *Bulletin monumental* 164, no. 1, 61–66.

Pringle, Denys. 1993–2009. *The Churches of the Crusader Kingdom of Jerusalem*, 4 vols. Cambridge: Cambridge University Press.

—. 2007. "The Churches of Crusader Acre: Destruction and Detection," in *Archaeology and the Crusades*, ed. Peter Edbury and Sophia Kalopissi-Verti. Athens: Pierides Foundation Publications, 111–32.

Sherif, Lobna Abdel Azim. 1988. "Layers of Meaning: An Interpretive Analysis of Three Mamluk Buildings," Ph.D. dissertation, University of Michigan.

Speiser, Philipp. 2008. "The Sultan al-Nasir Muhammad Madrasah in Cairo: Restoration and Archaeological

Investigation," *Mamluk Studies Review* 12, no. 2, 197–221.

—. 1994. "Restaurierungsarbeiten an der al-Nasriyya Madrasa in Kairo," in *XXV Deutscher Orientalistentag*, ed. Cornelia Wunsch. Stuttgart: Steiner Verlag, 527–39.

Swelim, Tarek. 2015. *Ibn Tulun: His Lost City and Great Mosque*. Cairo: American University in Cairo Press.

Tabbaa, Yasser. 1986. "Monuments with a Message: Propagation of Jihad under Nur al-Din," in *The Meeting of Two Worlds: Cultural Exchange Between East and West During the Period of the Crusades*, ed. Vladimir Goss and Christine Verzár-Bornstein. Kalamazoo: Medieval Institute Publications, 223–40.

Talbot, Alice-Mary. 2001. "Building Activity Under Andronikos II," in *Byzantine Constantinople: Monuments, Topography and Everyday Life*, ed. Nevra Necipoğlu. Leiden: Brill, 329–43.

Taragan, Hana. 2006. "Signs of the Times: Reusing the Past in Baybar's Architecture in Palestine," in *Mamluks and Ottomans: Studies in Honour of Michael Winter*, ed. David Wasserstein and Ami Ayalon. London: Routledge, 54–66.

Thorau, Peter. 1992. *The Lion of Egypt: Sultan Baybars I & the Near East in the Thirteenth Century*. London: Longman.

Trachtenberg, Marvin. 2010. *Building-in-Time: From Giotto to Alberti and Modern Oblivion*. New Haven: Yale University Press.

van Berchem, Max. 1894. *Matériaux pour un Corpus Inscriptionum Arabicarum*. Paris: E. Leroux.

Velenis, George. 1988. "Thirteenth-Century of Architecture in the Despotate of Epirus: The Origins of the School," in *Studenica et l'art byzantin autour de l'annee 1200*, ed. Vojislav Korać. Beograd: Srpska Akademija Nauka i Umetnosti, 279–85.

Ward-Perkins, Bryan. 1999. "Re-using the Architectural Legacy of the Past, *entre idéologie et pragmatism*," in *The Idea and the Ideal of the Town Between Late Antiquity and the Early Middle Ages*, ed. Gianpaolo Brogiolo and Bryan Ward Perkins. Leiden: Brill, 225–44.

Warner, Nicholas. 2005. *The Monuments of Historic Cairo: A Map and Descriptive Catalogue*. Cairo: American University in Cairo Press.

Williams, Caroline. 2008. *Islamic Monuments in Cairo*. Cairo: American Unversity in Cairo Press.

II

Restoration and Rewriting

Chapter 4
The Limits of Palimpsest: Architectural Ruins, Reuse, and Remodeling among the Ancient Maya

Sarah Newman

The term "palimpsest" is evocative. It conjures the thrill of discovery, the challenges of sorting out successive layers of meaning (perhaps in several scripts and languages), the satisfaction of rescue from imminent oblivion. The word also has a precise origin. It denotes reuse of a particular kind: palimpsests are manuscripts from which an earlier text has been intentionally scraped away, whether completely or incompletely, to make a new surface available for writing. Behind that original meaning are specific attributes and processes, each of which is essential to the production of a palimpsest: the value of the material substrate, the irrelevance of earlier writing, the intentional erasure and reinscription, the subsequent detection of layered messages and meanings, and the revival of effaced—sometimes precious—texts.

If the goal of this volume is to develop the notion of "palimpsest" systematically, as a critical tool for understanding archaeological and architectural evidence, then this contribution attempts a rigorous—but not inflexible—analysis of the term's applications in Maya archaeology. "Palimpsest" has potential as a conceptual metaphor, but not simply as a synonym for layering. The word implies much more than that. It also involves rupture, forgetting, and renewed interest. These are constitutive elements that are as essential to its full meaning as the resulting textural strata.[1] Using the word loosely or only partially does violence to the term, reducing its hermeneutic value.[2]

In this chapter, I examine uses of the term "palimpsest" in archaeological and art historical scholarship from the Maya world, considering its applicability both in its original sense as an erased and rewritten manuscript, and in its extended, metaphorical sense as applied to architecture and urban design. I highlight particular examples that challenge the applicability of the word: cities where deteriorating ruins stood alongside new constructions, long-buried buildings that were actively venerated despite being invisible, and hieroglyphic texts that are not palimpsests themselves, but that give us insight into how the ancient Maya engaged with the material traces of the past. I argue that "palimpsest," especially when used metaphorically, should attend to the full, complex suite of features the word implies: not only acts of layering, but instances of irrelevance, erasure, and replacement.

The idea of "palimpsest" is far from home in the New World. In the original sense of the word—surfaces made and used for writing, later erased to make space for new writing—examples are exceedingly rare among the Maya. To apply the term, whether literally or metaphorically, requires varying degrees of semantic stretch.[3] For example, the Maya did not usually scrape away, but rather covered over. Concealing acts of additive erasure, whether textual or architectural, both obscured and preserved what lay beneath. Any so-called "palimpsest" from the Maya world, whether a bark-paper book or painted mural, thus varies from the original meaning of the word (which derives ultimately from the Greek word *psēn* meaning "to scrape"). Yet the intent and effect, if not the process, is sometimes the same: one message is erased from a surface in order to be replaced with another. Whether subtractive or additive, however, such intentional acts are fundamentally quite different from accumulations of signs of human activity, in superposition and contiguity, which can be observed simultaneously when earlier layers are not obscured. My aim in this chapter, then, is not to suggest that "palimpsest" cannot be applied to Maya cases, but rather to do so with both caution and care, probing the limits of the term's capacity to describe architectural reuse, remodeling, and ruins in a context far from its cultural and temporal origins.

Pre-Columbian palimpsests?

European parchment was rare and expensive. The tanned hides that are manuscript pages had intrinsic value that prompted recycling, entirely apart from the text they originally bore. Those sturdy animal skins allowed ink to be scraped off, with slight damage to the surface. In a palimpsest, the original textual content of a manuscript is almost fully obliterated, but the manuscript's form and purpose are maintained—initially used as a background for writing, the page is reused for an identical purpose. The particular type of reuse involved in the production of a palimpsest happened only when an initial text became irrelevant to its owners. The useless text was intentionally erased, scraped away as the word "palimpsest" conveys, and replaced with something of interest. In sequential layers, the new covered up the old. But do the palimpsests of the Old World have counterparts in the New?

There were many Maya manuscripts, but seemingly few palimpsests. Pre-Columbian screenfold books—generally made of wild fig or mulberry bark, but also animal leather in some cases, with a smooth coating of calcium-based plaster—are depicted on polychrome vessels and mentioned in hieroglyphic texts (fig. 4.1). Archaeological finds, including mortars and pestles for pigment preparation, shell ink pots, bark beaters (grooved stones used to break down the long, fibrous strands of the bark), and elite scribal residences, shed light on the production of codices and demonstrate their prestige. Early colonial documents even hint at the existence of large archives of codices (alongside accounts of their destruction as implements of idolatry). A precious few—four, to be exact—have survived to the extent that they may be read. Known as the Grolier, Dresden, Madrid, and Paris Codices (each named for the city or library where it now resides), these manuscripts all date to the Postclassic period (*c.* 1200–1519 CE) and contain genealogies; divinatory, agricultural, and ritual almanacs; and astrological charts and calculations.[4] In short, the Maya world presented the necessary conditions for palimpsests akin to those in Europe.

Unlike European parchment or vellum, however, Mesoamerican bark-paper was cheaply produced and procured, available in ample quantities, and used for a variety of purposes beyond writing. In Central Mexico, the sixteenth-century Codex Mendoza lists bark-paper in quantity as a form of tribute paid by towns under the control of the Aztec empire; one province sent sixteen thousand sheets to the capital at

4.1. Painted vase (K1523) showing the Hero Twins (prominent, semi-divine figures in Maya mythology) as scribes, Late Classic period (*c.* 600–800 CE). Each twin paints an open screenfold book with jaguar skin covers.

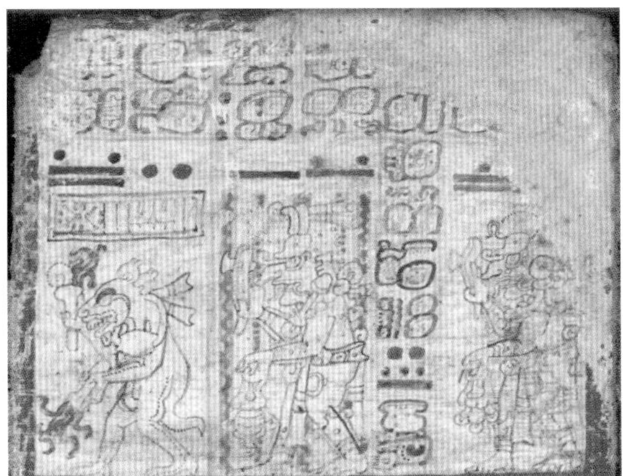

4.2. A page from the Dresden Codex showing vertical and horizontal guides in faint red paint to grid out locations for glyph blocks and figural proportions.

Tenochtitlan annually.[5] A bark-paper headband was used as the "crown" of Classic Maya kings, presented in royal accession events described in hieroglyphic texts as "headband-fastening" rituals.[6] Strips threaded through the earlobes of captives and slaves, in place of usual ear adornments, debased their wearers.[7] An offering in itself, but also a vehicle for transmitting important substances like blood, incense, or liquid rubber (spattered onto its surface), bark-paper was often burned, sent up as smoke to nourish gods and ancestors.[8] Mesoamerican paper was thus highly valued, but not for its difficult and costly production like European parchment.[9]

The four legible Maya manuscripts show evidence of multiple scribes and instances of painting, slight modifications, and occasional overlapping marks in the form of underlying sketches excluded from the final versions.[10] The scribes used underlying vertical and horizontal guide-lines in light red or black paint to grid out locations for glyph blocks and rough proportions for accompanying figural deities (fig. 4.2). The Grolier Codex is unique in that it shows evidence of both fully outlined content and grids for hieroglyphs. In the Grolier Codex, the underlying drawings are largely followed in the final version, whereas a single page of the Dresden Codex bears traces of faint glyphs that were sketched out, but never included in the final lines painted with darker pigment.[11] Similar techniques were employed by the Maya in the production of painted murals on stucco walls, where faint lines in red or black paint can be seen to underlie, and often correspond closely with, final brighter pigments.[12] Never meant to be seen, but also never removed, the guidelines and sketches in Maya manuscripts and murals attest to multiple interventions and interactions involved in artistic production, but none of these are palimpsests.

A few examples of actual palimpsests do exist, however.[13] Multispectral imaging of a much earlier codex (dating to the fifth or sixth century CE) suggests that its pages may have been fully re-plastered, the text and imagery completely replaced. Although the remains of this Early Classic codex are poorly preserved and completely illegible—the largest fragment is little more than 3 centimeters across at its widest point—at least two complete layers of plaster and paint were revealed through magnification and infrared light.[14] Beyond screenfold books, palimpsests are also found in the context of painted Maya murals. A spectacular series of seventh-century paintings, depicting scenes of a Classic Maya marketplace, covered a building at Calakmul, Mexico, in three separate phases of paint. Each phase appears to be distinct in both the images depicted and the color palette used.[15] Architectural murals at Chichén Itzá, in Yucatán, adorn the walls of the Temple of the Warriors and its buried substructure, the Temple of the Chacmool. In some areas, the murals comprise 131 individual layers of plastered stucco.[16] Although not all were painted, the strata include incised and painted sketches and guidelines, as well as final paintings of widely variable workmanship.[17] Finally, in what has been described as "a palimpsest in the most literal sense of the word,"[18] minute texts at the site of Xultún, Guatemala were painted or incised among the figural scenes of architectural murals, but without connection to the royal rituals depicted in the paintings (fig. 4.3). These small texts were plastered over, patched and inscribed anew—up to three layers of writing can be observed in some places. These "microtexts" include calendrical and astronomical calculations, similar to the tables and almanacs of the Post-

4.3. Multiple levels of replastering and reinscription on the east wall of Structure 10K–2 at Xultun.

classic Maya codices, which archaeologists and archaeoastronomers speculate might represent what "mathematicians might do on a blackboard, erasing and writing over earlier texts in search of numerical convergences, or commensurations among various cycles."[19]

The soft, stucco surfaces that covered Maya masonry were a favorite substrate for improvisational texts as well. Graffiti, whether incised or painted, are found at most Maya sites.[20] Unlike comparative examples known from Old World contexts, Maya graffiti are predominantly figural; only rarely do they convey a textual message.[21] Perhaps because of this, those who study Maya graffiti do not employ the term "palimpsest," despite the superpositioning that characterizes the composition of the scrawling, sprawling art.[22] Maya graffiti are generally rough and haphazard; it is not clear that they are meant to convey or replace a specific message. More importantly, they lack the key intermediate moment of erasure between an original inscription and a later reinscription.[23]

Although literal palimpsests are uncommon in the Maya world, their purported metaphorical counterparts are more often attested. Ancient Maya cities, in particular, are described as "palimpsests." Wendy Ashmore and Jeremy Sabloff view Maya cities as "architectural palimpsests," in which individual sites and their layouts are the result of many localized decisions made over generations, each altering or maintaining an existing spatial order to reflect the political or ideational messages that were considered important in specific times and places.[24] Ashmore further argues that an "unsorted palimpsest of decisions" can make it particularly difficult to "read" the civic layouts of Maya centers with turbulent political histories.[25] Separately, Shawn Morton writes that the heart of the ancient Maya city was "a palimpsest of complementary and self-referencing symbols," while Lisa LeCount and Jason Yaeger claim that "generations of accretionary growth resulted in a complex palimpsest of buildings and plazas" at most Classic Maya city centers.[26] On a larger scale, Rani Alexander, in a study of long-term agrarian practices among the Maya of Yucatán, sees the landscape as "a dynamic palimpsest that reflects critical relationships among four factors: population density; the physical attributes of the environment … technological and managerial use strategies … and political and economic policies…"[27] Olivia Navarro-Farr and Ana Lucía Arroyave Prera, on the other hand, apply the metaphor to a single public ceremonial shrine at the ancient Maya city of El Perú-Waka' in northern Guatemala, using Geoff Bailey's term to describe the successive ritual manipulations at the structure, carried out over more than a century, as a "cumulative palimpsest" (though it is difficult to imagine what a "non-cumulative" palimpsest might be).[28]

Some Mesoamerican archaeologists use "palimpsest" to refer to the "problem" of complex stratigraphy, an impediment to identifying or reconstituting individual episodes of past activities. In an edited volume on ancient households of the Americas, John G. Douglass and Nancy Gonlin suggest that one chapter's focus on spatial and diachronic patterns among groups of households, rather than individual residences, "offer[s] analytical advantages in allowing archaeologists to ignore the palimpsest nature of individual house floors."[29] Olivier de Montmollin refers to "palimpsest effects leading to contemporaneity problems" and to the "palimpsest problems" of the foothills of the Rosario Valley of Chiapas, Mexico, where high site loss and settlement instability bias population estimates against the valley floor.[30] Dylan Clark and Carmen Muñoz-Fernández use "palimpsest" as a metaphor to capture the competing, and at times conflicting, narratives presented to tourists at the eco-archaeological theme park of Xcaret, an ancient Maya site in Quintana Roo, Mexico. Following a similar analysis by Quetzil Castañeda at Chichén Itzá, Clark and Muñoz-Fernández describe layered "archaeonarratives" that they view as intrinsically "palimpsestic:" grouped together, superimposed, overriding one another. They position the archaeological ruins of Xcaret as the original text, which may still be "visited, climbed, admired," but is overlaid by official and non-official signage and mapping, modern reconstructions made to represent ruins (including two large ball courts, despite the fact that no such structures appear to have been constructed at the site), guided cultural tours, and the "Xcaret México Espectacular" show where actors, lights, and music are used to reenact episodes of Mexican history and folklore. For Clark and Muñoz-Fernández, the successive narratives do not physically erase the underlying layers, but rather create "new hybrid images."[31]

Whether they involve land- or cityscapes, an individual pyramid or the inherent "problems" of archaeology, these examples of metaphorical palimpsests rely on their authors emphasizing only certain characteristics of the original object on which the metaphor rests (usually only layering), while omitting most others. Rarely, however, is it made clear which aspects of a palimpsest apply to the case study and which should be ignored. Lack of precision makes for a poor metaphor. For example, how might we imagine Rani's "palimpsest" in which abstract political and economic policies are layered in (above or below?) the physical attributes of the environment?

An all-purpose metaphor lacks hermeneutic value. Take, for example, Geoff Bailey's statement that

> … it has become increasingly difficult to identify any situation or location, whether from the archaeological past, or in the contemporary world, whether it is in the built environment of a modern city or an archaeological context, in an institutional building or outdoors, that does not constitute some sort of palimpsest. Even individual objects do not escape the palimpsest phenomenon … palimpsests are universal, an inherent feature of the material world we inhabit.[32]

If palimpsests can be found everywhere, regardless of historical, cultural, or regional context; if the term can be applied to objects regardless of material, scale, or form; or if the intentions of a purported palimpsest's makers are irrelevant, then the term loses its explanatory power and the specificity of the object it references—the very things that make it such an enticing metaphor in the first place. This all-purpose metaphorical extension obscures more than it illuminates, becoming a synonym for "recycling" or "reuse." After all, anything that explains everything, in the end explains nothing.[33] If we consider the original meaning of "palimpsest"—attending not only to sequential layering, but also to the intentional erasure of an original text, the lasting value (and perhaps scarcity) of the message-bearing medium or materials being reused, and the subsequent renewed interest in the underlying writing—then palimpsests do not exist in Maya architecture and epigraphy. Put simply, the Maya had different ideas about the stratigraphy of the past than either the creators or contemporary readers of palimpsests. They did not adhere to a strictly linear chronology in which new layers cover over and completely replace older ones in a superimposed sequence. They often remembered and revered underlying or deteriorating objects and architecture, bringing the past into the present through repeated commemorations, even reincarnations, of things that could no longer be used or were no longer seen.

Ruining ancient Maya cities

Despite familiar artists' renderings of Maya cities with freshly painted temples, straight walls, and level platforms, the reality was somewhat different. As Stephen Houston reminds us,

> [t]he sun beat down, drying and cracking plaster. Rain fell in torrents, colors streaked, fungus spread, and stone structures sagged or collapsed under the rigors of tropical climate… At any one time, Maya cityscapes juxtaposed buildings in good repair with those in a state of advanced dilapidation.[34]

While some buildings were repeatedly restored or remodeled (see below), others simply remained. Abandoned or obsolete, houses, palaces, and pyramids at times persisted for centuries, exposed and deteriorating alongside structures in use.[35] Although Maya cities have been described as palimpsests, they were something rather different: complex concurrent landscapes of old and new, with lived-in and decaying spaces existing side by side, rather than in relatively neat successive layers.

An iconic depiction of the Acropolis of Piedras Negras, Guatemala, by Tatiana Proskouriakoff, imagines the city at its heyday (fig. 4.4). Impressive and impeccable, the complex is not only completely free of dilapidation, but is almost entirely devoid of inhabitants, save for the few individuals drawn in the foreground or atop distant temples for scale. A different extreme can be observed in *Tikal Abandoned*, a series of paintings by Russell Hoover, commissioned by the University Museum of the University of Pennsylvania in 1985, in which the artist imagines the site of Tikal, Guatemala, as it might have appeared in the tenth century CE, well after its royal dynasty had fallen and most of the city had been abandoned (fig. 4.5). In Hoover's illustrations, gone are the clean lines and bare plazas frozen in time. Instead, green creeps over

4.4. Tatiana Proskouriakoff, *Acropolis at Piedras Negras, Guatemala* (restored view), watercolor, 1939.

4.5. Russell Hoover, *Tikal Abandoned* (reconstruction of Tikal after its dynastic collapse), oil painting, 1985.

temple stairs and sprouts from crumbling roofcombs. Scattered smoke suggests farmers on a shrinking periphery as the jungle encroaches on the former spaces of civilization.

The reality of the Classic Maya city, however, fell somewhere between Proskouriakoff's manicured scene and Hoover's apocalyptic vision. Archaeological excavations at Piedras Negras revealed that architecture within the South Group, the location of the earliest known occupation at the site (southeast of Acropolis), saw episodes both of remodeling and of sustained neglect. Between 400–50 CE, population and construction boomed at Piedras Negras. The natural landscape was artificially leveled and monumental works, including ballcourts, sweatbaths, temples, funerary shrines, administrative buildings, and inscribed monuments, all suddenly appeared across the city during this period. In the South Group, this building frenzy included a number of pyramids and temples, some of which were constructed directly atop the area's earlier small-scale architecture, with significant shifts in style and orientation. The South Group remained the ceremonial heart of Piedras Negras into the seventh century CE (later rulers are responsible for the efforts illustrated in Proskouriakoff's Acropolis).[36] Two large, central pyramids, however, were left to decay, even as new structures rose around them.

The first, Structure R-16, sits along a major causeway that facilitated access from the southern end of the city to the areas to the north (including the Acropolis). Although it consists of two architectural phases— its initial construction and a remodeling—both took place before the end of the sixth century CE. While new buildings took shape adjacent to Structure R-16, it remained in ruins.[37] The second, Structure R-3–1st, represents the founding temple built at the South Group by the city's initial dynastic rulers. The early phase of this pyramid was never sealed beneath subsequent constructions, but rather retained its fifth-century façade throughout later sixth- and seventh-century building programs. After a few centuries, the Early Classic Structure R-3–1st was completely surrounded by Late Classic pyramids and temples, but remained a central focus of the South Group. Mark Child and Charles Golden see this preservation and presentation of earlier architecture as a way of both memorializing and manipulating the local past, a means of reinforcing new traditions while connecting with a well-established place of legitimation.[38]

In a palimpsest, parchment is scraped and reinscribed to replace an older text that is no longer deemed useful or relevant. As a metaphor for an ancient city, then, a palimpsest implies an indifference to what came before, an elision of a now-irrelevant past to make room for a more-important present. The Maya, on the other hand, deliberately situated new constructions atop and around earlier ones, not only taking existing architecture into careful consideration, but reiterating, manipulating, and extending its meaning. A city is a particularly difficult entity to convey via metaphor or analogy, as Joseph Rykwert has written:

> ... town planners, when talking about the way towns live and grow, invoke images drawn from nature when they consider town plans: a tree, a leaf, a piece of skin tissue, a hand and so on, with excursions into pathology when pointing to crises. But the town is not really like a natural phenomenon. It is an artefact—an artefact of a curious kind, compounded of willed and random elements, imperfectly controlled. If it is related to physiology at all, it is more like a dream than anything else.[39]

If we wish to use a textual metaphor for an ancient Maya city—or any city, for that matter—is it not more like a library than a single document? Rather than one text layered over and obscuring another, we can think of an assortment of books (some, perhaps, palimpsests), each recalling a particular moment, context, and purpose, collected and curated side by side, some with great care, others for practical purposes, some treasured, others rotting, many simply there.

Buried, but not forgotten

The monks who scraped and smoothed away earlier texts in medieval abbeys to reuse valuable parchment had no interest in the content they removed. The Maya, however, sometimes

4.6. Cutaway illustration showing the buried buildings, especially the intentionally preserved Rosalila, beneath Structure 10L–16 at Copán.

went to great lengths to ensure the protection of earlier architecture that would ultimately be covered over. Ancient Maya pyramids are sometimes likened to Russian *matryoshka* dolls: later structures erected atop earlier architectural phases gradually formed "mountains" of nested buildings; temples within temples, tombs atop tombs.[40] Earlier phases were often destroyed or partially dismantled in order to increase the stability of subsequent architecture, but they were neither obliterated nor forgotten. Certain structures, moreover, were not only spared systematic demolition, but were interred at the end of their use—entombed and perhaps even embalmed in the same way the Maya treated the dead.[41] These structures and their ornamentation were painstakingly protected—swept clean, reinforced with rubble and fill to prevent collapse, and selectively covered in fine earth. Though invisible, these monuments remained symbolically important, inciting reuse with their hidden presence. In exceptional instances, as we will see below, the buried buildings themselves were even commemorated in glyphic texts incorporated into later renovations, almost a kind of antithesis to the idea of palimpsest: it is the text that is preserved and reused, while the physical substrate is erased.

Perhaps the best-known example comes from the site of Copán, in northeastern Honduras. At the very center of the city's Acropolis, the anthropogenic hill where ritual and administrative affairs were conducted, sits Structure 10L–16. The reconstructed final phase of the building (the iteration visible to tourists today) was built during the reign of Copán's sixteenth ruler, around 776 CE. Beneath its pyramidal platforms, however, are the remains of at least seven earlier structures, each erected atop a single sacred center established by the burial of Copán's dynastic founder, K'inich Yax K'uk' Mo', in 437 CE (fig. 4.6).[42]

Structure 10L–16's multilayered architectural history incorporates a series of tombs and funerary shrines, each alluding to the origins and reign of the founder.[43] Some subsequent buildings were constructed to maintain access to buried offerings even after the construction of surmounting platforms, so that objects and offerings could be added and removed from the tomb of the founder's wife after her burial. The version of Structure 10L–16 built in the mid-sixth century CE, known as Rosalila, condensed multiple earlier structures beneath a brilliant polychrome temple, covered in imagery devoted to the cosmic roles of Copán's founder. When Rosalila was eventually buried beneath later constructions, the rooms, moldings, and niches of the colorful shrine were meticulously filled with clay and rocks, while the temple's elaborately ornamented, polychrome façade was covered with a thick layer of white stucco.[44] Finally, over three hundred years after the interment of the founder, the sculptural façades of the pyramid's last iteration imitated the Central Mexican style of the first structure in the sequence, now buried deep within the temple's strata.[45] A carved monument set just in front of Structure 10L–16's final version, Altar Q, depicts and recounts the continuity of royal rule at Copán from the city's first dynast to its last. Altar Q's form even mimics the burial slabs found in the royal tombs of the Acropolis, referencing the real and symbolic presence of the previous kings.[46]

The architectural sequence of Structure 10L–16 created, and recreated, a funerary monument that was not only commemorative, but cumulative.[47] Each subsequent phase condensed its underlying layers, reinforcing the power and authority that was concentrated in and came from the founder, physically entombed at the heart of the temple, merging the actual historical figure with the architectural testament to his enduring dynasty.

But Copán is not a singular case. Many Maya cities celebrated their dynastic origins through the continued commemoration of the lavish tombs and funerary shrines of their founders. At the site of El Zotz, in northern Guatemala, a funerary monument known as the Temple of the Night Sun, set atop the dynastic founder's vaulted tomb, was completely and carefully encased within later constructions, much like Copán's Rosalila.[48] The elaborate, bright red stucco façade for which the Temple of the Night Sun is named combines celestial and solar imagery (including depictions of the morning, noontime, and night versions of the Maya sun god) with themes of royal lineage, martial leadership, and legitimate succession, establishing the first El Zotz ruler at the center of both local and cosmic concerns.[49] When the Temple of the Night Sun was covered over and transformed into a higher pyramid, elements of the iconography of the original stucco façade were retained, recalling the hidden shrine buried below. Moreover, the Temple of the Night Sun defined the orientation of El Zotz's spatial layout and civic plan. In addition to the successive funerary monuments to the founder, all of the later causeways, pyramids, and palaces commemorated the city's long-buried dynastic origins.

Beyond the Maya, other kinds of objects and architecture in Mesoamerica were similarly buried, but not forgotten. Farther north, at Cacaxtla, Mexico, a series of Maya-style murals were carefully buried beneath subsequent buildings, but offerings made at the locations of the hidden murals continued to reference the styles and themes of the paintings.[50] At the first-millennium BCE Olmec site of La Venta, Mexico, buried deposits, such as an arrangement of small stone anthropomorphic figurines and upright celts known as Offering 4, point to the cultural breadth and temporal depth of such practices. Sometime after Offering 4's figurines and celts had been covered with clay, a small pit was excavated directly above the buried offering. The figurines were partially exposed (only the heads were uncovered) and the pit was filled back in. The placement of the pit suggests that the offering's caretakers remembered the particular locations of important buried objects.[51] Indeed, ceremonial acts of wrapping and bundling sacred objects throughout much of pre-Columbian and contemporary Mesoamerica suggest that a

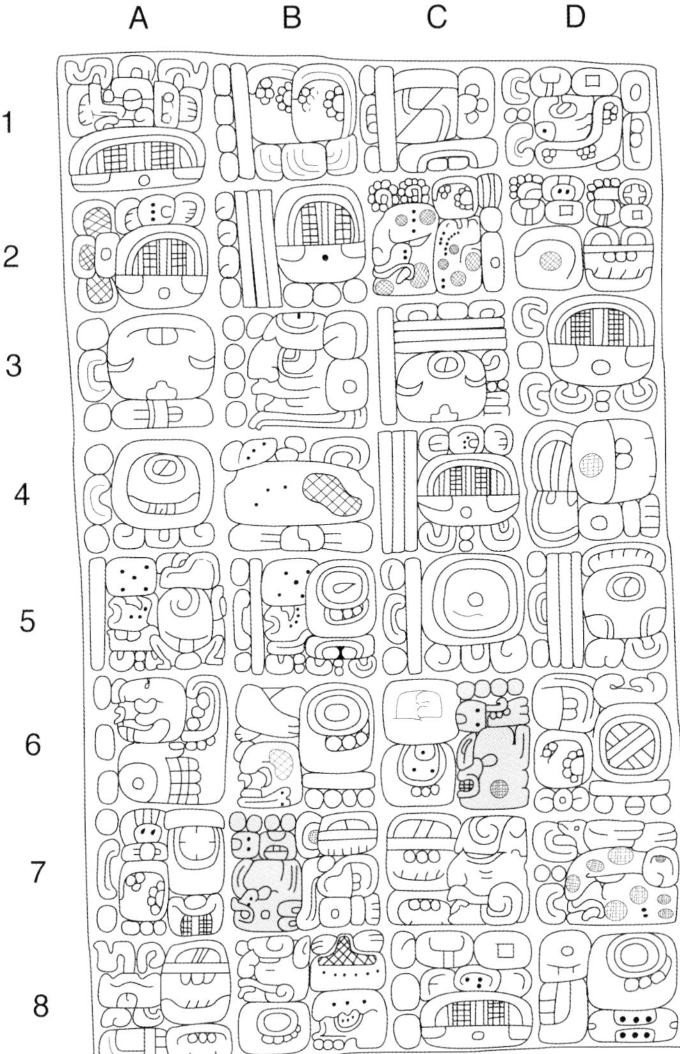

4.7. Lintel 21 from Structure 22 at Yaxchilán, Mexico. The shaded glyph at B7 names Structure 22 as the Four Bat Place constructed and dedicated in 454 CE; the shaded glyph at C6 names the renovated building once again as the Four Bat Place, during a later ceremony in 752 CE.

correlation between visibility and the ritual importance of objects, art, and architecture would be an exception, rather than the rule.[52]

A palimpsest is a tempting metaphor to convey this kind of simultaneous concealment and commemoration.[53] In these Mesoamerican examples, each layer completely covers over preexisting structures, but the underlying architecture also manages to peek through in later references to buried individuals or iconography. Yet, as Patricia McAnany and Ian Hodder point out, this kind of "entombment" should be seen as an active preserving or renewing agent.[54] For the Maya, subsequent architectural phases and buried offerings held meaning *because* of what lay beneath. Unlike a palimpsest, the underlying architecture not only motivated renovations, but transferred its message to subsequent constructions. At Copán, the architectural and iconographic references encoded in Structure 10L–16's final phase would have been unintelligible to its eighth-century audience without an understanding of the presence and persona of the fifth-century founder within.

Referring to these processes and buildings as palimpsests obscures the intent and meaning of their makers.

Rebuilt or reborn?

In the case of medieval palimpsests, the more complete the erasure, the better. The effaced texts often come to light only literally, when multispectral imaging technologies reveal the remnants of earlier ink, despite the attempts to scrape it away completely. In the case of Maya architectural restoration, however, complete erasure rarely occurs. Even when buildings were rebuilt rather than left to decay, they could be understood as reincarnations of their prior structures, a continuity not only of function and meaning, but of actual essence. Reused stones and reset hieroglyphic texts show that certain architectural renovations were more than restorations. A new building both commemorated its predecessor and continued to embody it: it was the same building. Among the Maya, cyclical conceptions of time and history allowed not only for reconstruction or reproduction, but also for the perpetuation of the past in the present.

Occasionally, hieroglyphic texts name specific buildings, providing a sense of individuality, perhaps even of identity, to Maya architecture.[55] At the site of Yaxchilán, Mexico, a building known as "Four Bat Place" (and to archaeologists as Structure 22) was first constructed and dedicated by the city's seventh ruler, in 454 CE.[56] Almost 300 years later, Yaxchilán's ambitious seventeenth king, Bird Jaguar IV, refurbished Four Bat Place. In his renovations, Bird Jaguar IV reserved and reset four carved stone lintels. Two of the reused texts appear to come from the earlier version of Structure 22 and were reset over two side entrances to the building, but the other two are from a slightly later, most likely altogether different building (dating to the reign of the city's tenth ruler), and were placed over two frontal entrances.[57] He also added a new, all-glyphic lintel, Lintel 21, which was carved in the style of the earlier texts from Structure 22 and set above the structure's central doorway on its front façade (fig. 4.7). Lintel 21 not only describes the original construction and dedication of Four Bat Place, but recounts a second commemorative ceremony conducted in Four Bat Place by Bird Jaguar IV, in 752 CE, shortly after his inauguration as king.[58] That is, the hieroglyphic text uses the same name for both the initial building, constructed in 454 CE, and its renovation 298 years later. More than a restoration, the building *was* its former self.

Another example comes from the city of Ceibal, Guatemala. There, Structure A-14, a long building running alongside one of the site's central plazas, was remodeled during the late ninth or early tenth century CE. Structure A-14's central, hieroglyphically-inscribed stairway, however, appears to have been reset from an earlier construction (possibly built when the stairway was dedicated in 751 CE).[59] The inscribed stairs are carved on a different type of limestone than that used in the final version of Structure A-14, the panels are slightly higher than the steps into which they were set and, most telling, the stairway bears calendrical dates from the mid-eighth century CE (roughly a century earlier than the ceramics found in the rooms and construction fill of Structure A-14's superstructure). The "new" building thus subsumed both the function and the identity of the previous version: it was labeled as a continuation of the former by the same textual information, conveyed by the very same stones.[60]

Lintel 21 from Yaxchilán and the hieroglyphic stairway from Ceibal, moreover, describe a particular kind of Maya retrospection. The texts record rituals contemporary with their carving, but convey the importance of those ceremonies by drawing parallels to events that occurred centuries earlier. At Yaxchilán, Lintel 21 recalls the moment when the Four Bat Place was dedicated in a "house-censing" ritual of 454 CE (an event in which fire was first brought into a structure to enliven and ensoul it), tying that original ceremony to the "seating ceremony" conducted by Bird Jaguar IV in the same house in 752 CE. At Ceibal, the stairway tells how in 747 CE, the burial chamber of a king, interred some 300 years earlier, was reopened, and a "fire-entering" (ritual burning) ceremony was conducted in order to renew his tomb.[61] These inscriptions underscore the continuation of not only the buildings themselves, remade into their originals, but also of their social functions, as places where the rituals of past rulers were continually reenacted by present kings.

Alexander Nagel and Christopher Wood offer a framework for understanding the simultaneous replacement and revival of the structures at Yaxchilán and Ceibal. For Nagel and Wood, pre-modern works of art and architecture could "retain [their] identity despite alteration, repair, renovation, and even outright replacement."[62] They call this mode of representation "substitution," a seemingly paradoxical process of creation in which "[m]odern copies of painted icons were understood as effective surrogates for lost originals … and new buildings were understood as reinstantiations … of prior structures."[63] Among many examples, Nagel and Wood point to the "ontological stability" of the so-called Ship of Theseus.[64] That mythical ship, allegedly built before the Trojan War, was said to be "preserved" until the late fourth century BCE by the Athenians, who continually replaced old, decaying planks with new, stronger timbers. For Nagel and Wood, "[t]he Ship of Theseus is a paradigm of the object that was defined by its structure rather than its material make-up. The age of the planks is accidental; essential is the form… The identity of such an object is sustained across time by the stability of its name and by the tacit substitution of its parts."[65]

Another, contemporary example can be found in the Ise Jingu, a Shinto shrine southeast of Kyoto, Japan.[66] In a ritual known as the *shikinen sengu*, the structure housing a representation of the sun goddess has been rebuilt every twenty years in a regular cycle dating back to the eighth century CE. Ancient techniques and tools of ancient design are used, though the building materials (timbers, silk, gold, and lacquer) are new and the rebuilding does not exactly occur *in situ* (the shrine, the *goshoden*, is erected in an adjacent vacant lot, the *kodenchi*, meaning that the *goshoden* and *kodenchi* swap locations with every *sengu* cycle).[67] Still, the *sengu* renovations do not alter the essence of the shrine or diminish its value. Rather, they create "an ephemerality that … can paradoxically yield 'lasting' or enduring achievements."[68] Although this may at first seem a distant concept, contemporary gardens are a more familiar example that can function in this way. Take, for example, the Central Garden created by artist Robert Irwin for the Getty Art Museum and Institute in Los Angeles. First designed in the early 1990s, the garden is included among the museum's permanent collections as a sculpture.[69] Yet the "sculpture" is completely transformed on a seasonal schedule—Irwin established distinct aesthetics for summer, spring, and winter plantings. Moreover, in recent years, California's severe water crisis has prompted garden supervisors at the Getty to replace non-native flowers with drought-tolerant species: green grasses have given way to redwood mulch, birds of paradise have been replaced with shrubs and succulents, none of which were part of Irwin's original plans. In the words of Irwin himself, inscribed into the plaza floor, the garden is "[a]lways changing, never twice the same."[70]

The "doubling or bending of time" and "plural temporality" described by Nagel and Wood for Renaissance art is a familiar practice among the Maya. David Stuart has described a similar flexible temporality for ancient Maya stone monuments, which served as direct and perpetual representations of ritual action and dioramas of royal ceremony, rather than static portraits. Rituals were continually reenacted as a result of literally being set in stone. Although each commemoration served as a unique event, its very enactment also recalled a deep, intrinsic history of reproduction.[71] Stephen Houston has also pointed to practices of "bending back" in Maya art, particularly in objects that display "archaic" imagery or forms with glyphic texts that reveal the artifacts to be of a much later date. The Maya intentionally produced temporally disjunctive texts, imagery, objects, and architecture.[72] The texts at Yaxchilán and Ceibal, like other multi-temporal Maya creations, collapsed what Nancy Farriss describes as the "elongated Slinky toy" of Maya time, aligning and effectively merging initial constructions and dedications in the past with reconstructions and commemorations in the present.[73]

It is easy to imagine how the buildings at Yaxchilán and Ceibal can appear like palimpsests. Constructed, partially demolished, and

4.8. A pseudo-color image of folios 110^{v}–105^{r} of the Archimedes Palimpsest, in which an ultraviolet image of both texts and an image showing only the prayers are manipulated to emphasize the contrast of both texts against the parchment. The overwriting is shown in neutral gray tones and the underwriting in red.

erected once again in the same location, there are certainly parallels to the inscription, erasure, and reinscription of a text upon a page. The metaphor only works, however, if we view architectural layers in a unilateral flow of time, moving steadily from what came before to what comes after, where each phase of construction replaces something earlier and the new necessarily covers over the old. Like Theseus' ship or the Ise Shrine, Structure 22 at Yaxchilán and Structure A-14 at Ceibal retained their identities despite the substitutions or reuse of their parts. Describing Maya architectural resuscitation as a palimpsest thus requires either stretching the meaning of "palimpsest" to uncomfortable limits, ignoring both the intended erasure and the layering process responsible for the creation of the object, or imposing a sense of linear chronology on what the Maya saw as a cyclical past.

Conclusions

The Archimedes Palimpsest (or Archimedes Codex) is one of the best known, and certainly among the most alluring, of palimpsests. Beneath the Christian texts of a thirteenth-century CE prayer book are seven tenth-century CE copies of treatises from the third century BCE mathematician Archimedes (including two otherwise unattested), speeches by the fourth-century BCE Athenian orator Hyperides, and a commentary on Aristotle's *Categories*, among other texts that remain illegible and a few pages of modern forgeries of portraits of the Evangelists, added in the twentieth century. In many ways, the Archimedes Codex is the archetypal palimpsest. Not only are the erased texts heralded by contemporary scholars as buried treasures, faintly and tantalizingly seen through the overlying layers (the original parchment pages were cut and rotated, so that the prayers are inscribed at right angles to the underlying writing), but the renewed interest in the original texts (especially that of Archimedes) effectively performs another erasure, this time of the thirteenth-century *euchologion*.[74] The prayer book, the object which brought together the various pages of parchment reused from other manuscripts, was dismantled to facilitate study of the underlying texts running into its gutter and renamed for the erased author whose works are considered most important from a contemporary perspective. Over the course of a decade, scholars and specialists, "have made the prayer book 'disappear,'" using multispectral imaging techniques to create individual, digital versions of the ancient texts that had been scraped off and overwritten (fig. 4.8).[75]

The example of the Archimedes Codex makes clear the complexities of the term "palimpsest." In the thirteenth century, the value of the parchment was greater than the earlier texts written upon it. The pages were cut, erased, transformed, and re-inscribed, even if incompletely. Many centuries later, however, the value shifted from the parchment itself to the effaced texts. An anonymous buyer paid $2,200,000 for the Archimedes Palimpsest at Christie's auction house in New York in 1998.[76] The palimpsest is the object, with its layers of writing and rewriting, but that object also signals an ongoing accumulation of interests and intentions, erasures and eliminations. This revived, modern appreciation for ancient underlying texts is yet another moment of revision in the history and production of a palimpsest. Contemporary scholars mimic medieval monks: effectively removing layers that they deem of lesser interest in order to recuperate the valuable stuff below. L. D. Reynolds and N. G. Wilson, for example, in describing palimpsests, bemoan the fact that

> ... the toll of classic authors was very heavy: amongst those palimpsested we find Plautus and Terence, Cicero and Livy, the Elder and Younger Pliny, Sallust and Seneca, Vergil and Ovid, Lucan, Juvenal and Persius, Gellius and Fronto ... Among the texts that have survived solely in this mutilated form are some of outstanding interest ... which succumbed in the late sixth of early seventh century to the Old Testament.[77]

The efforts made to recover earlier texts, even to make later writings digitally disappear, underscore a sense of supremacy afforded to modern connoisseurs of the past. We, in the present, are able to see what those in the past could not; we know what is valuable, we recognize the layers of the palimpsest and single out what is important, what was missed or neglected by earlier reusers. This chapter highlights the ability of the ancient Maya not only to see those layers, but to interact with them and emphasize multiple strata simultaneously.

Among the ancient Maya, ruins intentionally incorporated into otherwise vibrant cityscapes, temples that were venerated by means of being made invisible, and structures that maintained their identities despite remodeling challenge the capacity of "palimpsest" to describe the production, use, and renovation of ancient architecture. Reuse was not necessarily replacement; covering over could serve to commemorate. In order to apply the term to such examples, aspects of its meaning must be ignored. The benefit of "palimpsest," however, is that it incites us to focus on and tease out the specific dynamics of reuse. Even when the metaphor falls short of capturing multiple, overlapping architectural histories, its limits reveal the complexity of ancient creations, recreations, and meaningful engagements with the past.

Notes

I would like to thank Nadja Aksamija, Clark Maines, and Phillip Wagoner for their invitation to contribute to this volume and their diligence in bringing it to fruition. I would also like to thank Justin Kerr and Franco Rossi for generously allowing the use of their images and the Dean's Office at James Madison University for subventing the others. Felipe

Rojas, Stephen Houston, the editors, and an anonymous reviewer provided helpful comments, questions, and suggestions that have improved this chapter.

1 See McAnany and Hodder 2009, 10, for a review of stratigraphy-making processes that cannot be considered palimpsests, as well as Lucas 2005, 37, for a distinction between layering and a palimpsest, "a rather messier affair."

2 Geoff Bailey 2007, 204, for example, defines a "true palimpsest" and notes that it may be difficult to identify in the archaeological record. In response to such difficulties, Bailey creates and defines four new "types" of palimpsests—cumulative, spatial, or temporal palimpsests and palimpsests of meaning. It is telling that the word "palimpsest" must be variously glossed in order for it to apply to archaeological evidence.

3 Here, I am following G. E. R. Lloyd's notion of "semantic stretch" (see Lloyd 2014). Although Lloyd's discussion is focused on complex issues of linguistic, cultural, and ontological translation, the fundamental problem is the same: how many meanings can a term reference before it loses its specificity?

4 Images of screenfold books depicted on Maya ceramics are known from about 600 CE onward; see Coe 1973. Stuart 2012 traces out the conceptual connections between paper, particular Maya deities, and rulership. Implements used by scribes to produce codices have been recovered, for example, at Aguateca (Inomata 2001, 326–28) and Xultun (Rossi et al. 2015, 123), while residences with images of scribal gods have been found at Copán (Webster 1989). Sixteenth- and seventeenth-century accounts by Landa 1941 and Lopez de Cogolludo 2016, respectively, mention large archives of native books. Vail 2006 provides an overview of the history of research on the four Maya codices.

5 Berdan and Rieff Anawalt 1997, 41–46, 50, 52–53, and 82.

6 Stuart 2012.

7 Burdick 2016, 36.

8 Blood-spattered paper as an offering can be seen, for example, in Lintels 24 and 25 from Yaxchilán (Graham and von Euw 1977, 53, 55, 56). The sixteenth-century Franciscan Friar Bernardino de Sahagún describes paper as a vehicle for liquid rubber (Berdan and Rieff Anawalt 1997, 114).

9 According to Kraft 2007, note 21, the oldest surviving complete text of the Latin Bible consists of "1030 folios, each double thick skins measuring 27½ inches by 20½, and weighs over 75 lbs." and required about 1550 calves' worth of vellum.

10 Studies of style and handwriting in the codices suggest that the Dresden Codex was produced by more than one individual, while at least nine artists' hands have been identified in the Madrid Codex. See Vail 2015, 446.

11 Stephen Houston has traced the underpaintings in high-resolution photos of each page of the Grolier Codex, pinpointing where they coincide with or diverge from the final version of the manuscript. See Coe et al. 2015, 125–27.

12 See discussion of the murals at the Temple of the Warriors, Chichén Itzá, in Coe et al. 2015, 123–24. Underlying sketches have also been observed in the first-century BCE mural programs at San Bartolo, Guatemala, and seventh- and eighth-century CE paintings, respectively, at Calakmul and Bonampak, Mexico.

13 I have limited my discussion in this chapter to examples among the Maya. At least one screenfold book palimpsest, the Codex Selden, is known among neighboring Mesoamerican cultures. Images of underlying, Pre-Columbian layers of historical genealogies in the Codex Selden, a sixteenth-century CE Mixtec manuscript made of strips of gesso-covered leather, were recently revealed via multispectral imaging. See Snijders et al. 2016.

14 See Carter and Dobereiner 2016.

15 Carrasco Vargas and Cordeiro Baquiero 2012, 20–24.

16 Morris 1931, 383.

17 Morris describes one section of the murals as "one of the best examples of Maya painting which has ever been recovered" (Morris 1931, 379) and another as "the worst Maya mural that has ever come to light" (Morris 1931, 415).

18 Saturno et al. 2015, 132. Rossi et al. 2015, 120, also refer to the Xultún mural's east wall as a "literal palimpsest."

19 Aveni et al. 2013, 14. These repeated, related layers are comparable to the political posters, advertisements, and graffiti that Parslow (this volume) describes covering the *Praedia* of Julia Felix in Pompeii.

20 Some scholars exclude painted images from the umbrella term "graffiti." Here, I follow Jaroslaw Źrałka's definition: "[a]rchitectural graffiti are all representations (including those scratched, and painted) that do not pertain to the original design or context of a building and which are usually characterized by a crude style" (Źrałka 2014, 50–51). Under this definition, the Xultún texts are not graffiti, as they are part of the intended function of the walls, relate directly to the painted imagery, and include legible texts with complicated calculations (they are far from "crude").

21 Exceptions do, of course, exist, such as glyphic graffiti found at Tikal (e.g., Trik and Kampen 1983, fig. 78a).

22 See, for example, Kampen 1978, 166.

23 Bonde (this volume) highlights three layers of time that define the written or architectural palimpsest: the moment of original writing or construction, a subsequent moment of erasure, and a later moment of overwriting or rebuilding.

24 Ashmore and Sabloff 2002, 204. This idea builds on earlier work by Knapp and Ashmore 1999, 18, concerning the idea of the repetitive use and modification of a landscape as a palimpsest.

25 Ashmore 2007, 159.

26 LeCount and Yaeger 2010, 69; Morton 2012, 143.
27 Alexander 2006, 450.
28 Noting that a "true palimpsest" would imply the erasure of all pre-existing evidence, Navarro-Farr and Arroyave Prera 2014, 35, follow Bailey in his definition of a "cumulative palimpsest" as "the successive episodes of deposition, or layers of activity, [which] remain superimposed one upon the other without loss of evidence, but are so re-worked and mixed together that it is difficult or impossible to separate them out into their original constituents." See Bailey 2007, 204.
29 Douglass and Gonlin 2012, 28, referring to Beaule 2012, 381–406.
30 Montmollin 1988, 164; Montmollin 1989, 304–05.
31 Clark and Muñoz-Fernández 2009; see also Castañeda 1996.
32 Bailey 2007, 208–09.
33 Popper 1963.
34 Houston 2012, 392. See also Stanton and Magnoni 2008, 5; and Houston 2013, 48.
35 Halperin 2014, for example, describes a neighborhood of ancient Maya commoners centered around and interacting with ruins of long-abandoned monumental architecture at the site of Tayasal. Halperin also makes an important distinction between crumbling ruins covered by vegetation and buildings that would have been acknowledged as ancient but were not necessarily overgrown, since the plaza spaces and buildings around them were well-maintained and actively refurbished.
36 Houston et al. 2003, 224–25; Child and Golden 2008, 72–73; Martin and Grube 2008, 142.
37 Escobedo and Houston 2002, 139; see also Escobedo and Zamorra 2001, 376–77.
38 Child and Golden 2008, 77–78.
39 Rykwert 1976, 52–53.
40 See, for example, Drew 1999, 216.
41 McAnany and Hodder 2009, 13, use the term "entombment" to describe the anomalous preservation of Rosalila within the stratigraphic/architectural sequence of Structure 10L–16. Agurcia Fasquelle 2004, 102, relates the building's burial to embalming through comparison to contemporary mortuary practices among the Ch'orti' of Honduras and Guatemala. Drawing on the work of Girard 1949, and Wisdom 1961, he connects the cloaking of cadavers in white sheets to the process of covering Rosalila's iconographic program in white stucco.
42 Taube 2004, 265, terms this the "Copan Axis," the symbolic pivotal center of the city and the place of its founder.
43 Taube 2004 has highlighted the themes of fire rituals and founding events that characterize each element in the architectural sequence of Temple 16, as well as the symbolic connections to the Central Mexican metropolis of Teotihuacan.
44 Rosalila's replacement is poorly understood, as it was almost completely demolished by the construction of the final version of Structure 10L–16, built during the reign of Copán's sixteenth and final ruler. See Sharer et al. 1999, 19; Agurcia Fasquelle 2004, 101–02; and Agurcia Fasquelle and Fash 2005.
45 Taube 2004; Martin and Grube 2008, 193, 210.
46 Sharer et al. 1999, 10; Stuart 2000; Stuart 2004.
47 Just 2005, 70, sees the architectural structures encapsulated within later, larger renovations as conserving labor and raw materials, in addition to contributing accrued potency to a new structure.
48 Houston et al. 2015.
49 Taube and Houston 2015, 208–29.
50 Brittenham 2009, 150.
51 Gillespie 2008, 115. See Diehl 2004, 73, for other examples of buried caches at La Venta.
52 Guernsey and Reilly III, 2006.
53 Brittenham, for example, describes the Cacaxtla case as "both a palimpsest and a place of hidden memory" and also draws a comparison to Copán's architectural accretions. Brittenham 2009, 150, note 17.
54 McAnany and Hodder 2009, 12.
55 See Tremblay 2007.
56 Martin and Grube 2008, 119.
57 See Proskouriakoff 1964, 182; and Tate 1992, 128–29. Lintels 18 and 19 (those from Structure 22) do not contain dates, but are paleographically dated to the late fifth or early sixth century. Lintels 20 and 22 name the tenth ruler from Yaxchilán.
58 Stuart 1998, 390–92.
59 See Smith 1982, 63–77; as well as Mathews and Willey 1991, 50.
60 Just 2005, 70.
61 Stuart 1998, 391–93 and 397–99.
62 Nagel and Wood 2010, 8.
63 Nagel and Wood 2010, 29.
64 The example of the Ship of Theseus is also discussed by Aksamija (this volume), who draws similar parallels between the simultaneously old and new identities of the loggia of Brunelleschi's Ospedale degli Innocenti in Florence.
65 Nagel and Wood 2010, 8.
66 Houston 2011 highlights this example in an essay comparing Nagel and Wood's "substitutional" and "authorial" modes of representation in Renaissance art to the "archaicism" of certain Maya objects.
67 Lopes 2007, 77–84. Aksamija (this volume), also points to this example from Ise, but draws particular attention to the importance of the building's location. As she points out, the sanctuary and the adjacent empty lot always remain within the borders of the hallowed ground of the shine complex, which awards them authenticity, even if they do shift positions slightly.
68 Bognar 1997, 4 and 7.
69 Waldorf 2016.
70 Kilston 2015.

71 Stuart 1996, 160.
72 Houston 2011.
73 Farriss 1987, 572.
74 See also Wagoner (this volume), who discusses the model provided by the Archimedes Palimpsest and its application to architecture in detail, using the example of a fourteenth-century temple-turned-mosque in Bodhan, India. In particular, Wagoner highlights the differences in the semantic connections between layers (which rarely exist in the case of texts and rarely do not exist in the case of architecture) and the focus of later scholars, more often interested in the obscured elements than the visible ones.
75 *The Archimedes Palimpsest.*
76 Netz and Noel 2007, 6.
77 Reynolds and Wilson 1974, 86.

Bibliography

Agurcia Fasquelle, Ricardo. 2004. "Rosalila, Temple of the Sun-King," in *Understanding Early Classic Copan*, ed. Ellen E. Bell, Marcello A. Canuto, and Robert J. Sharer. Philadelphia: University of Pennsylvania Museum of Archaeology and Anthropology, 101–12.

Agurcia Fasquelle, Ricardo, and Barbara W. Fash. 2005. "The Evolution of Structure 10L–16, Heart of the Copán Acropolis," in *Copán: The History of an Ancient Maya Kingdom*, ed. E. Wyllys Andrews and William L. Fash. Santa Fe: School for American Research Press, 201–37.

Alexander, Rani T. 2006. "Maya Settlement Shifts and Agrarian Ecology in Yucatán, 1800–2000," *Journal of Anthropological Research* 62, no. 4, 449–70.

The Archimedes Palimpsest, http://archimedespalimpsest.org/digital/google-book.php (accessed 24 July 2016).

Ashmore, Wendy. 2007. *Settlement Archaeology at Quirigua, Guatemala.* Philadelphia: University of Pennsylvania Press, University of Pennsylvania Museum of Archaeology and Anthropology.

Ashmore, Wendy, and Jeremy A. Sabloff. 2002. "Spatial Orders in Maya Civic Plans," *Latin American Antiquity* 13, no. 2, 201–15.

Aveni, Anthony F., William Saturno, and David Stuart. 2013. "Astronomical Implications of Maya Hieroglyphic Notations at Xultún," *Journal for the History of Astronomy* 44, no. 1, 1–16.

Bailey, Geoff. 2007. "Time perspectives, palimpsests, and the archaeology of time," *Journal of Anthropological Archaeology* 26, no. 2, 198–223.

Beaule, Christine. 2012. "Interhousehold versus Intracommunity Comparisons: Incipient Socioeconomic Complexity at Jachakala, Bolivia," in *Ancient Households of the Americas: Conceptualizing What Households Do*, ed. John G. Douglass and Nancy Gonlin. Boulder: University Press of Colorado, 381–406.

Berdan, Frances F., and Patricia Rieff Anawalt. 1997. *The Essential Codex Mendoza.* Berkeley: University of California Press.

Bognar, Botond. 1997. "What Goes Up Must Come Down: Recent Urban Architecture in Japan," *Harvard Design Magazine* 3, 1–8.

Brittenham, Claudia. 2009. "Style and Substance, or Why the Cacaxtla Paintings were Buried," *RES: Anthropology and Aesthetics* 55/56, 135–55.

Burdick, Catherine E. "Held Captive by Script: Interpreting "Tagged" Prisoners in Late Classic Maya Sculpture," *Ancient Mesoamerica* 27, no. 1, 31–48.

Carrasco Vargas, Ramón, and María Cordeiro Baquiero. 2012. "The Murals of Chiik Nahb Structure Sub 1–4, Calakmul, Mexico," in *Maya Archaeology 2*, ed. Charles Golden, Stephen Houston, and Joel Skidmore. San Francisco: Precolumbia Mesoweb Press, 8–81.

Carrasco Vargas, Ramón, Verónica A. Vázquez López, and Simon Martin. 2009. "Daily Life of the Ancient Maya Recorded on Murals at Calakmul, Mexico," *PNAS* 106, no. 46, 19245–49.

Carter, Nicholas P., and Jeffrey Dobereiner. 2016. "Multispectral Imaging of an Early Classic Maya codex fragment from Uaxactún, Guatemala," *Antiquity* 90, no. 351, 711–25.

Castañeda, Quetzil E. 1996. *In the Museum of Maya Culture: Touring Chichén Itzá.* Minneapolis: University of Minnesota Press.

Child, Mark B., and Charles W. Golden. 2008. "The Transformation of Abandoned Architecture at Piedras Negras," in *Ruins of the Past: The Use and Perception of Abandoned Structures in the Maya Lowlands*, ed. Travis W. Stanton and Aline Magnoni. Boulder: University Press of Colorado, 65–89.

Coe, Michael. 1973. *The Maya Scribe and His World.* New York: Grolier Club.

Coe, Michael, Stephen Houston, Mary Miller, and Karl Taube. 2015. "The Fourth Maya Codex," in *Maya Archaeology 3*, ed. Charles Golden, Stephen Houston, and Joel Skidmore. San Francisco: Precolumbia Mesoweb Press, 116–67.

Clark, Dylan J. and Carmen Muñoz-Fernández. 2009. "Sights, Sounds, and Spectacle: The Palimpsest of Archaeonarratives at Xcaret (P'ole'), Quintana Roo, Mexico," paper presented at the annual meeting of the American Anthropological Association, Philadelphia, December 2–6.

Diehl, Richard. 2004. *The Olmecs: America's First Civilization.* London: Thames & Hudson.

Douglass, John G., and Nancy Gonlin. 2012. "The Household as Analytical Unit: Case Studies from the Americas," in *Ancient Households of the Americas: Conceptualizing What Households Do*, ed. John G. Douglass and Nancy Gonlin. Boulder: University Press of Colorado, 1–44.

Drew, David. 1999. *The Lost Chronicles of the Maya Kings.* Berkeley and Los Angeles: University of California Press.

Escobedo, Héctor, and Stephen D. Houston. 2002. "Arqueología e Historia en Piedras Negras, Guatemala: síntesis de la temporadas de campo de 1997-2000." In *XV Simposio de Investigaciones Arqueológicas en Guatemala, 2001*, ed. Juan Pedro Laporte, Héctor Escobedo, and Bárbara Arroyo. Guatemala City: National Museum of Archaeology and Ethnology, 135-44.

Escobedo, Héctor, and F. Marcelo Zamorra. 2001. "PN 47: Excavaciones en la Estructura R-5," in *Proyecto Arqueológico Piedras Negras, Informe Preliminar No. 4, Cuarta Temporada, 2000*, ed. Héctor L. Escobedo and Stephen D. Houston. Guatemala City: Report submitted to the Guatemalan Institute for Anthropology and History, 199–216.

Farriss, Nancy M. 1987. "Remembering the Future, Anticipating the Past: History, Time, and Cosmology among the Maya of Yucatan," *Comparative Studies in Society and History* 29, no. 3, 566–93.

Gillespie, Susan D. "History in Practice: Ritual Deposition at La Venta Complex A," in *Memory Work: Archaeologies of Material Practices*, ed. Barbara J. Mills and William H. Walker. Santa Fe: School for Advanced Research Press, 109–36.

Girard, Rafael. 1949. *Los Chortis ante el problema Maya*. Mexico City: Editorial Cultura.

Graham, Ian, and Eric von Euw. 1977. *Corpus of Maya Hieroglyphic Inscriptions*, vol. 3, part 1. Cambridge: Peabody Museum of Archaeology and Ethnology, Harvard University.

Guernsey, Julia, and F. Kent Reilly III, eds. 2006. *Sacred Bundles: Ritual Acts of Wrapping and Binding in Mesoamerica*. Barnardsville: Boundary End Archaeology Research Center.

Halperin, Christina T. 2014. "Ruins in Pre-Columbian Maya Urban Landscapes," *Cambridge Archaeological Journal* 24, no. 3, 321–44.

Houston, Stephen D. 2013. "Ping-Pong, Polygons, and Virgins: Graphic Representation of the Ancient Maya," in *Re-Presenting the Past: Archaeology Through Text and Image*, ed. Sheila Bonde and Stephen Houston. Joukowsky Institute Publication 2. Oxford and Oakville: Oxbow Books and The David Brown Book Company, 35–48.

—. 2012. "Telling it Slant: Imaginative Reconstructions of Classic Maya Life," in *Past Presented: Archaeological Illustration and the Ancient Americas*, ed. Joanne Pillsbury. Washington, D.C.: Dumbarton Oaks Research Library and Collection, 387–412.

—. 2011. "Bending Time among the Maya." *Maya Decipherment*. https://decipherment.wordpress.com/2011/06/24/bending-time-among-the-maya/ (accessed 25 June 2011).

Houston, Stephen D., Héctor Escobedo, Mark Child, Charles Golden, and René Muñoz. "The Moral Community: Maya Settlement Transformation at Piedras Negras, Guatemala," in *The Social Construction of Ancient Cities*, ed. Monica L. Smith. Washington, D.C.: Smithsonian Institution Press, 212–53.

Houston, Stephen, Sarah Newman, Edwin Román, and Thomas Garrison. 2015. *Temple of the Night Sun: A Royal Tomb at El Diablo, Guatemala*. San Francisco: Precolumbia Mesoweb Press.

Inomata, Takeshi. 2001. "The Power and Ideology of Artistic Creation: Elite Craft Specialists in Classic Maya Society," *Current Anthropology* 42, no. 3, 321–49.

Just, Bryan R. 2005. "Modifications of Ancient Maya Sculpture," *RES: Anthropology and Aesthetics* 48, 69–82.

Kampen, Michael. 1978. "The Graffiti of Tikal, Guatemala." *Estudios de Cultura Maya* 11, 155–80.

Kilston, Lyra. 2015. "Getty Gardens: Brown is the New Green." *The Iris: Behind the Scenes at the Getty*. http://blogs.getty.edu/iris/getty-gardens-brown-is-the-new-green/ (accessed 22 June 2016).

Knapp, A. Bernard, and Wendy Ashmore. 1999. "Archaeological Landscapes: Constructed, Conceptualized, Ideational," in *Archaeologies of Landscape: Contemporary Perspectives*, ed. Wendy Ashmore and A. Bernard Knapp. Oxford: Blackwell Publishers, 1–30.

Kraft, Robert A. 2007. "Para-mania: Beside, Before and Beyond Bible Studies," *The Journal of Biblical Literature* 126, no. 1, 5–27.

Landa, Diego de. 1941. *Relación de las cosas de Yucatán*. Trans. and ed. Alfred M. Tozzer. Papers of the Peabody Museum of Archaeology and Ethnology 18. Cambridge: Harvard University.

LeCount, Lisa J., and Jason Yaeger. 2010. "A Brief Description of Xunantunich," in *Classic Maya Provincial Politics: Xunantunich and its Hinterlands*, ed. Lisa J. LeCount and Jason Yaeger. Tucson: University of Arizona Press, 67–78.

Lloyd, G. E. R. 2014. "On the Very Possibility of Mutual Intelligibility," *Hau: Journal of Ethnographic Theory* 4, no. 2, 221–35.

Lopes, Dominic McIver. 2007. "*Shikinen Sengu* and the Ontology of Architecture in Japan," *The Journal of Aesthetics and Art Criticism* 65, no. 1, 77–84.

López de Cogolludo, Diego. 2016. *Historia de Yucatán*. Barcelona: Linkgua Historia.

Lucas, Gavin. 2005. *The Archaeology of Time*. New York: Routledge.

Martin, Simon, and Nikolai Grube. 2008. *Chronicle of the Maya Kings and Queens: Deciphering the Dynasties of the Ancient Maya*. London: Thames & Hudson.

Mathews, Peter, and Gordon R. Willey. 1991. "Prehistoric Polities of the Pasión Region: Hieroglyphic Texts and their Archaeological Settings," in *Classic Maya Political History: Hieroglyphic and Archaeological Evidence*, ed. T. Patrick Culbert. Cambridge: Cambridge University Press and School of American Research, 30–71.

McAnany, Patricia, and Ian Hodder. 2009. "Thinking about Stratigraphic Sequence in Social Terms," *Archaeological Dialogues* 16, no. 1, 1–22.

Montmollin, Olivier de. 1989. "Land Tenure and Politics in the Late/Terminal Classic Rosario Valley, Chiapas, Mexico," *Journal of Anthropological Research* 45, no. 3, 293–314.

—. 1988. "Scales of Settlement Study for Complex Societies: Analytical Issues from the Classic Maya Area," *Journal of Field Archaeology* 15, no. 2, 151–68.

Morris, Ann Axtell. 1931. "Murals from the Temple of the Warriors and Adjacent Structures," in Earl H. Morris, Jean Charlot, and Ann Axtell Morris, *The Temple of the Warriors at Chichén Itzá, Yucatán*, vol. 1. Washington, D.C.: Carnegie Institution of Washington, 347–484.

Morton, Shawn G. 2012. "Ritual Procession and the Creation of Civitas Among the Ancient Maya: A Case Study from Naachtún, Guatemala," *Canadian Journal of Archaeology* 36, no. 1, 141–65.

Nagel, Alexander, and Christopher S. Wood. 2010. *Anachronic Renaissance*. New York: Zone Books.

Navarro-Farr, Olivia C., and Ana Lucía Arroyave Prera. 2014. "A Cumulative Palimpsest Effect: The Multilayered Meanings of Late-to-Terminal Classic Era, Above-Floor Deposits at Structure M13–1," in *Archaeology at El Perú-Waka': Ancient Maya Performances of Ritual, Memory, and Power*, ed. Olivia C. Navarro-Farr and Michelle Rich. Tucson: University of Arizona Press, 34–52.

Netz, Reviel, and William Noel. 2007. *The Archimedes Codex: How a Medieval Prayer Book is Revealing the True Genius of Antiquity's Greatest Scientist*. Philadelphia: Da Capo Press.

Popper, Karl R. 1963. *Conjectures and Refutations*. London: Routledge and Kegan Paul.

Proskouriakoff, Tatiana. 1964. "Historical Data in the Inscriptions of Yaxchilán, Part II," *Estudios de cultura maya* 4, 177–201.

Reynolds, L. D., and N. G. Wilson. 1974. *Scribes and Scholars: A Guide to the Transmission of Greek and Latin Literature*. Oxford: Oxford University Press.

Rossi, Franco D., William A. Saturno, and Heather Hurst. 2015. "Maya Codex Book Production and the Politics of Expertise: Archaeology of a Classic Period Household at Xultún, Guatemala," *American Anthropologist* 117, no. 1, 116–32.

Rykwert, Joseph. 1988. *The Idea of a Town: The Anthropology of Urban Form in Rome, Italy, and the Ancient World*. Princeton: Princeton University Press.

Saturno, William, Heather Hurst, Franco Rossi, and David Stuart. 2015. "To Set Before the King: Residential Mural Painting at Xultún, Guatemala," *Antiquity* 89, no. 343, 122–36.

Sharer, Robert J., Loa P. Traxler, David W. Sedat, Ellen E. Bell, Marcello A. Canuto, and Christopher Powell. 1999. "Early Classic Architecture Beneath the Copán Acropolis," *Ancient Mesoamerica* 10, no. 1, 3–23.

Smith, A. Ledyard. 1982. "Major Architecture and Caches," in *Excavations at Seibal, Department of Petén, Guatemala*, gen. ed. Gordon R. Willey. (Memoirs of the Peabody Museum of Archaeology and Ethnology 15, no. 1.) Cambridge: Harvard University, 1–263.

Snijders, Ludo, Tim Zaman, and David Howell. 2016. "Using Hyperspectral Imaging to Reveal a Hidden Precolonial Mesoamerican Codex," *Journal of Archaeological Science: Reports* 9, 143–49.

Stanton, Travis W., and Aline Magnoni. 2008. "Places of Remembrance: The Use and Perception of Abandoned Structures in the Maya Lowlands," in *Ruins of the Past: The Use and Perception of Abandoned Structures in the Maya Lowlands*, ed. Travis W. Stanton and Aline Magnoni. Boulder: University Press of Colorado, 1–24.

Stuart, David. 2012. "The Name of Paper: The Mythology of Crowning and Royal Nomenclature on Palenque's Palace Tablet," in *Maya Archaeology 2*, ed. Charles Golden, Stephen Houston, and Joel Skidmore. San Francisco: Precolumbia Mesoweb Press, 265–96.

—. 2004. "The Beginnings of the Copán Dynasty: A Review of the Hieroglyphic and Historical Evidence," in *Understanding Early Classic Copán*, ed. Ellen E. Bell, Marcello A. Canuto, and Robert J. Sharer. Philadelphia: University of Pennsylvania Museum of Archaeology and Anthropology, 215–48.

—. 2000. "'The Arrival of Strangers': Teotihuacan and Tollan in Classic Maya History," in *Mesoamerica's Classic Heritage: From Teotihuacan to the Aztecs*, ed. Davíd Carrasco, Lindsay Jones, and Scott Sessions. Boulder: University Press of Colorado, 465–513.

—. 1998. "'The Fire Enters His House': Architecture and Ritual in Classic Maya Texts," in *Function and Meaning in Classic Maya Architecture*, ed. Stephen D. Houston. Washington, D.C.: Dumbarton Oaks Research Library and Collection, 373–425.

—. 1996. "Kings of Stone: A Consideration of Stelae in Ancient Maya Ritual and Representation," *RES: Anthropology and Aesthetics* 29/30, 148–71.

Tate, Carolyn. 1992. *Yaxchilán: The Design of a Maya Ceremonial City*. Austin: University of Texas Press.

Taube, Karl. 2004. "Structure 10L–16 and its Early Classic Antecedents: Fire and the Evocation and Resurrection of K'inich Yax K'uk' Mo'," in *Understanding Early Classic Copán*, ed. Ellen E. Bell, Marcello A. Canuto, and Robert J. Sharer. Philadelphia: University of Pennsylvania Museum of Archaeology and Anthropology, 101–12.

Taube, Karl, and Stephen Houston. 2015. "The Temple Stuccos," in Stephen Houston, Sarah Newman, Edwin Román, and Thomas Garrison, *Temple of the Night Sun: A Royal Tomb at El Diablo Guatemala*. San Francisco: Precolumbia Mesoweb Press, 208–29.

Tremblay, Adrienne M. 2007. *Building the Sacred: A Study of Proper Names of Monuments and Structures in Classic Maya Inscriptions*. Ph.D. dissertation, Tulane University.

Trik, Helen, and Michael Kampen. 1983. *The Graffiti of Tikal*. (Tikal Report No. 34.) Philadelphia: The University Museum, University of Pennsylvania.

Vail, Gabrielle. 2015. "Scribal Interaction and the Transmission of Traditional Knowledge: A Postclassic Maya Perspective," *Ethnohistory* 62, no. 3, 445–68.

—. 2006. "The Maya Codices." *Annual Review of Anthropology* 35, 497–519.

Waldorf, Sarah. 2016. "Your Questions about the Getty Gardens, Answered." *The Iris: Behind the Scenes at the Getty.* http://blogs.getty.edu/iris/your-questions-about-the-getty-gardens-answered/ (accessed 22 June 2016).

Webster, David, ed. 1989. *The House of the Bacabs, Copán, Honduras.* Studies in Pre-Columbian Art and Archaeology 29. Washington, D.C.: Dumbarton Oaks Research Library and Collection.

Wisdom, Charles. 1961. *Los Chortis de Guatemala.* Guatemala City: Ministerio de Educación Pública.

Źrałka, Jaroslaw. 2014. "Maya Graffiti in a Wider Cultural and Geographic Context," in *Artistic Expressions in Maya Architecture: Analysis and Documentation Techniques*, ed. Cristina Vidal Lorenzo and Gaspar Muñoz Cosme. (BAR International Series 2693.) Oxford: Archaeopress.

Chapter 5
Buildings and their Doubles: Restoration, Authenticity, and the Palimpsest in Italian Renaissance Architecture

Nadja Aksamija

This essay tackles the multifaceted problem of erasure and rewriting of the material substance of Italian Renaissance buildings by focusing on the uniquely challenging case of what will be termed "restoration palimpsests"—that is, palimpsests created through centuries of maintenance, partial remodeling, and total rebuilding whose layered materiality is not easily legible today.[1] Unlike with some other types of architectural palimpsests studied in this volume, the temporal episodes of erasure discussed in this paper were triggered by predominantly natural (e.g. decay, collapse) rather than ideological causes, while the episodes of subsequent reinscription entailed the rewriting of the architectural "text" as closely as possible to the original so as to provide a sense of continuity. As this study will argue, though the traces of erasure and reinscription on these monuments were often left purposefully faint, their material substance was altered—sometimes significantly—from when they were first constructed, an indisputable marker of their status as palimpsests. The physical extent and the temporal dimensions of that transmutation will be examined in relation to the fundamental issue of authenticity, which in turn underlies and affects both practical (subsequent restorations) and theoretical (scholarly research) questions and decisions regarding these structures.

In reflecting on the complex relationship between materiality and time with regards to architectural restoration, the ancient philosophical quandary concerning the structural upkeep of the ship of King Theseus may be productively evoked. As Plutarch recounts,

> [t]he ship wherein Theseus and the youth of Athens returned had thirty oars, and was preserved by the Athenians down even to the time of Demetrius Phalereus, for they took away the old planks as they decayed, putting in new and stronger timber in their place, insomuch that this ship became a standing example among the philosophers, for the logical question of things that grow; one side holding that the ship remained the same, and the other contending that it was not the same.[2]

Though various versions of this thought puzzle have engaged European philosophers from Heraclitus and Plato to Hobbes and Locke, its implications for the field of architectural history seem to have resonated almost exclusively with regards to monuments and traditions furthest removed from the Western conception of authenticity in architecture.[3] Well-known cases such as the Ise Shrine (Ise Jingu) in Japan—where sacred buildings are completely rebuilt every twenty years on sites adjacent to their current locations[4]—have led scholars such as Dominic McIver Lopes to identify and theorize an alternative ontology of architecture, one that embraces impermanence, highlights temporality through ritual cycles of making and remaking, and produces "instances" (or better, temporal "events") of architectural monuments that can be understood as simultaneously old (in their type) and new (in their current iteration).[5]

By contrast, the "standard," Western ontology of architecture in Lopes's view "survives the replacement of some parts and does not survive the simultaneous replacement of all its parts … it is unclear whether it survives the gradual replacement of all its [original] parts."[6] In other words, authenticity is directly related to the ways in which the material and temporal aspects of architecture intersect: maintenance and partial restoration over time do not seem to compromise it, while total destruction and rebuilding do, since they produce facsimiles and those are always suspect, carrying negative connotations related to the loss of the "aura"[7] and thus to the alleged falsification of the original aesthetic experience. In fact, the problem of copies is essential to Lopes's definition of architectural ontology in the West. He maintains that "to see a replica of the Seagram Building is not to see the Seagram Building," and that "we cannot appreciate Europe's great architecture by means of a trip to Las Vegas."[8] While those claims are certainly indisputable, they are not quite to the point since they do not take into account the crucial importance of the site. In fact, what bestows authenticity on Europe's historic structures is not only their (more or less) original material presence but also their (more or less) unchanged physical location. As a key anchor of authenticity, the site—often infused with layered meanings itself—can be understood as the foundational layer of an architectural palimpsest, a "writing tablet" for the three-dimensional text. In this, Lopes's Western and Japanese models are actually not fundamentally different: while the buildings at Ise do indeed "move" between the two adjacent locations during the rebuilding process (the current sanctuary, or *goshoden*, is located right next to the *kodenchi*, the empty site awaiting its next iteration), they never "leave" the hallowed grounds of the shrine complex. Here too, the site continuously provides an essential "infusion" of authenticity to the ever-changing architectural bodies and ritual practices on its surface.[9]

The ontological status of building materials is the second crucial aspect to consider with regards to the notions of authenticity in Western architecture. Returning to the Ship of Theseus dilemma and to Lopes's assertions regarding physical change, what percentage of new materials can a building tolerate before it becomes a *de facto* replica of itself? Does this percentage shift depending on whether it is the building's hidden structure or its visible surfaces that have been substituted? How is the status of a fully reconstructed building affected if its original location has not changed? Conversely, how authentic is a monument that has retained most or all of its original materials but has been moved to a different location?[10] Testing Lopes's claims against the actual cultural context that defines the buildings' authenticity, this paper addresses the concept of "invisible" restoration palimpsests by referencing select iconic examples from early modern Italy. It also calls attention to the frequent scholarly disregard of the palimpsestual nature of these monuments, making a case for the need to produce more inclusive biographies of important buildings in expert studies, as well as to present more nuanced discussions of their "temporal density"[11] in survey texts targeting students and non-specialists.

★★★

For over two millennia, architecture has held the status of a paradigmatic political, religious, and cultural signifier on the Apennine peninsula. Despite the widespread damage to, and destruction of, much of its built environment over the course of a history replete with wars and (ongoing) seismic activity (figs. 5.1 and 5.2), the abundance of Italy's surviving architectural patrimony from various periods is nevertheless extraordinary, presenting constant challenges to maintenance and conservation efforts. Architectural restoration there has also had a very long and complicated history in its own right. After centuries of "invisibility," it emerged as a modern (i.e. detectable and extensively documented) praxis at the end of the nineteenth century. Informed by an ongoing dialogue with practitioners and theorists in other European countries facing similar challenges, it developed in response to the urgent need to preserve an overwhelming amount of architectural heritage that was becoming increasingly vulnerable in the industrial age, with its dramatic expansion and reconfiguration of historic cities, as well as due to environmental pollution. The very identity of Italy, a country created only in 1861, was understood as being firmly rooted in that heritage, which came to serve as an ideological foundation for the newly unified nation and thus had to be protected as much as possible.[12]

The prominent Roman architect, critic, and art historian Camillo Boito (1836–1914) was vital in articulating a set of new principles guiding

5.1. Castello delle Rocche (Castello Estense), Finale Emilia, early fifteenth century. View of the courtyard. Documented in 2006.

5.2. Courtyard of the Castello delle Rocche at Finale Emilia after the May 2012 earthquake.

architectural restoration in this period. Credited with having defined a middle road between Eugène-Emmanuel Viollet-le-Duc's creative reinvention of monuments and John Ruskin's view that restoration equaled destruction, Boito produced a manifesto of modern restoration, the so-called *Prima Carta del Restauro*, in 1883.[13] His charter specified that consolidation and repair of architectural monuments were preferable to their full-blown restoration;[14] if the latter was absolutely necessary, however, the original and the new parts had to be clearly differentiated in both style and materials.[15] Moreover, all restored structures had to carry commemorative plaques describing the changes made, which were also thoroughly documented in photographs, drawings, and written reports submitted to the official authorities.[16] One of the great conceptual shifts that occurred in this period as articulated by Boito thus had to do with the notion of falsification: restorers had to make sure that viewers would not be deceived by the results of their work.[17] This view challenged the centuries-long paradigm of "invisibility" in architectural restoration, completely reversing the earlier efforts to hide all signs of temporal layering through the use of identical building materials and carving techniques. The new, highly self-conscious practice thus greatly increased the viewer's ability to see restoration palimpsests, while simultaneously (and somewhat ironically) granting authorial visibility to the restorers: though the layers they added purported to be the most neutral vis-à-vis the originals, they were, in fact, the most competitive with them.

It is crucial to remember, however, that architectural restoration—ranging from simple upkeep, such as repainting, to comprehensive substitution of structural and/or decorative elements—had had a long history prior to the advent of Boito and his contemporaries, who inherited monuments that were, in many instances, already heavily "layered." Those early strata, furthest removed from the more modern notions of "proper" restoration practices, are frequently completely imperceptible today, especially if they have left little or no documentary trace. Nevertheless, it is worth framing any historical inquiry with the supposition that they do exist and could, in fact, be part of a significant chapter in the biography of an architectural monument. Indeed, it is likely that an early modern Italian building of any significance can tell us as much about the history of its restoration as it can about its original design.

To start, exterior surfaces of buildings—especially those that appear extremely well preserved—invite us to consider the historical aspects of environmentally dictated maintenance. Bricks crumbled, moldings detached, porous stones "melted" under the elements. The famous *pietra serena*, the bluish-gray sandstone of choice for architectural decoration in Renaissance Florence, for instance, deteriorated rather quickly when exposed to water seepage and seasonal temperature shifts, and had to be substituted regularly every fifty to sixty years.[18] Buildings such as the enigmatic mid-sixteenth-century Palazzo Bocchi in Bologna,[19] with its now eroded sandstone cornice and window pediments (fig. 5.3), demonstrate just how unbecoming a monumental palace would look if the weathered materials on its facade were not periodically exchanged. Indeed, the great ecclesiastical, civic, and representative residential structures of medieval and early modern Italy were not abandoned after they were built; understood as living and aging entities, they required constant structural and superficial upkeep to survive. As long as their practical and symbolic value could be maintained and redefined as necessary, they continued to perdure thanks to an integral "life support" system rooted in the generational transfer of technical knowledge and artistic skill, as well as the ongoing availability of quarries and depositories from which identical building materials could be retrieved to replace whatever was damaged or destroyed. It is telling that it was these two constants that enabled the seamless expansion—a sort of "grafting" in the original style—of some of the most important Early Renaissance palaces in Florence, such as Palazzo Medici-Riccardi (fig. 5.4), Palazzo Pitti, and Palazzo Rucellai, which were enlarged by several matching bays in the subsequent centuries.[20] As "parasitic" palimpsests, these additive clones erased and radically rewrote the buildings and spaces that once delimited the original structures.

5.3. Giacomo Barozzi da Vignola or Achille Bocchi (attr.), Palazzo Bocchi, Bologna, begun 1545. Detail of the front façade.

The recurring practice of material substitution also went well beyond the facades to transform the structural substance of Renaissance buildings when they reached unsafe levels of decay due to age or natural disasters. A telling example is the iconic nine-bay loggia of the Ospedale degli Innocenti facing the Piazza Santissima Annunziata in Florence (fig. 5.5), whose initial conception is linked to the period from 1419 to 1432 and the towering figure of the Early Renaissance "starchitect" Filippo Brunelleschi (1377–1446).[21] The complex history of the Ospedale as a whole has received surprisingly limited attention in recent scholarship, with only a single minor publication specifically addressing the cultural/architectural biography of this important orphanage complex and briefly touching on the principal episodes of reconfiguration of its spatial layout in response to the shifting programmatic needs.[22] Similarly, the quest to understand Brunelleschi's original design for the loggia, a structure that has profoundly shaped our ideas regarding the genesis of Renaissance architecture and Brunelleschi's trailblazing ingenuity that ushered in a new era of rational design,[23] has led to remarkably concise and dismissive treatments of the structure's later strata, which subsequently come across as inconvenient obstacles that cloud our vision and confuse our narrative concerning the loggia's distinguished beginnings.[24] Yet, its cumulative materiality profoundly complicates our efforts to read its originating moment without acknowledging the palimpsest first. Failing to do so smooths over the building's rich history, creating a sort of nostalgic, frustrated longing for the elusive moment of its creation.

5.4. Michelozzo di Bartolomeo, Palazzo Medici-Riccardi, Florence, begun 1444, with later changes. View of the seventeenth-century extension along Via Cavour. Documented *c.* 1890.

5.5. Filippo Brunelleschi, loggia of the Ospedale degli Innocenti, Florence, begun 1419, with later changes. Documented in 2008.

Several episodes from the post-quattrocento life of Brunelleschi's structure, however, are well documented in the archival and visual sources.[25] To briefly mention just a few later ones, in 1794 both the pavement underneath the loggia and the stairs facing the piazza were replaced in their entirety, following a contentious debate among experts regarding which materials to use and how much to restore.[26] Though the total substitution of the crumbling columns, their damaged columnar bases, and the cracked vaults was identified as a priority during this campaign, the grand-ducal authorities decided to hold off on exchanging them, so that a more comprehensive restoration project could be developed for the entire complex. The early decades of the nineteenth century saw a dramatic reconfiguration of the interior spaces and courtyards, but nothing happened with the loggia until 1842, when its structural integrity was seriously threatened following an earthquake that caused major damage to the already compromised architectural members. Under the leadership of engineer Gaetano Coli and architect Leopoldo Pasqui, the columns with their capitals and the vaults were finally replaced in their entirety at this time. Pasqui, moreover, seized this opportunity to "complete" the façade, with the intention of regularizing the loggia's connections to the surrounding structures and thus giving a more uniform character to the piazza as a whole.[27] In 1896, an attic storey was added, only to be removed again during the 1966–70 restoration campaign.[28] The loggia was restored once again in 1994, and again during the 2012–16 major overhaul of the Museo degli Innocenti by the Florentine architectural firm Ipostudio.[29] This

5.6. Ipostudio, new brass gates to the Museo degli Innocenti, Florence, 2016.

most recent renovation included the addition of two glistening brass gates in Pasqui's later bays located on the southern end of the building (fig. 5.6), which were promptly criticized for their "insolent" opulence that assaulted the formal equilibrium of Brunelleschi's "sober" masterpiece.[30]

Brunelleschi's loggia is thus in many ways an architectural Ship of Theseus: simultaneously old and new, it is nevertheless a unique instance of itself for each subsequent community of users who re-appropriate it for their own needs and in the process redefine its value and authenticity. Different parts of the monument—some original, others substituted, yet others added centuries later—have caused its material substance to inhabit several different temporalities concurrently. The creatively enhanced restoration palimpsest that we encounter in Piazza Santissima Annunziata today certainly carries the genetic signature of its Renaissance progenitor, but it is also a different, cumulative presence in our time. Given the building's age, this condition should not be seen as surprising or negative, nor does its authenticity—deeply rooted in its iconic design and its original site—suffer because of it. Indeed, in this and many other cases, the transmutation of the original fabric is easily tolerated precisely because the building has not "moved" and because the process of material change has been gradual, allowing each new layer of the palimpsest to acquire its own "age-value"[31] over time.

However, in the case of a sudden and radical transformation of a structure's physical makeup, the situation is very different. When a building of great symbolic value is destroyed in a traumatic event such as a war or an earthquake, its original substance at times acquires an almost sacred, relic-like status: in recent practices, bro-

5.7. Ponte Santa Trinita, Florence. Constructed by Bartolomeo Ammannati in 1567–69, destroyed in 1944, rebuilt (with some original materials) in 1958.

ken pieces of such structures have been carefully collected and then symbolically reused in the "resurrected" versions of those monuments, with the goal of infusing their facsimiles with a degree of authenticity associated with the lost originals. For example, the stones of the celebrated elliptical arch bridge at Santa Trinita in Florence—built by Bartolomeo Ammannati between 1567 and 1569 and destroyed by the retreating German troops in August 1944—were retrieved from the river Arno and, combined with new materials obtained from the same quarry, used to reconstruct the bridge in 1958 (fig. 5.7).[32] Cases such as this one complicate the notion of what constitutes an architectural palimpsest even further: the extremely short temporal episode of total erasure is followed by the slightly longer one of total rewriting of the monument in its original location, based on its original design, and using much of its original substance. Yet, because of the (relatively) highly compressed duration of those combined episodes—even if they do not result in physical changes that are significantly different from those created through longer processes of palimpsestual layering—the authenticity of the reconstructed monument as a historical monument is seriously compromised (though not necessarily completely obliterated), no matter how painstakingly accurate the outcome. An abrupt interruption of a building's duration may, however, eventually become just one of the many episodes in its long life as an architectural palimpsest, but in the short run, that is, while the memory surrounding the erasure of the original is still alive in the community that had witnessed it, the monument's precise ontological status remains unresolved.

5.8. Rubble of the Campanile di San Marco and the Loggetta in Venice, 1902.

When a community accepts the more flexible notion that a philologically accurate refabrication of a destroyed building can be understood as a legitimate iteration of that building in the *longue durée*, however, it is possible to move away from an understanding of architecture as analogous to painting or sculpture (in terms of the inviolability of the original material substance) and instead focus on its dialectical relationship with the broader urban network of which it is a part and through which it engages and affects its surroundings. This is exactly how the rebuilders of the Campanile and the Loggetta di San Marco in Venice approached the reconstruction of the two monuments between 1902 and 1912, in the wake of the devastating collapse of the thousand year-old Campanile on 14 July 1902 that essentially annihilated both buildings (fig. 5.8).[33] In response to this catastrophic event and despite the vehement objections from some more "forward-looking" figures in the architectural community,[34] Venice's Communal Council decided that the bell tower, as well as the sumptuously decorated Renaissance loggia that once stood at its base (fig. 5.9), had to be replaced *com'erano, dov'erano* ("as they were, where they were") in order to restore to the Venetian skyline the "supreme harmony of lines and colors consecrated by time"[35] that was painfully distorted by their absence.[36] The Council's insistence on reproducing the original (exterior) form of the two buildings in their original locations stemmed from a firmly-held belief that the tragic episode of their destruction was but a short interruption in their ongoing "march through the centuries"[37] and that the soul—and thus, the authenticity—of those cherished monuments could indeed be reclaimed through their faithful replicas.[38] In the case of Jacopo Sansovino's 1538–45 Loggetta, the resurrected form was additionally

5.9. Jacopo Sansovino, Loggetta di San Marco, 1538–45, Venice. Documented before 1874.

legitimized through the integration of numerous surviving sculptural fragments into the new architectural "skin" of the monument (figs. 5.10 and 5.11), which masked its modern, reinforced concrete structure. As a result of this hybrid approach, the Loggetta still occupies a very ambiguous place in architectural history as both a reconstituted original and a copy.[39] Further complicating its status is the fact that scholarly literature hardly ever mentions—let alone explains—its complex biography, presenting it as a straightforward Renaissance masterpiece by Sansovino.[40]

For a facsimile to "feel" authentic enough to suture the temporal fracture in the life of an architectural monument, two fundamental conditions need to be met: the building's form needs to be flawlessly reproduced and the replica needs to be constructed in the original location.[41] The "charge" provided by the authentic site is what allows the facsimile to pick up where the original left off, and to begin to age itself as the original's legitimate heir. No matter how perfect their form and how accurate their materials, facsimiles can make no claims to authenticity once they are detached from the original site, as evidenced by the recent, high-quality scale reproduction[42] of the Monumental Arch of Palmyra (destroyed in October 2015), which has been displayed in strategic locations and in conjunction with culturally significant events in London, New York, Dubai, and Florence (fig. 5.12).[43] Though the primary purpose of this object was to raise awareness about the ongoing destruction of cultural heritage under ISIS, it also looked completely unintelligible without the complex network of signification created by the spatial, proportional, coloristic,

5.10. Detail of the Loggetta showing a reconstituted sculptural relief on the façade.

5.11. Facsimile (with integrated original sculptural elements) of Jacopo Sansovino's Loggetta, Venice, 1912.

and environmental relationships present at the original site in Syria. This same set of relationships is what determines the level of authenticity in buildings that have been moved from one location to another, an infrequent practice usually driven by preservation concerns.[44] If their physical context remains more or less unchanged despite their slight dislocation—as was the case with the Gothic church of Santa Maria della Spina in Pisa, which was dismantled in 1871 and reassembled on higher ground to safeguard against the repeated flooding by the Arno (fig. 5.13)—the building may indeed retain some of its site-based authenticity. Nevertheless, since in the case of Santa Maria della Spina the building's transposition also involved an extensive and philologically inaccurate transformation of its architectural and sculptural fabric, its "age-value," "historical value," and "relative art-value," to borrow Riegl's terms,[45] have all been perceived as deeply problematic ever since John Ruskin first bemoaned the church's unfortunate transformation at the hands of his Italian contemporaries.[46]

★★★

There is little doubt that one of the main reasons for why many early modern Italian monuments have not been widely recognized as palimpsests is the fact that scholarship continues to present them as materially immutable and temporally static entities. As we have seen with the loggia of the Ospedale degli Innocenti in Florence, despite the extensive and well-known changes to both its exterior surfaces and its invisible structure—which in some cases involved the presumably unmodified rewriting of the same architectural "text" (i.e. the decayed original elements being substituted with the matching new ones) and in others entailed dramatic alterations to it—virtually all classic surveys of Renaissance architecture completely dismiss the fact that the current iteration of the loggia is not identical to the initial instance of that building in the fifteenth century. Similarly, the memory of the now distant events of the destruction of the Venetian Loggetta in 1902 and its rebirth as a creatively enhanced facsimile in 1912 has been effectively erased from most scholarly literature. The interest in the building's originating moment continues to prevail, producing nothing more than an occasional footnote regarding its traumatic modern history in studies that focus narrowly on the achievements of the great sixteenth-century architect Jacopo Sansovino (1486–1570). The field of Renaissance architectural history thus appears to be suffering from a severe case of chronophobia; it may be more accurate to think of it as a history of architectural design and patronage, focused on investigating monuments as design concepts and intellectual and creative acts on paper that were "corrupted" as soon as buildings as physical entities began to exist and change in time. Though there are, of course, notable exceptions to this trend in specialized literature, such as Marvin Trachtenberg's magisterial study of "Building-in-Time" in fifteenth-century Florence,[47] survey books targeting students continue to promulgate a very flat temporal picture of the extremely layered Renaissance monuments.[48] Consequently, those generations of "new users" never quite learn why the old buildings they study may be relevant to them and why those structures even matter at all in the current day and age. Moreover, the lack of explicit acknowledgment of, and inquiry into, the buildings' palimpsestual nature has led to significant misunderstandings regarding the history of their restoration and the associated problems of style, materials, and other physical and ideological aspects. In other words, the successive layers of the palimpsest have at times been confused and conflated with the elusive "original" layers precisely because the later ones have not been well understood. The underlying fear in the field seems to be that if an iconic building's layered temporality and "messy" materiality as a palimpsest were to be recognized and examined, its perceived authenticity and canonical status could be challenged and potentially destabilized.

Part of the reason for why we continue to consider monuments from a limited temporal perspective may also be the lack of disciplinary competencies that would allow us to confront them through a multi-synchronic lens. In fact, the separation in scholarship between studies posing questions about the originating moment and those directed towards an understanding of changes in monuments over time reflects a profound disciplinary rift between architectural and restoration/conservation histories. The field of architectural history rarely intersects with the practice of restoration; moreover, restoration/conservation history is a recent field that has only produced a limited bibliography on select structures. To complicate matters even further, archaeologists of architecture, that is, experts focusing on the material stratification of standing structures, work almost exclusively with pre-Renaissance monuments. While medieval archaeology has become a highly developed field in Italy (as well as in other European countries), Renaissance structures there are much less frequently the subject of archaeological scrutiny. To study them, architectural historians and historians and practitioners of restoration rely mostly on documentary archives, which seldom provide enough evidence for a comprehensive account. While it may well be true that some

5.12. The Institute for Digital Archaeology, scale replica of the Palmyra Arch in Piazza della Signoria, Florence. Documented in April 2017.

5.13. Santa Maria della Spina, Pisa. Erected *c.* 1230; enlarged after 1325; dismantled and rebuilt (on a higher level) in 1871.

of the now "invisible" episodes of restoration of these buildings could be described as "the mundane connective tissue" rather than the "highs and lows"[49] in their biography, much of the layered data contained in the monuments themselves continues to be left unexplored and many basic questions that could lead to new venues of investigation are never even asked. "Decompressing" the layers of the palimpsest, rather than fighting the palimpsest as an inconvenient byproduct of history, should be an equally important and urgent venue for future research if the goal is to truly understand and protect the rich and complex architectural heritage that has reached us from the Renaissance.

Notes

I am grateful to Azra Aksamija, Francesco Ceccarelli, Clark Maines, Phillip Wagoner, and the anonymous peer-reviewer for the insightful comments that have helped improve this paper.

1 In his unpublished paper "Seeing Palimpsests: Materiality and the Visibility of Temporal Density," Finbarr Barry Flood underscores the fact that even when the different layers of the palimpsest are visible, they may not be easily legible due to the absence of metadata such as inscriptions or archival documents. In such cases, the building itself becomes the primary archive, albeit frequently an inaccessible one. Flood 2014, 3.

2 Plutarch, *Theseus*, trans. John Dryden, http://classics.mit.edu/Plutarch/theseus.html (accessed 18 April 2016).

3 A notable exception is the recent study by Nagel and Wood, which points to the Ship of Theseus paradigm as a way to understand the process of "substitution" in medieval and early modern art and architecture, through which copies could become legitimate replacements for the lost (or geographically distant) originals. See Nagel and Wood 2010, 8, 29. These issues are also recognized and productively discussed by Newman in this volume.

4 For a detailed discussion of the ritual rebuilding tradition (*shikinen sengu*) at the Ise Shrine and the range of rituals that constitute it, see Adams 1998. Though the transmission of traditional construction technologies through the exact reproduction of its predecessor has been understood as one of the key goals of the cyclic reconstruction at Ise, Adams underscores the fact this has been a highly dynamic process (with several long periods of interruption, for example during wartime between 1463 and 1585) and that some of the principal changes over the thirteen centuries have included "the placement and orientation of buildings, the number and dates of rituals, the number of shrines included, and some of the architectural details (the list goes on)." Adams 1998, 57.

5 It is telling that these questions are still explored primarily by scholars of philosophy/aesthetics (Wicks 1994; Lopes 2007), rather than by architectural historians. Investigating the ontology of architecture—both traditional and contemporary—in Japan, Lopes sees it as opposite to the "standard," Western understanding of architecture where "copies of a building are not instances of a work." Lopes 2007, 81. He also recognizes that "*sengu* allows for changes in material and spatial specifications from one rebuilding to the next" and that "a constitutive feature of Ise Jingu is that it involves twenty-year cycles of building, weathering, decay, rebuilding, and demolition." This element of temporality is what makes the architectural "instances" (i.e. various iterations of Ise shrines) into "events of about twenty years' duration." Lopes 2007, 82.

6 Lopes 2007, 81.

7 The defining theoretical text for the notion of the aura in art is Benjamin's 1936 essay; see Benjamin (1936) 1968. On the aura and contemporary facsimiles of works of art, see Latour and Lowe 2011.

8 Lopes 2007, 81.

9 Comparable examples can be found throughout history and in many different architectural traditions. For example, Branfoot has demonstrated that when the ancient Tamil temples of India were renovated (i.e. replaced) during the much later Nayaka period of the late sixteenth and seventeenth centuries, the new shrines did not replicate the architecture of the old structures, but they retained their dimensions and were built on the exact same sites. Branfoot 2013, 28.

10 In their discussion of Factum Arte's impeccable facsimile of Paolo Veronese's *Wedding Feast at Cana* (1563), through which the painting was "repatriated" to its original location at the refectory of San Giorgio Maggiore in Venice while the original remained at the Louvre, Latour and Lowe make a compelling case against the modern obsession with originals as the only way to understand and appreciate works of art. In their view, "facsimiles, especially those relying on complex (digital) techniques, are thus the most fruitful way to explore the original and even to redefine what originality is." Latour and Lowe 2011, 278. Though Factum Arte's remarkable facsimile of Veronese's painting does not "pretend" to be the original painting, its insertion into the original architectural context provides something much more authentic as far as the viewing experience is concerned than does the Louvre picture, which is framed (rather than surrounded by walls) and hanging too low for its painted architecture (originally created as a virtual extension of the Palladian refectory) to make sense to the viewer.

11 The concept of "temporal density" is developed in Flood 2014.

12 On the politics of culture (including architecture) in Italy in the post-Unification period, see Körner 2009.

13 For a summary of Boito's eight points in the *Prima Carta*, see Dezzi Bardeschi 2007, 48. For recent contextual studies of his theoretical and practical contributions, see Zucconi 1997; and Zucconi and Castellani 2000. For the idea that architectural conservation is a modern phenomenon (with an emphasis on Viollet-le-Duc, Ruskin, and Riegl), see Arrhenius 2012.

14 "I monumenti architettonici, quando sia dimostrata incontrastabilmente la necessità di porvi mano, devono piuttosto venire consolidati che riparati, piuttosto riparati che restaurati, evitando in essi con ogni studio le aggiunte e le rinnovazioni." http://mestrado-reabilitacao.fa.utl.pt/disciplinas/jaguiar/boitocartadelrestauro1883.pdf (accessed 2 July 2016).

15 "… le aggiunte o rinnovazioni si devono compiere con carattere diverso da quello del monumento, avvertendo che, possibilmente, nell'apparenza prospettica le nuove forme non urtino troppo con il suo aspetto artistico." http://mestrado-reabilitacao.fa.utl.pt/disciplinas/jaguiar/boitocartadelrestauro1883.pdf (accessed 2 July 2016).

16 "Dovranno eseguirsi, innanzi di por mano ad opere anche piccole di riparazione o di restauro, le fotografie del monumento, poi di mano in mano le fotografie dei principali stati del lavoro, e finalmente le fotografie del lavoro compiuto. Questa serie di fotografie sarà trasmessa al Ministero della pubblica istruzione insieme con i disegni delle piante degli alzati e dei dettagli e, occorendo, cogli acquarelli colorati, ove figurino con evidente chiarezza tutte le opere conservate, consolidate, rifatte, rinnovate, modificate, rimosse o distrutte." http://mestrado-reabilitacao.fa.utl.pt/disciplinas/jaguiar/boitocartadelrestauro1883.pdf (accessed 2 July 2016).

17 "… allora converrà in ogni modo che i pezzi aggiunti o rinnovati, pure assumendo la forma primitiva, siano di materia evidentemente diversa, o portino un segno inciso meglio la data del restauro, sicché neanche su ciò possa l'attento ossevatore venire tratto in inganno." http://mestrado-reabilitacao.fa.utl.pt/disciplinas/jaguiar/boitocartadelrestauro1883.pdf (accessed 2 July 2016).

18 Malesani and Vannucci 1974, 37. The authors argue that the process of decay of *pietra serena* (used for decoration) and *pietra forte* (used for construction) has significantly accelerated in modern times due to the effects of air pollution. For a recent study of *pietra serena*, its properties and principal quarries in Tuscany, see Fratini et al. 2014.

19 Considered one of the most enigmatic palaces of the Italian Renaissance, Palazzo Bocchi was built for the Bolognese humanist and professor, Achille Bocchi, starting in 1545, and became famous as the seat of his private academy dedicated to Hermes and Athena. The façade of the palace—featuring prominent inscriptions in Hebrew and Latin—has been studied in relation to Bocchi's 1555 emblem book *Symbolicarum quaestionum*. See Watson 1993; and Kiefer 1999. Unfortunately, the existing scholarship has not dealt with this building's biography after the sixteenth century, including its current state of disrepair.

20 On this phenomenon and for additional bibliography, see Frati 2013. Frati identifies more than twenty cases of subsequent "doubling" of Early Renaissance Florentine buildings in the same style and using identical materials. Today, only the most perceptible of beholders can detect the slight differences in surface treatment between the original and later parts of these facades. On the extension of Palazzo Medici-Riccardi, a building whose later changes and uses have been well documented, see Millen and Wolf 1987. On its early restorations, see Acidini 1992. The bibliography on Florentine palaces is vast and among the richest for Italian Renaissance architecture in terms of the buildings' more comprehensive biographies.

21 The bibliography on the Ospedale degli Innocenti is extensive; the most comprehensive discussion of Brunelleschi's project is Saalman 1993. A useful summary is provided in Goldthwaite 1996.

22 See the individual essays in Sandri 1996. For an early history of the Ospedale's activities, see Bruscoli 1900.

23 In one of the pioneering survey texts in English on Early Renaissance architecture, Ludwig Heydenreich argues that Brunelleschi's "formal elements reveal the desire to achieve a kind of classical order offering a sharp contrast to the Late Gothic syntax current at the time." He also suggests that the architect's originality lay in the "almost austere purification of these medieval forms" and "was characterized by a practical mathematical ratio in the proportions" that created "absolute harmony which was the culmination of the new concept of beauty." Heydenreich (1974) 1999, 15.

24 Though he does significantly more than many other scholars in terms of discussing the loggia of the Ospedale as a palimpsest, Saalman dedicates just a few succinct paragraphs to its later history, presenting as a continuous distortion of Brunelleschi's original design. He writes, for example, "[t]he Brunelleschian design, already unbalanced by the *aggiunta* of 1427, was further distorted by the extra arcade at the northern end. The façade was becoming progressively more asymmetrical and this asymmetry was accentuated by the erection of three bays of a loggia with stilted arcades over the northern (Annunziata) end of the upper storey. It was left to the academic classicist Leopoldo Pasqui in 1843 to give the façade a symmetry it had never previously achieved." Saalman 1993, 64–65.

25 These episodes are cogently summarized in Romby 1996. The visual evidence illustrating the changes to

the loggia is published in Mendes Atanásio and Dallai 1966.

26 The 1794 restoration is discussed in Cisternino (2007/08) 2010.

27 For details regarding Pasqui's interventions, see Romby 1996, 30.

28 For the 1966–70 restoration, see Morozzi and Piccini 1971.

29 See Barletta 2016.

30 The scorching review of these "golden" gates was published by the art historian Tomaso Montanari in one of Italy's premier newspapers, *La Repubblica*. Montanari argues that, in contemporary Florence, art has become synonymous with ostentation, and the city—with its precious works of art and architecture—has been reduced to nothing but a playground for the wealthy. See Montanari 2016.

31 The concept of "age-value" as a facet of the modern "cult of monuments" was articulated by Riegl at the turn of the twentieth century. See Riegl (1903) 1982, 31–33.

32 For the history of the bridge from 1557 to 1958, see Belluzzi and Belli 2003. It is important to underscore that Ammannati's bridge succeeded several earlier wooden and stone ones, constructed in the same location since the thirteenth century and periodically destroyed during the extreme flooding of the river Arno. For restorers and restoration theorists working in the middle of the twentieth century, i.e. close to when the Santa Trinita bridge was "resurrected," one of the guiding principles was to preserve the meaning of a reconstructed monument as a work of art, while adapting its use to the contemporary context. See Dezzi Bardeschi 1964, 95. A similar, more recent case of post-war reconstruction of an ancient bridge using some of its suriving pieces is the Stari Most (Old Bridge) over the Neretva River in Mostar, Bosnia and Herzegovina, which was built by the Ottoman architect Mimar Hayruddin in 1566 and destroyed by Croatian gunners on 9 November 1993. Part of a UNESCO World Heritage Site, Stari Most was reconstructed between 2001 and 2004. See Petrovic 2013.

33 For a discussion of this event, the subsequent debates on how to proceed with the rebuilding, and the actual process of reconstruction of Jacopo Sansovino's Loggetta, see Aksamija 2013.

34 The most outspoken critic of the plan to replace the bell tower with an exact facsimile was the Viennese Jugendstil architect Otto Wagner (1841–1918), who advocated for both the modern style and the change of location of the new Campanile. See Plant 2002, 237; Aksamija 2013, 233.

35 Fradeletto 1912, vi.

36 Aksamija 2013, 233–34.

37 Fradeletto 1912, vii.

38 Aksamija 2013, 241. Glendinning provides a helpful summary of the values that were recovered: "In the terms set out by Riegl the following year, Beltrami's facsimile Campanile was a logical and 'authentic' expression of several key monument values. It displayed historical value, present-day art-value, newness-value, and even use-value, given the requirement of the tourist industry for a recognisable skyline image…" Glendinning 2013, 193. In his discussion of the Venice Campanile a year after its destruction, Riegl offered a positive and very hopeful view of the future of facsimiles, stating that "the development of modern techniques of reproduction promises that in the near future (especially since the invention of color photography and facsimile reproduction) new and perfect means of compensating for the loss of originals will be found." Riegl (1903) 1982, 37–38.

39 It is important to mention that only the front façade of the Loggetta was reproduced as closely to the original as possible. Its lateral elevations, which were considered inferior and not the work of Jacopo Sansovino, were stylistically "improved" on the facsimile; they also significantly extended the new building's footprint on each side. See Aksamija 2013, 239–41.

40 Even the most recent survey books are guilty of such omissions. Frommel, for instance, focuses on the Loggetta's material opulence, without even mentioning that most of the materials on the façade are not original: "The appeal of the Loggetta derives from the contrast between white and pink marble, the precious columns, the masterly bronze statues (sculpted by Sansovino himself) and the marble reliefs." Frommel 2007, 168. Concina similarly concludes: "With its polychrome marbles, this elaborate little work (1538) established a precise—and, for Sansovino, unusual—symmetry with the fifteenth-century portal opposite." Concina 1998, 186. Before them, Lotz commented on the triumphal arch motif adopted by Sansovino for the Loggetta, which had previously been employed by Giuliano da Sangallo in his designs for the façade of San Lorenzo in Florence. Lotz 1974 (1995), 86.

41 Approaching this problem from a philosophical standpoint, Wicks offers three additional ways in which architectural facsimiles can be more than mere replicas of original buildings: "(1) architectural refabrications can be authentic, in so far as architectural plans are like musical scores, (2) since the Platonic model of architectural restoration is frequently unavoidable, and since this model suggests that 'the work' resides in the buildings multiply instantiable 'look', that architectural refabrications can be authentic when viewed in light of this model, and (3) since a 'successful restoration' generates hermeneutical problems parallel to the interpretation of old texts, and since—to add a further implication—works of literature are themselves multiply instantiable, then architectural works may be considered to be such as well, even if the multiple instantiation of the work is restricted to the work's original site." Wicks 1994, 168.

42 The scale replica in Carrara marble is about 1/3 of the *c.* 20-meter original Monumental Arch of Palmyra. The significantly reduced size of the copy (*c.* 6 meters) is one of the reasons why it is perceived as an illustration of, rather than a stand-in for the original.

43 For the display of the replica of the Palmyra Arch in London's Trafalgar Square for the UNESCO World Heritage Week in April 2016, see Shea 2016; for its display at New York's City Hall Park in September 2016, see Jalabi 2016. The replica was also shown in Dubai during the World Government Summit in February 2017, and in the Piazza della Signoria in Florence in March-April 2017, on the occasion of the G7 Culture Summit.

44 Though moving of entire buildings (as opposed to parts of buildings, even very large ones, which we think of as *spolia*) was certainly a rare practice in early modern and modern Italy, much more research needs to be done to determine the range of circumstances under which it took place. There are records of it occurring in the Renaissance, such as with the celebrated instance in 1455 of the architect Aristotele Fioravanti moving the fourteenth-century Torre della Magione in Bologna (destroyed in 1825) by some 13 meters in order to position it closer to the apse of the church of Santa Maria del Tempio. See Malagola 1874; Tugnoli Pattaro 1976, 41–44.

45 Riegl (1903) 1982, esp. 21–38, 44–49.

46 For Ruskin's reaction, see Burresi 1990, 10. Burresi effectively summarizes the changes inflicted upon the monument during the 1871 rebuilding campaign: "L'edificio che oggi vediamo è stato dunque smontato dalla sua antica sede, alterato nelle proporzioni, nelle forme e nelle funzioni, incrostato di un paramento lapideo esterno in materiale prevalentemente diverso dall'originale sul quale si innesta un apparato scultoreo anch'esso in gran parte manomesso da restauri e sostituzioni. È stato inoltre spogliato, all'interno, delle vestigia dei suoi arredi scultorei e pittorici, che avevano segnato, nei secoli, tappe importanti della sua storia. È perciò ormai difficile riconoscerlo come edificio medievale ed appare, invece, in tutta la sua ambiguità, reinterpretazione moderna, di un edificio antico." Burresi 1990, 19. For a discussion of the monument at the time of its nineteenth-century reconstruction, see Martelli 1871.

47 Trachtenberg 2010.

48 There are, of course, significant limitations, often imposed by the publishers, in terms of what authors are able to do in textbooks and surveys, which is certainly one of the reasons this narrow and counterproductive approach has persisted over several generations.

49 Flood 2014, 6.

Bibliography

Acidini, Cristina, ed. 1992. *I Restauri nel palazzo Medici Riccardi: Rinascimento e Barocco*. Cinisello Balsamo: Silvana.

Adams, Cassandra. 1998. "Japan's Ise Shrine and Its Thirteen-Hundred-Year-Old Reconstruction Tradition," *Journal of Architectural Education* 52, no. 1, 49–60.

Aksamija, Nadja. 2013. "The Loggetta's Skin," in *Reflections on Renaissance Venice: A Celebration of Patricia Fortini Brown*, ed. Blake de Maria and Mary Frank. Milan: Five Continents, 230–47.

Arrhenius, Thordis. 2012. *The Fragile Monument: On Conservation and Modernity*. London: Artifice Books and Black Dog Publishing.

Barletta, Mariagrazia. 2016. "Apre a Firenze il nuovo Museo degli Innocenti con il restyling di Ipostudio," *Il Sole 24 Ore*, 24 June. http://www.ediliziaeterritorio.ilsole24ore.com/art/progettazione-e-architettura/2016-06-23/apre-firenze-museo-innocenti-il-restyling-ipostudio-144941.php?uuid = ADxv4kh (accessed 15 June 2017)

Belluzzi, Amedeo, and Gianluca Belli. 2003. *Il ponte a Santa Trinita*. Florence: Polistampa.

Benjamin, Walter. (1936) 1968. "The Work of Art in the Age of Mechanical Reproduction," in Walter Benjamin, *Illuminations*. New York: Schocken Books, 217–51.

Birth, Kevin K. 2012. *Objects of Time: How Things Shape Temporality*. New York: Palgrave Macmillan.

Branfoot, Crispin. 2013. "Remaking the past: Tamil sacred landscape and temple renovations," *Bulletin of the School of Oriental and African Studies* 76, no. 1, 21–47.

Bruscoli, Gaetano. 1900. *Lo Spedale di Santa Maria degli Innocenti di Firenze dalla sua fondazione fino ai giorni nostri*. Florence: E. Ariani.

Burresi, Mariagiulia. 1990. *Santa Maria della Spina in Pisa*. Cinisello Balsamo: Silvana.

Cisternino, Alfredo. (2007/08) 2010. "Il restauro della Loggia degli Innocenti del 1794," *Bollettino della Società di Studi Fiorentini* 16/17, 199–201.

Concina, Ennio. 1998. *A History of Venetian Architecture*. Cambridge: Cambridge University Press.

Dezzi Bardeschi, Chiara. 2007. "Camillo Boito e la Prima Carta Italiana del Restauro (1883)," in *Archeologia e Conservazione. Teorie, metodologie e pratiche di cantiere*. Santarchangelo di Romagna: Maggioli, 48–50.

Dezzi Bardeschi, Marco, ed. 1981. *Il monument e il suo doppio: Firenze*. Florence: Fratelli Alinari.

—. 1964. "La mostra internazionale del restauro a Venezia, 1964," *Marmo* 3, 78–95.

Flood, Finbarr Barry. 2014. "Seeing Palimpsests: Materiality and the Visibility of Temporal Density," paper presented at the Art History Symposium *Monuments as Palimpsests*, Wesleyan University, February 28-March 1, 1–20.

Fradeletto, Antonio. 1912. "Prefazione," in *Il campanile di San Marco riedificato: studi, ricerche, relazioni*, ed. Antonio Fradeletto. Venice: C. Ferrari, v–xxi.

Frati, Marco. 2013. "Identità formale, varietà materiale. La ripetizione dei moduli progettuali nelle facciate dei palazzi muniti fiorentini (cantieri fra XIII e XX secolo)," in *Architettura e identità locali*, vol. 2, ed. Howard Burns and Mauro Mussolin. Florence: Leo S. Olschki, 585–604.

Fratini, Fabio, et al. 2014. "Pietra Serena: the stone of the Renaissance," in *Global Heritage Stone: Towards International Recognition of Building and Ornamental Stones*, Geological Society Special Publication no. 407, ed. Dolores Pereira et al. London: The Geological Society, 173–86.

Frommel, Christoph Luitpold. 2007. *The Architecture of the Italian Renaissance*. London: Thames & Hudson.

Glendinning, Miles. 2013. *The Conservation Movement: A History of Architectural Preservation*. London and New York: Routledge.

Goldthwaite, Richard A. 1996. "La prima campagna edile e il mondo del lavoro, 1419–1432," in *Gli Innocenti e Firenze nei secoli. Un Ospedale, un archivio, una città*, ed. Lucia Sandri. Florence: S.P.E.S., 15–20.

Heydenreich, Ludwig H. (1974) 1996. *Architecture in Italy 1400–1500*. Revised by Paul Davies. New Haven and London: Yale University Press.

ICOMOS. 1964. *International Charter for the Conservation and Restoration of Monuments and Sites (The Venice Charter 1964)*. http://www.icomos.org/charters/venice_e.pdf (accessed 15 June 2016)

Jalabi, Raya. 2016. "Replica of Syrian arch destroyed by Isis unveiled in New York City," *The Guardian*, 20 September. https://www.theguardian.com/us-news/2016/sep/20/palmyra-arch-syria-new-york (accessed 14 June 2017)

Jokilehto, Jukka. 1999. *A History of Architectural Conservation*. Oxford: Butterworth-Heinemann.

Kiefer, Marcus. 1999. *Emblematische Strukturen in Stein. Vignolas Palazzo Bocchi in Bologna*. Freiburg im Breisgau: Rombach Verlag.

Körner, Axel. 2009. *Politics of Culture in Liberal Italy: From Unification to Fascism*. New York and London: Routledge.

Labadi, Sophia. 2013. *UNESCO, Cultural Heritage, and Outstanding Universal Value: Value-based Analyses of the World Heritage and Intangible Cultural Heritage Conventions*. Lanham: AltaMira Press.

Latour, Bruno, and Adam Lowe. 2011. "The Migration of the Aura, or How to Explore the Original through Its Facsimiles," in *Switching Codes: Thinking Through Digital Technology in the Humanities and the Arts*, ed. Thomas Bartscherer and Roderick Coover. Chicago: University of Chicago Press, 275–97.

Lopes, Dominic McIver. 2007. "*Shikinen Sengu* and the Ontology of Architecture in Japan," *The Journal of Aesthetics and Art Criticism* 65, no. 1, 77–84.

Lotz, Wolfgang. (1974) 1995. *Architecture in Italy 1500–1600*. Revised by Deborah Howard. New York and London: Yale University Press.

Malagola, Carlo. 1874. "Del trasporto della torre di S. Maria del Tempio in Bologna detta della Magione," *Il Politecnico* 22, 203–09.

Malesani, Piergiorgio P., and Sergio A. Vannucci. 1974. "Decay of Pietra Serena and Pietraforte, Florentine Building Stones: Petrographic Observations," *Studies in Conservation* 19, no. 1, 36–50.

Marconi, Paolo. 1999. *Materia e significato. La questione del restauro architettonico*. Rome: Editori Laterza.

Martelli, Giuseppe. 1871. *Sul Proposto Restauro del Tempio di Santa Maria della Spina di Pisa*. Florence: Successori Le Monnier.

Mendes Atanásio, Manuel Cardoso, and Giovanni Dallai. 1966. "Nuove indagini sullo Spedale degli Innocenti a Firenze," *Commentari* 17, 83–106.

Millen, Ronald F., and Robert E. Wolf. 1987. "Palazzo Medici into Palazzo Riccardi: the extension of the façade along via Larga," *Mitteilungen des Kunsthistorischen Institutes in Florenz* 31, 81–120.

Montanari, Tomaso. 2016. "Firenze, lo Spedale degli Innocenti: quell'oro sfacciato contro la sobrietà del Brunelleschi," *La Repubblica*, 21 July. http://firenze.repubblica.it/cronaca/2016/07/21/news/firenze_lo_spedale_degli_innocenti_quell_oro_sfacciato_contro_la_sobrieta_del_brunelleschi-144560666/ (accessed 13 June 2017)

Morozzi, Guido and Attilio Piccini. 1971. *Il restauro dello spedale di Santa Maria degli Innocenti 1966–1970*. Florence: Giunti-G. Barbèra.

Nagel, Alexander, and Christopher S. Wood. 2010. *Anachronic Renaissance*. New York: Zone Books.

Petrovic, Jadranka. 2013. *The Old Bridge of Mostar and Increasing Respect for Cultural Property in Armed Conflict*. Leiden and Boston: Marinus Nijhoff Publishers.

Plant, Margaret. 2002. *Venice: Fragile City 1797–1997*. New Haven and London: Yale University Press.

Riegl, Alois. (1903) 1982. "The Modern Cult of Monuments: Its Character and Its Origin," trans. Kurt W. Forster and Diane Ghirardo, *Oppositions* 25, 21–51.

Romby, Giuseppina C. 1996. "Le vicende architettoniche nei secoli," in *Gli Innocenti e Firenze nei secoli. Un Ospedale, un archivio, una città*, ed. Lucia Sandri. Florence: S.P.E.S., 21–32.

Saalman, Howard. 1993. "The Hospital of the Innocents," in *Filippo Brunelleschi: The Buildings*. University Park: Pennsylvania State University Press, 33–81.

Sandri, Lucia, ed. 1996. *Gli Innocenti e Firenze nei secoli. Un Ospedale, un archivio, una città*. Florence: S.P.E.S.

Shea, Christopher D. 2016. "Palmyra Arch Replica is Unveiled in Trafalgar Square in London," *New York Times*, 19 April. https://www.nytimes.com/2016/04/20/arts/international/replica-of-palmyra-arch-is-unveiled-in-trafalgar-square.html?mcubz = 0&_r = 0 (accessed 13 June 2017)

Stanley-Price, Nicholas, Mansfield Kirby Talley, and Alessandra Melucco Vaccaro, eds. 1996. *Historical and Philosophical Issues in the Conservation of Cultural Heritage*. Los Angeles: Getty Conservation Institute.

Trachtenberg, Marvin. 2010. *Building-in-Time: From Giotto to Alberti and Modern Oblivion*. New Haven and London: Yale University Press.

Tugnoli Pattaro, Sandra. 1976. "Le opere bolognesi di Aristotole Fioravanti architetto e ingegnere del secolo quindicesimo," *Arte Lombarda* 44–45, 35–70.

Watson, Elizabeth See. 1993. *Achille Bocchi and the Emblem Book as Symbolic Form*. Cambridge: Cambridge University Press.

Wicks, Robert. 1994. "Architectural Restoration: Resurrection or Replication?" *The British Journal of Aesthetics* 34, no. 2, 163–69.

Zucconi, Guido. 1997. *L'invenzione del passato. Camillo Boito e l'architettura neomedievale 1855–1890*. Venice: Marsilio.

Zucconi, Guido, and Francesca Castellani, eds. 2000. *Camillo Boito. Un'architettura per l'Italia unita*. Venice: Marsilio.

III

Buildings Inscribed

Chapter 6
Cut 'n' Paste:
Reconstructing the Façades of the *Praedia* of Julia Felix in Pompeii

Christopher Parslow

Political and social life in ancient Pompeii was conducted in the streets and public spaces, but while these are today mute and lifeless, the posters and graffiti once plastered across the façades of buildings offer a vivid and animated record of these activities. While individuals used sharp points and charcoal to scrawl greetings to friends, expressions of love, and quotations from classical literature, troupes of professional sign painters (*scriptores*) fanned out to paint political and commercial notices, known today as *dipinti*, on the facades of buildings across the city. These were executed in elegant cursive letters of black and red paint, often set off against preparatory patches of whitewash (fig. 6.1).[1] Many of the posters advocating the election of political candidates, known specifically as *programmata*, were tailored to the neighborhoods in which they appeared by calling upon local inhabitants, shop owners and their clientele, professional guilds, and patrons of public buildings to lend their support to specific candidates. In most cases they neither sought the owners' permission nor bothered to cover their work at the end of the campaign season; in other cases, they whitewashed over old notices to solicit support for new candidates. The result is a palimpsest: a rich, layered, and detailed prosopographical record of the names of leading citizens and politicians, religious and commercial organizations, homeowners and shopkeepers, slaves, and even children, extending over many decades and unparalleled in the Roman world.[2]

The ephemeral nature of these inscriptions, in antiquity as well as today, means that there are few examples in Pompeii where their full palimpsestic qualities can be deployed to shed light on questions about a building's architectural history and its role in the political and social life of the city. The excavators left most inscriptions *in situ* on the walls, but time and the unrelenting forces of nature have left them largely illegible, where they have not been obliterated completely. While photographs captured some of these inscriptions in context beginning in the twentieth century, when photography was introduced as a means of recording the archaeological discoveries, the records allow the provenance of most others to be identified in very general terms, as coming from a particular house or building.

One exception to this is the *Praedia*, or Properties, of Julia Felix in Pompeii, a complex of structures that include a small neighborhood bath, three shops, second storey rental apartments and richly decorated garden dining rooms situated north of the amphitheater at the eastern edge of the city (fig. 6.2).[3] More than half of the *Praedia*'s painted inscriptions were cut down from the walls on which they had been posted soon after their discovery in the Bourbon era and survive in the storerooms of the Museo Archeologico Nazionale in Naples (hereafter abbreviated MAN) to this day. The remainder, found later and fully documented and published, were left *in situ* and are regrettably now lost.

This study concentrates on the inscriptions originally painted on the west end of the *Praedia*'s north façade where the most detailed and varied evidence exists for reconstructing their appearance and identifying their palimpsestic aspects. In this case, the "parchment" is the wall's masonry, smoothed over with stucco, onto which inscriptions were painted and graffiti scrawled over the course of several years. The inscribed portions of the wall removed by the Bourbons preserve evidence for the sequential accretion of the inscriptions. By referencing the excavation records and reconstructing the physical context, scaled reproductions of the inscriptions can be

6.1. Political *programmata* covering the eastern half of the south façade of the House of Trebius Valens (*Regio* III.ii.1) as discovered in 1915.

returned to their proper location on the façade and the relationships between them established. Their importance goes beyond illuminating how these vertical canvasses of stone and plaster were used and reused in antiquity. They also shed light on the possible function of the *Praedia*'s spaces and may even reveal the names and livelihoods of their occupants and patrons.

The *Praedia* were excavated on four separate occasions over the course of two hundred years, with each campaign contributing to the corpus of inscriptions. The first set of 19 *dipinti* was recovered from the western half of the north façade during the earliest systematic excavations in the *Praedia* sponsored by Charles of Bourbon (1716–88), King of Naples and Sicily, from 1755 to 1757.[4] Among the discoveries was a unique painted notice providing the proper name of the properties ("*Praedia*") and their owner ("Julia Felix, daughter of Spurius") and advertising for rent the baths, shops, and second storey apartments within them (fig. 6.3).[5] Immediately recognizing these inscriptions' historical value and fragile nature, the Bourbon excavators dealt with them as they did the wall paintings they had encountered here and elsewhere: they cut them down, mounted them as individual panels, and accessioned them in the royal collection of antiquities at nearby Portici. Stripped as well of most of their artistic finds, and with their structures heavily damaged as a consequence of both the eruption of Vesuvius in AD 79 and the Bourbon excavations, the *Praedia* were reburied and the land returned to cultivation.

It was not until 1935 that the entire north façade was exposed during the course of excavations aimed at clearing the full length of the so-called Via dell'Abbondanza, the main east-west commercial thoroughfare onto which the *Praedia* face. In the course of this work nine more *dipinti* and additional graffiti were revealed on the eastern half of the north façade, an area left unexplored by the Bourbons.[6] The stucco on which these had been painted was in generally

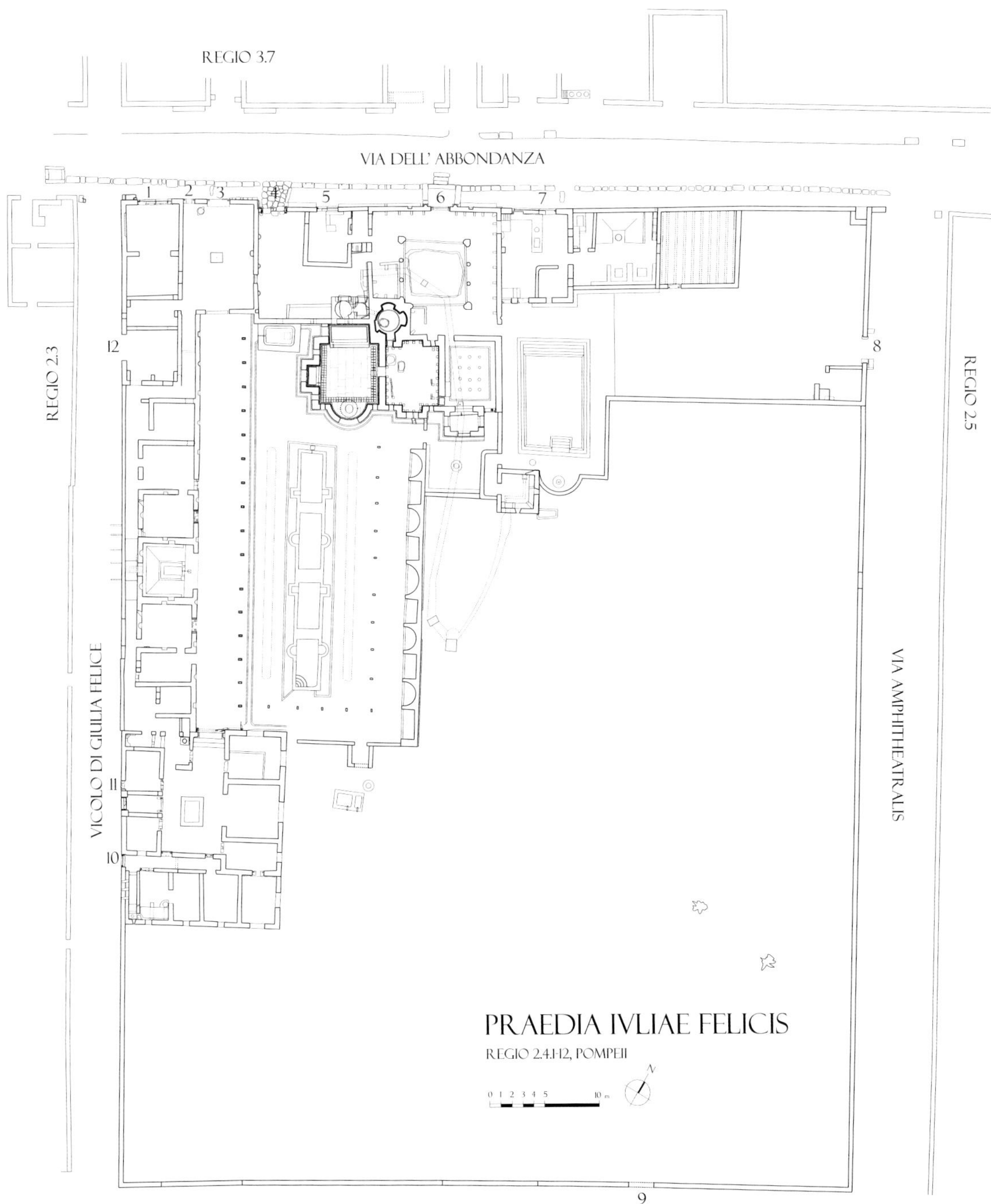

6.2. Plan of the *Praedia* of Julia Felix, *Regio* II.iv.1–12, Pompeii.

good condition at the time, but the entire façade was subsequently left exposed to the elements and so the process of deterioration began soon after the excavations.

Finally, in 1952, the entire west façade was cleared, revealing a large number of graffiti scrawled in chalk or etched with a sharp point on the stucco outside one of the *Praedia*'s principal entrances (*Regio* II.iv.10), but no additional *dipinti* were recovered. At that same time, the entire site was cleared, some of the standing walls were restored or consolidated, and several key spaces were covered in modern roofs. The newly discovered inscriptions were published

6.3. Panel in the Museo Archeologico Nazionale in Naples (MAN 4713) containing *CIL* 4.1136 naming the *Praedia* of Julia Felix along with five other *dipinti* (*CIL* 4.1137–1141), as it appears today.

but the *Praedia* as a whole were left to their fate and remain unpublished.[7] The paint of the earlier *dipinti* vanished long before the stucco containing them succumbed to the elements, leaving now only a few featureless patches whose edges have been consolidated with concrete in an attempt to keep them anchored to the walls. Moreover, much of the masonry of the façades has been repointed and recapped at least twice since the 1950s, obscuring any differences between the ancient and the modern. Today, only a single *dipinto* survives *in situ*.

The Bourbon-era sources for reconstructing the western half of the north façade are remarkably complete and detailed, as they are for the site as a whole.[8] The excavators, unfamiliar with the paleography and the abbreviations used by the ancient sign painters, had transcribed the texts as best they could and these are preserved in their inventories, some now published and others in archives. Of particular relevance here are the texts of two *programmata* from the *Praedia* transcribed in the field by one of the excavators. These not only preserve the names and abbreviations as they were deciphered at the moment of their discovery, they also record characteristics such as over painting and damage to the texts (figs. 6.4 and 6.5).[9] The supervisor of the excavations, the Swiss military engineer Karl Jakob Weber (1712–64) documented the precise provenance of each inscription by placing a number at the corresponding location on detailed plans he drew of the site at the conclusion of the investigations (hereafter abbreviated KW, with the relevant number) and providing the full text in an accompanying legend (fig. 6.6). Most remarkably, five of the seven panels of *dipinti* removed in this period survive in the storerooms of the Naples museum, though their paint has flaked and faded considerably and the texts are largely

6.4. Left image: Tracing of the text of *CIL* 4.1142–1143 (MAN NR 834; now lost) as copied by the Bourbon excavators at the time of its discovery in 1756. Right image: Proposed reconstruction.

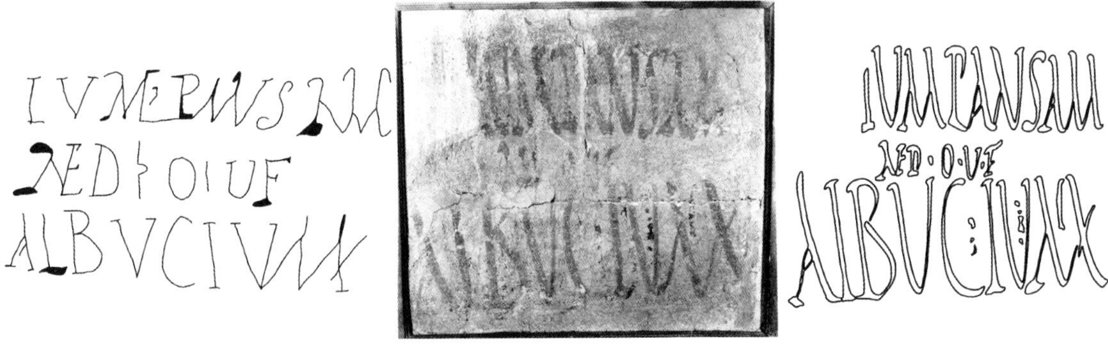

6.5. Left image: Tracing of the text of *CIL* 4.1153–1154 as copied by the Bourbon excavators at the time of its discovery in 1756. Center image: MAN 4667. Right image: Tracing based on MAN 4667 and Rosini 1797, plate 12.3.

illegible today.[10] Fortunately, scaled engravings of the principal *dipinti* were produced soon after their removal and later published with commentary.[11] This is the only site in Pompeii for which such a full set of these engravings exists.

The sources from the later excavations are much less complete. The excavation daybooks are frustratingly terse and vague about where they are in the site, and this renders it difficult to ascertain the exact provenance of even the most important discoveries. A single, overall plan was produced at the conclusion of the 1950s excavations.[12] All the inscriptions uncovered from 1912 through 1952 had been read and published by a single individual: Matteo Della Corte (1875–1962), who worked in the excavations at Pompeii from 1902 to 1956. While he kept detailed inventories and vellum tracings of the roughly 4000 inscriptions uncovered in the ruins during his time there, his documentation was selective—he would record the overall width of an inscription and might indicate its location relative to others nearby, but he rarely indicated where it had been found on a wall—and his readings are idiosyncratic and at times seemingly fantastical.[13] Unfortunately, most of his readings cannot be checked because the original inscriptions have now vanished. Photographs were made of some of the graffiti, but the quality is not always sufficient to discern the let-

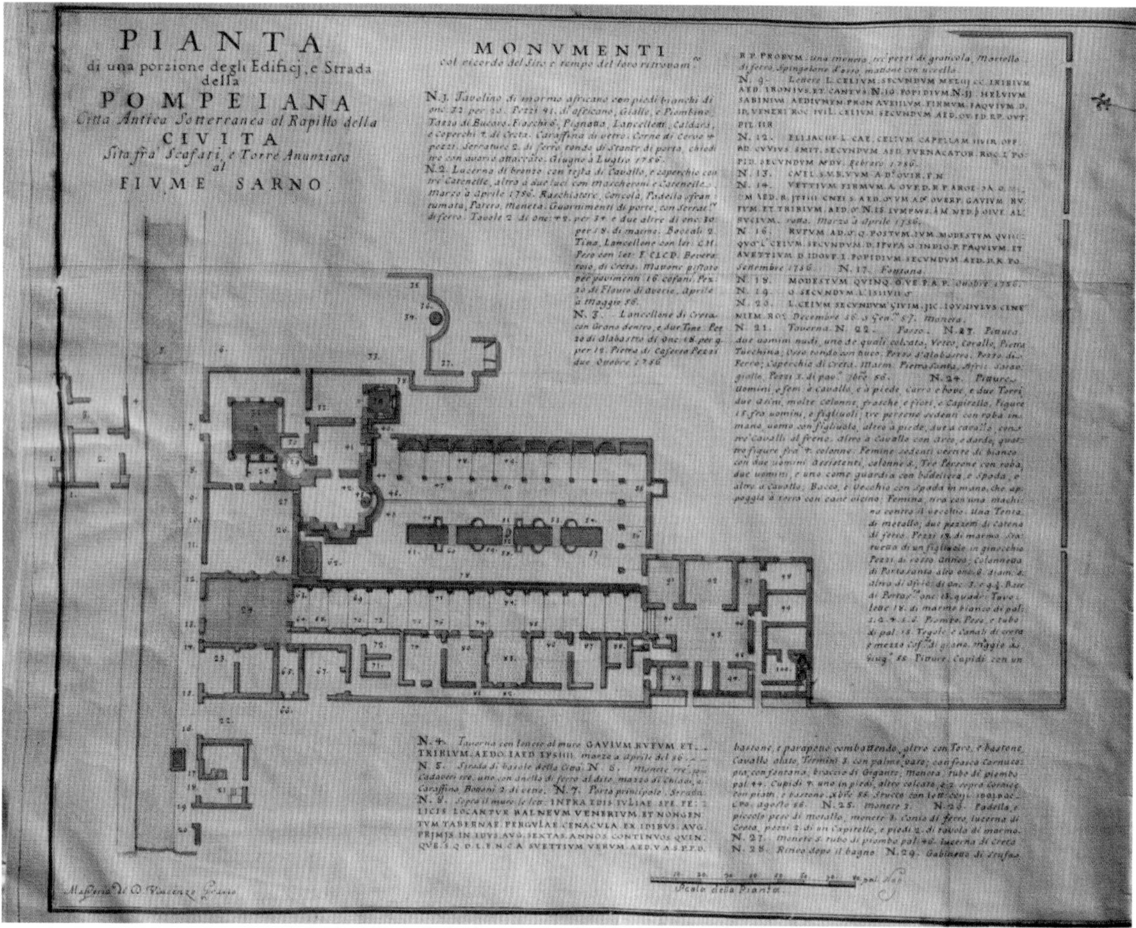

6.6. Karl Weber, Plan of the *Praedia*, 1757.

ters.[14] More valuable are the photographs of the *dipinti* recovered in his period, though only the best preserved were documented in this manner and the emphasis was on the content not the context.[15] Nevertheless, the extant written and visual documentation is sufficient not only to identify where on the façade most of the *dipinti* recovered in these more recent excavations had been displayed but also to determine, if not their exact position above the ground, then at least their proper relationship between one another.

Supplementing the photographs of the individual inscriptions are several photographs that document the physical remains of the north façade as they appeared when first cleared in 1935 (fig. 6.7). These reveal the dismal state in which the Bourbons had left the structures and what little remained even before they had been abandoned to the elements for 20 years, a process of deterioration documented in turn by photographs from the 1950s excavations.[16] All of these clearly show that the greatest damage to the structures was to the western portion of the façade, corresponding precisely with the areas where the Bourbon records indicate they had cut down the greatest number of *dipinti*. Additional voids in the stucco on the eastern portion of the façade of the bath complex visible in the excavation photographs suggest the Bourbons had removed other *dipinti* from there as well, but the records provide no clear evidence for what these might have been.

The Bourbon records catalogue the texts of nineteen individual *dipinti* removed from the western end of the façade.[17] These were mounted on seven framed panels, two of which are now lost. Two of these panels are of substantial size. Indeed, these are significantly larger than the average figural painting or small painted vignette

6.7. North façade of the *Praedia* as it appeared immediately after re-excavation in January 1935.

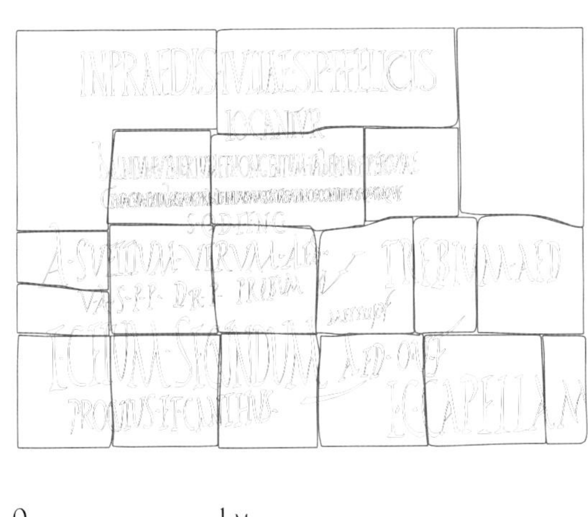

6.8. MAN 4713 consisting of *CIL* 4.1136–1141 divided up into nineteen fragments of stucco and remounted together. Composite tracing based on original panel and on Rosini 1797, plate 4.

6.9. MAN 4672 containing *CIL* 4.1145–1150 in eleven fragments of stucco. Based on original and Rosini 1797, plate 10.2.

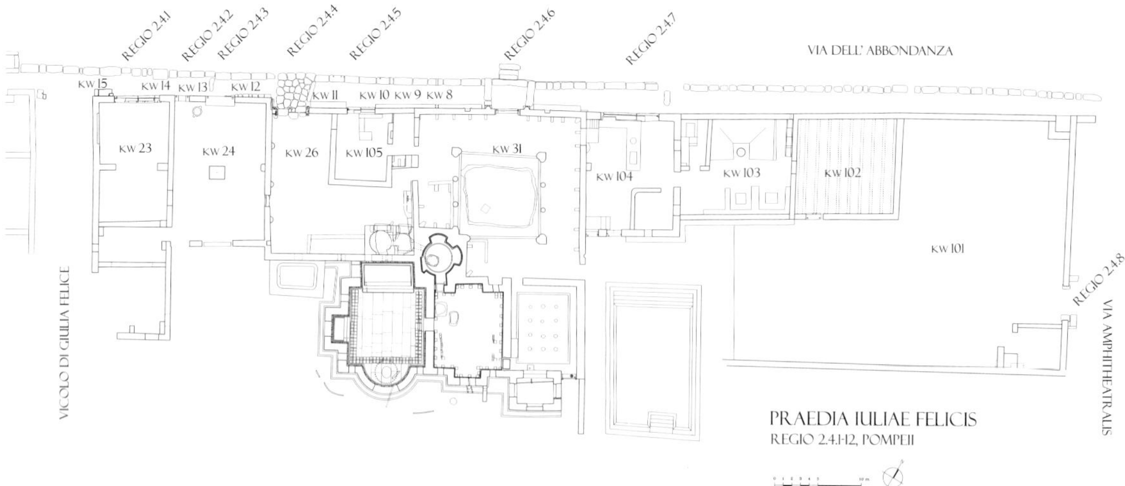

6.10. North façade of the *Praedia* with segments of wall labeled according to the numerical colocation employed by Karl Weber.

the Bourbons had extracted in precisely the same manner from the painted stucco adorning the interior rooms. The only example approaching the scale of these two panels is the entire wall of a room they had removed from the *Praedia* some months earlier, an undertaking they would repeat on only one other occasion in this period.[18]

The largest of the panels (MAN 4713) is actually made up of 19 fragments of stucco pieced back together to form an irregular grid (fig. 6.8). This vividly illustrates the crude method employed in the removal of such painted artifacts in these earliest years of the excavations. The outer margins of the desired product were scored before a chisel was used to undercut the surface stucco, separate it from the underlying masonry, and slice it off in pieces that, in this case, reached little more than one meter long and a half meter wide and likely only a few centimeters thick. If they had reinforced the surface first by, for example, adhering a sheet of linen cloth with paste or coating it with a consolidant like gesso, there is no surviving evidence for such a practice. The need to successfully extract and then transport the fragments to the royal museum in Portici for reassembly in their proper order must have influenced the decision to reduce such large surface areas into sections of a more manageable size, though at what point in the entire process these smaller sections occurred is unclear. As was the procedure with the figural paintings, the fragments subsequently were repositioned on a bed of mortar backed by a slab of slate and then the whole mounted in a wooden frame.[19]

Mounted together in this largest panel were the rental inscription (*CIL* 4.1136), four political *programmata*, and one other *dipinto* (*CIL* 4.1137–4.1141).[20] The pattern of the grid shows that the excavators had taken little account of the lines of text, cutting their way randomly through letters and splitting one part of a *dipinto* off from another to produce regular sections of a manageable size (fig. 6.8). Yet, this had the felicitous consequence of showing that all these *dipinti* were bound together as a unit, proving that this mounted panel is not a montage of inscriptions removed from different areas of the façade, as might be expected from their separate listings in the Bourbon records.[21] The same is true of the second largest panel (MAN 4672) containing the texts of six *programmata* (*CIL* 4.1145–4.1150) cut down in a somewhat more regular grid of eleven sections, which again take no account of the text of the inscriptions (fig. 6.9). The other three surviving panels removed during the Bourbon-era excavations of the north façade were significantly smaller in size, made up of fewer fragments, and contained only one or two inscriptions each. The two smaller of these are, however, in markedly worse states of preservation today.

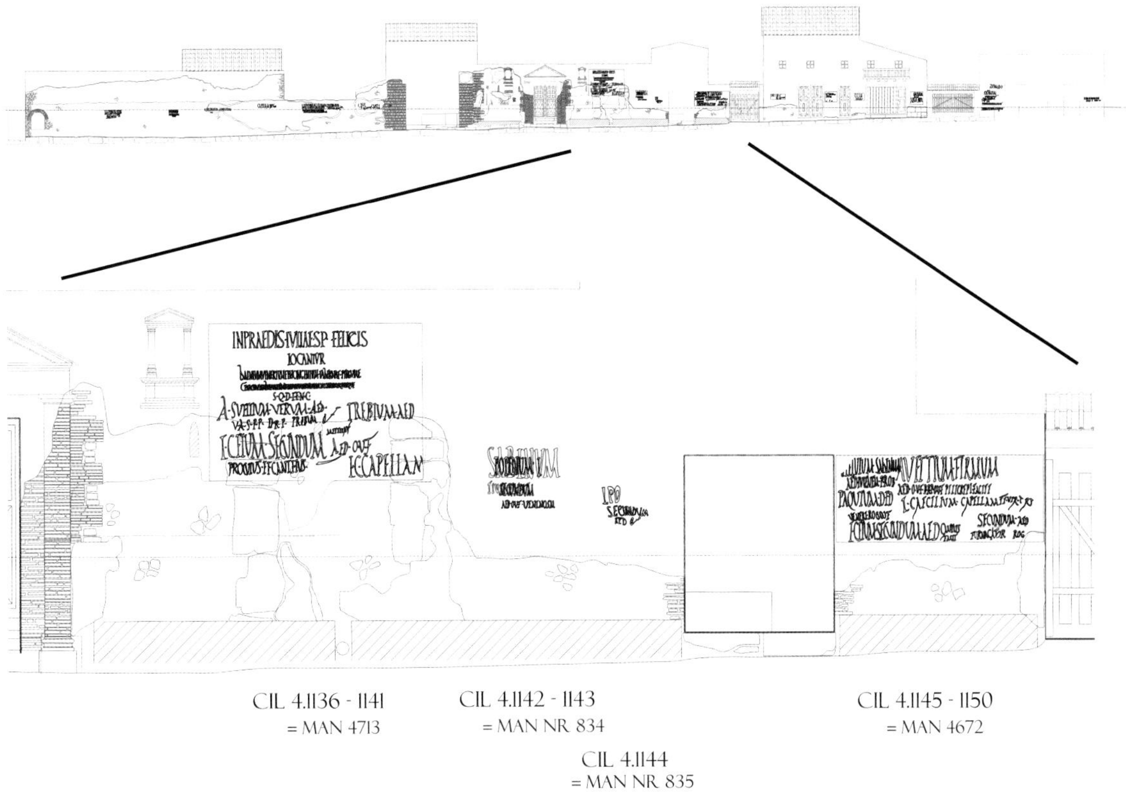

6.11. The provenance of the *programmata* from the central portion of the north façade (*CIL* 4.1136–1150).

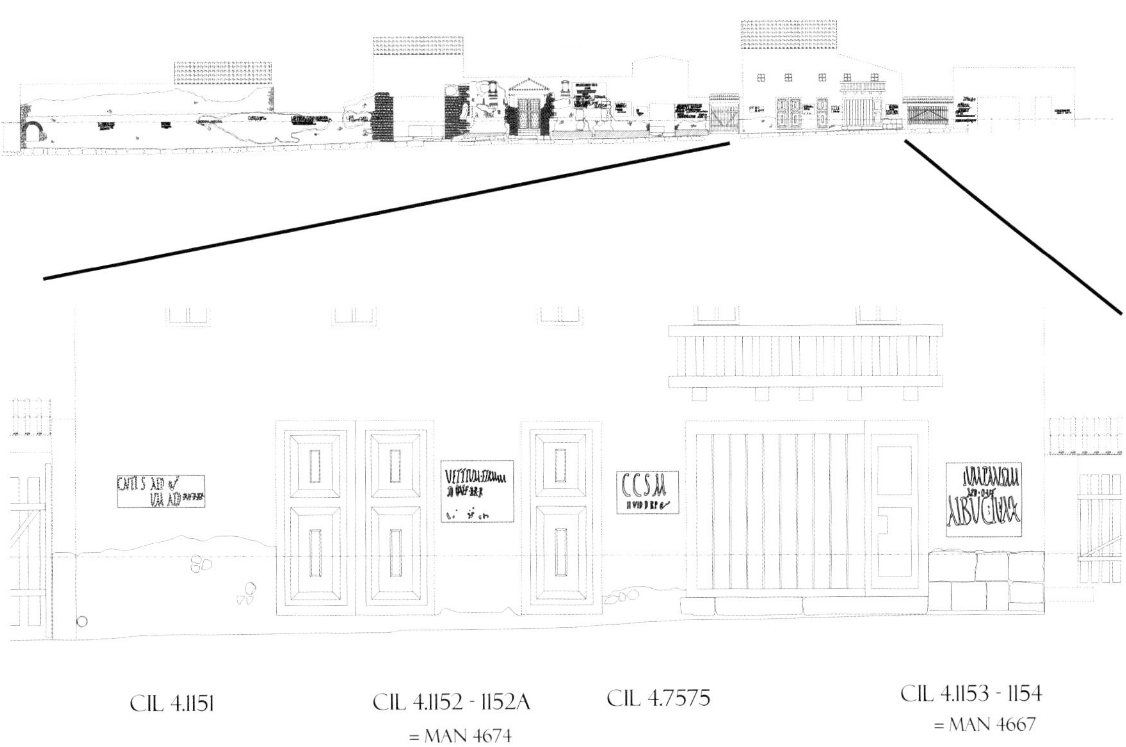

6.12. The provenance of the *programmata* from the west end of the north façade (*CIL* 4.1151–1154).

6.13. Left image: MAN 4674 containing *CIL* 1152–1152a. Right image: Tracing based on Rosini 1797, plate 12.4.

That the large panels consisted of *dipinti* from a single section of wall is further confirmed by the fact that their dimensions all conform to those given in the excavation daybooks. These measurements appear to have been taken in the field prior to the removal of the *dipinti* and therefore reflect the dimensions of the desired product, not always what was ultimately acquired. But in this case the two correspond. The dimensions, in turn, facilitate the process of restoring them to their proper location on the façade, given the limitations imposed by the spaces on the available walls. Moreover, the structural remains can serve as further guideposts for relocating the *dipinti* since the process of removing them had damaged the façade's masonry and stucco to varying degrees. In some cases the masonry remained unscathed and only the stucco applied on top of the masonry, on which the *dipinti* had been painted, was sliced off; in others, the masonry was so heavily compromised that it later collapsed.[22]

The width of the second largest panel (MAN 4672), for example, corresponds closely to the width of a narrow stretch of wall between the wide doors to one of the small shops (*Regio* II.iv.5; KW 105a) and an open courtyard (*Regio* II.iv.4; KW 27): 2.65 meters for the panel and 2.70 meters for the wall (fig. 6.10). Weber had in fact recorded the text of the inscriptions making up this panel in two different locations, on opposite sides of the latter of these doors, but again the manner in which the letters of the inscriptions overlap the seams between fragments proves that these inscriptions had been displayed together on this single section of wall (KW 11) (fig. 6.11).[23] The extraction of these inscriptions likely contributed to the destruction of the masonry: virtually the entire current wall is a reconstruction of the 1950s. Similarly, the provenance (KW 8 and KW 9) given on Weber's plans for the *dipinti* on the first and largest panel (MAN 4713) corresponds nicely with a section of the façade which the excavation photographs show had lost the upper portion of its masonry along with a substantial patch of stucco from the surviving lower portion: a neat horizontal margin along the top of the stucco marks the point where the upper stucco had been peeled off. Missing too is the section of wall between this largest panel and the door to the small shop. Weber documented the removal of three inscriptions from here (*CIL* 4.1142–4.1144) and this, combined with its shoddy construction, led to the destruction of much of this wall. In this case, these were cut down as two panels, with two *programmata* overlapping on the first one and a single *programma* on the second (fig. 6.4).[24]

Only five *dipinti* were found on the westernmost part of the north façade, which comprised four sections of wall separated by two wide and one narrow door openings (fig. 6.12). The masonry here had collapsed almost entirely by the 1950s, and was completely reconstructed after

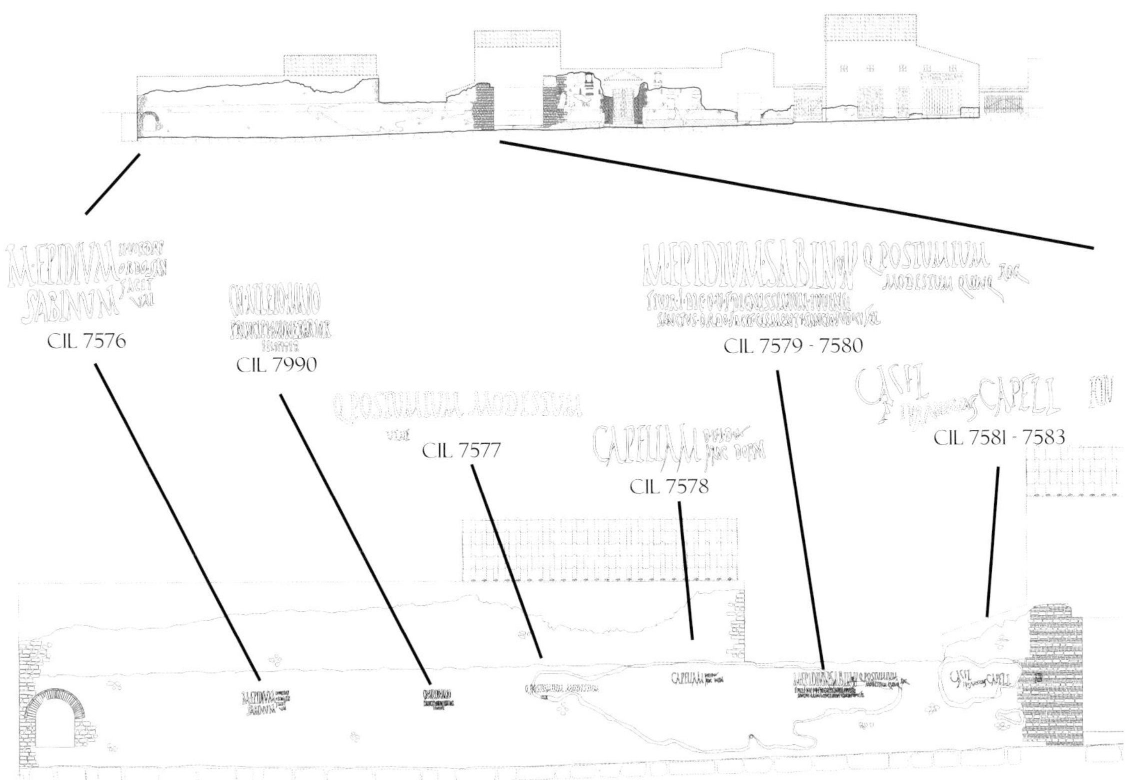

6.14. The *dipinti* on the eastern half of the north facade (*CIL* 4.7576–7583, 7990).

the excavations of that decade, so the excavation records provide the only clues for restoring these to their proper location. Of the five, four were removed by the Bourbon excavators while one had been documented but left *in situ* in the 1930s. The latter (*CIL* 4.7575) is no longer extant and because it consisted of abbreviations alone must not have been of any interest to the Bourbons: it appears to have been inventoried in the excavation records but they did not remove it.[25] It must have occupied the narrow jamb between the door to the shop (KW 23; *Regio* II.iv.1) at the northwest corner and the narrow door (*Regio* II.iv.2) into the building's main vestibule (KW 24) since no other finds are recorded from here. The remaining four were distributed on the other three sections of wall. One *programma* (*CIL* 4.1151), already scarcely readable when discovered and also now lost, must have been posted on the eastern section.[26] A second (*CIL* 4.1152) was cut down, engraved by Rosini, and still survives, though it is in very poor condition (MAN 4674) (fig. 6.13).[27] The last pair of *programmata* (*CIL* 4.1153–4.1154) had been painted one above the other. These too were first documented in the field by the excavators, whose transcription provides a remarkably accurate copy of the text, even if they failed to differentiate between the size of the lettering. The panel containing these two was also engraved by Rosini and is extant (MAN 4667) (fig. 6.5).[28] Weber's documents indicate the provenance of the first of these was the section of wall between the two doors (*Regio* II.iv.3 and *Regio* II.iv.2; KW 13 and KW 14) into the *Praedia*'s main vestibule (KW 24). He assigned the second to the narrow wall at the building's northwest corner (KW 15). The dimensions of each allow them to be easily accommodated on these walls. As elsewhere, their exact position on these segments of walls relative to the ground and to the adjacent door openings is impossible to determine, but the *scriptores* tended to paint their *dipinti* at eye-level and above.

These clusters of *programmata* accumulated over several years, with new ones added with each election cycle. While most of the examples in Pompeii were painted on whatever space was available, many overlapped earlier ones, either partially or by being painted on a new white background that cancelled out an older one. Studies of the manner in which these relate to one another have led to the creation of a rough chronology of the years in which specific candidates sought election to the available annual seats, the two *duoviri* and two *aediles*. Some clearly date from the early first century but most fall within the last years of the city, specifically the Flavian period from the years 72 to 79. While the proposed chronology for the slates of candidates in these final years has not been universally embraced, it does provide a working framework for reconstructing the process by which these *dipinti* came to be layered on the *Praedia*'s façade.[29]

The reconstruction of their placement on the entire north façade shows that, apart from the two large clusters of postings that came to make up the two largest panels (MAN 4713 and MAN 4672), most stood in isolation. This is especially the case on the long expanse of featureless, high wall making up the eastern half of the façade where the *dipinti* were either spaced far apart or placed right next to each other (fig. 6.14). This may reflect the fact that there was less traffic along this stretch of the Via dell'Abbondanza, or that traffic was more transitory and not prone to idle, as it would in front of the shops and more public spaces of the western half. Apart from this tendency to cluster around the most heavily trafficked areas, there is no clear pattern to the arrangement of *dipinti* on the western half. The earliest ones for 72 and 73 were painted higher on the walls and all those for candidates in 76—at least two for Lucius Ceius Secundus for *aedile* and two for Lucius Caecilius Capella for *duovir*—were among the lowest on the walls.[30] But late inscriptions also surround early ones, and posters supporting the same candidate for the same office can be in close proximity.[31] There are only two examples of overlapping posters. One supporting the candidate Lucius Popidius Secundus in the year 79 (*CIL* 4.1143) was painted directly over one for the candidate Marcus Epidius Sabinus dated to 77 (*CIL* 4.1142), leaving only faint traces visible underneath. The circumstances behind this particular overpainting are unclear, though many of Secundus's other *dipinti* overlap or overlay those of other candidate's throughout the city (fig. 6.4). Another *programma* advocating the election of Cnaeus Helvius Sabinus dated to 79 (*CIL* 4.1145), the year of the eruption, slightly overlaps one of the earliest, supporting Aulus Vettius Firmus, from 72 (*CIL* 4.1147).

The overall picture is not exactly one of fervid political activity, with proponents of one candidate seeking to muscle out another. In contrast, façades just up the street from the *Praedia* were covered with *dipinti* almost in their entirety. On the *Praedia*, the process of accretion was quite gradual, with only six posters painted between the years 72 and 75, a total of six in the year 76 alone, and the remaining twelve dating from the last three years of the city. In all, 26 political posters supporting 15 candidates were painted on the full 68.50 meters of the *Praedia*'s north façade, yielding an average of only one poster every 2.65 meters, a relatively low frequency for a façade on this busy main thoroughfare.[32]

On the basis of the chronology of the election posters, portions of the stucco on the *Praedia*'s façade can date no earlier than 72. This may only be valid for the stucco itself because the masonry of the bath complex, for example, indicates it was operational by the early first century AD. It cannot be ruled out that such façade stucco was subject to routine renewal as it succumbed to the elements and as renovations and additions to a building were made. This should explain at least in part the two clusters of *dipinti* making up the largest panels, with their *programmata* spanning the years 72 to 79. The first of these occupies the northwest corner of the bath complex, while the other fills the west façade of the small shop to the west (*Regio* 2.4.5; KW 105a). Both clusters are directly above fixed masonry benches built against the façade in order to accommodate patrons, but that these *dipinti* were concentrated in high traffic areas cannot be the sole explanation since the bench extends the entire length of the baths' façade. A more likely explanation is that the east façade of the shop running between these two sections of the façade was rebuilt later as a result of modifications to the shop's interior.

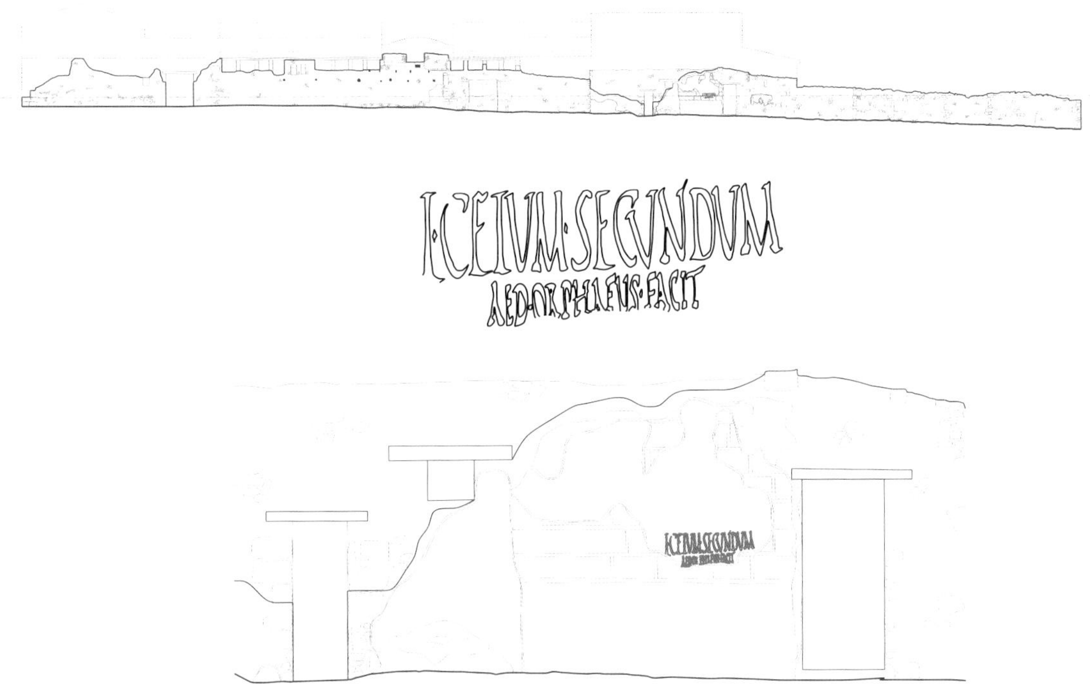

6.15. The *programma* of Orphaeus in support of L. Ceius Secundus revealed under the final coat of stucco on the west façade outside the entrance (*Regio* II.iv.10) to the second floor apartments.

Not only does the pattern of painted stucco here differ from that on the baths, but also the earliest of the three *programmata* dates to 77. The fact that the other two are for the same candidate in 79 seems to confirm that this section of wall only became prime realty for the sign painters late in the city's life. On the other hand, a single *programma* (*CIL* 4.1152) was painted strategically in the center of the western portion of this façade in 72, while the remaining wall space was respected until four *programmata* were posted in 78 and 79.

This process of alteration and renovation is further attested by an example of a *dipinto* that came to light many years after the site had been excavated and restored. This had been posted on the west façade immediately outside a rear entrance (*Regio* II.iv.10) into the *Praedia* that led to a stair to the rented apartments arranged on the second storey. The poster called upon an individual named Orphaeus to support the election of Lucius Ceius Secundus, the candidate for *aedile* in 76 also named in at least two *programmata* on the north façade.[33] But here the text is of less interest than its context, for unlike those on the north façade this had been painted on the initial rough layer of plaster that had been applied during the course of renovations being made to this façade (fig. 6.15). This work must have extended into the campaign season of 76, but the lack of a finish coat of stucco did not inhibit the sign painters. What must have made this location attractive, and made painting a professional campaign poster here financially worthwhile, was the expectation of high visibility, even if only for a short time. This, in turn, indicates that this entrance to the *Praedia*, though off the main thoroughfare down a narrow alley, received a good deal of foot traffic.[34] Soon thereafter the *dipinto* was stuccoed over and remained concealed for over 1900 years until the winter rains of 1998 caused the thinner finish coat to buckle and fall away.

The finish stucco covering the *dipinto* naming Orphaeus had remained free of political posters in the last three years of the city but it came to be cluttered with graffiti. Unfortunately, all of these were carried off together when the finish coat came down. Most consisted of the names of individuals who, like Kilroy, were simply recording their presence here: Habitus, whose graffiti appears elsewhere in the *Praedia*; Pithia Prima, a woman idling here along with someone nicknamed Sparitundiolus, perhaps a gladiator; Scutularius, likely the nickname of another gladiator, together with his girl Africana; and Popidius, whose attempts to reinvent himself by taking on various new careers was mocked in one of the longest graffiti in Pompeii.[35] Many must have been scrawled by the occupants of the apartments, but several may have been addressed to patrons entering the *Praedia* from the direction of the amphitheater. The overall tone is one of the exchange of banter between acquaintances, but these graffiti nevertheless are important documents for the light they shed on the *Praedia*'s occupants and patrons, and for illuminating how an entrance such as this one had become a focal point of social interaction.

Even some of the otherwise formulaic political posters from the north façade help to reanimate the *Praedia* by being addressed to specific individuals and groups. One group identified as the *Pilicrepi*, evidently ball players who may have practiced or performed in the baths, are asked to support Aulus Vettius Firmus for aedile in one of the earliest *dipinti* (*CIL* 4.1147). Another group calling themselves the *Veneri*, a name perhaps derived from that of the baths and applied generically to the baths' patrons, lent their support to at least one candidate.[36] Two call upon Proculus and Canthus to help elect Lucius Ceius Secundus. The location of these suggests they were proprietors of one or two of the *Praedia*'s shops. In another, posted outside the room containing the baths' furnace, Secundus's campaign is supported by the *fornacator*, the stoker of the furnace and doubtless a popular character in the neighborhood for his role in maintaining the baths (fig. 6.9). These examples illustrate the importance of understanding the inscriptions' proper context and underscore how this virtual process of pasting the façades back together is essential for reconstructing the role of the *Praedia* in the politics and society of Pompeii and establishing their importance as a center of neighborhood life in this corner of the city.

This reconstruction calls attention to two distinctive aspects of the palimpsest model not encountered in the other studies in this volume. The first is methodological. Discerning the layers and understanding their temporal relationships is crucial, as it is in most of the other cases illustrated here. Even more fundamental, however, is the need to reconstruct virtually the fragmentary evidence created by the several excavators of the site and then determine how the reintegrated wholes related both to one another and to important features within the architectural fabric of the site, like the baths, the shops, and the apartments. It is as if a palimpsest manuscript has been unbound and all its individual pages torn into fragments. Before the palimpsest itself can be comprehended, the individual pages must first be reassembled and then their proper relative sequence established. Only when the text can be read in its proper sequence—that is, only when the graffiti and the *dipinti* can be read in their proper spatial and architectural context—can the palimpsest reveal its full meaning.

The second aspect illuminated by the *Praedia* has to do with the question of intentionality. When the buildings were originally constructed, no one intended that they should bear a specific programmatic meaning generated through the inscribing of graffiti and *dipinti* on their façades. As cumulative precipitates of everyday life and social interaction added in the natural course of the *Praedia*'s use, they document the nature of these past interactions. *Programmata* did not accumulate randomly but were often concentrated at points of high visibility, where people tended to congregate. In the case of the *Praedia*, the painters of later *programmata* generally respected earlier ones, with only two *dipinti* overlapping older ones and two being covered over entirely. As a consequence, the *Praedia*'s façades bear witness to the names of candidates and their supporters accrued over almost a decade, suggesting that here, as elsewhere in Pompeii, there was a conscious desire to build a record of these campaigns without regard to the winners and losers. This process not only speaks vividly to the nature of political life in the city, it also rescues from oblivion the names of Pompeians who moved through the spaces of the *Praedia*, sponsoring and reading these political posters while engaged in the routines of their daily lives.

Notes

1 The *dipinti* and graffiti from Pompeii were published in the fourth volume of the *Corpus Inscriptionum Latinarum* (hereafter *CIL* 4, followed by the relevant inscription number). The Pompeian *dipinti* numbered *CIL* 4.1 to 4.9986 were recently re-edited, with new readings and updated bibliography in Weber et al. 2011.

2 The principal studies of the political *programmata* are Franklin 1980; Mouritsen 1989; and Chiavia 2002. Among the many more specialized studies, but those most relevant to this inquiry, are Castrén 1975; Franklin 1978; Biundo 1996; Mouritsen 1999; and Biundo 2003.

3 The modern "address" for the *Praedia* is *Regio* II.iv.1–12. This identifies it as the fourth city block in the city's second region with twelve entrances providing access to the structures within the block. The entrance to the baths is at *Regio* II.iv.6; those to the small shops at *Regio* II.iv.1, *Regio* II.iv.5, and *Regio* II.iv.7; and the apartments at *Regio* II.iv.10.

4 For an overview of these Bourbon-era excavations, see Parslow 1995, 107–22.

5 *CIL* 4.1136: *In · Praedis · Iuliae · Sp(urii) · f(iliae) · Felicis / locantur / Balneum · Venerium · et · Nongentum · Tabernae · Pergulae / Cenacula · ex · Idibus · Aug(ustis) · primis · in · Idus · Aug(ustas) · sextas · annos · continuos · quinque / S · Q · D · L · E · N · C* · "In the properties of Julia Felix, daughter of 'Spurius,' are available for rent the *venerium* and *nongentum* baths, shops, lofts, and second storey apartments, for five years from the Ides of August." In this case "Spurius" is not the name of her father, as would be expected in such formulaic expressions, but identifies her as free-born but without a known father. The multivalent meanings of *venerium* and *nongentum* complicates their translation beyond what can be dealt with here but they likely were intended to evoke the sophisticated nature of both the facilities and the class of clientele they served (see below, note 36). The seven-letter abbreviation at the end has not been satisfactorily deciphered; it likely provides instructions on how interested parties should proceed.

6 These consisted of eight *programmata* (*CIL* 4.7576–7583) and one *dipinto* (*CIL* 4.7990) offering greetings to Cnaeus Alleius Nigidius Maius, *princeps munerariorum*. The inscriptions were published originally in Della Corte 1936, 336–43.

7 The inscriptions were published in Della Corte 1958, 123–32, 159, 162–63, 168, 172, 178. An overview of the discoveries was provided by the principal excavator, Amedeo Maiuri, in two short articles: Maiuri 1954, 285–99; and Maiuri 1983, 51–54 (originally published in 1958). I am completing a monographic study of the *Praedia*.

8 The documentation is discussed in Parslow 1989, 37–48; and Parslow 1996, 115–32.

9 The field notes with the transcribed texts of two *programmata* (*CIL* 4.1143 and 4.1153) are archived in the library of the Società Napoletana di Storia Patria, "Rapporti," between 31 January and 7 February 1756, *Fondo Cuomo* Ms. 20–5–3, Naples, Italy. An edited transcription of all the relevant records for the Bourbon excavations was published in Fiorelli 1860, 38–43 (8 February to 28 August 1756). See Parslow 1995, 282–90, for the text of the legend to Weber's preliminary draft of his plan of the *Praedia* (Museo Archeologico Nazionale di Napoli, *Archivio Disegni* 71), and Fiorelli 1860, 95–101, for an edited text of the legend to Weber's final published plan of the *Praedia* (Museo Archeologico Nazionale di Napoli, *Archivio Disegni* 72). On both plans, the relevant *dipinti* are listed under entry numbers KW 8 to KW 15 in the legends and on the plan.

10 Of the two missing panels, one contained two overlapping *programmata* (*CIL* 4.1142 and 4.1143) and the other probably consisted of two *programmata* as well, one above the other, but was published as only a single *programma* (*CIL* 4.1151).

11 Rosini 1797, 63–66, plates 4, 10.2, 12.3, and 12.4.

12 The final site plan, by R. Oliva, was first published in Maiuri 1954, 285–99, and remains the most commonly reproduced, despite minor errors.

13 Della Corte held various positions in the excavations, ultimately rising from inspector to director. Among his important contributions were his work to identify the occupants of houses and shops throughout the city on the basis of the *dipinti*, graffiti and engraved bronze stamps; see Della Corte 1965. His personal field notes are archived in the Getty Research Institute (Halsted B. Vander Poel Campania Collection, Matteo Della Corte Papers, Box 53, Folder 2 [5 September 1951 to 27 July 1952]); copies exist as well in the archives of the Soprintendenza Archeologica di Pompei. For cautionary remarks on Della Corte as a source, see Mouritsen 1989, 23–27.

14 The extant photographs of the graffiti have been published in Varone 2012, 107–12 (for the *Praedia*).

15 The extant photographs of the *dipinti* have been published in Varone and Stefani 2009, 209–20 (for the *Praedia*).

16 The earliest photograph of the north façade was taken in January 1935, and provides a long view of the façade from the entrance to the shop at *Regio* II.iv.7 toward the northwest corner (Soprintendenza Archeologica di Pompei, Archivio Fotografico C2098). A second photograph that must have been taken a short time later reveals how rapidly the structures began to deteriorate; for this (Soprintendenza Archeologica di Pompei, Archivio Fotografico A378) and a selection of photographs taken during the 1950s excavations, see Pugliese Carratelli and Baldassarre 1990, 184–310.

17 Weber inventoried these on his plans under KW 8 to KW 15, which covers roughly 26.00 meters from the northwest corner of the building east to near its midpoint.

18 The south wall of the *tablinum* (Room 92) was removed in the last week of July 1755. The painting is now MAN 8598 and measures 4.74 meters wide and

2.98 meters high. The other paintings removed from the *Praedia* range from as small as 0.10 meters square to 2.34 meters wide and 1.00 meters high. MAN 8594, removed on 13 October 1759 from a house on the opposite side of Pompeii (*Regio* VI.17, *Insula Occidentalis*, 41), measures 2.94 meters wide by 2.10 meters high.

19 While paintings certainly were damaged or destroyed by this crude process, the overall rate of success is remarkable. For the process, the precise details of which remain somewhat obscure, see Rossignani 1967, 7–43; and D'Alconzo 2002, esp. 15–45.

20 *CIL* 4.1139 was read as *Metelli cf*, a name not associated with any political candidates in this period and so is not considered one of the *programmata* here.

21 MAN 4713 is 2.69 meters long by 1.93 meters high, which closely matches the inscriptions documented as removed on 27 March 1756, which measured 2.77 by 1.98 meters. This is the same as Rosini 1797, plate 4.

22 The same pattern of damage is true for the wall paintings, though those of small dimensions were more often gouged out of the wall, leaving only a hole in the masonry.

23 MAN 4672 is 2.65 meters wide by 1.07 meters high; the fragment removed on 27 March 1756 measured 2.70 meters wide by 1.11 meters high. Weber had located the last of these *dipinti* (*CIL* 4.1150) to the east (KW 12) of the wide doorway to the courtyard while placing all the others to the west (KW 11).

24 The first panel, containing *CIL* 4.1142–1143, bears an old inventory number in the MAN (NR 834) and appears to be lost; the reconstruction of the text offered here is based on details provided in the documentation and is a composite of lettering copied from the extant inscriptions (fig. 6.4). Among these documents is the copy of the text made in the field by one of the excavators, the first line of which has a smaller "P" overlapping a larger "S," thus showing how the later inscription of "Popidium" (*CIL* 4.1143) was painted directly over that of "Sabinum" (*CIL* 4.1142). Letters and markings at the end of the line are also likely to be traces of the earlier inscription. This transcription is also the source of the odd "veninosm," the meaning of which remains a puzzle because it is either incomplete or incorrectly copied. According to the Bourbon inventories, MAN NR 834 measured 1.32 meters wide and 1.10 meters high. The second panel (*CIL* 4.1144) also has an old inventory number (MAN NR 835) but survives; for a photograph, see Varone and Stefani 2009, 211 (D110634 [a. 2004]). MAN NR 835 measures 1.10 meters wide and 0.73 meters high. Combined, these two fit easily on this section of wall, which measures 2.95 meters wide.

25 Fiorelli 1860, 137 (21 August 1756): an entry documenting an inscription measuring 0.53 meters by 0.79 meters with the letters *CCSJL*. The full text of the two-lined *CIL* 4.7575 is *C(aius) C(alventius) S(ittius) M(agnus) / IIv(ir) i(ure) d(icundo) d(ignum) r(ei) p(ublicae) o(ro) v(os) f(aciatis)*. In publishing this inscription, Della Corte recorded only its overall height (0.57 meters) and the height of the lettering in the first (0.30 meters) and second (0.10 meters) lines; the text was published in the standard font used in the *CIL*. Consequently, the appearance of this *programma* has been reconstructed here on the basis of the information provided in the published sources and represents a composite of lettering copied from the extant inscriptions. The section of wall on which it was painted had collapsed sometime between the 1930s and the 1950s excavations.

26 The documents indicate *CIL* 4.1151 measured 1.14 meters wide and 0.40 meters high. The text and appearance of this *programma* has also been reconstructed on the basis of the available evidence and is a composite of lettering copied from the extant inscriptions.

27 MAN 4674 measures 0.94 meters wide and 0.77 meters high. For the engraving, see Rosini 1797, plate 12.4; for a photograph, see Varone and Stefani 2009, 205 (D110638 [a. 2004]), where it is inexplicably catalogued under the property to the west (*Regio* II.iii). MAN 4674 shows traces of letters in the lower left portion which were published as *AROF) A6* (*CIL* 4.1152a). This might be another heavily abbreviated *programma* but because its exact contents are unknown, it has been left out of consideration here.

28 MAN 4667 is 0.96 meters wide by 0.84 meters high. For the engraving, see Rosini 1797, plate 12.3; for photographs, see Varone and Stefani 2009, 209 (D95571 [a. 1997], D110640 [a. 2004]).

29 Franklin 1980, 33–58; Mouritsen 1989, 37–44; Chiavia 2002, 126–40, esp. 134–35, table 29. Chiavia's chronology parallels Franklin's in the early and late years; Mouritsen groups them all as "Flavian" without breaking them down into annual slates of candidates. On the sign painters themselves, see Franklin 1978, 54–74.

30 *CIL* 4.1147 supporting Aulus Vettius Firmus for *aedile* is dated to 72 and is at the upper right of MAN 4672; *CIL* 4.1138 supporting Aulus Trebius Valens for *aedile* in 73 is at the upper right of MAN 4713. Lucius Ceius Secundus is supported in *CIL* 4.1140 by Proculus and Cantus, perhaps the proprietors of the shop at *Regio* II.iv.5 (KW 105a) and by Cantus alone in *CIL* 4.1149. A third (*CIL* 4.1150) with only the cognomen SECUNDUM, whom the *fornacator* (stoker of the bath's furnaces) supported for the office of *aedile*, might be either this candidate or Lucius Popidius Secundus, a candidate for *aedile* in 79. Lucius Caecilius Capella's *programma* (*CIL* 4.1141) for *aedile* stands to the right of Secundus's (*CIL* 4.1140) in MAN 4713 and above and to the right in *CIL* 4.1148 in MAN 4672.

31 The *programma* supporting Cnaeus Helvius Sabinus for *aedile* in 79 (*CIL* 4.1145), for example, appears at the upper left of MAN 4672. Two *programmata* (*CIL* 4.1143, *CIL* 4.1144) supporting Lucius Popidius Secundus for *aedile* were painted side-by-side to the east of the entrance to the shop at *Regio* II.iv.5 (KW 105a).

32 A good example is the famously cluttered façade (now largely destroyed) of the House of Aulus Tre-

bius Valens, himself a candidate for *aedile* in 73, at *Regio* III.ii.1, with 23 *dipinti* on roughly 16.00 meters, or one *dipinto* per 0.70 meters; for photographs, see Varone and Stefani 2009, 232–40 (fig. 6.1). The façade of *Regio* III.vii, directly across from the *Praedia*, had 27 *dipinti* on 45.00 meters, yielding one for every 1.66 meters; see Varone and Stefani 2009, 286–94.

33 Orphaeus is an otherwise unattested supporter (*rogator*) of political candidates, and he does not appear in other inscriptions from Pompeii.

34 Confirmation of this high volume of foot traffic is provided by a second *programma* posted directly opposite this on the otherwise blank façade of *Regio* II.iii. This (*CIL* 4.9890) advocated the election of Quintus Postumius to the office of *quinquennial duovir* in 75, an important office held only once every five years. Though only his name is preserved here, two other *programmata* supporting him were posted on the east portion of the *Praedia*'s north façade (*CIL* 4.7577 and *CIL* 4.7580).

35 Habitus: *CIL* 4.10160 and 4.10161, the latter a multi-line text written in red chalk and extending 2.85 meters long with some of the letters of the first line reaching 0.20 meters high; Pithia Prima: *CIL* 4.10153 and 4.10157; Pithia Prima with Sparitundiolus: *CIL* 4.10151, 4.10154, and 4.10156; Scutularius with Africana: *CIL* 4.10155; Popidius: *CIL* 4.10150 and 4.10152, the latter's 206 letters were scratched into the façade's stucco with a sharp point and measured 2.00 meters long with letters 0.055 meters high.

36 The *Veneri* clearly advocated the election of Publius Paquius to *duovir* in 74 (*CIL* 4.1146), though the reading *Veninosm* (...) in the *dipinto* supporting Lucius Popidius Secundus for *aedile* in 79 (*CIL* 4.1143) is questionable. The precise meaning of the name applied to the bath complex, the *balneum venerium et nongentum*, in the rental inscription (*CIL* 4.1136), and whether the patrons took their name from the baths or vice versa, is well beyond the scope of this paper.

Bibliography

Biundo, Raffaella. 2003. "La propaganda elettorale a Pompei: La funzione e il valore dei *programmata* nell' organizzazione della campagna," *Athenaeum* 91, no. 1, 53–116.

—. 1996. "I rogatores nei programmata elettorali pompeiani," *Cahiers du Centre Glotz* 7, 179–88.

Castrén, Paavo. 1975. *Ordo populusque Pompeianus: Polity and society in Roman Pompeii* (Acta Instituti Romani Finlandiae, 8). Rome: Bardi.

Chiavia, Catherine. 2002. *Programmata: Manifesti elettorali nella colonia romana di Pompei.* Turin: S. Zamorani.

D'Alconzo, Paola. 2002. *Picturae excisae: Conservazione e restauro dei dipinti ercolanesi e pompeiani tra XVIII e XIX secolo* (Studi della Soprintendenza archeologica di Pompei, 8). Rome: L'Erma di Bretschneider.

Della Corte, Matteo. 1965. *Case ed abitanti di Pompei.* Naples: Fausto Fiorentino.

—. 1958. "Pompeii: Iscrizioni scoperte nel quinquennio 1951–56," *Notizie degli Scavi di Antichità* ser. 8.2, 123–32, 159, 162–63, 168, 172, 178.

—. 1936. "Pompei: Nuove scoperte epigrafiche," *Notizie degli Scavi di Antichità* n.s. 12, 336–43.

Fiorelli, Giuseppe, ed. 1860. *Pompeianarvm antiqvitatvm historia qvam ex cod. mss. et a schedis divrnisqve R. Alcvbierre.* Naples: n.p.

Franklin, James L. 1980. *Pompeii: The electoral programmata, campaigns and politics,* AD *71–79* (Papers and monographs of the American Academy in Rome, 28). Rome: American Academy in Rome.

—. 1978. "Notes on Pompeian Prosopography: *Programmatum scriptores*," *Cronache Pompeiane* 4, 54–74.

Maiuri, Amedeo. 1983. "Giulia Felice, gentildonna pompeiana," in *Pompei ed Ercolano fra case e abitanti*, ed. Amedeo Maiuri. Florence: Giunti Martello, 51–54.

—. 1954. "Due iscrizioni veneree pompeiane," in *Saggi di varia antichità*, ed. Amedeo Maiuri. Venice: Neri Pozza, 285–99.

Mouritsen, Henrik. 1999. "Electoral campaigning in Pompeii: A reconsideration," *Athenaeum* 87, no. 2, 515–23.

—. 1989. *Elections, magistrates and municipal élite: Studies in Pompeian epigraphy* (Analecta Romana Instituti Danici, Supplementum 15). Rome: L'Erma di Bretschneider.

Parslow, Christopher. 1996. "Additional documents illustrating the Bourbon excavations in the Praedia Iuliae Felicis at Pompeii," *Rivista di Studi Pompeiani* 7, 115–32.

—. 1995. *Rediscovering Antiquity: Karl Weber and the excavation of Herculaneum, Pompeii, and Stabiae.* New York: Cambridge University Press.

—. 1989. "Documents illustrating the Bourbon excavations in the Praedia Iuliae Felicis at Pompeii," *Rivista di Studi Pompeiani* 2, 37–48.

Pugliese Carratelli, Giovanni, and Ida Baldassarre. 1990. *Pompei, pitture e mosaici.* Rome: Istituto della Enciclopedia Italiana.

Rosini, Carlo Maria. 1797. *Dissertationis isagogicæ ad Herculanensivm volvminvm explanationem.* Naples: Ex Regia Typographia.

Rossignani, Maria Pia. 1967. "Saggio sui restauri settecenteschi ai dipinti di Ercolano e Pompei," in *Contributi dell'Istituto di Archeologia Università Cattolica, Milano* 1, 7–43.

Varone, Antonio. 2012. *Titulorum graphio exaratorvm qvi in C.I.L. vol. IV collecti svnt imagines, I–II* (Studi della Soprintendenza Archeologica di Pompei, 31). Rome: L'Erma di Bretschneider.

Varone, Antonio, and Grete Stefani. 2009. *Titulorum pictorum Pompeianorum qui in CIL vol. IV collecti sunt: Imagines* (Studi della Soprintendenza archeologica di Pompei, 29). Rome: L'Erma di Bretschneider.

Weber, Volker, Antonio Varone, Roberta Marchionni, and Janaeds Kepartova, eds. 2011. *Corpus Inscriptionum Latinarum: Inscriptiones parietariae Pompeianae*, vol. 4, suppl. pars 4, fasc. 1: *Ad titulos pictos spectantem.* Berlin: De Gruyter.

Zangemeister, Karl, ed. 1871. *Corpus Inscriptionum Latinarum*, vol. 4: *Inscriptiones parietariae Pompeianae Herculanenses Stabianae.* Berlin: G. Reimerum.

Chapter 7
Early Modern Palimpsests and Medieval Portal Sculpture: Three Case Studies in the History of Iconoclasm and Religious Transformation

Clark Maines

For about a year during the French Revolution, citizens of France engaged in corporate acts of iconoclasm, systematically mutilating and hammering away monumental sculpted images on the exteriors of churches throughout the nation.[1] The recently revealed, mutilated western portal of the priory church of Saint-Pierre-des-Minimes in Compiègne provides us with insight into the visual impact that Revolutionary iconoclasm had during the 1790s (figs. 7.1 and 7.2).[2] Because this portal was completely masked by another building during much of the twentieth century, the Revolutionary damage appears fresh today and its effect is enhanced by the substantial remains of paint on the vestiges of sculpture that survive and will help us understand the portals in this study.

Physically on, or near, this mutilated iconography, Revolutionary groups painted or carved textual palimpsests that announced the presence, within the buildings, of new rational cults that were to replace, however briefly, the "superstitions" and "fanaticism" of Roman Catholicism.[3]

The simpler of these palimpsests, *TEMPLE DE LA RAISON*, began to appear in autumn of 1793. One of them survives carved into the doorway arch of the west portal of the parish church of Saint-Loup in Bléneau (Yonne) (figs. 7.3 and 7.4). This inscription was itself mutilated, presumably when it, and the cult it announced, were superseded in spring/summer of 1794 by the more elaborate, *LE PEUPLE FRANÇOIS RECONNOIT L'ÊTRE SUPRÊME ET L'IMMORTALITÉ DE L'ÂME*. These words were taken from a decree of 7 May 1794 issued by the Convention, based on a speech given by Maximilien Robespierre (1758–94) as part of an attempt to mediate between the more abstract cult of Reason and the desires of the greater populace for some form of deity.[4] The issuance of the decree gives us a sure *terminus post quem* for imposition of this palimpsest on church façades and doorways.

It is worth observing that inscribing a tympanum or a doorway was hardly a new idea. Beyond the painted or carved inscriptions on banderoles held by sculpted and painted figures, the frames of tympana and the borders of doors of medieval churches of France were often inscribed. Church interiors were also replete with inscriptions, many of which are lost today.[5] The Revolutionary portal inscriptions can thus be thought to have played to citizens' expectations that were based in centuries of shared experience.

As we will see, mutilation of the monumental sculpture in church portals was part of a larger process that involved re-inscribing the sculpted surface with new texts and included purging church interiors of the signs of superstition and fanaticism as well as generating a body of new religious practice. Put another way, Revolutionary iconoclasm and the creation of palimpsestual inscriptions in the place of the medieval imagery was but one part of an attempt to transform the religious life and practice of the French people.

The time frame for much of Revolutionary iconoclasm can be quite accurately defined as extending from October 1793 to early autumn 1794, though there were certainly examples outside both ends of the frame.[6] Of what once were hundreds of monumental palimpsests, as few as thirty-one are known to survive on twenty-seven monuments, though more are known to have existed on the basis of municipal records.[7] These thirty-one Revolutionary inscriptions come from twenty different departments, another indication of their once widespread presence.

7.1. Priory church of Saint-Pierre-des-Minimes, Compiègne. View of the mutilated west portal.

7.2. Saint-Pierre-des-Minimes, detail of the west portal showing the present state of the tympanum, lintel, and figured archivolt.

Only five churches retain the earlier Temple of Reason inscription, while inscriptions of the Supreme Being survive on twenty-five.[8] The inscriptions appear on churches of every rank, from cathedrals like Clermont-Ferrand (Puy-de-Dome) and monasteries like Bassac (Charente) to parish churches like Saint-Martin in Ivry-la-Bataille (Eure) and Croixrault (Somme). Some of them were painted, like those at Monthiers (Aisne) and Houdan (Yvelines). Others were carved, like those at Dompierre-les-Tilleuls (Doubs) and Saint-Loup de Bléneau (Yonne).

This paper looks closely at the west portals of the collegiate church of Saint-Thomas de Cantorbéry in Crépy-en-Valois (Oise), the important parish church of Saint-Pierre in Gonesse, near Paris and the collegiate pilgrimage church of Notre-Dame-en-Vaux in Châlons-en-Champagne (formerly Châlons-sur-Marne). It does so from two perspectives. The first revalues the actions of what has been called "vandalism" to consider the positive aspects of religious reform.[9] The second examines the ways in which the social memory of Christian religious functions continued to exert a powerful influence during the French Revolution, both in the creation of a new rational religion, and in that religion's failure to attract and sustain a cult following.[10]

Three case studies

Turning to the first of our three case studies, Crépy-en-Valois best shows us the relationship between the original sculptures, the act of iconoclasm itself and the imposition of a palimpsest. Gonesse is one of four churches that still retain both the Temple of Reason and the Supreme Being inscriptions.[11] Notre-Dame-en-Vaux allows us to consider site lines and the Revolutionary use of space as factors in the placement of the palimpsests.

7.3. Parish church of Saint-Loup, Bléneau. View of the west portal showing the placement of both Revolutionary cult inscriptions.

Crépy-en-Valois: from a medieval iconography to a Revolutionary one

Originally located just outside the walls of the expanding medieval town of Crépy-en-Valois,[12] the collegiate church of Saint-Thomas de Cantorbéry was begun around 1165 and consecrated in 1182, though probably not completed until well into the fourteenth century.[13] The new religious institution formed part of a service complex that included the contemporaneous foundation of a new hospital.[14] The new church also

7.4. Saint-Loup de Bléneau, detail of the partially effaced inscription "Temple de la Raison."

served as a parish for townspeople living in the growing outskirts of Crépy and its secular canons served as teachers, presumably for children of the bourgeoisie and the local nobility. Together with the Hopîtal Saint-Michel, it formed a monumental focal point at the opposite end of Crépy from the comital castle and the Cluniac abbey of Saint-Arnoul. Crépy-en-Valois grew in size during the eighteenth century. By the time of the French Revolution, the population had reached more than 2500 souls. The church of Saint-Thomas de Cantorbéry remained outside the walls, but was fully within the town.

Of this collegiate church and hospital complex, there remains only the western tower block of the church of Saint-Thomas (fig. 7.5).[15] Its single west façade portal, which served the canons and is the one concerning us here,[16] was systematically mutilated by iconoclasts during the Revolution and its tympanum painted over with a Revolutionary inscription honoring the Supreme Being (fig. 7.6).

On the tympanum, now essentially stripped of its sculpture, one can still discern the faint contours of three figures that have been hammered back to the relief ground. In fact, the contours are so faint that they are clearly visible only in the raking light of sunset. At the center, along the left side, the outline of a throne is clear. Again in the center, contour lines trace the outer limits of the clothing covering the legs, hips, and lower torso of the figure once seated on the throne. Near the apex of the tympanum remains a partial contour of a circle that once represented a nimbus. To the left and right of this enthroned central figure are the partial contours of two other figures that reveal the position of their legs and hips. The angle of these contours suggests that the two figures were represented kneeling. Traces of an elongated, ovoid form remain on the tympanum border at the left. Only part of a similar form remains on the right. Both of these vestiges appear behind and slightly above the kneeling figures.

As for the medieval iconography of this tympanum, it is obvious that the sculptures represented an enthroned figure, flanked by two angels (fig. 7.7).[17] This seated figure is no longer identifiable. It could have been a representation of Christ, and thus similar to the north portal tympanum of the west façade of the collegiate church at Mantes-la-Jolie, or of the Virgin as one finds on the tympanum of the lateral portal of the collegiate church of Donnemarie-en-

7.5. Collegiate church of Saint-Thomas de Cantorbéry, Crépy-en-Valois. View of the west façade from the southwest. Documented in 2001.

Montois.[18] The most likely personage represented, however, would probably have been Saint Thomas of Canterbury, to whom this church was dedicated and who was canonized a mere eight years after the church was begun.

Equally important to scholarship as is the lost medieval iconography, is the early modern, aniconic palimpsest that replaced it (fig. 7.8):

LE PEUPLE FRANÇOIS
RECONNOIT L'ÊTRE SUPRÊME
ET
L'IMMORTALITÉ DE L'AME

First of all, the inscription occupies the lower two-thirds of the tympanum area. Comparison with popular images of the time reveals that there could have been an image of the sun or the all-seeing eye above the inscription, motifs that form part of the iconography of the Revolution.[19] No trace of either motif is visible, perhaps because the upper portion of the tympanum has been plastered over. No such motifs, however, occur on any of the other monuments that retain this inscription. We need therefore to take account of the "void" and to consider what the blank space may have signified.

7.6. Saint-Thomas de Cantorbéry, view of the tympanum of the west portal in 2001.

7.7. Reconstruction drawing of the medieval iconography of the west portal tympanum at Crépy.

7.8. Reconstruction drawing of the medieval iconography of the west portal tympanum at Crépy with the Revolutionary inscription superimposed on it.

7.9. Saint-Thomas de Cantorbéry, detail of the lower right portion of the tympanum showing the chisel marks on the mutilated sculpture.

Important to notice are the traces of the iconoclastic act (fig. 7.9). Not simply the remaining contours of the figures that indicate their former presence, but the actual marks of the chisel in the surface of the stone where the figures once were, attest to the actions of iconoclasts. This is most obvious today in the lower portions of the figures of the enthroned saint and the kneeling angels, but was probably originally visible in the less well-preserved upper portions of the tympanum as well.[20] It is on top of both the remains of the three figures and some of the chisel marks that the palimpsestual statement is inscribed. One thinks here of Heidegger's notion of *sous rature*, where the deleted text remains visible through the evidence of its deletion.[21] The tympanum's multi-temporality presents the viewer with traces of the past, with the moment of transformation in the iconoclastic act and with the unfolding present in the Revolutionary inscription.[22] The visibility of this three-layered palimpsest should be understood as deliberate.

The thoughtfulness of the stages of the Revolution's palimpsestual process brings us back to an important point mentioned earlier. Even the writings of Michel Vovelle, the important French historian of the relationship between Christianity and the Revolution, maintain the popular notion that Revolutionary iconoclasm resulted from mob activity.[23] As we have seen, this idea is negated by the physical evidence of the monument. Moreover, it is also negated by written sources. In a seldom-cited article published in the *American Historical Review* in 1954, Stanley Idzerda showed convincingly on the basis of municipal records that many acts of iconoclasm were commissioned by local Revolutionary governments.[24] We can thus distinguish here what Clay has identified as unofficial and official iconoclasm.[25]

Further, one can contextualize the palimpsest at Crépy. Revolutionary clubs in Crépy, notably the *Société Populaire*, were at first slow to respond to the creation of new Revolutionary cults. Once authorized by the *Municipalité* (the Revolutionary town council),[26] however, they embraced the idea with enthusiasm. The *Société Populaire* of Crépy moved quickly to catch up, organizing a grandiose ceremony for the rededication of the church of Saint-Thomas as a Temple of Reason on 29 January 1794.[27] Later that spring the *Société* was moved to further Revolutionary activity as the Temple of Reason was rededicated anew as a Temple of the Supreme Being.[28]

It would seem then, that the medieval sculptures were carefully and deliberately mutilated, with the aim of creating a flattened but not fully erased surface destined both to receive its Revolutionary palimpsest and to show the removal of the original sculpture. It would have been easy to plaster over the entire tympanum, hiding both the images of superstition and the act of their erasure, to provide a fresh, clean surface on which to inscribe the palimpsest.[29] Instead, the act of erasure is preserved to remind contemporary citizens of Crépy of the removal of the imagery of superstition, for whom remembrance of the actual images would have held far more poignancy than we can achieve today. Finally, the inscription itself was added to signal the new cult and the new function of the building.

Sometime between 2001 and 2008, the Revolutionary inscription was restored and the tympanum at Crépy "cleaned up," adding yet another palimpsestual layer on the portal. This recently restored inscription celebrates anew the destruction of the religious iconography that preceded it, a celebration that probably was not possible before the 200th anniversary of the French Revolution at the end of the previous century. The inscription "looks better" today than it did in 2001, but the work was done without concern for a close reading of traces of pigment or faint contours of the carving that may have been visible only from a scaffold. It is ironic that the desire to celebrate the Revolution in the twenty-first century has resulted in a secondary act of iconoclasm of both the original sculpted imagery and the palimpsest that replaced it.

Saint-Pierre de Gonesse: a case of Revolutionary conflict?

The large parish church of Saint-Pierre de Gonesse presents a complex palimpsestual problem (fig. 7.10). Located in the Val d'Oise just north of Paris, the town of Gonesse was a sub-diocesan center of one of the rural *doyennés* (administrative subdivisions) of the diocese of Paris, a

7.10. Parish church of Saint-Pierre, Gonesse. View of the west façade. Documented in 2013.

position later reflected in its choice as head of a district during the Revolution.[30] It had not only a royal *grange* (farm), but also a royal residence from which charters in the king's name were issued throughout the thirteenth century.[31] It was, throughout its medieval and early modern history, a populous and prosperous town.

A church dedicated to Saint Peter is known from the early ninth century on the basis of documents,[32] but it may date from the sixth century on the basis of recently excavated burials within the existing building.[33] Evidently an *Eigenkirche* (proprietary church) belonging to the Montmorency family, Saint-Pierre was given around 1110 to the abbey of Saint-Florent de Saumur (Maine-et-Loire) by Hervé de Montmorency, as part of the endowment for the foundation of a Saumurian priory at Deuil-la-Barre, about five kilometres west of Gonesse.[34]

Today, the church consists of a twelfth-century Romanesque tower adjacent to the crossing bay in the south side-aisle, and two Gothic phases, a late twelfth-century chevet and a thirteenth-century nave.[35] The Romanesque tower can probably be associated with Hervé de Montmorency's gift of the parish and related revenues to the abbey of Saint-Florent. It has also been suggested that the first Gothic phase began as a royal thank-offering for the birth of Philip Augustus, *Dieudonné*, though there is no evidence one way or the other.[36]

7.11. Saint-Pierre de Gonesse, view of the west portal in 2013.

7.12. Saint-Pierre de Gonesse, view of the west portal tympanum from below in 2013.

It is the thirteenth-century portal of the west façade that concerns us here. Framed by stepped embrasures borne on a splayed socle and three elaborate archivolts, the focus of the portal is a large tympanum and a lintel supported by a trumeau (fig. 7.11). The trumeau and its statue are modern[37] and the lintel has recently been cleaned and restored. Today, the tympanum carries two inscriptions datable to the Revolutionary period.

Originally, however, the tympanum certainly bore relief sculpture.[38] Seen from an angle, its surface undulates, the inward depressions corresponding to areas where carvings were removed. Further evidence of iconoclastic alteration to the tympanum surface is visible from directly below (fig. 7.12). At the lower left and right corners, the tympanum surface comes all the way up to the edge of the enframing archivolt. Above that point, which corresponds to the depression in the surface on each side, the tympanum is cut back, away from the archivolt. It was in this area that more sculpture must have been carved away to prepare the tympanum area to receive the Revolutionary inscriptions. Unlike Saint-Thomas at Crépy-en-Valois, no contours of the sculptures remain at Gonesse.

During the 1890s, the historian Marechal claimed to be able to see a *TEMPLE DE LA RAISON* inscription beneath the whitewash covering the tympanum.[39] Over time, the surface became darker, dirtier, and stained so that, as recently 1991, no inscription was visible on the tympanum (figs. 7.13 and 7.14). Shortly after the year 2000, and thus around the same time as the restoration of the inscription at Crépy-en-Valois, the tympanum at Gonesse was cleaned, revealing two inscriptions against a dark ground. The inscription honoring the Supreme Being is immediately visible, its bright, yellow-gold majuscules standing out clearly against the darker ground:

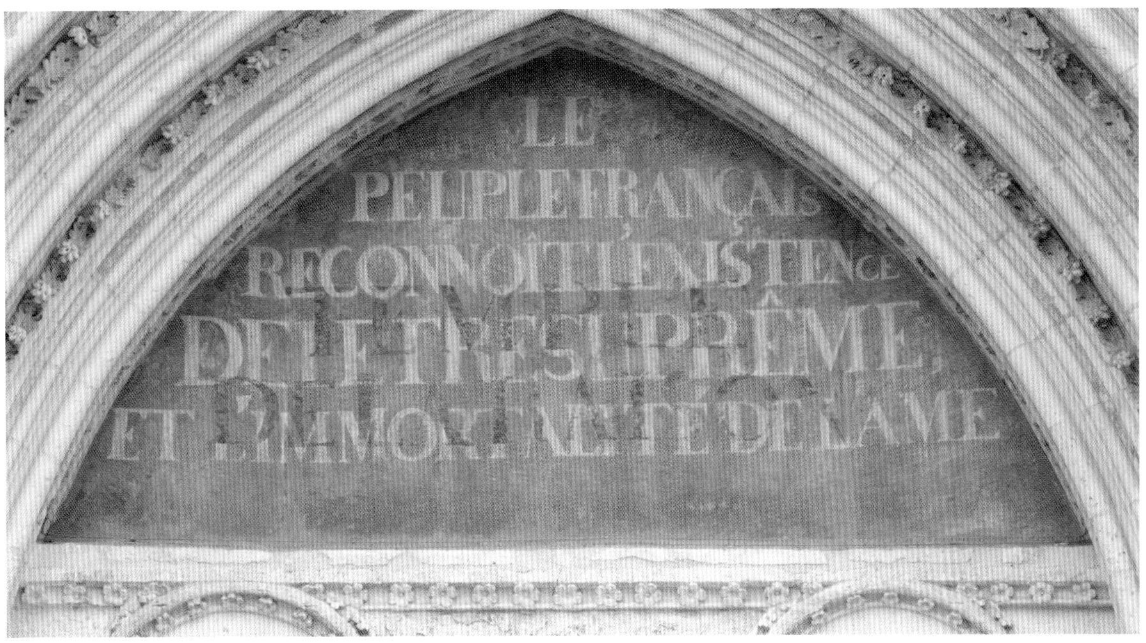

7.13. Saint-Pierre de Gonesse, view of the west portal tympanum in 2013.

7.14. Saint-Pierre de Gonesse, view of the tympanum in 1991.

LE
PEUPLE FRANÇAIS
RECONNOIT L'EXISTENCE
DE L'ÊTRE SUPRÊME
ET L'IMMORTALITÉ DE L'ÂME.

Written in large letters, the palimpsest fills nearly the entire relief field. The epigrapher's attempt at a careful composition fell short, however, at the end of the second and third lines where letters had to be reduced in size to fit the remaining space. It is perhaps useful to observe that, on the fourth line that contains the words *DE L'ÊTRE SUPRÊME*, the letters are markedly larger than those of the rest of the palimpsest, thereby emphasizing the significance of those words.

Also visible against the dark ground are the darker letters of the words, *TEMPLE DE LA RAISON*, giving us another striking example of a double Revolutionary palimpsest.[40] Records of the *Municipalité* indicate that the phrase TEMPLE DE LA RAISON was inscribed on the tympanum of Saint-Pierre during early January 1794.[41] Records of the *Municipalité* also reveal that a festival in honor of the Supreme Being took place in Gonesse on 8 June 1794,[42] by which time the Robespierrean inscription was presumably in place. Given the chronological relationship of the two cults, it should be the case that the Supreme Being palimpsest overlays both the Temple of Reason one and the altered sculptural field. The relationship between the letters of the two inscriptions, however, suggests the opposite, indicating that the TEMPLE DE LA RAISON is the more recent layer. Given the restoration of the tympanum early in this century, it is impossible now to be certain, whether what we see is a reaction among local radicals (Hébertists),[43] re-inscribing the tympanum after the fall of Robespierre in the summer of 1794, or the result of restoration work that blurred the material and temporal relationship between the two inscriptions.[44] Clay has emphasized the struggle between various Revolutionary factions that could easily have resulted in a "reversal" of the chronological and physical layering of these two palimpsests.[45] Given the multi-temporal layering we saw on the tympanum of Crépy, it is also not impossible that, at Gonesse, both inscriptions were once visible at the same time, just as they are today. The result is a palimpsest of meaning, the accumulation and transformation of successive, partially preserved acts that result in multi-layered meanings that are different from, and more than, the sum of the constituent parts even if in this case we cannot be certain of their chronological order.[46]

Prior to 1793–94, the plaza in front of Saint-Pierre was actually a cemetery. During that time, the cemetery was transformed, creating the relatively broad, open space we see today (fig. 7.10).[47] Mona Ozouf has demonstrated, in her magisterial study of Revolutionary festivals, the importance of open spaces for Revolutionary festival planners, who saw them as free, egalitarian, and democratic.[48] Ozouf also recognized that such spaces were not easy to find within towns.[49] We should see the creation of the plaza in front of Saint-Pierre in Gonesse as one local response to the desire for such open, democratic spaces, one which was then, as it is again today, overlooked by the Revolutionary palimpsests on the tympanum of Saint-Pierre's central portal.

Notre-Dame-en-Vaux: seeing where the inscription was

Because the palimpsests of Crépy and Gonesse were inscribed on the west portals of their churches, it is easy to overlook the importance of the visibility of these Revolutionary inscriptions. Notre-Dame-en-Vaux in Châlons-en-Champagne allows us to see just how much attention was paid to the placement of the inscription and to the sight lines that made it visually accessible.[50]

The collegiate church was, and is, located alongside the main street running past the cathedral at the west end of the city to the town gate at the east (fig. 7.15). The west façade of Notre-Dame faces a narrow street that borders one of the town's several rivers. For this reason, the church's main ceremonial entrance was, and is, the lateral portal on the south side of the nave that opens onto the main road. This once beautiful Early Gothic portal, and the flamboyant porch that precedes it, stand as testimony to the destruction wrought on exterior sculpture. Records of the *Municipalité* tell us that this portal was mutilated beginning on 6 November 1793,[51] and on 2 February 1794 it was decided that the church would be inscribed TEMPLE DÉDIÉ AU CULTE DE LA RAISON, above which would be suspended a *drapeau tricolore*.[52] The Conseil Municipal decided that this inscription should be placed above the *trois entrées* of Notre-Dame-en-Vaux.[53]

No traces of the palimpsest are visible today, but it must have been inscribed above the central of the three portals on the west façade. In the spandrel area above that portal is a set of seven carefully arranged holes, two on each side of the portal and three above (fig. 7.16). I suggest here that the two on either side anchored plaques with the words TEMPLE DE LA RAISON, while the three above the apex of the portal anchored plaques bearing a painted *tricolore* (fig. 7.17).[54] What is important in terms of visibility is that

7.15. Collegiate church of Notre-Dame-en-Vaux, Châlons-en-Champagne. View of the west façade from the southwest.

7.16. Notre-Dame-en-Vaux, detail of the west façade showing the placement of seven symmetrically arranged holes in the spandrel area above the central portal.

7.17. Notre-Dame-en-Vaux, detail of the same spandrel area with a reconstruction of the *drapeau tricolore* and the inscription "Temple de la Raison."

one typically approached Notre-Dame from the western end of town, coming eastward past the market area in the town center. As one approaches Notre-Dame-en-Vaux, it is the west façade rather than its mutilated southern lateral portal that has greatest visibility.

Revolutionary inscribers at Notre-Dame-en-Vaux were not alone in the consideration paid to sight lines and visibility. At the monastic priory of Notre-Dame in Monthiers (Aisne), a painted inscription honoring the Supreme Being wraps around two sides of a stair turret, now also serving as a clock tower, that is attached to the south side of the choir (figs. 7.18 and 7.19).[55] The monastic enclosure of the priory and the curve of the road leading to the newly consecrated temple make this placement of the inscription on the turret maximally visible to those in or accompanying processions approaching the building from the town center. Like Notre-Dame-en-Vaux, Monthiers makes clear that sight lines were a principal factor in choosing the location for a Revolutionary inscription.

Portals in context: festival processions and temple ceremonies

In our close reading of the portals of these three churches, we have seen multiple levels of intentionality and have come to understand more completely the significance of these Revolutionary era inscriptions. Yet in looking closely at the portals, we miss their larger context. We cannot fully understand the portals unless we consider their urban context and the churches of which the portals were a part.

Celebrations of Reason and the Supreme Being also extended outside the temples. Indeed, ceremonies inside temples were typically preceded by processions that were as much a remaking of religious processions as the inscribed, mutilated portals were a remaking of their medieval predecessors. The processions inevitably had a terminus and, where the sources allow us to see it, that terminus was the new Temple of Reason or, months later, the Temple of the Cult of the Supreme Being.

In the case of Gonesse, written evidence allows us to know the route of Revolutionary processions in honor of the new cults and to discern the place of the temple within them.[56] Taking the festival in honor of the Supreme Being as an example, the procession formed in the area above the hospital founded in the thirteenth century (fig. 7.20). It comprised twelve young boys and twelve young girls dressed in white, decorated with tricolor ribbons, each holding a basket of fruits and flowers. They were followed by farmers holding bouquets of green branches and stalks of wheat tied with thin ribbons, and by other participants.

The cortège descended the Rue de l'Hôpital to the Rue de Paris where it turned left and continued to the Rue de la Fontaine Saint-Nicolas. There, it turned right and continued down that street to the Rue Galande, where it again turned right and continued on. Here the sources are lacking, but the next location given is the Place du Marché, easily identifiable on the earliest cadaster of the town, just south of the church of Saint-Pierre.[57] In all likelihood, this means that the procession continued along the Rue Galande to the Rue Saint-Nicolas where it turned to go back up the hill. It crossed the Rue de Paris again and continued up the former Rue de la Cage (now Rue Général Leclerc) to the Place du Marché, where celebrants visited two symbolic monuments, the mountain and the obelisk.[58] In front of each, a speech was given invoking the Revolutionary martyrs and railing against the enemies with whom France was at war. Each speech included an invocation of the Supreme Being. Following these events, the procession continued on to the temple, passing through the inscribed portal for yet a third speech in which the orator demonstrated the existence of the Supreme Being and the immortality of the soul. Organ music accompanied the singing during the service.

Connerton and Peterson have emphasized the performative aspects of social memory and the role of bodily practices, like modes of movement and types of dress.[59] We might add to the performative aspects the choice of youths and farmers as participants in the procession and the significance of the objects that they carry. Commemorative rituals, such as this procession in honor of the Supreme Being, were essential

7.18. Priory church of Notre-Dame de Montiers. View of the church from the main road through the village.

7.19. Notre-Dame de de Monthiers, detail of the stair tower on the south side of the choir showing the remains of the painted Revolutionary inscription.

7.20. Satellite view of the center of the old town of Gonesse showing the location of key monuments (in white) and the route of Revolutionary processions (in red).

to creating a new Revolutionary social memory for a town like Gonesse, and were intended to replace similar processions in the Catholic tradition. They were, in a sense, recurrent palimpsests.

What is striking in this example is the parallel with religious processions. Organizers of Revolutionary festivals, especially in larger towns and cities, sought to avoid traditional processional routes, but this does not seem to have been the case in the much smaller Gonesse.[60] Beginning near the Hôtel Dieu, Revolutionary processions made a circuit of the town's two parishes, Saint-Nicolas and Saint-Pierre. While the former is

7.21. Pierre-Antoine Demachy, *Fête de l'Être Suprême*, 1794.

7.22. Anonymous artist, popular print of the *Vue de la Montagne Élevée au Champs de la Réunion (Fête de l'Être Suprême)*.

today destroyed, its general location is preserved in the names of two of the streets processed. The stops in the Place du Marché seem analogous to the stops of medieval and early modern processions at outdoor crosses and similar religious monuments. While we do not have medieval or early modern texts that identify religious processional routes in Gonesse, we do know that such processions were a regular occurrence everywhere and in smaller towns typically made a circuit of the parishes.[61]

Portals in context: temple ceremonies

Popular prints and registers recording the meetings and decisions of *Municipalités* are our best source for what took place in Revolutionary Temples of Reason and the Supreme Being (figs. 7.21 and 7.22). Destruction of images on the exterior and the emptying of the interior of church plate, religious paintings, and statues, as well as the dismantling of liturgical furnishings, has standardly been characterized as despoliation and vandalism, seeing these actions only from the perspective of the past and of what was removed. Some of these actions may have been nothing more than vandalism. Yet, in the light of what we have seen regarding portals, it becomes possible to see these actions positively, as necessary preparation for installing the new cult(s).[62]

A best-case example comes from registers of Châlons-en-Champagne, regarding the collegiate church of Notre-Dame-en-Vaux (fig. 7.23). Along with the inscribing of the west façade, the Council decided that there would be an elaborate inauguration festival, about which Barbat quotes extensively from municipal records:

> With the aim of throwing the Hydra of fanaticism to the ground, that most cruel enemy of all popular government, and of raising, on the smoking debris of error and superstition, the altars of Reason, the popular and republican Society wanted to consecrate a temple of Reason. The area in the front of the church of Notre-Dame was cleaned and arranged for the exercise of this cult. They placed at the front of the sanctuary a colossal statue of Reason; one read on her pedestal: *Do to the other what you want done to you*. Before the statue, an altar in the antique style, and to the sides, columns supporting vases for the burning of incense, and, on four square pillars placed at the corners of the sanctuary, four projecting consoles were set to support the busts of Brutus, the father of the Republic and the example of republicans; Marat, the faithful friend of the people; Lepelletier, who died for the Republic; and a fourth, the immortal Challier.[63]

Châlons-en-Champagne was, and is, a cathedral town, larger and wealthier than either an important comital town like Crépy-en-Valois or a district center like Gonesse. There is, however, no reason to suppose that the description of the interior of Notre-Dame-en-Vaux, cleaned and prepared for the occasion, and outfitted with a neo-classical altar and a large statue personifying the deified concept of Reason, surrounded by incense burners placed on columns and busts of the martyr-saints of the Revolution set on square pillars, is radically different in kind than similar celebrations that took place in smaller and less important towns throughout France (or larger ones, as a popular print[64] representing the celebration of the Cult of Reason in Paris Cathedral reveals). What is particularly striking are the references to preparing the temple and the similarity to the interior of a typical eighteenth-century church: altar, image of the deity, the role accorded to the sense of smell, and, finally, the presence of icons of the martyr-saints of the Revolution. Whether with the aim of reassuring the worshippers or simply because this was considered the most appropriate way to proceed, the power of past modes of adorning sanctuary interiors, recalled through social memory, seems to have shaped the choices made by the Revolutionaries.

Conclusion

What then shall we make of these palimpsests, and of their place in the portals of former churches that were the foci of the Revolutionary cults and *termini* of the processions associated with them? The layered inscriptions formed part of the Revolution's public iconography, as essential to the temples as were inscriptions on

7.23. Notre-Dame-en-Vaux, Châlons-en-Champagne. View of the medieval choir reconstructed as a Temple of Reason.

the exteriors of medieval churches. Iconoclasm and re-inscription formed, however, only one dimension of the larger phenomenon of the transformation of religious signs.

What the Revolution set out to do in the realm of religion was to create "a whole system of Revolutionary rituals, symbols and language which aimed to replace Christianity."[65] The goal was nothing less than a complete cultural transformation. Churches were purged of all signs of the old superstitions in order to be purified to serve as temples of the new cults, first Reason and then the Supreme Being. New symbols (the oak, the mountain, the all-seeing eye) were created and a new body of religious practice was formed. Portals were inscribed to identify, celebrate, and advertise those new faiths, and new processions were invented to incorporate entire towns in the new religions.

Certainly, there was resistance to both Reason and the Supreme Being from the very beginning and throughout the Reign of Terror during which they came into being. This came not only from the Church and its priesthood, but also from women, wives, and mothers, in towns and villages throughout the nation.[66] On the other hand, while churches were returned gradually to the Christian cult after the fall of Robespierre in July 1794, republican cults were still being celebrated in Châlons-en-Champagne, for example, into early 1797.[67]

This radical religious transformation lasted little more than a year. The brevity of the religious phase of the French Revolution stemmed in significant part from the force of the social memory of traditional Catholicism and its ability to provide comfort to believers in times of need. The Revolutionary appropriation of Catholicism's architecture and its entrances would seem more impressive to us today had the power of social memory, which the Revolution tried to manipulate and use by modeling aspects of the new cults on the old, been less strong. The strength of the old superstitions was too great, as was already recognized by Robespierre in his shift in cult from Reason to the Supreme Being.

7.24. Parish church of Saint-Pierre, Nanteuil-le-Haudouin. View of the portal on the south side of the church.

As Connerton has pointed out, recollected knowledge of the past is communicated and maintained by ritual performance.[68] In a Shakespearean sense, the tragedy of the Revolution's more egalitarian and human-centered cults lay within them, in their appropriated Christian spaces, in their transformed signs, and in the performance of their rituals, all of which were intended to create a new set of social memories, but which too closely recalled the social memories of Catholicism that they were intended to replace.

The resurgent Catholicism, first in the gradual return to limited freedom of worship in the Thermidorian period (February 1795–autumn 1797) and then in the nineteenth century, gives us a final, ironic example of the Revolution's failure to transform the faith of the French people. On the tympanum of the southern lateral portal of the parish church of Saint-Pierre in Nanteuil-le-Haudouin (Oise), one can still

7.25. Saint-Pierre de Nanteuil-le-Haudouin, detail of the lateral portal tympanum showing the remains of a post-Revolutionary inscription.

read, inscribed in paint, on the portal's mutilated tympanum (figs. 7.24 and 7.25):[69]

C'EST ICI (LA) MAISON
DE (D)IEU
ET LA (PORTE) DU CIEL.

Notes

This study is part of a larger, ongoing investigation of early modern iconoclasm in France. I would like to thank Denis Defente for facilitating my work at Saint-Pierre-au-Parvis, in Soissons where the larger project began; Victor Lassalle for inviting me to participate in the École antique de Nîmes in 1997, where it entered its second phase; and Sheila Bonde for comments and suggestions on an earlier version of this study. I am also grateful to Emma Maines and Benjamin Maines for their patience in visiting more churches with mutilated portals than they would care to remember.

1 On Revolutionary period iconoclasm, see Sprigath 1980, 510–35, who provides a Marxist critique of the prehistory of the term "vandalisme." Idzerda 1954, 13–26, clarifies the role of municipalities in paying for the disfigurement of images. Wrigley 1993, 182–95, discusses different types of iconoclasm and nuances ways of interpreting them. Noyes 2013, 95–110, takes a political view, linking iconoclasm and the struggle for political power in the construction of a state identity in Revolutionary France. Clay 2007, 93–122; Clay 2012; and Clay 2013, 97–122, take a semiotic approach to argue that for iconoclasm to be understood, it must be considered in the context of the transformation of *signs*, a term that encompasses statuary, paintings, prints, and drawings in the case of the kings, and sculpture, paintings, relics, reliquaries, prints, ex votos, and other associated objects in the case of a saint's cult. Other recent important studies include: McClanan and Johnson 2005; Boldrick and Clay 2007; Boldrick, Brubaker, and Clay 2013; Noyes 2013; and Kolrud and Prusac 2014.

2 The portal, which is usually dated to 1160–70, was revealed during the 1991–95 restoration of the church.

On the portal of Saint-Pierre before its recent unmasking, see Lefèvre-Pontalis 1922, 208–09; Philippot 1937; and Lapeyre 1960, 174–75. Recently, see Martinuzzi 2012, 61–63. On Compiègne during the Revolution, see Bernet 1978, esp. 422–25; and Bernet 1988, esp. 169–77. Compiègne celebrated the cults of Reason and the Supreme Being. The town also had active iconoclasts as its three surviving churches have mutilated or missing exterior sculpture. No trace of a Revolutionary inscription survives on any of them. The parish church of Saint-Jacques was rededicated as a Temple of Reason during the Revolution, but nothing seems to be known about Saint-Pierre or the other churches.

3 On what is called "dechristianization," see Vovelle 1991 (original French edition 1976); and Clay 2012, 240–72. For the generally accepted view that dechristianization was intense, short-lived and destructive, but had no lasting effect, see Cobb 1961, vol. 2, 660, 667. For a different view of the long-term effects, see Tallet 1991, 1–28.

4 Scholars have noted that one reason for the failure of Revolutionary cults was that neither, and especially not the cult of Reason, provided a special being to turn to in time of need, as the cult of saints in Roman Catholicism did. See, for example, Tallet 1991, 3–4.

5 Clay 2012, 206–07. Hamburger's 2014 essay on script as image in medieval manuscripts has much of use for thinking about monumental inscriptions.

6 Though much less studied, there was a second round of iconoclasm that followed the left-wing coup d'état of September 1797 that lasted until the end of 1799. See Desan 1990, 11–13.

7 It may ultimately be possible to verify the survival of an additional five inscriptions through site visits.

8 The thirty-first inscription is different in location and words. On the abbey gate of Lagny-sur-Marne, the words "*Liberté, Égalité, Fraternité ou la Morte*" are painted. They constitute the Revolutionary version of what later became the national motto of France.

9 Classic early, and entirely negative assessments of Revolutionary iconoclasm begin with Grégoire 1794, and include Réau (1958) 1994; and Souchal 1993, the latter two with additional bibliography. For remarks by historians of medieval sculpture, see recently Joubert 2008, 24–28.

10 For recent work on social memory, see Connerton 1989; Fentress and Wickham 1992; Jones 2007; Mills and Walker 2008; Meskell 2008, 233–43; and Peterson 2012, 266–83. For a historical survey of work on social memory, see Olick and Robbins 1998. See also Olick, Vinitzky-Seroussi, and Levy 2011.

11 The others are Saint-Loup de Bléneau, mentioned above; Criteuil-le-Madeleine (Charente) and Saint-Vaast de Rebreuviette (Pas-de-Calais).

12 For a recent overview of the history and evolution of the town, see Riés 1999, 167–74. Important early modern sources include, Muldrac 1662; and Carlier 1764, vol. 1, 506–11. The great merit of Muldrac and Carlier lies in their access to documents destroyed during the French Revolution to which the authors often make reference. See also Bourgeois 1867, 3–65; 175–248; Bourgeois 1868, 115–55; and Tomasini 1987, esp. 39–47 on the medieval period, and 99–113 on the Revolution. Bourgeois depends on Carlier for the history, but he contributes numerous observations on the monuments. Tomasini depends principally on Muldrac and Carlier for the medieval period, and while he provides a good bibliography, his work contains no footnotes and his sources are often not fully cited.

13 On the foundation and history of the church of Saint-Thomas, see Muldrac 1662; and Carlier 1764, vol. 1, 506–11. See also Bourgeois 1868, 145–55; and Tomasini 1987, 211–15, on the collegiate church of Saint-Thomas. Among the guidebooks for the site, one needs to cite, Moreau-Neret (s.d.) 1976, 6–14 and 30 (which depends on Carlier 1764; and Batillot 1987), which includes a good image of the portal at that time.

14 Both the church and the hospital were established through the benefaction of Philippe of Alsace, Count of Flandres and of the Valois, and his wife Countess Elisabeth. On the foundation of hospitals at this time, see Mollat 1978, 111–16, and 118–24.

15 A length of the north side-aisle wall of the nave also survives partially in elevation. According to Tomasini 1987, 215, the church façade was restored in 1838 by the town and in 1878 by the architect Selmarsheim for the *Commission des Monuments historiques*.

16 The church also had an elaborate thirteenth-century lateral portal in the bay just east of the south tower of the west façade. This portal, which is almost entirely demolished, served the parish community. See de Fleury 1884, 314.

17 Methods for iconographic reconstruction of mutilated portals, as well as for their compositional and stylistic analysis, were first articulated by the author in Maines 1982, 178–98, and later refined in Maines 1999–2002, 107–30, where an earlier discussion of the portal at Crépy-en-Valois appears (113–14). The potential for new directions in the study of mutilated sculptures can be seen in recent French work such as Rollier and Vilain 2016.

18 See Sauerländer 1972, plates 48 (top) and 141 (bottom), respectively.

19 See, for example, the print issued by the Parisian publisher Paul-André Basset, *c.* 1794, which shows a radiant sun above the inscription and a symbolic landscape. An original is held in the collection of the Bibliothèque nationale de France, Cabinet des Estampes and is available at: http://frda.stanford.edu/en/catalog/ch030yz4084.

20 It is worth observing that, regardless of whether the uncarved surfaces of the tympanum were weathered or painted, they would have contrasted sharply with the cream color of the freshly revealed limestone, making the traces of iconoclastic action that much

more obvious to anyone standing in front of the portal, much as we can now see on the tympanum of Saint-Pierre-aux-Minimes (fig. 7.1).

21 See Spivak 1967, xiv. Application of the concept to Revolutionary iconoclasm was first suggested by Wrigley 1993, 185, though not in relation to relief sculpture as is done here. For an analogous instance of deliberately preserving traces of the iconoclastic act, see Wagoner in this volume, esp. fig. 1.12.

22 On the multi-temporality of palimpsests, see Lucas 2005, 37–43; and Bailey 2007, 203–10.

23 Notwithstanding the earlier work of Idzerda, Vovelle 1991, still wrote of spontaneous acts of iconoclasm, linking them to the *auto-da-fe* (symbolic burnings) and burlesques. While there certainly were spontaneous acts of iconoclasm, spontaneity hardly applies to the systematic mutilation of monumental sculpture, as is clear from Clay's discussion of the iconoclastic efforts of the sculptor Daujon. Clay 2012, 209–15, and 257–59. The two types of iconoclastic acts correspond to Clay's unofficial and official iconoclasm.

24 Idzerda 1954, 13–26. Roquet-Hoffet 2001, 390 and 392, makes the same point concerning Strasbourg, though without reference to Idzerda. It has been only recently that Idzerda's work has begun to be regularly cited.

25 Clay 2012, 13–27, and 217–24, respectively.

26 *Municipalités* constituted a system of town administration that was created during the French Revolution. See Forrest 1996, 64–71, and 91–92.

27 Bernet 2007, xxix, and note 122. For the procès-verbal for the inauguration of the Temple of Reason (29 January 1794), see Bernet 2007, 100–05.

28 Bernet 2007, xxix–xxx. The *Société Populaire* was installed in the choir of the chapel of the Hôpital Saint-Michel near to the church of Saint-Thomas. Bernet 2007, 286. It does not seem to be known whether the tympanum of Saint-Thomas originally bore a "Temple de la Raison" inscription prior to being inscribed with the existing one less than four months later. See Picot-Bocquillon 2012a, 86.

29 This is known to have occurred, for example, at Donnemarie-en-Montois, near Provins.

30 For the history of Gonesse, see Lebeuf (d. 1760) 1883, vol. 2, 259–73; and Marechal 1895, the latter of which is particularly useful for local records. Marechal 1895, 107–08, identifies Gonesse as a district center. The reconfiguration of France into *départements* occurred during the Revolution. Districts were the first major subdivision of departments and were in turn divided into cantons, and the latter into communes.

31 Marechal 1895, 8. No trace of the residence or the *grange* has been identified materially. The "rue du chattel" located south and west of the church as an extension of the former "rue des huilliers" on the cadaster of 1819, may be the best indicator of where the royal residence once was. Whether the residence was a *château*, or a *maison forte* (perhaps attached to the *grange*) thus remains unknown. For the cadaster, see http://archives.valdoise.fr/archive/fonds/FRADO95 côte 3P 2490 tableau d'assemblage.

32 Lebeuf (d. 1760) 1883, 260. Charters are known from 1218, 1236, 1247, 1254 and 1262.

33 Excavations were recently carried out by archaeologists from INRAP; late sixth-century burials were recovered in 2010. I am grateful to the archaeologists for sharing information about the results of their work. On the excavations, see now http://www.inrap.fr/reprise-des-fouilles-archeologiques-gonesse-val-d-oise-5245 and http://www.inrap.fr/1-000-ans-d-inhumations-dans-l-eglise-de-gonesse.

34 Lebeuf (d. 1760) 1883, 260 and 268; Marchegay 1878, 138–39.

35 On the church, see Lefèvre-Pontalis 1888, 55–64; Lambin 1898, 59–63; Aubert 1951, 424–28; Bontemps 1981, 209–28; and Foussard 2008, 134–38. On early modern funerary inscriptions in Saint-Pierre, see de Guilhermy 1880, vol. 2, 542–48.

36 de Guilhermy 1880, vol. 2, 542; followed by Lefèvre-Pontalis 1888, 58. This notion is largely based on the nineteenth-century belief that the king was born in Gonesse, though this is unlikely since he was baptized in Paris the morning after. See Bradbury 1998, 1–3.

37 First identified as "moderne" by Lefèvre-Pontalis 1888, 59, and followed by Lambin 1898, 62, though without any documentation by either author. Marechal 1895, 152, on the basis of fabric records, states that, "[l]a statue de St-Pierre est remise à sa place d'autrefois, devant le grand portail de l'Église." It would be easy to interpret this sentence meaning that the present statue is the original, medieval one. More likely, Marechal meant that a new image replaced the lost original.

38 Lebeuf (d. 1760) 1883, 261, is the only author to discuss the portal before the French Revolution. His remarks are general: "Le portail de cette Eglise est aussi du XIII siècle, mais fort simple et sans beaucoup d'ornemens." Against the backdrop of fully decorated portals like those of Notre-Dame de Paris, Lebeuf's comment could easily be describing a portal with sculptures only on the tympanum. Lefèvre-Pontalis 1888, 58, believed that the tympanum was originally sculpted, though he did not state why.

39 Marechal 1895, 126.

40 Both inscriptions appear together in the west portal of the parish church of Criteuil-la-Madeleine (Charente), but there they appear one above the other on separate archivolts. The portal has recently been cleaned and the incised letters painted a bold red, making a strikingly effective visual statement.

41 Marechal 1895, 126.

42 Marechal 1895, 129–30.

43 Hébertists, followers of Jacques-René Hébert, were more rigorously atheistic and were advocates of the more abstract cult of Reason. See McPhee 2002, 145–46, and the brief biographical sketch in Jones 2003, 140. A re-inscription during the dechristianization of 1797–99 is also possible.

44 Marechal 1895, 137, seems to suggest that the Temple of Reason inscription was effaced (overwritten?) in spring of 1794. Close inspection with high-resolution photographs has not resolved the question and even a close reading of the physical evidence from a scaffold might not prove decisive.

45 Clay 2012, 224–40.

46 The term "palimpsests of meaning" is borrowed from Bailey 2007, 203–09.

47 Marechal 1895, 123. During late September 1793 and in the name of *egalité*, tombstones were broken up by masons and the monumental cross in front of the façade was thrown down and removed.

48 Ozouf 1988, 126–57.

49 Ozouf, 1988, 137.

50 On the history of the town, see Barbat (1855) 2003. In his (unpaginated) preface, Barbat details his sources, explaining that he spent the years 1817–20 in the archives of the prefecture and the *mairie*.

51 Barbat (1855) 2003, 466.

52 Barbat (1855) 2003, 494. Without being specific with regard to Notre-Dame, Barbat later on wrote that during May 1794, following Robespierre's declaration of the cult of the Supreme Being, "sur le frontispice des édifices, où l'on avait écrit: Temple de la Raison, on écrivait: À l'Être-Suprême." Barbat (1855) 2003, 500. It is not known whether Barbat was writing about France in general or whether he was referring to the five republican cult buildings in the city, including Notre-Dame-en-Vaux. No surviving Revolutionary inscription to the cult of Reason corresponds to the words called for in the records of the *Municipalité*. For that reason, I have followed Barbat and used the phase "Temple de la Raison" in the reconstruction proposed in what follows.

53 Barbat (1855) 2003, 494.

54 Compare the arch above the door of the parish church of Saint-Sulpice-sur-Loire where a painted *tricoleur* bears, in gold letters, the Robespierrean inscription to the Supreme Being.

55 On Monthiers, see Moreau-Nelaton (1913) 2002, vol. 2, 483–88, who mentions the Revolutionary inscription.

56 The following discussion is taken from Marechal 1895, 113, and 129–30, with reference to section C of the cadastral plan of Gonesse dated to 1819, available at http://archives.valdoise.fr/n/ressources-en-ligne/n:41. Evidently, all the Revolutionary processions in Gonesse followed the same route.

57 The earliest *plan cadastral* for the town of Gonesse dates to 1819 and is known as the *cadastre Napoléonien*. It is available on line at http://archives.valdoise.fr/archive/fonds/FRADO95 côte 3P 2495 le Bourg and provides earlier street names. See also note 31 above.

58 See Ozouf 1988, 134–35, on the meanings and function of symbols. The *montagne* took its name from the Montagnards, the radical Revolutionary group in Paris. It, and the obelisk, were moral signs, suggesting elevation in the context of open space and the sky and contrasting with the narrow, crowded streets and limited vistas of medieval towns and cities.

59 Connerton 1989, 10–12, and 58–61. Peterson 2012, 277–80, follows Connerton's performative approach and further develops it.

60 Ozouf 1988, 137–47, acknowledges the limited processional options in villages, something that should probably be extended to modest towns like Gonesse. Unlike the varied processional routes that avoided a "tour" of the city, like those in Caen which Ozouf describes, the routes in Gonesse seem to have remained the same and to have made a tour of the town's major monuments and spaces: the hospital, the two parishes, and the open market area.

61 Bonde and Maines 2015, 65–66.

62 Useful analogies can be drawn here with the cleansing of pagan temples in preparation for their use as Christian churches, of which the church of Santa Maria ad Martyres (Hadrian's Pantheon) in Rome is the best-known example. Muslims in Spain and Portugal converted churches into mosques, as for example at Mértola, Almonaster, and Badajoz, all in Portugal. That process was also reversible, as the Great Mosque of Cordoba became the Catedral Santa Maria following the *Reconquista*. Contemporary scholarship holds that few of these conversions are reducible to the reuse of available structure. Rather they were more likely all (and I would include the Revolutionary ones discussed in this study) transformations of the nature of cult at sites of recognized holiness.

63 "Dans le but de terrasser l'hydre du fanatisme, l'ennemi le plus cruel de tout gouvernement populaire, et d'élever, sur les débris fumants de l'erreur et de la superstition, des autels à la Raison, la Société populaire et républicain voulut consacrer un temple à la Raison. La ci-devant église de Notre-Dame fut nettoyée et disposée pour l'exercice de ce culte. On plaça dans le ci-devant sanctuaire une statue colossale de la Raison; on lisait sur son piédestal: *Fais à autrui ce que tu veux qui te soit fait*. Au-devant de la statue, un autel antique; aux alentours, des colonnes supportant des vases pour brûler des parfums, et, sur quatre piliers carrés placés aux coins du sanctuaire, quatre consoles saillantes étaient disposées pour recevoir les bustes de Brutus, le père de la République et le modèle des républicains; de Marat, le fidèle ami du peuple; de Lepelletier, mort pour la République, et d'un quatrième, l'immortel Challier." Barbat (1855) 2003, 488–89. For the inauguration of the Temple of Reason, Barbat's citation goes on to describe participants, costumes, and symbols, as well as the processional route itself.

64 The anonymous image is well known and is titled *Fête de la Raison: le decadi 20 brumaire de l'an 2.e de la République française*. Dated 1793, it is available at : http://www.bnf.fr/fr/collections_et_services/bibliotheques_numeriques_gallica.html. This print served as the basis for the reconstruction (fig. 7.23).

65 Desan 1990, 2.

66 Hufton 1971, 90–108; and Desan 1990, 197–216.

67 Barbat (1855) 2003, 508–09.

68 Connerton 1989, 70–71.

69 Traces of black remaining on both sides of the second line of the catholic inscription suggest that there may have been a Revolutionary inscription that has since been effaced by post-Revolutionary one. The clear presence of an upright rectangular block in the center of the tympanum strongly suggests the former presence of a central (enthroned?) figure and provides indirect evidence of its mutilation. There is little scholarship on the church of Saint-Pierre; the most extensive description is https://fr.wikipedia.org/wiki/Église_Saint-Pierre_de_Nanteuil-le-Haudouin.

Bibliography

Aston, Nigel. 2000. *Religion and Revolution in France, 1780–1804*. Washington, D.C: Catholic University of America Press.

Aubert, Marcel. 1951. "L'église de Gonesse (Seine-et-Oise)," *Bulletin monumental* 109, 424–28.

Aulard, Alphonse. 1925. *Le christianisme et la révolution*. Paris: F. Rieder et Cie.

—. 1892. *Le culte de la raison et de l'être suprême*. Paris: F. Alcan.

Bailey, Geoff. 2007. "Time Perspectives, Palimpsests and the Archaeology of Time," *Journal of Anthropological Archaeology* 26, no. 2, 198–223.

Barbat, Louis. (1855) 2003. *Histoire de la ville de Châlons-sur-Marne et ses monuments depuis son origine jusqu'en 1854*. Châlons-sur-Marne: T. Martin (repr. ed. Paris: Le livre d'histoire-Lorisse).

Batillot, Pierre. 1987. *Crépy-en-Valois et environs: Sites, monuments* (ser. Petites Monographies des Grands Édifices de la France). Paris: Henri Laurens.

Bernet, Jacques. 2007. *Procès-Verbaux de la Société populaire de Crépt-en-Valois (Oise) (septembre 1793-avril 1795)* (ser. Collection des documents inédits sur l'histoire de France, Section d'histoire moderne, de la Révolution française et des révolutions-Série Procès-Verbaux des Sociétés populaires, vol. I). Paris: CTHS.

—. 1988. "La crise révolutionnaire (1789–1799)," in *Histoire de Compiègne*, ed. Élie Fruit. Dunkerque: Éditions des Beffrois, 159–82.

—. 1978. "Les origines de la déchristianisation dans le district de Compiègne (septembre-décembre 1793)," in *La déchristianisation de l'An II* (special issue: *Annales historiques de la Révolution française*, 233), 405–32.

Boldrick, Stacy, Leslie Brubaker, and Richard Clay, eds. 2013. *Striking Images: Iconoclasms Past and Present*. Farnham: Ashgate.

Boldrick, Stacy, and Richard Clay, eds. 2007. *Iconoclasm: Contested Objects, Contested Terms*. Aldershot: Ashgate.

Bonde, Sheila, and Clark Maines. 2015. "Performing Silence and Regulating Sound: the Monastic Soundscape of Saint-Jean-des-Vignes," in *Resounding Images: Medieval Intersections of Art, Music and Sound*, ed. Susan Boynton and Diane J. Reilly. Turnhout: Brepols, 47–70.

Bontemps, Daniel. 1981. "La nef de l'église Saint Pierre de Gonesse et ses rapports avec l'abbatiale de Saint Denis," *Bulletin monumental* 139, 209–28.

Bourgeois, Dr Alfred. 1867 and 1868. "Histoire de Crépy et de ses dépendances, de ses seigneurs, de ses châteaux et de ses autres monuments depuis l'époque la plus reculée jusqu'à nos jours," *Comité archéologique de Senlis, Comptes-rendus et mémoires* V, 3–65, 175–248; and VI, 115–55.

Bradbury, Jim. 1998. *Philip Augustus, King of France 1180–1223*. London and New York: Longmans.

Bremmer, Jan N. 2008. "Iconoclast, Iconoclastic, and Iconoclasm: Notes Towards a Genealogy," *Church History and Religious Culture* 88, 1–17.

Carlier, Claude. 1764. *Histoire du duché de Valois, ornée de cartes et de gravures, contenant ce qui est arrivé dans ce pays depuis le temps des Gaulois, depuis l'origine de la Monarchie françoise jusqu'en l'année 1703*, 3 vols. Paris and Compiègne: Guillyn and Louis Bertrand.

Clay, Richard. 2013. "Sainte Geneviève, Iconoclasm and the Transformation of Signs," in *Striking Images: Iconoclasms Past and Present*, ed. Stacy Boldrick, Leslie Brubaker, and Richard Clay. Farnham: Ashgate, 97–112.

—. 2012. *Iconoclasm in Revolutionary Paris: The Transformation of Signs* (ser. SVEC, 11). Oxford: Voltaire Foundation.

—. 2007. "Bouchardon's statue of Louis XV: iconoclasm and the transformation of signs," in *Iconoclasm: Contested Objects, Contested Terms*, ed. Stacy Boldrick and Richard Clay. Aldershot: Ashgate, 93–122.

Caviness, Madeleine H. 2003. "Iconoclasm and Iconophobia: Four Historical Case Studies," *Diogenes* 50, no. 3, 99–114.

Cobb, Richard. 1961. *Les armées révolutionnaires: instrument de la Terreur dans les départements, avril 1793*, 2 vols. Paris: Mouton.

Connerton, Paul. 1989. *How Societies Remember*. Cambridge: Cambridge University Press.

Desan, Suzanne. 1990. *Reclaiming the Sacred, Lay Religion and Popular Politics in Revolutionary France*. Ithaca: Cornell University Press.

Dupeux, Cécile, Peter Jezler, and Jean Wirth, in collaboration with Gabriele Keck, Christian von Burg, and Susan Marti. 2001. *Iconoclasme, Vie et mort de l'image médiévale*. Paris: Éditions d'art SOMOGY.

Elsner, Jas. 2003. "Iconoclasm and the Preservation of Memory," in *Monuments and Memory, Made and Unmade*, ed. Robert S. Nelson and Margaret Olson. Chicago: University of Chicago Press, 209–31.

Fentress, James J., and Chris Wickham. 1992. *Social Memory: New Perspectives on the Past*. Oxford: Blackwell.

de Fleury, Paul. 1884. *La collégiale de Saint-Thomas-le Martyr-les-Crespy, Coup d'oeil sur l'histoire du Valois et principalement de Crépy*. Senlis: E. Payen.

Flood, Finbarr Barry. 2003. "Pillars, palimpsests, and princely practices: Translating the past in sultanate Delhi," *RES: Anthropology and Aesthetics* 43, 95–116.

Forrest, Alan. 1996. *The Revolution in Provincial France, Aquitaine, 1789–1799*. Oxford: Clarendon Press.

Foussard, Dominique. 2008. "Gonesse - Saint-Pierre-Saint-Paul," in *Églises du Val-d'Oise: Pays de France, vallée de Montmorency*. Gonesse: Société d'histoire et d'archéologie de Gonesse et du Pays de France, 134–38.

Freedberg, David. 1985. *Iconoclasts and their Motives*. Maarssen: Gary Schwartz.

Fricke, Beate. 2005. "Fallen Idols and risen saints: western attitudes towards the worship of images and the 'cultura veterum deorum,'" in *Negating the Image, Case Studies in Iconoclasm*, ed. Anne McClanan and Jeff Johnson. Aldershot: Ashgate, 67–95.

Goujard, Philippe. 1978. "Sur la déchristianisation dans l'Ouest," in *La déchristianisation de l'An II* (special issue: *Annales historiques de la Révolution française*, 233), 433–50.

Grégoire, abbé. 1794. *Trois rapports à la Convention sur le vandalisme*. Paris: Imprimerie nationale.

de Guilhermy, Ferdinand. 1880. *Inscriptions de la France du Ve siècle au XVIIIe: ancien diocèse de Paris*, 2 vols. (ser. Collection de documents inédits sur l'histoire de France publiés par les soins du ministre de l'Instruction publique). Paris: Imprimerie nationale.

Hamburger, Jeffrey. 2014. *Script as Image* (ser. Corpus of Illuminated Manuscripts, 21). Leuven: Peeters.

Hufton, Olwen. 1971. "Women in Revolution, 1789–1796," *Past and Present* 53, 90–108.

Idzerda, Stanley J. 1954. "Iconoclasm during the French Revolution," *American Historical Review* 60, no. 1, 13–26.

Jones, Andrew. 2007. *Memory and Material Culture*. Cambridge: Cambridge University Press.

Jones, Peter M. 2003. *The French Revolution 1787–1804*. London: Pearson-Longman.

Joubert, Fabienne. 2008. *La sculpture gothique en France, XIIe-XIIIe siècles*. Paris: Picard.

Kennedy, Emmet. 1989. *A Cultural History of the French Revolution*. New Haven: Yale University Press.

Kennedy, Michael. 2000. *The Jacobin Clubs in the French Revolution, 1793–1795*. New York and Oxford: Berghahn Books.

Kolrud, Kristine, and Marina Prusac, eds. 2014. *Iconoclasm from Antiquity to Modernity*. Farnham: Ashgate.

Lambin, Émile. 1898. *Les églises de l'Île-de-France* (ser. Bibliothèque de la Semaine des constructeurs). Paris: Aux Bureaux de la Semaine des Constructeurs.

Lapeyre, André. 1960. "Des façades occidentales de Saint-Denis et Chartres aux portails de Laon." Ph.D. dissertation, University of Paris-Sorbonne.

Lebeuf, abbé Jean (d. 1760). 1883. *Histoire de la ville et de tout le diocèse de Paris*, 2 vols. Paris: Librairie de Fechoz et Letouzey.

Lefèvre-Pontalis, Eugène. 1922. "Tympan du portail des Minimes à Compiègne," *Bulletin monumental* 81, 208–09.

—. 1888. "Monographie de l'église de Gonesse," *Mémoires de la Société historique et archéologique de l'arrondissement de Pontoise et du Vexin* 11, 55–64.

Lucas, Gavin. 2005. *The Archaeology of Time*. London and New York: Routledge.

McClanan, Anne, and Jeffrey Johnson, eds. 2005. *Negating the Image: Case Studies in Iconoclasm*. Aldershot: Ashgate.

McPhee, Peter. 2002. *The French Revolution, 1789–1799*. Oxford: Oxford University Press.

Maines, Clark. 1999–2002. "Iconoclasme moderne et sculptures médiévales: Bilan provisoire sur l'étude des portails mutilés en France lors du XVIe et du XVIIIe siècles," *Bulletin de l'École Antique de Nîmes* 25, 107–30.

—. 1982. "Le portail ouest mutilé de St-Pierre-au-Parvis, Soissons (Aisne): reconstitution iconographique," *Révue Archéologique de Picardie* 1, 178–98.

Marchegay, Paul. 1878. "Chartes et autres titres du monastère de Saint-Florent près Saumur concernant l'Ile-de-France de 1070–1220," *Mémoires de la Société de l'histoire de Paris et de l'Île-de-France* 5, 132–57.

Marechal, abbé F. 1895. *Essai sur l'histoire religieuse de Gonesse au diocèse de Versailles depuis ses origines jusqu'à nos jours*. Villiers-le-Bel: Minouflet Imp.

Martinuzzi, Francis, in collaboration with François Callais, Éric Blanchegorge, and Nathalie Mathian. 2012. *De Compiègne à Pierrefonds, architectures monumentales et singulières*. Compiègne: Société historique de Compiègne.

Mathiez, Albert. 1925. *Autour de Robespierre*. Paris: Payot.

—. 1927. *The Fall of Robespierre and Other Essays*. New York: Alfred Knopf.

—. 1909. *Robespierre et la déchristianisation*. Paris and Le Puy: Imprimerie Peyriller, Rouchon & Gamon.

McPhee, Peter, ed. 2013. *A Companion to the French Revolution*. Oxford and Malden: Wiley-Blackwell.

Meskell, Lynn. 2008. "Memory Work and Material Practice," in *Memory Work: Archaeologies of Material Practices*, ed. Barbara J. Mills and William H. Walker. Santa Fe: School for Advance Research Press, 233–43.

Mesqui, Jean. 1994. "Le château de Crépy-en-Valois, Palais comtal, palais royal, palais féodal," *Bulletin monumental*, 152, 257–61.

Mills, Barbara J., and William H. Walker, eds. 2008. *Memory Work: Archaeologies of Material Practices*. Santa Fe: School for Advance Research Press.

Mollat, Michel. 1978. *Les pauvres au moyen age*. Paris: Hachette.

Moreau-Nelaton, Étienne. (1913) 2002. *Les églises de chez nous, Arrondissement de Château-Thierry*, 3 vols. Paris: Henri Laurens. (repr. ed. Paris: Le livre d'histoire-Lorisse).

Moreau-Neret, André. (s.d.) 1976. *Crépy-en-Valois*. Paris: Nouvelles Éditions Latines.

Muldrac, Fr. Antoine. 1662. *Le Valois royal amplifié et enrichi de plusieurs pièces curieuses extraites des cartulaires et archives des abbayes, églises et greffes du Valois*. Bonne-Fontaine: n.p.

Nelson, Robert S. 1996, "Appropriation," in *Critical Terms for Art History*, ed. Robert S. Nelson and Richard Shiff. Chicago: University of Chicago Press, 116–28.

Noyes, James. 2013. *The Politics of Iconoclasm: Religion, Violence and the Culture of Image-Breaking in Christianity and Islam.* London and New York: I. B. Tauris.

Olick, Jeffrey, and Joyce Robbins. 1998. "Social Memory Studies: From 'Collective Memory' to the Historical Sociology of Mnemonic Practices," *Annual Review of Sociology* 24, 105–40.

Olick, Jeffrey, Vered Vinitzky-Seroussi, and David Levy, eds. 2011. *The Collective Memory Reader.* Oxford: Oxford University Press.

Ozouf, Mona. 1988. *Festivals and the French Revolution.* Trans. Alan Sheridan. Cambridge: Harvard University Press.

—. 1976. *La fête révolutionnaire. 1789–1799.* Paris: Gallimard.

Peterson, Rick. 2012. "Social memory and ritual performance," *Journal of Social Archaeology* 13, no. 2, 266–83.

Philippot, Jacques. 1937. *Le prieuré de Saint-Pierre-des-Minimes de Compiègne.* Compiègne: Imprimérie de Compiègne.

Picot-Bocquillon, Sophie. 2012a. "Crépy-en-Valois vu par Pierre Lelu au lendemain de la Révolution," in Éric Blanchegorge, et al., *Trésors du Valois.* Crépy-en-Valois: Association des Amis du Musée de l'Archerie et du Valois, 86-88.

—. 2012b. "Le patrimoine religieux, Collégiale Saint-Thomas," in Éric Blanchegorge, et al., *Trésors du Valois.* Crépy-en-Valois: Association des Amis du Musée de l'Archerie et du Valois, 90-91.

Réau, Louis. (1958) 1994. *Histoire du vandalisme, les Monuments détruits de l'art française*, 2nd rev. ed. Michel Fleury and Guy-Michel Leproux. Paris: Robert Laffont.

Riés, Guillaume. 1999. "Crépy-en-Valois," *Revue archéologique de Picardie* special no. 16, 167–74.

Rollier, Juliette and Ambre Vilain, eds. 2016. *Portails romans et gothiques menacés par les intempéries, Le relevé laser au service du patrimoine, Portails en 3D* (ser. Archéovision, 7). Bordeaux: Ausonius Éditions.

Roquet-Hoffet, Anouk. 2001. "La révolution française à Strasbourg," in *Iconoclasme, Vie et mort de l'image medieval*, ed. Cécile Dupeux, Peter Jezler, and Jean Wirth. Paris: Éditions d'art SOMOGY, 390–99.

Sauerländer, Willibald. 1972. *Gothic Sculpture in France, 1140–1270.* Trans. Janet Sondheimer. New York: Abrams.

Souchal, François. 1993. *Le Vandalisme de la Révolution.* Paris: Nouvelle Éditions Latines.

Spivak, Gayatri Chakravorty. 1976. "Translator's Preface," in Jacques Derrida, *Of Grammatology.* Baltimore: Johns Hopkins Press, ix–lxxxvii.

Sprigath, Gabriele. 1980. "Sur le vandalisme révolutionnaire (1792–1794)," *Annales historiques de la Révolution française* 52, no. 242, 510–35.

Tackett, Timothy. 1986. *Religion, Revolution, and Regional Culture in Eighteenth-Century France, the Ecclesiastical Oath of 1791.* Princeton: Princeton University Press.

Tallet, Frank. 1991. "Dechristianizing France: the Year II and the Revolutionary Experience," in *Religion, Society and Politics in France since 1789*, ed. Frank Tallet and Nicholas Atkin. London: Hambledon Press, 1–28.

Tomasini, Jean-Marie. 1987. *Crépy-en-Valois, Mille ans d'histoire.* La Ferté Milon: Corpus 9 Éditions.

Vovelle, Michel. 1991. *The Revolution against the Church: From Reason to the Supreme Being.* Columbus: Ohio State University Press.

—. 1976. *Religion et Révolution, la déchristianisation de l'an II.* Paris: Hachette.

Wrigley, Richard. 1993. "Breaking the code: interpreting French Revolutionary iconoclasm," in *Reflections of Revolution, Images of Romanticism*, ed. Alison Yarrington and Kelvin Everest. London and New York: Routledge, 182–95.

IV

Site Transformations

Chapter 8
Considering Kadwaha as Palimpsest: Continuities, Discontinuities, and Layers In-Between

Tamara Sears

In December of 2012, I found myself walking around a small *gadhi* (fortress) at Kadwaha (fig. 8.1), a remote village in central India, and engaging in a lively discussion with Ram Barosi Sharma, a recently retired schoolteacher and local history enthusiast. As we moved within the enclosure, we talked about the inscriptions that were still embedded in the *gadhi*'s walls, and we considered the functions and relative chronology of the buildings still standing *in situ*. But our main focus was on their relationship to the site's oldest monument, an enormous stone monastery that once served as the abode of a prominent lineage of Shaiva ascetics. Established in the late ninth and early tenth centuries, the monastery and its accompanying temple served as the main impetus for the development of a larger village, which, within two centuries, had become a formidable temple town possessing no fewer than fifteen temples. The fortress walls, by contrast, were erected only in the thirteenth and fourteenth centuries. Scholarly opinion on the history revealed through the inscriptions has not achieved a consensus, and I had just recently crystallized my own revisionist conclusions based on a first-ever disentanglement of the site's architectural layers.[1]

As we walked around the site working through the material, we began to draw a crowd of interested villagers, for whom the histories that we were describing were quite new. Despite the fact that the *gadhi* and its monuments stand prominently at the village center, Kadwaha today no longer carries the same associations as it did in earlier centuries. Instead of revolving around a monastic order that worshipped the god Shiva, it has become well known instead as a place sacred for the goddess Bijasan Devi, whose temple has been drawing crowds to the village for as long as any local can remember (fig. 8.2). Every two weeks, during the goddess's biweekly festival, the streets fill up with devotees and merchants seeking a sacred viewing (*darshan*) of the main icon, and the open field (*maidan*) across the street becomes a makeshift market where craftsmen and farmers can come to peddle their wares. In truth, the Bijasan Devi temple at Kadwaha dates back only as far as the late eighteenth or early nineteenth century, which is approximately when the goddess herself likely achieved broader regional currency in central India.[2] Unlike the monuments in the *gadhi*, the goddess temple stands not at the center of the village but rather at what was once its northern outskirts, in an area that had, at the time of Kadwaha's inception, served as a fluid boundary between the core settlement and the dense forests beyond (fig. 8.3). Development over the past century and a half, however, has expanded Kadwaha's urban fabric such that the Bijasan Devi temple blends seamlessly into the rest of the village in a way that conceals discontinuities in the site today.

This essay examines the ways in which Kadwaha can be seen as a palimpsestic surface that has been formed through multiple, overlapping layers that have accumulated over time. In thinking about the concept of the palimpsest, I follow Sarah Dillon in recognizing the palimpsest as "an involuted phenomenon where otherwise unrelated texts are involved and entangled, intricately interwoven, interrupting and inhabiting each other."[3] In addressing Kadwaha as a site, I follow the editors' lead in thinking about site as a practiced place. In doing so, I follow both Tuan and De Certeau in considering place as a stable and concretely distinguishable entity, differentiated from its surroundings through the ordering of its physical features, and enlivened through movement and

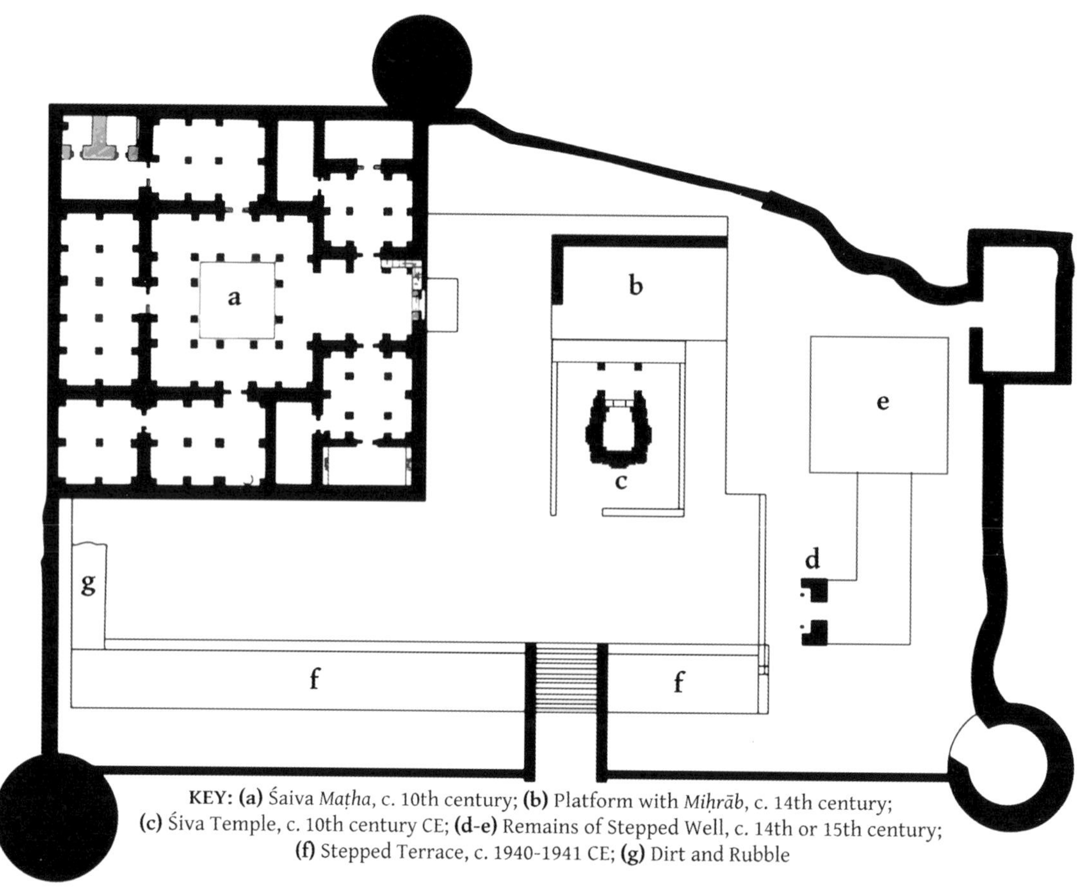

8.1. Plan of the monuments in the fortress (*gadhi*), Kadwaha, tenth–fifteenth century.

8.2. Bijasan Devi temple, Kadwaha, late eighteenth or early nineteenth century.

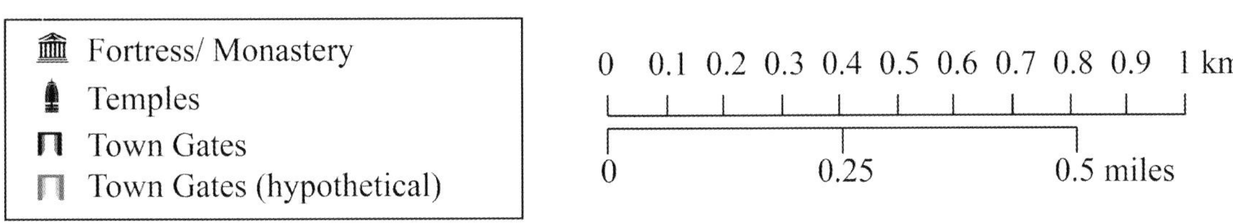

8.3. Map of the village of Kadwaha showing the reconstructed contours of the lake.

human experience.[4] My goal is more specifically to historicize the ways in which the transformation of Kadwaha's physical fabric contributed to fundamental transformations in its meaning and status at key transitional moments. I focus on specific acts of addition and erasure, some of which were intentionally enacted for political reasons and others of which represent non-intentional and more gradual changes in demographics that have resulted in significant shifts in the experience and perception of the site.

Sifting through Kadwaha's many layers is not an easy task for two reasons. The first is that the layers themselves are thoroughly imbricated in a way that makes them difficult to disentangle. The second is linked to a paucity of textual sources. At Kadwaha, everywhere one turns, one encounters striking juxtapositions. On the northeastern edge of the settlement, just before the extension of fields, a modern sculpture workshop abuts a stone wall set up by the Archaeology Survey within the past decade to protect a pair of tenth-century temples (fig. 8.4). Closer to the center of the village, just up the street from the medieval monastery, is a small colonial-era memorial pavilion (*chattri*), unob-

8.4. View of modern sculpture workshop against the backdrop of the Nahalvar group of temples, Kadwaha, tenth-twenty-first century.

8.5. Colonial-era *chattri* set in a gap between two houses, Kadwaha, nineteenth century.

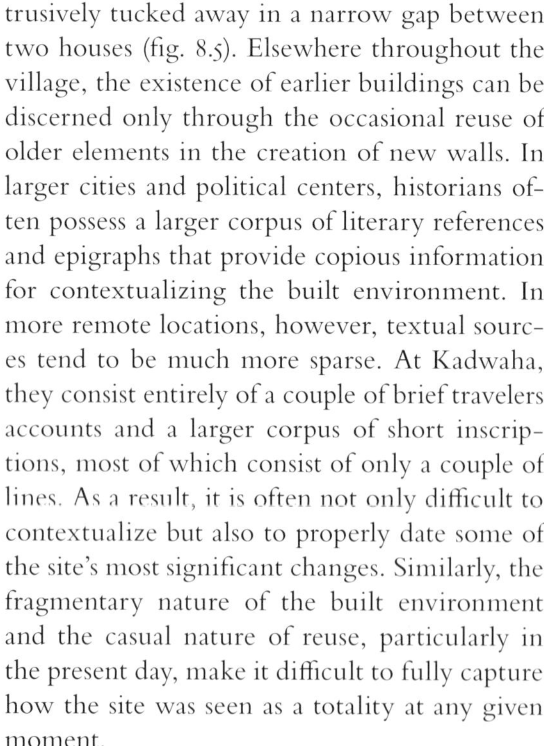

trusively tucked away in a narrow gap between two houses (fig. 8.5). Elsewhere throughout the village, the existence of earlier buildings can be discerned only through the occasional reuse of older elements in the creation of new walls. In larger cities and political centers, historians often possess a larger corpus of literary references and epigraphs that provide copious information for contextualizing the built environment. In more remote locations, however, textual sources tend to be much more sparse. At Kadwaha, they consist entirely of a couple of brief travelers accounts and a larger corpus of short inscriptions, most of which consist of only a couple of lines. As a result, it is often not only difficult to contextualize but also to properly date some of the site's most significant changes. Similarly, the fragmentary nature of the built environment and the casual nature of reuse, particularly in the present day, make it difficult to fully capture how the site was seen as a totality at any given moment.

Nonetheless, Kadwaha's diachronicity offers a different kind of insight, one that emphasizes the ways in which continuities and discontinuities often co-existed simultaneously. While shifts in political affiliation were often reinforced through radical reconfigurations in the architectural landscape, they were usually targeted at individual or small groups of monuments rather than at the site as a whole. A good case in point can be seen through the conversion of Kadwaha's *gadhi* from a Hindu monastic complex into an Islamicate *ribat* (frontier outpost) endowed with a mosque. As will be discussed in greater detail later in this essay, this conversion did little to change the actual structure of Kadwaha as a broader site or to alter in any significant way the daily forms of worship that unfolded within the site's many temples.

In my consideration of Kadwaha, I expand my notion of site to include all aspects of the built environment, incorporating both monuments and patterns of urban planning, and also the shaping of the natural landscape. In many cases, it is this latter element that is the hardest to historicize, since, unlike monuments, landscape has often been conceived of as immutable and not often subject to radical change. However, at Kadwaha, the manipulation of landscape at various moments has been revealed by the existence of a particularly rich textual source, the *Baburnama*, the memoir of the Mughal emperor Babur (1483–1530), which includes a detailed passage providing a survey-like overview of the site as a whole. As a result, this essay takes Babur's account of Kadwaha's landscape as a point of departure first for examining the layered history that preceded his arrival, and then, by way of conclusion, for examining how his account makes even more obvious the ways in which the site has changed in the present day.

Encountering outlying landscapes

On 17 January 1528, the Mughal emperor Babur set up camp on the outskirts of a "fine little place" known to him as Kachwaha, which is synonymous with the present-day village of Kadwaha.[5] The journey, which had begun a month earlier in Agra, was aimed at reclaiming the central Indian fortress at Chanderi, which had recently fallen to allies of his Rajput rival, the Maharana Sangram Singh. Located less than forty kilometers from his final destination, Kadwaha might have easily been just a day's travel away (fig. 8.6). However, at the time of Babur's journey, Kadwaha was a relatively rural outpost, and, while roads had been long established, they had been overgrown by dense forests and had become covered with pits and potholes. Passing might not have been much of a problem had he been traveling only with horsemen and infantry. But his army was also outfitted with unwieldy carts and a cannon. Thus, he employed local overseers and shovelers to clear a path in order to enable his artillery to pass. The task took two days, during which Babur made use of the time to survey the local landscape and to take note of its tactical advantages.

This particular campaign is described in some detail in the *Baburnama*, or Babur's memoirs, which was written in Chaghatay and later translated into Persian in 1589 during the reign of the Mughal emperor Akbar (1542–1605). Although Babur's original manuscript subsequently disappeared from the imperial library a century later,

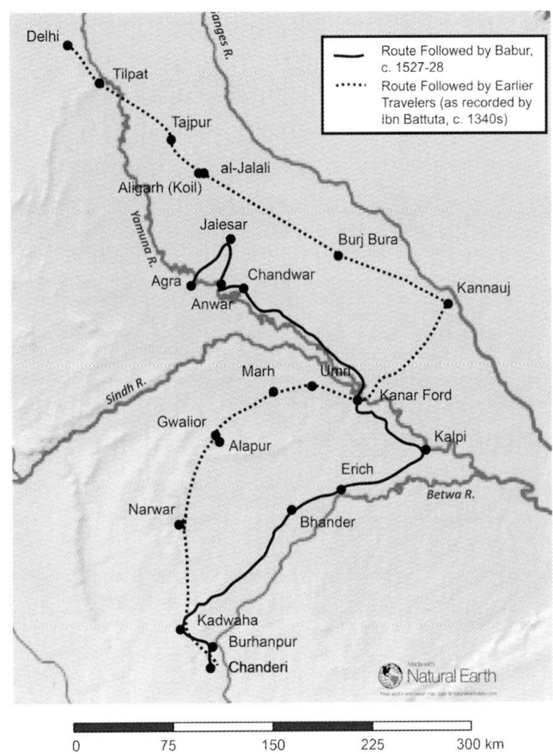

8.6. Map displaying routes of travel through Central India, as described by Ibn Battuta (*c.* 1340s) and Babur (*c.* 1527–28).

the Persian version was repeatedly reproduced and embellished with paintings executed by the finest artists of the Mughal atelier.[6]

To anyone familiar with the *Baburnama*, it will not be surprising that Babur's account of Kadwaha is dominated by a description of hills, forests, and waterways. Even during his own time, Babur was known for his obsessive love of nature and his cultivation of gardens. Accordingly, his memoirs are filled with numerous opinions and observations of India's landscape, both natural and manipulated.[7] His judgment was not always favorable, as Babur made it abundantly clear that he preferred the mountains and steppes of his homeland to the flat plains and thorny trees of the subcontinent. He particularly bemoaned the lack of good sources of running water, and he disdained the disordered gardens of India's previous rulers.[8] To rectify these problems, he fostered the creation of new gardens, lakes, and irrigation canals.[9]

Within this context, it is notable that Babur's account of Kadwaha expresses neither praise nor disdain, but rather an attentiveness to key topographical and hydrological features of the surrounding landscape.[10] The privileging of the site's tactical advantages was no doubt related to the fact that he was in the middle of a military campaign, which, although ultimately directed towards Chanderi, also offered Babur the opportunity to solidify political control over other key outposts along the way. Accordingly, his first act upon setting up camp at Kadwaha was to place the town under the authority of the son of one of his allies, giving the people of Kadwaha safe quarter, effectively incorporating them as subjects within the burgeoning Mughal Empire. From there, Babur turned to the task of surveying Kadwaha's natural environment. In addition to being surrounded by little hillocks, Kadwaha was also protected by a large artificial lake with a perimeter of approximately a dozen miles—something that added significantly, in his estimation, to its defensibility.[11]

From the perspective of an architectural or urban historian, this portion of the *Baburnama* is of particular interest, as it records not only the specifics of the lake's size but also its mode of construction. According to the account, Kadwaha's lake was formed by a dam built to harness a stream flowing down from the mountains situated to the southeast of the site. The resulting lake was like a moat, protecting Kadwaha on three sides, giving way only at the northwest, where stood the town gate. In addition to serving as a moat around the village, Babur observed that the lake provided a safe haven for residents in times of extreme danger. In his own words, "whenever the people need to flee, they get into the [small] boats [kept along the banks of the lake] and [find safety by going] out into the middle of the water."[12] What made Kadwaha's lake impressive was not its singular nature but rather its large size. He wrote that "before reaching Kachwaha, we saw two other places where dams were built across hills to form lakes, but the lakes were smaller than the one at Kachwaha."[13] Thus Kadwaha represented for Babur a particularly grand example of a broader pattern of urban planning that could be observed on a smaller scale at other sites in central India.

8.7. Morayat (or Mulayata) temple group, Kadwaha, tenth-eleventh century. View of fields around the temples from the south.

The significance of Babur's account for historicizing Kadwaha's landscape cannot be understated since without it, it would be nearly impossible today to know that the village plan once featured a large body of water. Unlike the old road between Chanderi and Kadwaha, which remains overgrown and pitted even today, the lake that so captured Babur's attention has completely disappeared. When I first visited Kadwaha during the monsoon season in August of 1999, I saw no sign of a large expanse of water surrounding the village. Instead, the village's outskirts gave way to verdant fields (fig. 8.7). During subsequent trips, in 2001–02, I noted traces of dismantled *ghats* (steps leading down to a body of water) in the boundaries between plowed tracts. By December 2012, the area of cultivated land had visibly increased as had the size of the residential area, with new streets, vendor's stalls, and homes beginning to sprawl beyond the historic village center.

The expansion of fields around the village of Kadwaha is not surprising given the increasing push for investment in agro-business across India, and particularly within the present-day state of Madhya Pradesh, whose agricultural growth has surpassed nearly every other state over the course of the past two decades.[14] This development has led to a wide-scale diversion of groundwater and seasonal streams for the purpose of irrigation and also to the draining of older artificial lakes. The fact that the lake's disappearance is relatively recent is attested to by archival photographs. Only a few decades ago, it was still possible to see a large body of water extending beyond the entrance to the impressive Toteshvara Mahadeva temple, which stands today at the far eastern edge of the village.[15] Perhaps because the lake's loss is recent, its approximate original contours can be discerned through satellite imagery, which reveals a large area of water-saturated ground extending beyond the village (fig. 8.8). As in Babur's account, the saturated area appears to give way only at the north side, where one of the remaining medieval gates can still be found today. Similarly, Babur's description of the lake as formed by a dam slung across two hills to the southeast matches up well with maps of the local topography, which reveal a narrow stretch of land bounded by hillocks and watered by streams in precisely the right location.

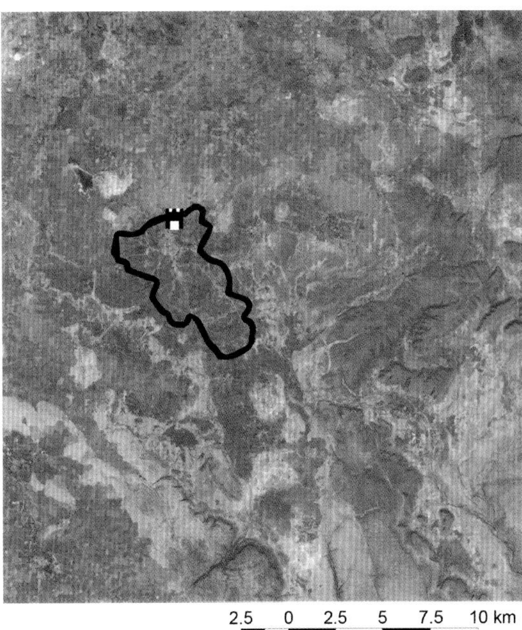

8.8. Maps displaying the extent of saturated groundwater around Kadwaha. Left: Physical map. Right: Satellite map.

Although Babur's account appears relatively late in Kadwaha's settlement history, it reveals an important element of the original site plan that would otherwise remain invisible. As noted above, Kadwaha's origin can be traced back to the monastic complex at its center, which consisted at the time of its foundation of a residential dwelling, an accompanying temple and a stepwell (fig. 8.1). In addition to forming a monumental grouping in its own right, this complex also served as the impetus both for further architectural growth and development on a local level and for the strengthening of routes of travel that connected Kadwaha to dozens of distant places.[16] Built by a guru belonging to a prominent lineage known as the Mattamayuras, the monastery functioned as a key political and religious node within a larger monastic network that extended not only across central India, but also much further, into the Deccan and southern India. By the eleventh and twelfth centuries, the Mattamayuras had become associated with branching lineages of sages extending eastward towards Orissa and Bengal, and southward into Maharashtra, Karnataka, and Tamil Nadu. While some of their monastic dwellings functioned as forest retreats and were built beyond the boundaries of a nearby settlement, others served as institutional hubs of larger temple towns.[17] Kadwaha was a prime example of this latter type. The monastery stood at the center of the growing settlement that was encircled, in turn, by clusters of temples. The temples served to define and delimit the space of the village. They marked the furthest extent of Kadwaha's architectural fabric, approximately a half kilometer out from the monastic complex at the center, and were positioned along three of the four cardinal directions, to the east, west, and north.

The ways in which the lake's reconstructed contours, as noted above, skirt the edges of this built environment suggests that the intention of its makers was to create a lakefront for Kadwaha's temples (fig. 8.3).[18] The act of juxtaposing temples and water was quite common in medieval India. It was a hallmark of sacred sites and pilgrimage centers, where temples were frequently built along the banks of rivers, lakes, or tanks. In addition to fostering the performance of daily ritual activities, the water would also function as an extension of a sacred arena. At Kadwaha, the water would have functioned in a way that was both religiously meaningful and deeply pragmatic. While the positioning of Kadwaha's temples would have symbolically marked the village's outermost extents, the water would have concretized the boundaries and enhanced both the sustainability and defensibility of the growing settlement.

Historicizing the residential center

While Babur's account is useful for conceptualizing the horizontal extents of Kadwaha's surface, it ultimately describes the village in a way that is hollow. In contrast to his careful detailing of Kadwaha's landscape, he says next to nothing about its many monuments. This is strange because by the time of his visit, Kadwaha had become radically transformed over the centuries, from a Hindu monastic center into an important Islamicate outpost that stood at a crucial position along the routes connecting two of central India's most important frontier fortresses at Narwar and Chanderi. Narwar and Chanderi were notably two among a trio of regional military centers (which also included Gwalior) that, when all three were held together, made it possible to control not only the region but the longer-distance routes connecting onward towards the Deccan. Whereas Gwalior was geographically well within the reach of the north Indian imperial centers of Kanauj and later Delhi, Narwar, and Chanderi were situated deeper in the wilderness frontier. Located approximately halfway between Narwar and Chanderi, Kadwaha became a natural outpost and stopping point for travelers of many types, ranging from traders and pilgrims to fully equipped armies, such as the one led by Babur. However, it was Kadwaha's abundant lake that would have made it particularly useful as a stop for anyone traveling with horses and pack animals needing to be watered.

At the time of Babur's campaign against Chanderi in 1527–28, Gwalior was already under the emperor's control, and, although Narwar was not on Babur's immediate path, it had

8.9. Monastery and fortress wall, Kadwaha, tenth-fifteenth century. View of exterior from the west.

been conquered many times in earlier centuries by Hindu and Muslim rulers. Originally established as a capital under the Hindu Kachhapaghatas in the eleventh and twelfth centuries, Narwar subsequently fell to the Yajvapala dynasty that succeeded them at some point in the 1230s or 40s. In the thirteenth century, it became a contested ground between multiple Hindu and Muslim dynasties. The Yajvapalas, who continued to hold it through the end of the century, managed to thwart assaults by their Hindu rivals, the Chandellas, who ruled over the region of Bundelkhand to the east.[19] At the same time, Narwar was periodically targeted by the Muslim sultans of Delhi. All three fortresses were overtaken briefly in 1251–52, by the general and later sultan Ulugh Khan Balaban. But their final conquest occurred only at the turn of the fourteenth century under the leadership of 'Ala' al din Khalji.[20] The Khalji usurpation of the region at that moment had staying power, and the trio remained under the control of subsequent sultanate dynasties. The ability to police the larger region, however, was contingent on also holding smaller outposts, such as at Kadwaha.

At Kadwaha, this layered history of conquest, mobility, and travel became inextricably etched into the physical fabric in ways that are best described as palimpsestic. The most radical changes were felt at the very center through the changing shape of the monastic complex. While the monastery continued to serve as the abode of Shaiva ascetics through at least the early fourteenth century, the status of the monastery became increasingly contested, especially towards the end. By the last quarter of the thirteenth century, fortifications were built around the monastery.[21] These had the effect of transforming the sacred site into the veritable *gadhi* that still stands today. The builders of the *gadhi* made economical use of the existing structure of the monastic complex in their design. Instead of building a completely new wall, they built it as an extension of the monastery's southern and western sides (figs. 8.1 and 8.9). As a result, the monastery ceased to be an independent, free-standing structure and was instead incorporated into the broader fortress walls.

The ascetics likely remained in possession of the monastery for only a few more decades, until both Narwar and Chanderi were fully inte-

8.10. Fortress (*gadhi*), Kadwaha, tenth-fifteenth century. View of the temple, monastery, and fragmentary *qibla* wall of the mosque from the northeast.

grated into the Khalji Kingdom. The very last trace of ascetic presence can be found just two or three years prior to the conquest of Chanderi by the Khaljis in 1312, through an inscription built into the floor near the temple accompanying the monastery. According to the inscription, a sage named Bhuteshvara performed special worship of the temple's icon, a Shiva *linga*, after the take-over of the area by *mlecchas* (i.e., Muslims), which resulted in damage to the nearby stepwell in 1309–10. In addition to repairing the well, Bhuteshvara practiced severe penance, most likely as an attempt to prevent further incursions.[22] Unfortunately, Bhuteshvara's penance seems to have been unsuccessful. By the early fourteenth century, the *gadhi* that had encompassed the monastery was fully converted into a Muslim *ribat*.

The conversion of the monastic complex into a *ribat* was established vertically through the creation of a tall platform that completely subsumed the entirety of the original Shiva temple (figs. 8.1 and 8.10). In fact, the temple's existence was completely forgotten in the centuries that followed. It was only rediscovered in 1939, when the Archaeological Survey of India decided to remove the "accretions of earth and debris of later structures" that obstructed its vision.[23] Although acts of Islamic conversion are often understood in terms of the destruction or desecration of temple sites, in this case, the temple was left almost fully intact. In palimpsestual terms, it had been primarily subject to additive erasure, covering over the original fabric with mounds of earth, but leaving the original structure preserved within. Only the temple's tower was subjected to subtractive erasure, being dismantled stone by stone. It remains unknown why the mosque's builders might have chosen to preserve the body of the temple in this way. I would suggest, however, that the key factor was related to the height of the original temple tower. The platform that supported the mosque was very deliberately extended at the same level

8.11. Fortress (*gadhi*), Kadwaha, tenth-fifteenth century. Digital rubbing of inscriptions on the windowsill of the third-storey room in the monastery.

8.12. Fortress (*gadhi*), Kadwaha, tenth-fifteenth century. View of the ruined mosque and temple from the south.

8.13. Fortress (*gadhi*), Kadwaha, tenth-fifteenth century. View of the recently excavated stepwell.

8.14. View of the northern town gate, Kadwaha.

as the curved eave that would have functioned as the base of the tower extending above the temple's sanctum. As a result, the mosque would have, in effect, usurped a crucially symbolic vertical position, one that would have been, just prior to its construction, synonymous with the most visible portion of the temple.

The establishment of a mosque on a tall platform was not the only way in which the focus of the site was drawn upwards. The monastic dwelling, too, was heightened through the creation of a third story, which survives today only in the form of a small room situated just to the west of the building's north-south axis. Although its precise chronology remains unknown, the room possesses over a half dozen inscriptions dating between 1409 and 1447 (fig. 8.11).[24] These make it clear that Kadwaha's alliances broadened during this period as it became increasingly incorporated into the kingdom of the regional sultans of Malwa, who were based at Mandu, not far from the city of Indore today.[25] Set up higher than any other monument within the *gadhi*, the third story may have served as a lookout point that would have enabled surveillance of the landscape far beyond the fortress's walls. It would have also enabled easy viewings of the mosque's *mihrab*, which stood almost directly on axis below (fig. 8.12). The shift in viewpoint was particularly significant. Prior to its making, the monastery's only other significant aperture would have been a central balcony that would have overlooked the site from the center of the monastery's upper facade. In writing about such balconies elsewhere, I have suggested that they would have facilitated acts of *guru-darshana*, or the sacred viewing of the resident preceptor, and acted as highly mediated points of permeability between the interior and exclusive world of the monastic residence and the expansion of public ritual around the temples outside.[26] With the covering up of the temple, it would have been the mosque that would have commanded the primary view from the residence that had, in previous periods, functioned as a monastery.

Such later architectural interventions at Kadwaha's center moved not only upwards but also downwards through the excavation of an expansive stepwell in the northwest quadrant of the fortress (figs. 8.1 and 8.13). Only recently

8.15. Toteshvara Mahadeva Temple, Kadwaha, eleventh century. View of an inscription on the pedestal of the icon within the sanctum, *c.* 1523–24.

uncovered by the Archaeological Survey of India, this stepwell has not undergone systematic study. Nonetheless, even a cursory survey makes it clear that it was built in phases over many centuries. The earliest, and deepest, part was a fairly simple square tank, built of stone coursing that is similar in dimension and form to the tenth-century Shaiva monastery. The inscriptional record suggests that the well may have been expanded, repaired, and/or renovated much later, first by an individual named Kumarapala in 1294–95, and then by the sage Bhuteshvara in 1309–10, as noted above.[27] Although the precise nature of each of these phases is unknown, it is likely that they contributed to the enlargement of the stepped passage leading down to the original well. Certainly, by the time of Babur's visit in January of 1528, the stepwell would have been a prominent structure, with a visible entryway on the north side of the *gadhi*.

The gradual conversion of the earlier Hindu complex, first into a fortress and then a fortified *ribat*, over the course of the early sultanate period, effectively transformed the site's surface on both horizontal and vertical levels. The horizontal expansion was felt through the erection of thick walls with circular bastions. In addition to creating a clear boundary between the sacred realm of the monastic complex and the residential world beyond, these fortifications fundamentally reconfigured the spatial relationship between the monastery and its temple. The monastery became not a separate building, but an embedded part of the *gadhi*'s southwest quadrant. By contrast, the temple was situated along the main approach from the fort's entrance. This shift in focus can be understood as palimpsestic layering, through which the shift in the surface was produced both materially through architectural form and performatively through vision and movement.

Beyond the *gadhi*'s walls, new dwellings for local residents, built of similar materials, began to form a densely packed residential core, which, by the time of Babur's visit in the early sixteenth century, was surrounded again by a defensible wall and gateways. The overall plan of the fully developed medieval village can be reconstructed through the remnants still visible in the present day. The village walls created an approximate circle around the residential core, effectively creating a radial plan. This inner area was, in turn, divided into quadrants by a pair of perpendicularly oriented roads that established roughly north-south and east-west axes that culminated in four gateways, only two of which can still be found in traces today (figs. 8.3 and 8.14). In short, the village plan, in its medieval conception, was not haphazardly formed, but rather followed medieval Indian patterns of urban design.[28]

In contrast with the radical transformations occurring at its center, the physical structure of space around Kadwaha's edges seems to have remained remarkably stable through the centuries leading up to Babur's visit. The temples that were built to encircle the village in the tenth and eleventh centuries remained standing and in active use. This continuity is attested to through dozens of inscriptions that were scrawled across their surfaces. Although most consist simply of one or two lines recording the names of pilgrims, others are more substantial. These latter generally recorded a specific donation to a temple or a significant moment of renovation. A case in point can be found in the Totesvara Mahadeva temple, which once towered over the lake at Kadwaha's far eastern edge (fig. 8.7). Originally built in the late eleventh century and dedicated to the god Siva, the Totesvara Mahadeva temple possesses over a dozen inscriptions dating between the twelfth and sixteenth centuries.[29] Most are found in the pillared hall (*mandapa*) preceding the sanctum and attest to continuing ritual activity, even as their authors pay homage, through the text itself, to their Muslim overlords. The most significant of the records at the Toteshvara Mahadeva temple is one that is found on the rounded edges of a pedestal in the sanctum. It records the renewal of the icon proper by a priest in 1523–24, which is notably less than half a decade before Babur passed through town (fig. 8.15).[30]

That ritual activity continued even through periods of political transition is not surprising. Although inscriptions indicate that authority over Kadwaha shifted over the years, they also attest to threads of continuity within Kadwaha's communities. Almost all of Kadwaha's inscriptions are written in a local Devanagari script in either Sanskrit or Hindi, regardless of whether the ruling power was Hindu or Muslim. They thereby follow older local and regional linguistic traditions instead of adopting the Persian language of the Islamicate courts.[31] In fact, what the inscriptions highlight is that the transition to sultanate rule was felt not through the mass conversion of populace and place, but through the selective transformation of key spaces within the context of a larger site. At Kadwaha, the advent of the Delhi sultans had the greatest impact at the village center, through the usurpation of the fortress enclosing the earlier Hindu monastery. Because the monastery also served as a political and administrative center, its conversion was likely motivated less by religion than by the desire to cut its ties to earlier forms of political power.[32]

Revisiting the palimpsest in the present day

The process of working through these additions highlights the fact that sites are never static. Instead, like the monuments that populate them, they are experienced through embodied movements and sets of unfolding views that are subject to change with every addition and renovation. What is particularly notable at Kadwaha is that the most destructive changes have occurred not in the distant past but in the present day. For example, the Sultanate era transformation of the Hindu monastic site into an Islamicate *ribat* poses a stark contrast with early twentieth-century archaeological practices. What is notable

8.16. Toteshvara Mahadeva Temple, Kadwaha, eleventh century. View of the landscape from the interior of the temple.

about the fourteenth-century moment is that the surface of the site was radically transformed through a temporary "covering up" rather than a permanent "taking away." The temple next to the monastery was not dismantled, but rather buried. As such, it continued to serve a vital role in the ongoing life of the site by serving as the foundation for the mosque that took its place at the center of the *gadhi*. By contrast, the colonial-era efforts to recover the temple from beneath the platform constituted an act of irreversible destruction, through which later layers of building were excavated and removed in the effort to recover an earlier, original moment. This was one of many colonial-era incidents in which an earlier Hindu history was privileged over later obviously Muslim interventions.[33]

It is true that by the time of the dismantling of the platform and the excavation of the temple accompanying the monastery in the 1930s, Kadwha had long ceased to be a place associated with either Islam or Islamic rule. The Mughals likely remained nominally in control until the second half of the eighteenth century, at which point the Marathas took firm control over the region. It was then that the *ribat* may have lost its significance as the administrative and political center of the village. It is not surprising perhaps that it was this moment that also saw the construction of the Bijasan Devi temple that dominates the social, ritual, and economic life of Kadwaha and its outlying area today. It is uncertain precisely when the local goddess festival began attracting thousands of people to Kadwaha twice a month. However, what is clear is that the festival has also begun to take on political implications. In addition to coinciding with the marketing of goods from throughout the local area, Bijasan Devi festival days have been targeted also by political candidates running for election at both local and national elections. I myself was present in February of 2002 when the Maharaja of Gwalior, Jyotiraditya Madhavrao Scindia (b. 1971), was campaigning for the Congress Party seat in the Lower House (Lok Saba) of the Indian Parliament during a special election held to replace his father, who had passed away suddenly in a tragic helicopter accident. As I made my way through Kadwaha, I observed a parade of white Tata jeeps making their way through the congested streets to the open field by the Bijasan Devi temple. There I joined members of the local *panchayat* (governance board) and watched the Maharaja give his campaign speeches. Around me, local villagers stood watching with admiration. There was no question that he would sweep the district, where his family had long been thought of, ever since the Maratha conquest, as the beloved rulers.

As the social, ritual, and political heart of the site has moved outward towards the Bijasen Devi temple, the monastic complex at the physical center of the village has become redefined as an archaeological site important not because of its living presence, but because of its layered past. In recent years, the Archaeological Survey has taken increasing pains to preserve both the monuments in the *gadhi* and Kadwaha's many temples. In the past decade alone, most of Kadwaha's early medieval temples have undergone extensive restorations. In some cases, they were dismantled block by block and rebuilt carefully in order to secure their foundations and prevent further damage due to the settling of the ground. All of them have been outfitted with new walled and gated enclosures as a protective measure, presumably to secure the monuments from the potential threat of vandals.

It is perhaps unfortunate that these acts of preservation have had the additional effect of further removing Kadwaha's temples from the landscape environment that had once been so essential to their meaning. The disconnect can perhaps be most poignantly realized in the case of the Toteshvara Mahadeva temple, which, until a few decades ago, had stood directly above the banks of Kadwaha's erstwhile lake (fig. 8.16). Today, it stands behind a stone fence and a gated door that have created both a visual and physical separation from the fields that lie beyond. The fields, in turn, function as the latest etching upon Kadwaha's palimpsestic surface. The expansion of agricultural activity has irrevocably destroyed the water feature that had long been essential to Kadwaha's design and underlying conception. And the influx of migrant agrarian labor has been further changing the shape of Kadwaha's edges. New houses have begun to sprawl haphazardly along the roads leading in and out of town, and the families that have begun to occupy them have no memories of Kadwaha's recent history, let alone of its distant past. Such changes make it all the more essential that we, as historians, think of sites as palimpsestic and exert our energies not only into publishing our findings but also into conversing with locals in order to ensure that the many layers continue to speak to the local populace in the present day.

Notes

1 Sears 2014.

2 Although the history of Bijasan Devi is not well known, she appears to have spread rapidly across central India and Rajasthan in the eighteenth and nineteenth centuries. Kadwaha is only one of many villages that sponsors a periodic festival dedicated to the goddess, and she may have originated as a tribal deity associated with the Bhils and Gonds. In at least one instance, in the market town of Jahazpur in Rajasthan, she has been associated with potters, and it is possible that her movement might have followed the path of mobile artisan communities. See, for example *Central Provinces District Gazetteers: Hoshangabad District* 1908, 54; Gold 2017, 299, note 28.

3 Dillon follows Thomas De Quincey in defining the term "involuted" as describing "the relationship between the texts that inhabit the palimpsest as a result of the process of palimpsesting and subsequent textual reappearance." Dillon 2005, 245.

4 Although the editors do not use the term "practiced place" in this volume, their definition of site as place includes both the stability of site as a Cartesian geographic location and the production of its meaning through human activity and experience. In other words, their definition is not so much place in the more restricted sense of the term, but of a space that is effectively a "practiced place." See also Tuan 1977; De Certeau 1984, 117.

5 Thackston 1996, 396.

6 For a fuller history of the text and its translations, see Thackston 1996, 11–15.

7 For more on the importance of gardens and landscape in the production of Babur's cultural persona, see Dale 2004, 183–86.

8 Welch 1996.

9 Thackston 1996, 302, 330–34. See also Ruggles 2008, 110.

10 Babur's treatment of Kadwaha's landscape is similar to his description of other places encountered in the context of military campaigns. In this case, the most notable comparison can be found at Chanderi, where Babur fully exploited water channels and hills in order to obtain a quick and decisive victory. See Thackston 1996, 396–99.

11 The exact dimensions of the lake observed by Babur remains an open question. Babur describes it as having a perimeter of five to six *kos*. It is commonly assumed that the Mughal *kos* was equivalent to approximately 4.17 kilometers or 2.5 miles. However, the *kos* has historically varied significantly across localities and regions. While the Mughals were known for their efforts at standardization through the installation of new road markers, these came under the aegis of later Mughal rulers. See, for example, Gole 1989, 14; Parihar 2008, 14.

12 Thackston 1996, 396.

13 Thackston 1996, 396.

14 The state of Madhya Pradesh has experienced a dramatic 80% increase in agricultural production since 2002. The widening geography of cultivation has seen a similar demographic shift to reflect a rising population of primarily male agricultural laborers. For additional agricultural data, see Kumar 2014, 250–51.

15 A particularly useful photo can be accessed through the American Institute of Indian Studies photographic archive, accession no. 3085, negative no. 82.51. For an illustration, see Sears 2009, 20, fig. 14.

16 Only a small shrine dated to the late ninth century predates this monastic complex. See EITA 1998, vol. 2, pt. 3, 21–27.

17 For a more extensive discussion of the network, see Mirashi 1950; Sears 2014. For a Sanskrit edition, see Mirashi and Sastri 1968.

18 See, for example, Willis 2014.

19 For an overview of this history, see Trivedi 1978, vol. 1.

20 Wink 1997, 158; Jackson 1999, 144–45.

21 I have argued elsewhere that this transformation likely occurred in the second decade of the thirteenth century, after the Khalji conquest of the regional capital at Chanderi, which was similarly marked there by the establishment of a mosque datable by inscription to January 1312. See Sears 2009, 13–18.

22 Willis 1996, 22; Singh 2000, 230–31.

23 The removal of debris and the construction of a retaining wall to safeguard the temple are recorded in Garde 1939–1940, 8. For a more detailed discussion, see Sears 2009, 10–12.

24 Willis 1996, 14, 21–23, 26–30, 36, 39, 44, 45, 112–13; Singh 2000, esp. 230, 231, 234.

25 The name of the sultan of Malwa, Mahmud Khalji (r. 1436–69), is found among the inscriptions. See Willis 1996, 31.

26 Sears 2014, 88, 95, 119, 178–80.

27 Willis 1996, 21; Singh 2000, 232–33.

28 On patterns of urban planning, as correlated through textual and archaeological sources, see Michell 1992; Chattopadhyaya 1997; Heitzman 2008; Kaul 2011.

29 Although the inscriptions have yet to be assessed as a cohesive set, descriptions of individual records can be found in Willis 1996, and transcriptions of select inscriptions in Singh 2000, 231–32, 234–36. The chronological range is from 1106–07 through the sixteenth century.

30 Singh 2000, 232.

31 There is little evidence to support the idea of a local mass conversion to Islam, and, in fact, the names of local individuals found in Kadwaha's inscriptions are predominantly Hindu. For more on problems with assessing conversion in medieval India, see Eaton 1985.

32 This was typical practice in medieval India. See Eaton 2000.

33 For the contentiousness over complex communal histories and the privileging of pre-Muslim origins in colonial and post-colonial India, see Guha-Thakurta 2013.

Bibliography

Central Provinces District Gazetteers: Hoshangabad District. 1908. Calcutta: Thacker, Spink & Co.

Chakravarty, Kalyan Kumar. 1984. *Gwalior Fort: Art, Culture, and History.* New Delhi: Arnold-Heinemann.

Chattopadhyaya, B. D. 1997. "The City in Early India: Perspectives from Texts," *Studies in History* 13, no. 2, 181–208.

Dale, Stephen F. 2004. *The Garden of the Eight Paradises: Babur and the Culture of Empire in Central Asia, Afghanistan and India (1483–1530).* Leiden: Brill.

De Certeau, Michel. 1984. *The Practice of Everyday Life.* Berkeley: University of California Press.

Dillon, Sarah. 2005. "Reinscribing De Quincey's palimpsest: the significance of the palimpsest in contemporary literary and cultural studies," *Textual Practice* 19, no. 3, 243–63.

Eaton, Richard M. 2000. "Temple Desecration in Pre-Modern India," *Frontline* 17, no. 25, 62–70.

—. 1985. "Approaches to the Study of Conversion to Islam in India," in *Approaches to Islam in Religious Studies*, ed. Richard M. Martin. Tucson: University of Arizona Press, 106–23.

EITA. 1998. *Encyclopaedia of Indian Temple Architecture.* Vol. II, part 3 (text and plates), *North India: Beginnings of Medieval Idiom*, ed. M. A. Dhaky. New Delhi: American Institute of Indian Studies and Indira Gandhi National Centre for the Arts.

—. 1988. *Encyclopaedia of Indian Temple Architecture.* Vol. II, part 1 (text and plates), *North India: Foundations of North Indian Style*, ed. Michael W. Meister, M. A. Dhaky, and Krishna Deva. Princeton: Princeton University Press and New Delhi: American Institute of Indian Studies.

Fussman, Gérard, Dennis Matringe, Eric Ollivier, and Francoise Pirot. 2003. *Chanderi Du Xe Au XVIIIe siècle: naissance et déclin d'une qasba (sous la direction de Gérard Fussman et Kanhaiya Lal Sharma)*, 3 vols. Paris: Boccard.

Garde, M. B. 1939–40. *Annual Administration Report of the Archaeological Department of Gwalior State*. Gwalior: Alijah Darbar Press.

Gibb, H. A. R., and Charles Beckingham, trans. 1994. *The Travels of Ibn Baṭṭūṭa (AD 1325–1354)*. Vol. 4. Cambridge and London: The Hakluyt Society.

Gold, Ann Grodzins. 2017. *Shiptown: Between Rural and Urban North India*. Philadelphia: University of Pennsylvania Press.

Gole, Susan. 1989. *Indian Maps and Plans: From Earliest Times to the Advent of European Surveys*. Delhi: Manohar.

Guha-Thakurta, Tapati. 2013. "The Production and Reproduction of a Monument: The Many Lives of the Sanchi *Stupa*," *South Asian Studies* 29, no. 1, 77–110.

Hegewald, Julia A. B. 2002. *Water Architecture in South Asia: A Study of Types, Development, and Meanings*. Leiden: Brill.

Heitzman, James. 2008. *The City in South Asia: Asia's Great Cities*. London and New York: Routledge.

Jackson, Peter. 1999. *The Delhi Sultanate: A Political and Military History*. Cambridge: Cambridge University Press.

Jain-Neubauer, Jutta. 1981. *The Stepwells of Gujarat in Art Historical Perspective*. New Delhi: Abhinav Publications.

Kaul, Shonaleeka. 2011. *Imagining the Urban: Sanskrit and the City in Early India*. London: Seagull Books.

Kumar, Sarvesh, R. C. Sharma and M. K. Bankoliya. 2014. "Agricultural Production Scenario of Madhya Pradesh," in *Technologies for Sustainable Rural Development (TSRD–2014)*, ed. Jai Prakash Shukla. New Delhi: Allied Publishers, 250–56.

Michell, George. 1992. "City as Cosmogram: The Circular Plan of Warangal," *South Asian Studies* 8, no. 1, 1–18.

Mirashi, V. V. 1950. "The Saiva Acaryas of the Mattamayura Clan," *Indian Historical Quarterly* 26, 1–16.

Mirashi, V. V., and A. M. Shastri. 1968. "A Fragmentary Stone Inscription from Kadwaha," *Epigraphia Indica* 37, 117–24.

Parihar, Subhash. 2008. *Land Transport in Mughal India: Agra-Lahore Mughal Highway and its Architectural Remains*. Delhi: Aryan Books International.

Ruggles, D. Fairchild. 2008. *Islamic Gardens and Landscapes*. Philadelphia: University of Pennsylvania Press.

Sears, Tamara I. 2014. *Worldly Gurus and Spiritual Kings: Architecture and Asceticism in Medieval India*. New Haven and London: Yale University Press.

—. 2009. "Fortified Maṭhas and Fortress Mosques: The Transformation and Reuse of Hindu Monastic Sites in the Thirteenth and Fourteenth Centuries," *Archives of Asian Art* 59, 7–31.

Singh, Arvind Kumar. 2000. "Inscriptions from Kadwaha, Dist. Guna (M.P.)," *Prāgdhārā, Journal of the U.P. State Archaeological Organisation* 10, 229–39.

Smart, Ellen. 1986. "Yet Another Illustrated Akbari Baburnama Manuscript," in *Facets of Indian Art*, ed. Robert Skelton, Andrew Topsfield, Susan Stronge, and Rosemary Crill. London: Victoria and Albert Museum, 105–15.

Thackston, Wheeler M., trans. 1996. *The Baburnama: Memoirs of Babur, Prince and Emperor*. New York and Oxford: Oxford University Press.

Trivedi, H. V. 1978. *Inscriptions of the Paramāras, Chandēllas, Kachchapaghātas, and Two Minor Dynasties*, 3 vols. (ser. Corpus Inscriptionum Indicarum, 7). New Delhi: Archaeological Survey of India.

Welch, Anthony. 1996. "Gardens that Babur Did Not Like: Landscape, Water, and Architecture for the Sultans of Delhi," in *Mughal Gardens: Sources, Places, Representations, and Prospects*, ed. James L. Wescoat and Joachim Wolschke-Bulmahn. Washington, D.C.: Dumbarton Oaks Research Library and Collection, 59–94.

Willis, Michael, Pankaj Raj, O. P. Mishra, and Doria Tichit, eds 2014. *Patrimoine Culturel de L'Eau: Cities and Settlements, Temples and Tanks in Central India*. Bhopal: Directorate of Archaeology, Archives and Museums, Govt. of M.P.

Willis, Michael D. 1996. *Inscriptions of Gopakṣetra*. London: British Museum.

Wink, Andre. 1997. *Al Hind: The Making of the Indo-Islamic World*. Vol. 2: *The Slave Kings and Islamic Conquest in the 11th–13th Centuries*. Leiden: Brill.

Chapter 9
Temporal Palimpsests and Authenticity in Rwandan Heritage

Annalisa Bolin

Rwanda today exists in multiple times. It is impossible not to consider its turbulent history—the 1994 genocide that killed hundreds of thousands of ethnic minority Tutsi and politically moderate Hutu, the subsequent refugee crisis, and the wars in the Congo the genocide sparked. But at the same time, the word "genocide" hardly appears without "recovery," "reconciliation," "development:" Rwanda as model post-conflict country. Books for popular audiences lean heavily on this contrast between the violent past and the peaceful present.[1] Rwanda is looking ahead, the story goes; and the attraction of this narrative is its emphasis on how far Rwanda has come from 1994 to today and, implicitly, how much further it will go in the coming years.

Time is also an important axis for heritage practice both within and outside Rwanda. This chapter argues that time, as an element of authenticity at the Rwandan memorials to the country's past, becomes problematic for a default reading of heritage (here understood as the existence and uses of the material past in the present). Instead, we should take Rwanda's memorials on their own terms, which involve a temporal manipulability that enables certain interpretations. Many heritage professionals and scholars understand the past not to exist as such, but rather to be brought into being by the present for the present's own purposes. At the same time, heritage is multi-temporal—it cannot be entirely present-focused or it loses its depth and its reason for being—and so the past has a real, if somewhat invented, existence. The past is deployed in the present and, in this deployment, it is written—while still tethered to this material, "authentic" past. In this way, not only interpretations of the past but the material past itself becomes a palimpsest, written and rewritten according to the present's needs. It is this relationship of time to authenticity and materiality with which this chapter is concerned.

The chapter first reviews the default Western modes of reading meaning out of authenticity, which are on display in the application for UNESCO World Heritage status for some of Rwanda's genocide memorials. It then untangles how and why this normative reading creates problems for understanding what is actually a different construction of authenticity in Rwanda. Through a case study of the Presidential Palace Museum in Kigali (fig. 9.1),[2] it outlines how, far from being aberrant or nonsensical, as some have understood Rwandan heritage approaches, there is in fact a distinct relationship between time, authenticity, and politics at work. It focuses on the Presidential Palace Museum as a less-charged site at which to analyze uses of authenticity in Rwandan heritage, but references genocide memorialization where multi-sited analysis can reveal a widespread approach to heritage in the country. Moreover, as all major Rwandan heritage sites are managed by related government institutions, it is reasonable to suggest that a certain approach to heritage holds true across different types of sites, from memorials to museums.[3]

As this chapter demonstrates through the example of the Presidential Palace Museum, the prevailing practice of heritage in Rwanda, under the Rwandan Patriotic Front (RPF) government, both relies on the interaction of time and authenticity, and makes use of that relationship. Thus, the chapter shows not merely that the Rwandan heritage can be a political tool, but more specifically, it examines the conditions that make heritage available for contemporary political interpretation. These conditions originate in the palimpsestual nature of heritage in Rwanda—its ability to be written and shaped according to the needs of the present.

9.1. Presidential Palace Museum, Kigali. View from the southeast. Documented in 2014.

As the editors indicate in their introduction to this volume, sites become palimpsests when they are used, reused, reworked, and transformed for the needs and desires of different actors over time. A site's resultant significance may change even if its form does not, but form may change too; as such, "palimpsest" here serves as both a material and metaphorical description of such sites. In the case of Rwanda's Presidential Palace Museum, the physical form of the site, particularly the contents of the building, has been purposefully arrested at a particular historical moment, thus bringing the past into the present; but this very freezing of form has enabled a rewriting of the significance—historical and political—of the site for contemporary purposes. It is the understanding of authenticity and originality, the origin of a site in a previous time, that is in play here, mobilized and transformed within a larger political project for the state that owns and manages the site. Memorialization in Rwanda, then, becomes a process that not only preserves the past but also employs that preservation for powerful contemporary purposes—purposes that make use of the ability of a site to be palimpsestually overwritten, while coyly asserting the absence of this rewriting. In this, "authenticity" is key to understanding how the Rwandan approach works as a palimpsest, and contrasting conventional understandings of authenticity with the Rwandan mode elucidates the complex workings of heritage in Rwanda, in the use of temporal authenticity above all. This mode simultaneously leans on materiality and manipulates it by playing with time, enabling certain readings of heritage that are shaped by and reflect contemporary politics.

Authenticity: materiality, time, space

In searching for a baseline against which to compare the specifics of Rwandan heritage, we turn first to UNESCO. The UNESCO World Heritage List today stands as the largest and most powerful determiner of what heritage is and should be, bringing recognition, legitimacy, and possible financial benefits to listed sites. World Heritage status is awarded to sites which possess a so-called outstanding universal value which crosses national borders: "[t]he universalizing logic of World Heritage aims to transcend the heritage logic of the nation-state,"[4] despite the tension between this "transcendent" universalizing goal and the continuing salience of the nation-state framework to UNESCO inscription.[5] By examining Rwanda's application for World Heritage status, we can first see the international norms of heritage within which all countries applying to the list work; further, we can examine the well-established international frameworks which at present hold sway over the practice of heritage. In this chapter, these are referred to as "default" readings of heritage and authenticity.

World Heritage nomination is a major site of Rwandan heritage's articulation with international frameworks of legitimacy. In 2012, a set of sites were nominated to the List by Rwanda: the national memorials at Gisozi (Kigali), Nyamata, Murambi, and Bisesero.[6] In analyzing the nomination document, we must bear in mind that the approach to authenticity that emerges from it is that which is demanded by UNESCO and its World Heritage List. That is, the application exists in a liminal state, between a local heritage framework and an international one to which the Rwandan application—and by extension the memorials—must mold itself in order to attain World Heritage status. Accordingly, the default understanding of authenticity comes to the fore in Rwanda's nomination to the World Heritage List.

The application includes a "statement of authenticity and/or integrity" emphasizing material authenticity and its preservation. In part, the statement reads that evidence at the memorials "remains unchanged:" "sites and the material evidence of the genocide that they contain are conserved in an original state" which "testifies to the authenticity and integrity of the sites."[7] Authenticity at these sites avowedly depends on the authenticity of the material evidence of the buildings themselves and on what they contain being preserved and unchanging. Intervention compromising the "original [material] state" of the memorial site would therefore compromise the authenticity of the site as whole.

As in this application, the vast majority of States Parties connect authenticity to originality.[8] In these applications' interpretations of the UNESCO framework, authenticity is linked to purity, to a self-contained integrity uncontaminated by outside intervention: purity and authenticity in heritage involve "values akin to integrity and, in particular, integrity of the bond with origin."[9] The Rwandan application follows this logic of authenticity in three ways: material, spatial, and temporal.

First, the memorial sites are authentic because of the preservation of their buildings and the material evidence contained therein. The application refrains from specifying, but by "evidence" it means the bones and bodies of the dead, their clothing, often exhumed from mass graves, and the personal possessions left behind when victims were killed. These are displayed at all of the memorial sites covered in the application. Here, the continued existence of buildings and clothing, possessions, and human remains guarantees the authenticity of the site: these are the bones of the dead and the clothes they once wore.

Beyond material authenticity, the sites also display spatial and temporal authenticity. Spatial authenticity derives from the tie of the object to its place of origin. This is evident in the locations of the nominated genocide memorials: Nyamata and Murambi are buildings that were sites of massacres; Bisesero, the "hill of resistance," is a place where genocide victims took refuge and fought back.[10] The spatially-authentic materiality of the past has been saved *in situ*, not transported or interfered with, and so the "bond with origin" remains intact.

Spatial authenticity takes origin to be a location in space, but origin can also be perceived as a location in time, if we take the "bond with origin" to have a temporal dimension. An object in a museum, though it may have traveled some distance, can remain "authentic" if it fails to display evidence of intervention during the time between its past and present existence. That is, if such purity of material culture derives from a perceived link to its origin, the idea is that as the heritage object travels through time, it remains unchanged and therefore may as well *not* have traveled. It is a throwback to an earlier period or indeed a preservation of that period which possesses the ability to make the "perceived temporal distance between past and present [melt] away."[11] And this is what the memorials rely on when they not only preserve spatial and material authenticity, but also remain in a nearly or supposedly untouched state: time has been frozen here. At any rate, this is how the UNESCO application's default reading of heritage proceeds.

Authenticity against meaning

In fact, despite the UNESCO application's heavy reliance on authenticity, a degree of uncertainty exists about the origins of the evidence on display at the memorials. In particular, there is some question about whether all the human remains actually date to the 1994 genocide or if all belong to genocide victims. In the words of one Rwandan, "we cannot identify the people they put into the memorial sites. They took all bones."[12] At some sites, survivors have protested the burial of certain remains, claiming that they include not only genocide victims but also genocide perpetrators (*génocidaires*), possibly killed in retaliation.[13] However, these questions are *not* raised at or by the memorials, and the remains are presented as authentic without acknowledging the existence of debate. Of course, it would be both unreasonable and impossible to demand that the biography of every object on display at these sites—much less every bone—be similarly displayed, or even be known. Questioning authenticity at one of these sites would be perceived as insulting. The memorials assure us that what we encounter is authentic, and base their application to UNESCO upon the fact of material, spatial, and temporal authenticity. But why—beyond World Heritage recognition—does it even matter?

It matters because, despite lively debate over the meaning and value of "authenticity," revealing inauthenticity is still understood to devalue heritage, since in most conceptions heritage is still rooted in authenticity. It is also essential to note that beyond their role as heritage sites, the memorials are also spaces of mourning, where survivors go to honor and grieve their friends and relatives. The nature of the memorials' contents is thus of intense importance to survivors, who hold the reasonable expectation that genocide memorials do in fact contain the genuine remains of genocide victims. As Holtorf points out in a related context, "visitors to archaeological sites or museums experience authenticity and aura in front of ancient originals to exactly the same extent as they do in front of fakes or copies—as long as they *do not believe* them to be fakes or copies."[14] Inauthenticity, and especially the revelation thereof, violates a relationship, devaluing the experience of heritage and interfering in the process of interpretation.

Authenticity—which brings the past into the present—is therefore valuable because it underlies meaning: because heritage is meant to *speak to us*. The authenticity of the material remains of the past is not a static quality but a dynamic one, which reaches out across the gap between the past and the present to narrate its own existence. It is this that underlies the emphasis on authenticity in the UNESCO application's default reading: the principle that authentic materiality has the capacity to speak in a way that inauthentic materiality does not. Authenticity creates and enables valuable, interpretable meaning. Rwanda's memorials are authentic, in the senses in which we have come to understand that term; they should then produce meaning. They should speak to us.

It is on this understanding that some scholars and visitors to Rwandan heritage sites rely; it underlies their identification of a problem, which they describe as the actual absence of meaning. They argue that the authenticity-meaning chain has been somehow broken, and the visitor may listen but be unable to hear. Even faced with the bones of the dead, recounts Gourevitch, the genocide "was still strangely unimaginable. I mean one still had to imagine it."[15] Cook succinctly says that "the physical remains themselves do not 'tell the story'."[16] Guyer locates a "crisis of comprehension,"[17] in which the human remains at memorial sites "lead [not] to a clearer understanding of the genocide … but rather produce confusion, despondency, even senselessness: the bones at these sites resist a meaningful narrative."[18] The authentic materiality of genocide "resist[s] comprehension and meaning"[19] and "preserve[s] the non-sense of genocide."[20] These accounts identify a disconnect at Rwandan memorial sites that derives directly from the presence of human remains and the location of the memorials on the site of genocide—conditions on which so much of their authenticity depends. This is a failure that requires remediation, suggesting that materiality must be accompanied with or replaced by interpretive narrative in order to produce meaning.

Underlying this analysis is the unspoken framework of the default reading of heritage: if the evidence is authentic, it should lead to meaning. Cook and Guyer argue that meaning should be imposed through text and interpretation because, if the evidence is authentic and yet meaning is not conveyed, something in the process has broken down. For these visitors, the default reading is frustrated because—this chapter argues—there is a disjunction between default expectations of heritage and the Rwandan memorials. In fact, heritage in Rwanda does not actually work in this way; instead, it exists in its own situated context that should be taken into account when trying to "read" the memorials. It recasts the relationship between authenticity and meaning, and following this reorganized relationship leads to finding comprehensible sense in the memorials rather than overwhelming non-sense.

By turning to a different kind of Rwandan heritage site, the Presidential Palace Museum, this chapter demonstrates that material authenticity does not lead directly to meaning in the way that traditional readings of authenticity would have it, thus frustrating those who expect it. Rather, the dynamics of authenticity at the Rwandan sites are available for manipulation, and meaning is to some extent detached from authenticity rather than resulting from a direct relationship to it. Politics both powers and benefits from this disconnection, troubling the authenticity-meaning link and putting it to work.

The Presidential Palace Museum

The Presidential Palace Museum in Kigali is one of the museums managed by the Institute of National Museums of Rwanda (INMR).[21] The building began construction in 1976 (with assistance from European architects and designers) after President Juvénal Habyarimana's ascent to power in a 1973 coup. Completed in 1980, it was home to the Habyarimana family until 1994, when the 6 April plane crash that killed the president sparked the genocide.[22] The family fled in the following days—Habyarimana's wife, Agathe Kanziga, has been implicated in the planning of the genocide.[23] After the victory of the Rwandan Patriotic Front over the genocidal forces later in 1994, then-president Pasteur Bizimungu moved in.[24] In 2000, Bizimungu stepped down, and the building opened as a museum in 2008. The house bears no interpretive material to do with its construction or the presidents who inhabited it; museum tour guides narrate visits. Many of the rooms are furnished, though mainly with large items including chairs, tables, and beds. In its transformation into a museum, the house was not substantially restored, and so only a few decorative items persist, such as chandeliers and wall hangings. Of these, the most telling is a pair of portraits in the onetime presidential office, hanging over a large wooden desk: to one side, President Habyarimana; to the other, President Bizimungu.

The portraits are key to understanding how the Palace Museum approaches the problem of authenticity. The portraits are mirror images of each other: posed identically, of the same size, hanging at the same height on the wall. The interest lies not in what is present in the pictures, but rather in what they and the tour omit: namely, a real distinction between Habyarimana and Bizimungu. The first was an Army Chief of Staff who seized power in a coup and held it through two decades, only to die in a fiery crash that initiated the calamitous genocide which threw Rwanda into infamy on the world stage; the second, a president of the post-genocide RPF-ruled era of the Government of National Unity. But a lack of differentiation extends throughout the house, where visitors are encouraged to understand the residence as Habyarimana's alone. The office is called Habyarimana's office by tour guides; an attic room is described to visitors as a place where Habyarimana performed black magic with his witch doctor. Outside, a habitat once housed Habyarimana's pet python and the garage Habyarimana's cars. In the Habyarimana bedroom is the safe he filled with papers and foreign currency; upstairs, a pair of cabinets and a large mirror furnish the hair salon belonging to his wife. In the large foyer, where visitors are told that guests of Habyarimana could wait for appointments, cushy leather chairs sit in a circle. Each room and item, in sum, is identified by the purpose it served during Habyarimana's reign.

And yet the materiality of the house is not so easily established. After the plane crash that killed Habyarimana, his family fled the country, leaving most of the house's contents behind. In the violence that followed, the house was looted; as a result, only difficult-to-move items like armchairs and wardrobes remained. After the RPF took control of the country in July 1994 and Bizimungu became president, he moved in, furnishing the house with some of his own belongings but retaining some items left by the Habyarimana family. Upon his resignation in 2000, Bizimungu similarly ceded some of his furniture to the house. As a result, the furnishings come from a mix of origins. The master bedroom, for example, holds an array of items belonging to Habyarimana and Kanziga: a shelving unit, a large wardrobe, chandeliers original to the house, and a massive elephant-foot table. Others—including the bed, bedside tables, chairs, a dresser and mirror—were installed by the Bizimungu family. Similar mingling is found throughout the house.

However, should a visitor fail to inquire, she would not necessarily even know that Bizimungu had so much as lived in the building. Tour guides focus on Habyarimana's tenure to the near-exclusion of Bizimungu. Staff members are insistent that Bizimungu is not being *hidden* at the site, and indeed will discuss him if prompted; some point out, at the beginning of a tour, Bizimungu's residence in the building following Habyarimana's.[25] But when a visitor encounters the museum, she hears extensive stories of Habyarimana and his family, around whom the tour is formed. It is perhaps most telling that guides use the term "the president" interchangeably with "Habyarimana." The president, tour guides relate, met visitors here, in his office; in the dining room next door, they say, he took meals with his eight children (Bizimungu has three). In the master bedroom, visitors are told, the president and his wife slept; while always here "the president" is understood to indicate Habyarimana, the bedframe to which visitors' eyes are directed was never used by Habyarimana or Kanziga. The pastoral relief on the low wall of the dining room was commissioned by Bizimungu. No guest of Habyarimana ever sat in the large leather chairs in the foyer. It is not that Bizimungu is deliberately and sinisterly erased in favor of a story about Habyarimana. Rather, the important point is what occurs beneath the story—the way authenticity and materiality are used within it.

What happens here is a collapsing of time. Bizimungu's tenure folds into Habyarimana's, such that the materiality of the Bizimungu house becomes the materiality of the Habyarimana house. The purpose of the building, as it stands today, is to evoke a certain period in Rwandan history—beginning in the 1980s and ending with the genocide in 1994. It is spatially and materially authentic, certainly: its walls and its contents are where they have always been, largely unaltered, except through the loss of personal items and some objects of furniture and décor. But the temporal element is distorted—it does not represent the time it claims. The materiality of the house serves a different purpose, not its own; the link between authenticity and meaning is broken. That is, it *does not speak*. If meaning must be mediated through words, it is here being *determined*, not *interpreted*. This unexpected silence of materiality allows the museum itself to become a palimpsest of heritage, in which the site is both materially and spatially authentic, but also temporally layered. Such layering, the process of writing and rewriting meaning through the temporal dimension, enables the site to be harnessed for purposes that are not necessarily inherent to it, in the terms set by the default understanding of heritage. The subsequent question is then *why* should materiality function in this way—to what purpose and to whose benefit?

Politics and heritage in Rwanda

If materiality works in the way in which this chapter argues that it works at the Presidential Palace Museum, it stands to reason that meaning is dependent upon narrative. If authenticity does not speak for itself, then interpretation must speak for it, just as Guyer and Cook have maintained. But an alternative reading is possible—one which sees the failure of authentic materiality to speak for itself at Rwanda's memorials not as an obstacle to understanding, but as an a priori condition whose deployment we can then trace through a process of political sense-making.

The past is political in Rwanda, and interpreting it is a political endeavor, as a number of scholars have shown. Underneath the fraught project of history is the constant threat of a return to social division and potentially genocidal violence, and as a result, the stakes are high. The teaching of history in Rwanda is a profoundly contested project,[26] and at heritage sites where public history and memory are created and propagated, the contestations multiply. At memorial sites, only a narrow range of acceptable narratives exist,[27] erasing politically inconvenient genocide victims and reprisal killings.[28] The historical interpretations presented at these sites support a contemporary socio-politics of history, where the past entangles with power in the present.[29] Genocide remains are "an entrenched and constantly circulating tool of political power" within Rwanda,[30] and in the global arena, interpretations of history and heritage can be deployed for the purpose of affecting foreign policy and international relations.[31] On the whole, then, heritage is subsumed into a wider political project that puts the past to work for the present.[32]

But literature on heritage and memory or memorialization in Rwanda has not directly interrogated the question of authenticity in the country or the relationship of materiality to the "truth" of the past. When the politicization of heritage surfaces, there can easily be implicit an assumption that if heritage is put to political use, it is a perversion of a truthful inherent narrative. This chapter does not argue that the Rwandan government's political uses of heritage are unproblematic, but it is also untrue that either a normative conception of authenticity or the default UNESCO-style reading are the only lenses through which to look at Rwanda's heritage sites. Instead, the politics of memorialization in Rwanda lead to and benefit from an alternative understanding of authenticity and approach to heritage.

Debate over the idea of "authenticity" in heritage is longstanding and reflected in international instruments, which have evolved from default Western understandings of authenticity to a more diverse and global perspective. It has been argued that a global Authorized Heritage Discourse, derived from a Eurocentric and Global North perspective, constrains acceptable discourse around heritage and suppresses local and especially Global South interpretations.[33] Indeed, the conceptions of authenticity put forward by the Venice Charter,[34] a foundational document for heritage as practiced by international organizations, are highly material; the Charter is uncritical of the ideal that material authenticity as practiced and derived from a Western tradition (and as illustrated earlier in this chapter) is, and should be, paramount in heritage. A number of international attempts to push back against this document followed, including the Burra Charter in 1979 and, in 1994, perhaps the most high-profile attempt to specifically address authenticity, the Nara Document.[35] The Document and the Nara Conference that gave rise to it "reflect … skepticism toward the grand totalizing master narrative" of older charters.[36] The Document argues that while authenticity remains vital, of the highest importance is recognizing the cultural diversity of ideas of authenticity and broadening such conceptions away from mere material authenticity into intangibility and culturally contingent understandings. Such understandings allow, for example, cultural practices that periodically renew the material fabric of a heritage site not to be seen as violating its authenticity and integrity, whereas they might have been seen in this way in a purely material reading of authenticity. In the wake of the Nara Document, authenticity continues to be a highly contested concept. The universalizing logic of the UNESCO discourse is in flux, challenged in different ways by an increasing diversity of locally-specific understandings.[37] Some suggest that the pushback against Eurocentrism in heritage has tended toward essentializing different regions and their approaches to heritage,[38] or that even within a global framework of heritage that theoretically supports diversity, individual national heritages are reified and coopted.[39]

Within the continent of Africa exists a debate over Western and local approaches to heritage. African scholars have argued that Western-style museums, with exhibitions behind glass and interpretive signs, often fail to truly apply in African contexts; instead, they suggest that in order to achieve relevance to local communities, heritage in Africa should rather focus on intangible and landscape aspects of heritage over monumental, built heritage or artifacts.[40] In Rwanda, however, the Western-style museum persists in places such as the Ethnographic Museum's exhibits, the preserved living space of the Presidential Palace Museum, and the approach to memorialization taken at the national genocide memorials. In one sense, then, these sites are not strictly Rwandan. They draw on Western traditions of display and interpretation, and their layout (interpretive panels, tour guides, reconstructions) makes them instantly familiar to any visitor of Western museums. Indeed, as Vidal has pointed out, the very decision to display human remains to visitors, as at the genocide memorials, is not in line with traditional Rwandan death and funerary practices, which historically lent very little importance to the dead body as such.[41] The need to exhume and prepare human remains for exhibition is a new experience in Rwanda[42] and the display of genocide victims' remains is a far-from-settled topic in the country.[43] That said, the decision to display human remains, as with the decision to exhume and rebury victims' remains in mass graves, was a decision taken by the government[44]—which, questions of representation and internal divisions aside,[45] is a body made by and for Rwandans. The Institute of National Museums is run by Rwandans; though the British organization Aegis Trust designed the exhibitions at Gisozi and Murambi, and other international donors and organizations have been involved in the other memorials, the sites are primarily managed by Rwandan government institutions and staffed by Rwandans. Though these are not "customary" Rwandan heritage practices, then, neither is it appropriate to understand Rwanda's heritage sites merely as "Westernized" or, more severely, as a kind of Rwandan false consciousness about heritage practice. Rather, what is happening here is an appropriation of certain Western heritage management practices and a reworking of these practices for Rwandan purposes.

Even if the Authorized Heritage Discourse[46] and Eurocentric understandings of authenticity do not necessarily possess the totalizing power some assign to them, this chapter has argued above that the default materialist reading of authenticity derived originally from the Venice Charter—the one on which the Rwandan State Party relies in its UNESCO World Heritage List application—retains sufficient power to dictate how applications to the List are made (and, as a result, to dictate which sites receive the relatively coveted inscription and associated international acknowledgement). On the other hand, the same international heritage frameworks and conceptions of authenticity originally shaped by the Venice Charter are in the process of fragmenting into a myriad of culturally-contingent conceptions. In this sense Rwandan heritage becomes another example to be added to the ever-growing list of heritage "difference." What is at work in Rwanda is not, however, a fully oppositional concept of heritage, but rather a complex gradation of difference that takes some Venice Charter ideas of material authenticity, some Western traditions of museum display, and a set of local political demands, blending them into a new and subtle take on an old debate. Politics, this chapter argues, is at the root of why time and authenticity play out in the ways they do in Rwanda, and a particular attitude toward time and authenticity specifically enables the political manipulation of heritage.

The manipulability of the temporal aspect of authenticity—by blurring the temporal origins of materially and spatially authentic objects—creates the space for a certain political story, as we can see at the Palace Museum. The question, then, is: what is this political story, and to what end is time being manipulated at heritage sites? The RPF took power in 1994 after driving out the genocidal regime, and in its association with Habyarimana and the pre-genocide government, the house is obviously political. The RPF today thus has a straightforward interest in memorializing the site as a cautionary tale, a site of "negative heritage."[47] This does not, however, explain why the temporal manipulation of the museum centers around Bizimungu and Habyarimana; why should Bizimungu be implicated (or erased) at all?

Is it merely that Bizimungu is not considered to be of interest at this site? Visitors, to be sure, usually state that they have come to the museum to learn about Habyarimana and the genocide. Much interpretation of Rwandan history centers around the genocide, for understandable reasons, and Habyarimana's death was its spark. It is, however, also worth considering the recent history of Rwanda and the political dynamics that might drive a quiet reworking of heritage at this site; and, given this chapter's concern with types of authenticity, Bizimungu cannot simply be dismissed. In fact, as his home, the site possesses a second layer of political implications. Why indeed would a post-genocide president in the Government of National Unity live in the house of the dictator, sleep in his bedroom, sit at his dining table? Why, in the inverse scenario, would Bizimungu's additions to the house be coopted as Habyarimana's? To what end does materiality mix?

Bizimungu held the presidency as a member of the RPF from 1994 to 2000, when he resigned. His vice president, Paul Kagame, then assumed power, which he has held ever since. Accusations of fraud, corruption, and misconduct on the part of the ex-president followed swiftly,[48] although Bizimungu remained free for another year. In 2001, during a period in which domestic political dissent was being aggressively minimized,[49] he formed an opposition party, the *Parti démocratique pour le renouveau* (PDR-Ubuyanja). Political space was already closing at this time, and Bizimungu did not ensure the continuation of his political career by giving an interview to *Jeune Afrique*.[50] Bizimungu outlined his perception of what had happened toward the end of his presidency ("[w]hen I understood that they were going to get rid of me, I got ahead of it"); stated that after a history of ethnic division, "[w]e thought that with the RPF things were going to change, but we were disappointed;" and warned that if things continued as they had so far under the RPF, "the Hutu are going to prepare for war."[51]

Pursued by charges of "divisionism," a crime associated with genocide ideology,[52] Bizimungu was arrested amid accusations that the PDR was an ethnist Hutu party (he had been one of the few Hutu leaders in the primarily-Tutsi RPF) and the party was promptly banned. After a year and a half in pre-trial detention, in 2004 he was sentenced to a fifteen-year prison term[53] on the grounds of "embezzlement, inciting violence and associating with criminals," although he was cleared of threatening state security.[54] The trial received international attention; for example, the European Union issued a statement regarding Bizimungu and his codefendants, noting a concern about both the fairness of the trial and about the nature of the charges themselves.[55] After serving two years, Bizimungu was pardoned by President Kagame during the annual genocide commemoration in 2007, apparently as a gesture of "solidarity."[56] He has "led a secluded and very silent life since."[57]

Given the Rwandan government's wariness of political opposition[58] and Bizimungu's criminal status, the material association of Habyarimana with Bizimungu becomes clearer. The Palace Museum links the two spatially, given their residence in the same house.[59] They are then further connected through a material/temporal compression, in which Bizimungu's belongings occupy what is identified as Habyarimana's house, and the line between the pre- and post-genocide presidents is blurred. The divisionism charges which brought down Bizimungu, his ethnist party: these accusations draw their power from lessons of the era of genocide and the era of Habyarimana. Time collapses and authentic materiality does not "speak for itself"—otherwise, how could the borders be so unclear?

If we understand meaning to be intimately connected to politics in Rwanda, the Presidential Palace Museum and its frozen time are not about a lack of meaning. Rather than authenticity failing to speak to us, instead authenticity *never would* speak to us on its own behalf: its meaning comes not from inside but from outside. At the Palace Museum, heritage authenticity meshes Bizimungu with Habyarimana and compresses time into the particular temporal palimpsest connected to a particular meaning. In other words, temporal authenticity is harnessed within the political dynamic of the present, and meaning does not emerge organically, as the default heritage reading would have it. Pasteur Bizimungu is a ghostly presence at the Palace Museum: his mark is everywhere, if the visitor knows where to look, but it is easily missed. If extant, he is silent; his very offense may have been to speak.[60] In the words of one INMR employee, "Pasteur Bizimungu is very alive in Rwanda, but he is *soundless*." Today neither he nor the materiality of his life speak to us on their own.

Conclusion

Reading Rwanda's heritage sites as if they work in the way default Western narratives would have them work—expecting the authenticity of material heritage to speak to us—leads to an impasse. The problem of meaning at Rwanda's memorials is that rather than stemming from materiality, meaning serves something else. Reading Rwanda's heritage sites as politically determined restores meaning to them—not, perhaps, the meaning one would want or expect, but one which makes sense rather than non-sense.

Sites of memory are continually refashioned over their lifetimes; the political demands of one era—such as those of the post-Bizimungu period in Rwanda—might spur a shift in memory practice. "What may superficially appear to reflect continuity and memorialization might instead represent a palimpsest of meanings," as Meskell puts it.[61] Here, museum practice is not only about the changing shape of memory over time, but more importantly, about the changing shape of time in memory: how temporality wraps around materiality to tangle with authenticity. The Presidential Palace Museum is not a confusing mish-mash of materiality from different people and times, but instead a temporal palimpsest that creates politically useful links between two leaders. Here, the older narrative connected with Habyarimana manages to erase and overwrite the more recent one linked to Bizimungu. Materiality becomes not the determinant of narrative but instead a base on which narrative can be written, erased, or rewritten.

By following the manipulable elements of authenticity, we come to understand a particular Rwandan take on heritage that should hold a place in the landscape of increasingly diverse global understandings of heritage. Indeed, as Rwanda tries to remake itself, the formulation of a distinctive approach to heritage will help shape how this country tied to its past manages that relationship and moves forward.

Notes

Primary research for this chapter was carried out during the summers of 2013 and 2014, funded by Stanford University's Center for African Studies, Archaeology Center, and Department of Anthropology; follow-up research in 2015–16 was funded by a Fulbright study-research grant. I am grateful to my institutional affiliates, INMR and CNLG, for welcoming me to Rwanda. I am also indebted to the editors, Nadja Aksamija, Clark Maines, and Phillip Wagoner, for inviting me to contribute this chapter, and to Lynn Meskell for comments on earlier versions. All arguments made here are entirely my own, not those of (especially) the INMR, whose creative, capable, and generous staff always rises to the challenge.

1 For example, Kinzer 2008; Crisafulli and Redmond 2012.

2 Photography is prohibited inside the Presidential Palace Museum. Photos of the exterior and grounds are allowed, with the exception of the debris from President Habyarimana's plane. According to the INMR, this is because of the potential for such photographs to become political tools.

3 This said, memorials fall under the purview of the National Commission for the Fight against Genocide (CNLG), while museums are managed by the Institute of National Museums of Rwanda (INMR). However, both CNLG and INMR answer to the

Ministry of Sports and Culture and have institutional ties to each other; certain genocide memorials currently managed by CNLG were originally managed by INMR.

4 De Cesari 2014, 247.

5 Meskell 2014.

6 UNESCO 2012. The Gisozi memorial is operated by Aegis Trust and the other three by CNLG. As of 2017, these sites had not progressed beyond the Tentative List, although Rwandans involved in the application were optimistic.

7 My translation from the French.

8 Labadi 2010, 74.

9 Heinich 2011, 124; see also Labadi 2010.

10 The memorial at Gisozi is unique in that it is a purpose-built site.

11 Holtorf 2005, 115.

12 Buckley-Zistel 2011, 138.

13 Burnet 2008, 108.

14 Holtorf 2008, 126; italics in original.

15 Gourevitch 1998, 15.

16 Cook 2005, 302.

17 Guyer 2009, 157.

18 Guyer 2009, 169.

19 Guyer 2009, 162.

20 Guyer 2009, 171.

21 Information regarding the house, its construction, and its contents is derived from fieldwork in 2013 and 2014, especially interviews with INMR staff and participant observation at the Presidential Palace Museum.

22 The plane, a Falcon 50 carrying a number of passengers, including Burundian president Cyprien Ntariyamira, crashed into the grounds of the Habyarimana house after being shot down. The identity of the shooters has never been firmly established. The plane debris remains on the grounds of the museum and can be viewed by visitors, although photography is strictly prohibited.

23 Prunier 1995, 85–87; Straus 2006, 31–32.

24 During the genocide, the presidency was held briefly, for about three months, by Théodore Sindikubwabo, who later fled into the Democratic Republic of Congo and died in exile. During fieldwork I never heard Sindikubwabo mentioned by museum staff or guides; he is said to have never lived in the house.

25 My fieldwork in 2013 and 2014 included taking tours along with museum guides and a variety of visitors; unless I posed a direct question about Bizimungu, he was virtually never mentioned beyond this comment. However, I wish to emphasize that the staff are not engaged in any sort of deliberate misinformation campaign; rather, they operate within a highly politicized society, at a highly politicized site, and are aware of the limits of acceptable discourse.

26 Freedman et al. 2008; Buckley-Zistel 2009; Freedman et al. 2011.

27 King 2010.

28 Burnet 2009, 95; Waldorf 2011, 49.

29 Moore 2009; Brandstetter 2010.

30 Major 2015, 167.

31 Meierhenrich 2011; Bolin 2012; Giblin 2012.

32 Straus and Waldorf 2011; Pottier 2002.

33 Smith 2006.

34 ICOMOS 1964.

35 UNESCO 1994; Australia ICOMOS 2013.

36 Labadi 2010, 80.

37 Isar 2011.

38 Winter 2014.

39 De Cesari 2014.

40 Pwiti and Ndoro 1999.

41 Vidal 2004.

42 Major 2015, 169.

43 Burnet 2012, 99–101.

44 Vidal 2004.

45 See, for example, Burnet 2008; Ingelaere 2011; Thomson 2013; Ingelaere 2014.

46 Smith 2006.

47 Meskell 2002.

48 Reyntjens 2013, 15.

49 Reyntjens 2006; Reyntjens 2011.

50 Thorin 2001.

51 My translations from the French.

52 Tertsakian 2011; Waldorf 2011; Thomson 2013.

53 IRIN 2004.

54 BBC News 2004.

55 Council of the European Union 2004, cited in Reyntjens 2013, 33.

56 Beswick 2010, 235.

57 Reyntjens 2013, 33.

58 Straus and Waldorf 2011; Reyntjens 2013.

59 Current president Paul Kagame lives in a residence in central Kigali, several miles from the museum, which is located in the suburb of Kanombe near Kigali International Airport.

60 Beswick 2010, 235.

61 Meskell 2003, 36.

Bibliography

Australia ICOMOS. 2013. *The Burra Charter: The Australia ICOMOS Charter for Places of Cultural Significance.* Burwood: ICOMOS.

BBC News. 2004. "From President to Prison," *BBC News*, 7 Jun. http://news.bbc.co.uk/2/hi/africa/3728807.stm (accessed 29 December 2013).

Beswick, Danielle. 2010. "Managing Dissent in a Post-Genocide Environment: The Challenge of Political Space in Rwanda," *Development and Change* 41, no. 2, 225–51.

Bolin, Annalisa. 2012. "On the Side of Light: Performing Morality at Rwanda's Genocide Memorials," *Journal of Conflict Archaeology* 7, no. 3, 199–207.

Brandstetter, Anne-Marie. 2010. *Contested Pasts: The Politics of Remembrance in Post-Genocide Rwanda.* Wassenaar:

Netherlands Institute for Advanced Study. http://www.nias.knaw.nl/Content/NIAS/Publicaties/Ortelius/Ortelius_Lecture_6.pdf (accessed 11 October 2013).

Buckley-Zistel, Susanne. 2011. "Remembering to Forget: Chosen Amnesia as a Strategy for Local Coexistence in Post-Genocide Rwanda," *Africa* 76, no. 2, 131–50.

—. 2009. "Nation, Narration, Unification? The Politics of History Teaching after the Rwandan Genocide," *Journal of Genocide Research* 11, no. 1, 31–53.

Burnet, Jennie E. 2012. *Genocide Lives in Us: Women, Memory, and Silence in Rwanda*. Madison: The University of Wisconsin Press.

—. 2009. "Whose Genocide? Whose Truth? Representations of Victim and Perpetrator in Rwanda," in *Genocide: Truth, Memory, and Representation*, ed. Alexander Laban Hinton and Kevin Lewis O'Neill. Durham: Duke University Press, 80–110.

—. 2008. "Gender Balance and the Meanings of Women in Governance in Post-Genocide Rwanda," *African Affairs* 107, no. 428, 361–86.

Cook, Susan E. 2005. "The Politics of Preservation in Rwanda," in *Genocide in Cambodia and Rwanda: New Perspectives*, ed. Susan E. Cook. New Brunswick: Transaction Publishers, 293–331.

Council of the European Union. 2004. "Declaration by the Presidency on Behalf of the European Union on the Case of Pasteur Bizimungu." Brussels: Council of the European Union.

Crisafulli, Patricia, and Andrea Redmond. 2012. *Rwanda, Inc.: How a Devastated Nation Became an Economic Model for the Developing World*. New York: Palgrave Macmillan.

De Cesari, Chiara. 2014. "World Heritage and the Nation-State: A View from Palestine," in *Transnational Memory: Circulation, Articulation, Scales*, ed. Chiara De Cesari and Ann Rigney. Berlin: De Gruyter, 247–70.

Freedman, Sarah Warshauer, Harvey M. Weinstein, Karen L. Murphy, and Timothy Longman. 2011. "Teaching History in Post-Genocide Rwanda," in *Remaking Rwanda: State Building and Human Rights after Mass Violence*, ed. Scott Straus and Lars Waldorf. Madison: The University of Wisconsin Press, 297–315.

—. 2008. "Teaching History after Identity-based Conflicts: The Rwanda Experience," *Comparative Education Review* 52, no. 4, 663–90.

Giblin, John D. 2012. "Decolonial Challenges and Post-Genocide Archaeological Politics in Rwanda," *Public Archaeology* 11, no. 3, 123–43.

Gourevitch, Philip. 1998. *We Wish to Inform You That Tomorrow We Will Be Killed with Our Families: Stories from Rwanda*. New York: Farrar, Straus and Giroux.

Guyer, Sara. 2009. "Rwanda's Bones," *boundary 2* 36, no. 2, 155–75.

Heinich, Nathalie. 2011. "The Making of Cultural Heritage," *The Nordic Journal of Aesthetics* 40–41, 119–28.

Holtorf, Cornelius. 2008. "Is the Past a Non-Renewable Resource?" in *The Heritage Reader*, ed. Graham Fairclough, Rodney Harrison, John H. Jameson, and John Schofield. London and New York: Routledge, 125–33.

—. 2005. *From Stonehenge to Las Vegas: Archaeology as Popular Culture*. Walnut Creek: Altamira Press.

ICOMOS. 1964. *International Charter for the Conservation and Restoration of Monuments and Sites*. Venice: ICOMOS.

Ingelaere, Bert. 2014. "What's on a Peasant's Mind? Experiencing RPF State Reach and Overreach in Post-Genocide Rwanda (2000–10)," *Journal of Eastern African Studies* 8, no. 2, 214–30.

—. 2011. "The Ruler's Drum and the People's Shout: Accountability and Representation on Rwanda's Hills," in *Remaking Rwanda: State Building and Human Rights after Mass Violence*, ed. Lars Waldorf and Scott Straus. Madison: The University of Wisconsin Press, 67–78.

IRIN. 2004. "Rwanda: Former President Gets 15-Year Prison Term," IRIN, 8 Jun. http://www.irinnews.org/report/50150/rwanda-former-president-gets15-year-prison-term (accessed 29 December 2013).

Isar, Yudhishthir Raj. 2011. "UNESCO and Heritage: Global Doctrine, Global Practice," in *Cultures and Globalization: Heritage, Memory and Identity*, ed. Yudhishthir Raj Isar and Helmut K. Anheier. London: SAGE Publications, 39–52.

King, Elisabeth. 2010. "Memory Controversies in Post-Genocide Rwanda: Implications for Peacebuilding," *Genocide Studies and Prevention* 5, no. 3, 293–309.

Kinzer, Stephen. 2008. *A Thousand Hills: Rwanda's Rebirth and the Man Who Dreamed It*. Hoboken: John Wiley & Sons.

Labadi, Sophia. 2010. "World Heritage, Authenticity and Post-Authenticity," in *Heritage and Globalisation*, ed. Sophia Labadi and Colin Long. London and New York: Routledge, 66–84.

Major, Laura. 2015. "Unearthing, Untangling and Re-Articulating Genocide Corpses in Rwanda," *Critical African Studies* 7, no. 2, 164–81.

Meierhenrich, Jens. 2011. "Topographies of Remembering and Forgetting: The Transformation of Lieux de Mémoire in Rwanda," in *Remaking Rwanda: State Building and Human Rights after Mass Violence*, ed. Scott Straus and Lars Waldorf. Madison: The University of Wisconsin Press, 283–96.

Meskell, Lynn. 2014. "States of Conservation: Protection, Politics, and Pacting within UNESCO's World Heritage Committee," *Anthropological Quarterly* 87, no. 1, 217–43.

—. 2003. "Memory's Materiality: Ancestral Presence, Commemorative Practice and Disjunctive Locales," in *Archaeologies of Memory*, ed. Ruth M. Van Dyke and Susan E. Alcock. Malden: Blackwell, 34–55.

—. 2002. "Negative Heritage and Past Mastering in Archaeology," *Anthropological Quarterly* 75, no. 3, 557–74.

Moore, Lisa M. 2009. "(Re)covering the Past, Remembering Trauma: The Politics of Commemoration at Sites of Atrocity," *Journal of International and Public Affairs* 20, 47–64.

Pottier, Johan. 2002. *Re-Imagining Rwanda: Conflict, Survival and Disinformation in the Late Twentieth Century*. Cambridge and New York: Cambridge University Press.

Prunier, Gérard. 1995. *The Rwanda Crisis: History of a Genocide*. New York: Columbia University Press.

Pwiti, Gilbert, and Webber Ndoro. 1999. "The Legacy of Colonialism: Perceptions of the Cultural Heritage in Southern Africa, with Special Reference to Zimbabwe," *African Archaeological Review* 16, no. 3, 143–53.

Reyntjens, Filip. 2013. *Political Governance in Post-Genocide Rwanda*. New York: Cambridge University Press.

—. 2011. "Constructing the Truth, Dealing with Dissent, Domesticating the World: Governance in Post-Genocide Rwanda," *African Affairs* 110, no. 438, 1–34.

—. 2006. "Post-1994 Politics in Rwanda: Problematising 'liberation' and 'democratisation,'" *Third World Quarterly* 27, no. 6, 1103–17.

Smith, Laurajane. 2006. *Uses of Heritage*. New York: Routledge.

Straus, Scott. 2006. *The Order of Genocide: Race, Power, and War in Rwanda*. Ithaca: Cornell University Press.

Straus, Scott, and Lars Waldorf, eds 2011. *Remaking Rwanda: State Building and Human Rights after Mass Violence*. Madison: The University of Wisconsin Press.

Tertsakian, Carina. 2011. "'All Rwandans Are Afraid of Being Arrested One Day': Prisoners Past, Present, and Future," in *Remaking Rwanda: State Building and Human Rights after Mass Violence*, ed. Lars Waldorf and Scott Straus. Madison: The University of Wisconsin Press, 210–20.

Thomson, Susan. 2013. *Whispering Truth to Power: Everyday Resistance to Reconciliation in Postgenocide Rwanda*. Madison: The University of Wisconsin Press.

Thorin, Valérie. 2001. "Je Suis Prêt à Payer Le Prix Fort," *Jeune Afrique*, 3 July.

UNESCO. 2012. "Sites Mémoriaux Du Génocide: Nyamata, Murambi, Bisesero et Gisozi." http://whc.unesco.org/en/tentativelists/5753/ (accessed 15 December 2014).

—. 1994. "Nara Document on Authenticity, Report of the Experts Meeting, November 1994." Nara: UNESCO. http://whc.unesco.org/archive/nara94.htm (accessed 29 January 2014).

Vidal, Claudine. 2004. "La Commémoration du Génocide au Rwanda," *Cahiers d'Études Africaines*, no. 3, 575–92.

Waldorf, Lars. 2011. "Instrumentalizing Genocide: The RPF's Campaign against 'Genocide Ideology,'" in *Remaking Rwanda: State Building and Human Rights after Mass Violence*, ed. Lars Waldorf and Scott Straus. Madison: The University of Wisconsin Press, 48–66.

Winter, Tim. 2014. "Beyond Eurocentrism? Heritage Conservation and the Politics of Difference," *International Journal of Heritage Studies* 20, no. 2, 123–37.

Chapter 10
Ground Zero as Palimpsest: Erasure, Rebuilding, Rediscovery

Joseph Siry

The theme of the architectural palimpsest is one of great richness and adaptability to different scales, periods, and types of artifacts in the built environment. For built sites, the etymology of "palimpsest" is particularly suggestive, for it derives from the Latin *palimpsestum*, which in turn comes from the Greek *palimpseston*, the neuter form of *palimpsestos*, meaning "scraped again." This conjures the act of clearing an existing site of its older construction as the first step in building something new. The choice of this theme reflects a typically postmodern concern for studies of architecture in relation to cultural memory, where the built object is understood in terms of its layered history.[1]

Modernism in architecture and urbanism tended toward erasure of the past and denial of its continuity with the present. This attitude prevailed especially in creating the large sets of contiguous properties to provide sufficiently expansive ground area for new tall buildings. The tendency toward erasure was partly a corollary of modernism's utopian impulse, or what might be called its future-oriented or prophetic aspiration. But by adopting the premise of the palimpsest and its invocation of a site's multiple pasts, we engage with questions of who decides what aspects of a place's history are remembered. In other words, toward what ideological or political ends is the process of recovering memory directed? Perhaps equally important, what is the rationale for the timing of such an inquiry? Or, how is the act of unearthing or otherwise investigating a site's or object's layered past culturally situated? Who are its sponsors, its agents, and its audiences? Which layers are newly suppressed or privileged? Do these decisions shift over time?

Over the past sixteen years, no contemporary American site has been the focus of more anguish about its meaning than Ground Zero in Lower Manhattan. Awareness of the site's earlier history came to the fore after the destruction of the World Trade Center on 9/11, and that event immediately prompted a broad reconsideration of the architectural and historical significance of the lost Twin Towers (fig. 10.1). Upon their demise, the towers themselves and the mid-century urban development of which they were the central part became symbolic of an era suddenly past. The violent rupture in this site's history provoked a reevaluation of what had been lost, both in terms of appreciating what had disappeared and planning for appropriate rebuilding and commemoration. The end of the Twin Towers especially sparked a scholarly cycle of studying their beginnings. As with other such large redevelopment projects, these origins had their own disruptive quality.[2]

That narrative began in the late 1950s, when David Rockefeller (1915-2017), a grandson of John D. Rockefeller, Sr., and son of John D. Rockefeller, Jr., headed an effort to revive Lower Manhattan. Rockefeller was drawn into this process as the then head of Chase Manhattan Bank, which held sizeable mortgage interests on a large number of properties in the area whose value was then declining. Most of these properties were residential, but the population of Lower Manhattan shrank along with its earlier commercial functions in relation to shipping. David Rockefeller saw an analogy to the history of the Midtown site of what became Rockefeller Center, earlier a brownstone district, whose redevelopment into a cluster of tall office buildings had been headed by his father from 1929.[3] David Rockefeller formed the Downtown-Lower Manhattan Association (DLMA) to do much the same thing for the historic, and struggling, Wall Street area. In time, the World Trade Center and its Twin Towers emerged as the linchpin buildings of this larger scheme.

10.1. Minoru Yamasaki & Associates with Emery Roth & Sons, architects; Leslie Robertson, engineer. World Trade Center, New York City, 1962–77. Aerial view from southwest.

The concept of an international business center focused on super-tall office towers became the model for Lower Manhattan's redefinition and recovery, wherein the bank's properties would be revalued upward for their potential as office space. To advance this vision, Rockefeller needed the cooperation of the Port Authority of New York and New Jersey, a self-supporting corporate agency of these two states. It acquired the World Trade Center's future site through its powers of eminent domain, and could assist in raising capital for redevelopment. The Port Authority saw the new World Trade Center as a "port without water."[4] It would be a virtual port in a world-wide web of economic exchange. Its projected ten million square feet of floor space was to entice foreign business organizations, in order to trade with U.S. companies. In January 1960, Chase Manhattan Bank led in announcing plans for a "World Trade Center in the heart of the Port District," and the Port Authority joined in the project's planning that spring.[5]

In the late 1960s, twelve square blocks of low-rise commercial and residential buildings in Lower Manhattan were demolished to provide the sixteen-acre site for the series of buildings and interstitial spaces that constituted the World Trade Center. Thus the construction of the Twin Towers exemplified the classic capitalistic method of urban renewal known in traditional Marxist theory as "creative destruction," whereby cities transform themselves through financial investment that entails loss, rupture, and erasure.[6] Even the destruction of 9/11 did not erase the impulse to focus investment in the World Trade Center's site, because the forces that built the Twin Towers were more resilient than the buildings themselves, and would dictate the area's post-9/11 program.

As redevelopment went forward through the completion of the Twin Towers in 1974, there was effectively neither awareness of, nor concern for, the urban district that the towers effaced. This was an immigrant neighborhood with a long architectural and social history as part of the Lower West Side. As historians noted, the overall site of the World Trade Center overlapped with what had been home to the once largest Arab-American community in the

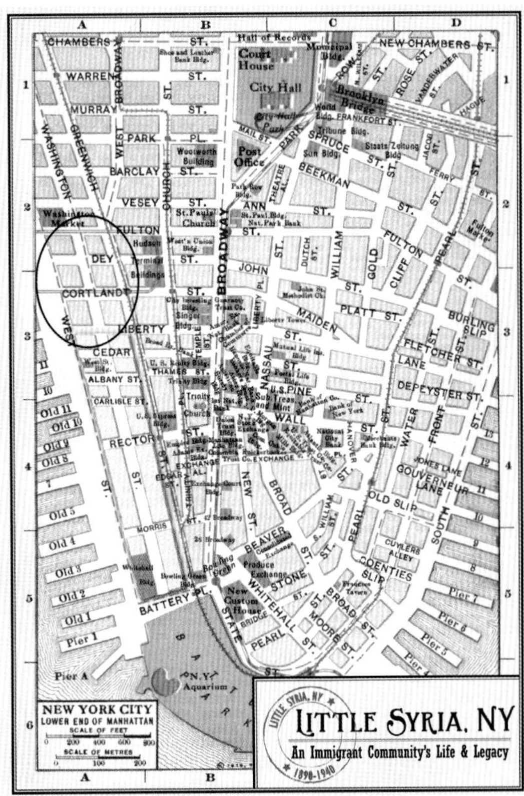

10.2. Little Syria, New York City, *c.* 1890–1940, postcard map with title of the Arab American Museum's 2012 exhibit on the community. The oval shows the site of World Trade Center, between Fulton (north), Liberty (south), Greenwich (east), and West (west) streets.

United States. The area was called the Syrian Quarter or Little Syria, a coherent neighborhood that thrived from the late 1880s to the 1940s and that included Arabic-speaking—though not all Muslim—people from Egypt, Iraq, Lebanon, Palestine, and elsewhere. This largely forgotten community was the focus of an exhibit created by the Arab American National Museum in 2012, the poster for which was based on an historic map of 1916 (fig. 10.2). The quarter had an internationally known, thriving bazaar, and was home to the leading Arab-American newspaper. In the late 1940s, some blocks of this part of Lower Manhattan were condemned and razed to create entrance ramps needed for the Brooklyn-Battery Tunnel, which opened in 1950 (fig. 10.3). The Arab American National Museum sought to preserve

10.3. "Relics of Old New York. At Battery Place. Homes of Greeks and Syrians," *c.* 1930.

this community's history after its locus in Lower Manhattan was transformed and its social network had dispersed.[7]

Although later historians have contested his assessment, the chief architect of the Twin Towers, Minoru Yamasaki, concluded of the site: "It was quite a blighted section, with radio and electronic shops in old structures, clothing stores, bars and many other businesses that could be relocated without much anguish … There was not a single building worth saving."[8] He wanted an open ground area so that his new structures could be seen from their nearby environs. By 1969 all older buildings on the World Trade Center site had been cleared away, and the local cultural history of the overlapping Little Syria would not return to broader public consciousness until after 9/11. Even in the 9/11 Memorial Museum, presentation of the site's history begins with a model of the Twin Towers. The 110-story towers that rose on the northwest edge of the former Little Syria had a gigantism that dramatically reconfigured the skyline of Lower Manhattan, and they were not well received critically. Terry Smith summarized a widely held opinion that the towers exhibited "a measure of formal invention so modest and a degree of social responsibility so small as to be scarcely discernible."[9] Yet the bulky parallelepipeds soon became iconic images of both the city and the nation, especially when seen from a distance. What such views did not show was their immediate spatial setting around their bases. There the former street grid was interrupted to create an open, notoriously windy plaza, unrelieved by greenery, whose scale and detachment from the neighborhood made it a fitting complement to the towers themselves. This approach aligned with the area's then relatively low residential density and related lack of activity along its streets. The World Trade Center plaza became more a space to walk through than a place to be in, and the memory of its urban deficiencies would influence the site's reconstruction after 9/11.

Initially there was next to no consideration for Ground Zero's layered history in the first period of design for its reconstruction that culminated in a public presentation of a master plan in July 2002. The organization that was created to act as overseeing client for the project was the Lower Manhattan Development Corporation (LMDC), which undertook to manage rebuilding on 3 December 2001. Its board members represented those interests with the largest financial and political stake in the area. These included the Port Authority, which still owned the site; the City of New York, which controlled the streets through the site; and those private leaseholders whose buildings had been lost on 9/11 and whose insurance payments provided the core of the funds for the reconstruction. In July 2001, less than three months before the attacks, the Port Authority sold 99-year leases on the Twin Towers to developer Larry Silverstein, who before 9/11 had hired architect David Childs "to fix up the Trade Center's image and turn it into a kind of downtown Rockefeller Center."[10] Silverstein would continue as the pivotal client for the site's renewal after 9/11, and Childs would become the chief architect of the Freedom Tower (later 1 World Trade Center). Other groups consulted included 9/11 survivors and families of victims, the police and fire departments, and area residents' organizations.

From a corporate and municipal viewpoint, the major planning issues were first the rethinking of the site's transportation and other technical infrastructure, and then the provision of sufficient new rentable retail and office space to recover the financial losses. In May 2002, with these aims in mind, the LMDC and the Port Authority commissioned a master plan for the World Trade Center site from architects Beyer Blinder Belle, who were selected from a short list of architectural, planning, and engineering teams. In July 2002 this firm presented six concept plans. However, there was an immediate and nearly universal dissatisfaction with these early proposals, which consisted mainly of new office towers around a central public open space with minimal acknowledgement of the tragic attacks.[11] Almost all these schemes proposed extensive new construction around, yet with little regard for, the memorial site, where the towers had been. Though these initial LMDC proposals for the rebuilding were soon set aside, they established a percentage of ground area dedicated to public space that remained relatively unchanged through later phases of planning. That percentage was dwarfed by the total amount of rentable office space to be created by the overall rebuilding. But what was soon closely reconsidered was the need to acknowledge the site's history in publicly legible symbols.

After 9/11, the site's palimpsestual nature was framed in terms of the Twin Towers as the lost substratum, rather than the earlier residential past. With the disastrous destruction of the towers, their remembered presence was the focus for collective civic and national grief, self-examination, and reassertion. These priorities informed the seven different master plans for Ground Zero's sixteen-acre site solicited by the LMDC for public presentation in December 2002. In its consideration of Ground Zero's multi-layered past, the winning design by Daniel Libeskind brings to mind the metaphor of the palimpsest, in the tradition of deconstructivist architectural theory since the 1980s, which held that a new building should unearth its site's past by exposing its history to view. Peter Eisenman described this approach in relation to his earlier Wexner Center for the Visual Arts, opened in 1990 at Ohio State University in Columbus. His building included a partial reconstruction of a demolished armory that formerly stood there. He wrote: "We used the site as a palimpsest: a place to write, erase and rewrite … Our building reverses the process of the site inventing the building. Our building invents the site."[12] With his center making visible forgotten layers of the past, "[i]t is as if the surface of the site were chiseled always and excavated to reveal the inlays of its own history and geography, the

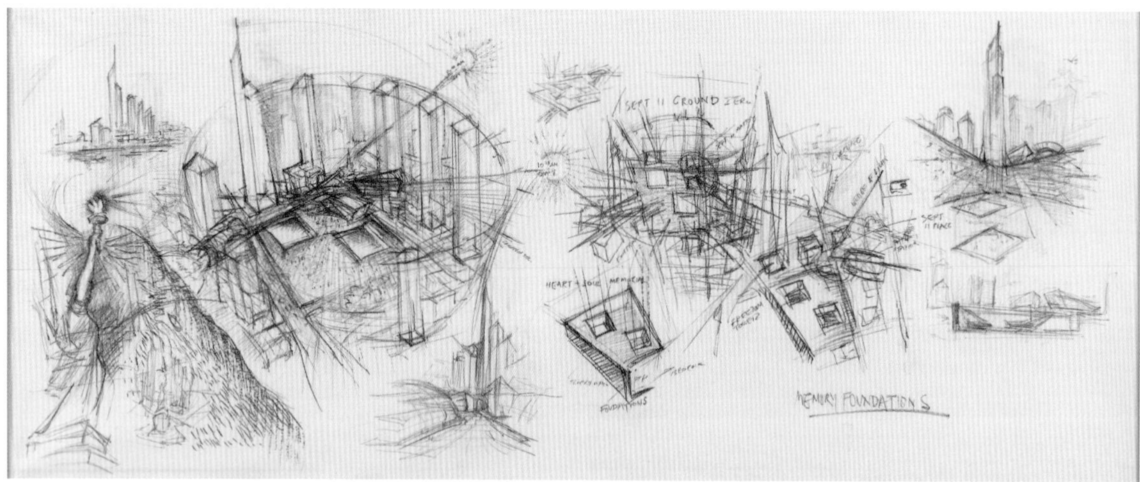

10.4. Daniel Libeskind, Studio Libeskind, concept sketches for Memory Foundations, Ground Zero master plan, New York City, 2002.

latent patterns and discontinuities which make something specific and real."[13]

Libeskind had developed this palimpsestual concept in his winning design for the Jewish Museum as an extension of the Berlin Museum, on which he began work in 1989 and which coincidentally opened (if without its exhibitions in place) on 11 September 2001.[14] It was Libeskind's first realized building, and Eisenman was among those contemporaries who cited the Jewish Museum as an important work. Here the idea of historical layering was multifaceted, as the museum was to encompass the past, present, and future of Berlin's Jewish community. The Jewish Museum was institutionally and physically appended to the Berlin Museum, housed in an early eighteenth-century Baroque building to its north. To enter the Jewish Museum, one passes first into the Berlin Museum and then descends to its underground level, where there is a long ramped passage that leads into Libeskind's building. Symbolically, one thus enters into local Jewish history through the experience of Berlin's overall past, so as to be confronted with their inseparability. As Libeskind wrote: "The existing building is tied to the extension underground, preserving the contradictory autonomy of both the old building and new building on the surface, while binding the two together in depth, underground."[15]

Speaking in 2003 of his master plan for Ground Zero, Libeskind similarly stated: "Architecture is about creating a multi-layered fabric of the city … It's not about prescribed things you should know about. People discover things on their own, discover architecture on more than one level."[16] Initially he proposed that visitors descend into the site's depth. Standing in the open pit of the memorial grounds, they were to experience that awareness of the tragedy that had moved Libeskind himself on his first visit there, and had inspired his vivid early sketches for the overall plan (fig. 10.4). Eventually this idea of descent was brought wholly indoors, from the ground-level entry to the 9/11 Memorial Museum down by stages to its near bedrock-level exhibits in their huge underground hall.

In this vein, Libeskind called his design for Ground Zero "Memory Foundations," presenting his ideas as those of a mourning citizen-participant in a long process of public grieving.[17] Although the spiraling arrangement of surrounding new office towers was carefully conceived, the architect insisted that he had not been focusing on these, but rather on the memorial. Libeskind's description did not foreground aesthetic issues, but rather presented a vision wherein the site's tragedy was central, and its commercial recovery would be peripheral. His project satisfied the LMDC's "strong preference for preserving the footprints of the twin towers for memorial or memorial-related elements." Above ground, the restored skyline was "to pro-

10.5. Daniel Libeskind, Studio Libeskind, winning design, Ground Zero master plan, New York City, December 2002.

10.6. Ground Zero, master plan revised, showing (left to right): David Childs, and Skidmore, Owings, and Merrill, 1 World Trade Center (formerly Freedom Tower); Bjarke Ingels, BIG, 2 World Trade Center; Sir Richard Rogers, 3 World Trade Center; and Fumihiko Maki, 4 World Trade Center.

vide a significant, identifiable symbol ... a new icon for New York City," since "a tall symbol or structure that would be recognized around the world is crucial to restoring the spirit of the city."[18] Libeskind proposed a group of five towers in an ascending spiral from the southeastern edge of the memorial site around its eastern side to the tallest new skyscraper, originally called the Freedom Tower (now 1 World Trade Center) on the northwest (fig. 10.5). As the project later evolved between the competition-winning version of 2002 and the definitive scheme of 2006, the group of five towers resolved into an L-shaped arrangement that retained this ascending order up to 1 World Trade Center, with its spire-like antenna (fig. 10.6). This grouping recalled the old World Trade Center's original cluster of five smaller buildings arrayed in a semicircle around the core five-acre plaza where the Twin Towers had stood.

The new master plan's reference to the old was another facet of the palimpsestual relationship between the phases of the site's history. An analogous process unfolded for the design of 1 World Trade Center, whose exterior was fashioned by Childs partly as a homage to the Twin Towers.[19] The new 1 World Trade Center's rooftop height (1,362 feet) would match that of the old Two World Trade Center, and its rooftop parapet would match the former One World Trade Center's height of 1,368 feet. Childs' tower would have a central spire-like antenna whose form recalled those atop the Twin Towers. But the 1,776-foot-high antenna atop 1 World Trade Center has another function. As Childs said: "It's the marker for the memorial. If you're coming in from Newark Airport, this is the one you'll look to. Somebody will say: 'You see that tall building? That's ground zero'."[20] This salient focus thus has meanings related to memory, erasure, and renewal.

After Yamasaki was hired in 1962, he had made a scale model of the World Trade Center site and had studied some 150 alternative ideas

10.7. Michael Arad and Peter Walker, *Reflecting Absence*, Ground Zero Memorial, designed and built 2004–11. View towards northeast showing footprints of North Tower (left) and South Tower (right), and (top center) Snøhetta Architects, National September 11 Memorial & Museum, entrance pavilion, opened 2014.

for his buildings' height, shape, and spatial arrangement. Finally he proposed the scheme of the Twin Towers, which were set at angles relative to each other in part to give maximal views for people working in them. The towers were arranged diagonally on their site, with a carefully calculated spatial gap of 110 feet (a distance equal to about half the 210-foot breadth of each tower) between their closest corners. Yamasaki detailed the towers' corners as chamfered 45-degree-angle surfaces through their full height (figs. 10.1 and 10.11), unlike the typically squared corners of Manhattan's iconic Art Deco and modernist skyscrapers. These canted corners, rising far higher than anything around them near the open southern tip of Lower Manhattan, glinted continually and memorably reflected occasional flashes of sunlight.

When Childs developed the design for 1 World Trade Center, he said that he made the canted corner, incidental but visually poignant in the Twin Towers, into the thematic concept for the massing of their monumental successor (fig. 10.6). While the Twin Towers had been nearly squared, 1 World Trade Center, though square at its base, was transformed above into an octagonal tower with its four lower corners becoming V-shaped canted wall planes rising like a parallelepiped in torsion to the building's top, where they resolved into another square, although one rotated ninety degrees from the base square. In plan, an octagonal tower provides not four but eight angled corner office areas on each floor, each of which would receive light from two sides and so become optimally rentable interior quarters. Also, an octagonal tower would decrease the lateral force of wind, the structural resistance to which is among the most challenging aspects of the design of very tall buildings. Canted surfaces allow wind to glance around the tower, reducing forceful downdrafts that are annoying and hazardous for pedestrians around a skyscraper's base. The complexities of designing an octagonal, torsional tower could be addressed through digital techniques unavailable to the engineers who designed the Twin Towers. Childs' new building thus proclaims its identity as a skyscraper of the twenty-first century and the icon of Ground Zero's renewal. Yet its angled corners are its architect's tribute to the Twin Towers, of which he had a living memory, now reinterpreted in their successor.[21]

The designers were required to restore the street grid that the Twin Towers had interrupted and to provide a grand pedestrian promenade on West Street. The rebuilt site also included Fulton Street (north), Greenwich (east), Liberty (south), and others. In this way, the urban design reasserted a lost layer of the site's spatial history. This decision was not just the result of a postmodern nostalgia for older, more humanely scaled urban spaces. Rather, the restoration of the grid and related concern for pedestrian movement reflected the fact that once the Twin Towers were near fully occupied, with ninety-six percent of their spaces leased by 2000, they housed more than 1,200 trading firms and other organizations. From 50,000 to 60,000 people worked in the buildings every day, and they attracted about 80,000 visitors per day.[22] Partly as a consequence of this huge influx of daytime population, there had been considerable residential construction nearby since the Twin Towers were built. The most important development along these lines had been the creation of Battery Park City on new land along the Hudson River.[23] Its ground platform had been built up from fill brought from demolition and excavation associated with the construction of the World Trade Center, for which Battery Park City was conceived from the start as an upscale residential complement mainly for workers in the financial district. There was a renewed need for reinstating the full criss-crossed street system in order to create multiple commercial areas and circulation patterns that would integrate the old streets of Lower Manhattan with Battery Park City along the river. Thus while the street grid's revival brought back to view an earlier layer in the site's history, at the same time it fulfilled the connective necessities of contemporary urban design.

If the restored grid reconstituted the site's pre-World Trade Center streetscapes, the post-9/11 symbolic program had to encompass a palimpsestual awareness of depths that made a pause in the present to enable visitors to remember the destructive trauma. In this spirit, Libeskind initially focused on the Slurry Wall, a massive basin of steel-reinforced concrete around the World Trade Center's site, tied below ground to bedrock foundations under the Hudson River's bed to hold back the river waters. A slurry wall is made when wet clay waterproofing is pumped into a trench in the shape of the wall. Concrete is then poured into the trench, driving out the slurry core to form the wall. Part of the west wall was incorporated into the 9/11 Memorial Museum (fig. 10.12). While the towers stood, their mass helped the Slurry Wall to resist the pressure of river water. After the towers fell, their debris performed the same structural function. Once the debris was removed, additional concrete panels and steel ties were inserted into new sections of the Slurry Wall flanking the surviving central part to anchor it more firmly to bedrock. So in the Slurry Wall we see in the museum, the pattern of older and newer ties is clearly distinguishable. We discern the layers of its history as an enduring, recently modified structural object. Having withstood the collapsing towers on 9/11, the Slurry Wall was celebrated as an engineering wonder, and direct contact with it is ultimately central to the museum's interior. It fulfilled Libeskind's premise that visitors engage with the site's depth, literally and historically. As he said: "We have to be able to enter this hallowed, sacred ground while creating a quiet, meditative and spiritual space. We need to journey down, some 70 feet into Ground Zero, onto the bedrock foundation, a procession with deliberation into the deep indelible footprints of Tower One and Tower Two."[24] The seventy-foot depth of the concrete Slurry Wall became the new datum for consciousness of the site's meaning; below this level one can descend no further. Yet invocation of this lower depth elided the site's human history before the World Trade Center had effaced it.

Libeskind's approach to planning Ground Zero engaged another level of meaning associated with the idea of the palimpsest, one that was less literally physical and site-specific. The challenges of the reconstruction were not only about the location of the tragedy and the commemoration of the lives lost. As Libeskind recognized, the issues were far broader, including the effect of the attacks on the city's and the nation's morale, and the role of architecture in helping New York and the United States recover a shared identity and collective purpose. From this perspective, the Slurry Wall took on a larger meaning: it became a general symbol of resilience and the capacity for renewal. Thus its preservation as a palimpsestual layer was fundamentally about restoring to public view an understanding of the urban and national capacity to revive and to reassert core values. Libeskind said: "The memorial site exposes ground zero all the way down to the bedrock foundations revealing the heroic foundations of democracy for all to see."[25] In this way, the issue of the site's meaning entailed both commemoration and resurgence, or finding an appropriate balance between memory and prophecy. Libeskind "realized that the challenge of Ground Zero was to address history; both the irreversible history of what happened there, but also the future. The question was how to assert life, how to assert something about liberty and freedom, and about how to reinforce that which New York represents to its inhabitants and to the world at large." In the pit, "feeling the potential of resilience," the goal became "asserting the vitality and vigour of Lower Manhattan."[26] As Libeskind wrote referring to the earlier Jewish Museum: "Good architecture anywhere ... continues to be something that does not simply haunt us in a negative sense, but instead it gives us breathing room to speculate and to think of new ways of being."[27]

The Slurry Wall was one key symbol, and as Libeskind and others acknowledged, the towers' footprints were another. 9/11 effectively created a new national community of commemoration, at the core of which were the truly bereaved who had lost loved ones in the attacks. Even before Libeskind's master plan was accepted early in 2003, much attention focused on the treatment of the footprints. New construction had to proceed around the footprints of the towers, which, as squares set into the earth, would record both the towers' former presence and their destruction. After 9/11, Governor George Pataki had promised the families of the dead that the towers' footprints would never be built upon, so as to remain a permanent sacred site. As Libeskind said, the directive to commemorate the former towers' footprints meant "you could not construct a building where people had perished; that it was no longer just ground to be built upon."[28]

The footprints became a central issue for the design of both the above-ground memorial and the below-ground museum. In keeping with Libeskind's master plan for the memorial space, designers were instructed to make the footprints of the towers visible, to leave the Slurry Wall exposed, to enable visitors to get to bedrock, and to list the names of the victims. The memorial design, by architect Michael Arad, entitled *Reflecting Absence*, was selected from a competition in 2004 that drew over 5,200 entries from sixty-three countries.[29] Developed with landscape architect Peter Walker, the altered memorial as built occupies about half of the sixteen-acre World Trade Center site. It includes over 400 swamp white oak trees planted in rows amid stone paving (fig. 10.7). The consistent canopy distinguishes the memorial from less carefully planted plazas. The near uniformly sized trees and their extensive drainage system form a green roof over the museum below ground, so the site has a layered environmental infrastructure. It is a public space accessible from almost the entire periphery of the grove, yet signs forbid singing, loud noise, recreation, and "behaving in a way that is inappropriate." As critics noted, at ground level, its park-like character, mainly visited by tourists and inviting touristic behaviors, to an extent competes with or compromises its memorial purpose.[30]

Yet that purpose powerfully reasserts itself once a visitor arrives at the footprints of the original Twin Towers. Aerial or other photographs cannot convey their acre-sized expanse as one encounters it on the site. Standing at their edge, measuring their breadth with one's eyes, and remembering that the Twin Towers matched the height of 1 World Trade Center,

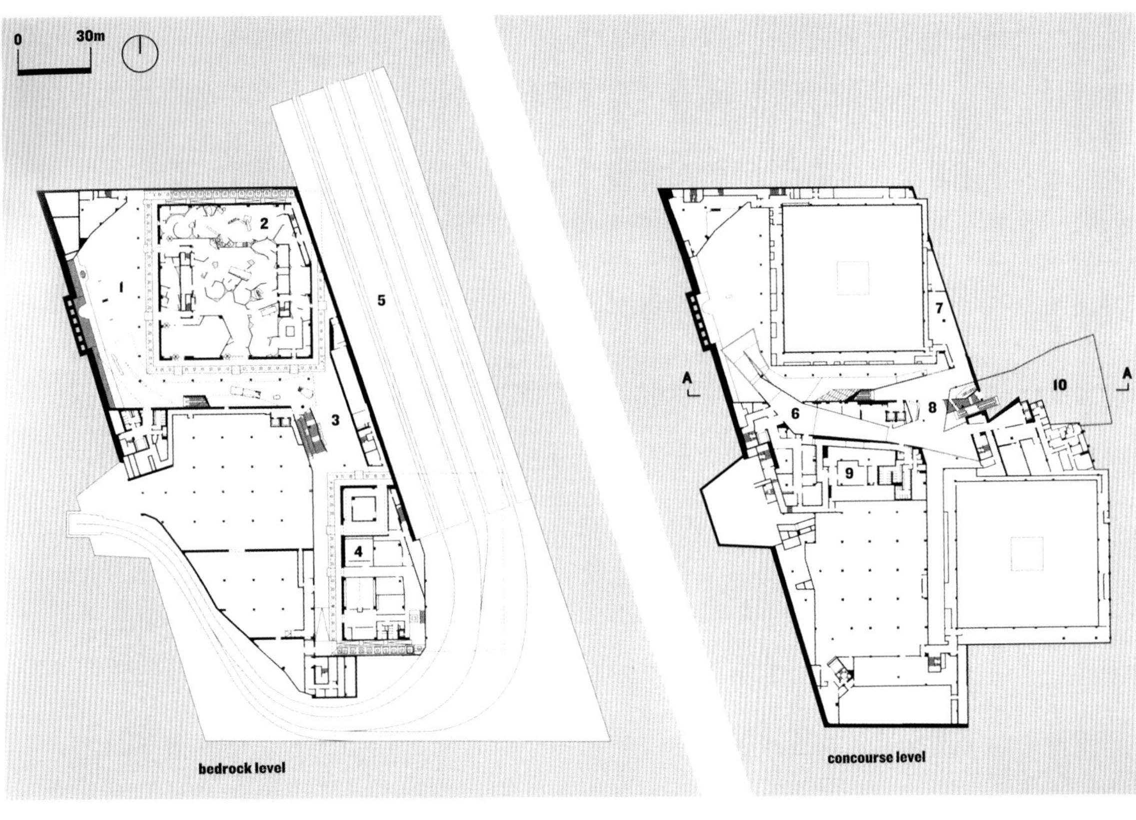

1 foundation hall
2 North Tower exhibition space
3 memorial hall
4 South Tower exhibition space
5 PATH station
6 ribbon descent
7 museum shop
8 concourse lobby
9 museum support
10 entry pavilion (above)

10.8. Davis, Brody, Bond, architects; National September 11 Memorial & Museum, 2011–14. Floor plans of (left) exhibition hall at bedrock level showing PATH train tracks within the footprint area of the South Tower and (right) concourse level.

which looms skyward to the north, induces awe at the enormity of their destruction and how horrific the events of 9/11 were. The memorial was to comply with the competition's condition of respecting the 210-foot-square footprints of the fallen towers. Yet this seemingly straightforward requirement turned out to be difficult to fulfill exactly, because the underground infrastructure made it hard to construct voids whose boundaries corresponded to the towers' perimeters. Competing priorities were visitors' ramps, underground circulation spaces, service roads, the electrical substation for the PATH commuter terminal, and the platform of the 1 and 9 subway trains.[31] Yet early in the design process, the LMDC stated: "We believe it's critical to delineate the original footprints." Arad stated: "I really think the footprints are the significant artifact of the site. To find a way of honoring it is my intention. I don't know that a literal tracing of the footprint is necessarily the only way to do it. What looks like a single square at the plaza level has many different layers of uses and programs."[32]

To 9/11 survivors and families of victims, the literalness of the footprints held great meaning,

10.9. Arad and Walker, Ground Zero Memorial, showing names of victims in "meaningful adjacency."

and the compromise of an approximation was disquieting. As the memorial design matured to its final form, square water pools were centered on the centers of the footprints of the original towers, but they are smaller. The recessed pools' interior dimension is 176 feet across; between the faces of the name panels on opposite sides is 192 feet. The first row of trees around each pool is 212 feet across, which was near the exterior dimension of the original towers.[33] In the museum underground, the North Tower's area is unencumbered. Yet only about half the South Tower's footprint area resides in the museum, since the PATH train tracks, which existed before the World Trade Center was built and ran underneath the South Tower, are again in use, operations having resumed in November 2003 (fig. 10.8).[34] The apparently literal representation of the towers' footprints is to a degree symbolic, because when the towers were built, they were not set in tight square holes, but rather were integrated with underground facilities. The pools are post-9/11 metaphors for foundational imprints, even though they look archaeological. They commemorate the towers' presence by imaging their absence.

The memorial version of the footprints became two square, below-ground pools, each nearly an acre, fed by thousands of rivulets that form sheets of water around their square perimeter. The water begins to flow at waist height above ground level just inside the periphery, cascades thirty feet into the gigantic squared pools, and falls another fifteen feet into smaller square central pools. The larger pools are called reflecting pools, but the constant cascade and churning of water perpetually prevents stillness on the surface. Instead, the continual falling of the water into the lower square core of each tower footprint is a compelling metaphor for catastrophic, sudden loss. The cascades may bring to mind the way in which the towers collapsed from their upper stories down to the ground, thus serving as a continual reenactment of the moments of destruction. As one visitor wrote: "the pools suggest the image of the event itself—the impossible fall of the buildings, the gray ash everywhere. That moment is shown through the fall of water, which looks ash-gray with a black stone wall behind it. From this point, the pools convey a powerful meaning."[35] Standing at the edge of the pools, one cannot see the bottom of the lower central pool, as if the water spills there into an abyss of indeterminate depth.

Yet water also connotes life and renewal. Libeskind had proposed waterfalls in his original master plan, although the concept was then criticized as bringing Niagara Falls to Lower Manhattan. He had reasoned that, if appropriately managed, the continuous sound of falling water would be helpful to the psychological efficacy of the memorial because it would mask the constant noise from streets all around the site. New York's great vitality was historically inextricable from its assertive soundscape. Hence, if the district around Ground Zero were to revive with its rebuilding, then the aural environs had to be partly screened out if the memorial were to serve effectively as a place of contemplation and quiet remembrance.[36] This is the effect of the built cascades. The water's fall and rush on all sides, with its noise reverberating inside the footprints' walls, creates its own soundscape that perceptually isolates the visitors at the footprints from the surrounding park, and induces a sense of removal from the encompassing city. In this way, the site's layered quality was not only visual and material, but also acoustic. The sounds from the memorial's periphery had to be muted in order to hallow its ground.

The seemingly secondary issue of acoustic control points up one of the central difficulties in creating a memorial for quiet contemplation in the midst of an extremely busy site. Indeed one challenge of the master plan was to integrate the memorial with paths that would facilitate the passage of people entering from Broadway and the related business side of Lower Manhattan on the east, and those moving across Ground Zero to and from the residential Battery Park City and the Hudson River on the west. Ideally a memorial would be located in a relatively open space, where the singular form of a built monument invites contemplation. A classic American example of this principle would be the Lincoln Memorial in Washington, D.C., designed and built 1911–22. As its architect Henry Bacon wrote of his project: "The power of impression by an object of reverence and honor is greatest when it is secluded and isolated, for then, in quiet and without distraction of the senses or mind, the beholder is alone with the lesson the object is designed to teach and inspire, and will be subject to its meaning."[37] Of course, such a privileged isolation was impossible for the Ground Zero memorial, but the details of its design are meant to lend the site a distinction appropriate to its commemorative function.

Along the tops of the square waterfalls that mark the footprints of the lost towers are continuous bronze parapet panels with the names of the deceased (fig. 10.9). The scale of the memorial pools is so vast that the names are diminished by comparison, as if the buildings themselves were casualties. Included among those memorialized were not only the 2,749 victims of 11 September 2001, in New York (revised as of January 2004), but also the 184 victims of terrorist attacks on that same day in the Pentagon and the 40 from the hijacked airplane that crashed near Shanksville, Pennsylvania, in addition to the six who died in the previous World Trade Center bombing on 26 February 1993. In conveying the scope of these losses, near and far, the memorial aspires to a national significance that transcends the site itself. Inspired by the Vietnam Veterans' Memorial in Washington, D.C., where names are etched on a vertical wall of polished, reflective granite, the effect of the names at Ground Zero is different. The tilted waist-high panels make the names experientially subordinate to the vast water cascades that they border. At Ground Zero, names are cut through the bronze panels above flowing water. At dusk, the perforated names are lit from within, transforming each letter from a dark daytime void into a light amid darkness. Mementoes of the deceased occasionally appear near their names, but the name panels are constantly inspected for graffiti, which is removed.

The biggest change to the original design was the loss, in 2006, of what Arad called the memorial galleries, or the below-ground walkways

10.10. Snøhetta Architects, National September 11 Memorial & Museum, entrance pavilion with "tridents" salvaged from World Trade Center.

in the footprints around the falls. Now visitors remain above ground, where the names were re-sited. The names are inscribed all around the great square footprints, including chamfered corner panels that recall the Twin Towers' splayed corners (fig. 10.9). The decision about the ordering of the names took two years, during which time the project was at a near standstill. There was hardly any fundraising or progress on design or construction until 2006. It was finally agreed to place the names according to an idea of "meaningful adjacency," meaning that victims who knew or worked with one another, as in the same company or police precinct, or who died close to one another, as in the same airplane, would be listed in close proximity. Victims' families were asked for specific names that they wanted listed next to their loved ones.[38] As with the adjustments to the towers' footprints, so with the arrangement of the names, the act of commemoration slightly reconfigured the conditions of the destruction, but there is no discernible clarification of what the process was. In other words, there is a palimpsest of alterations whose layered decisions we do not see.

A comparable dilemma of how to acknowledge both the site's difficult history— and its renewed condition as a zone of public remembrance—appears in the design of the 9/11 Memorial Museum.[39] When Ground Zero was cleared of debris (a process that took over eight months through May 2002), procedures were fraught with emotion among firefighters, construction workers, and other groups. From this scraping down of the site, its owner, the Port Authority of New York and New Jersey, retained about 700 artifacts, including the remains of police cars, fire trucks, steel columns, and part of the television antenna from the remains of the South Tower. The most visible aspect of the Twin Towers had been their closely spaced, tubular exterior steel columns clad in an aluminum alloy. The col-

10.11. World Trade Center, view of exterior with steel "tridents" clad in aluminum alloy.

umns constituted about seventy percent of each tower's surface, in contrast to the more wholly glass facades of many International Style buildings. As part of a structural system that provided an acre of open rentable office space on each floor, the towers' peripheral screen of columns was a programmatically desirable solution.[40] But that structure's vulnerability appeared when it was quickly weakened by fire caused by the crashing airplanes on 9/11. For weeks after the attack, jagged shards of the Twin Towers' skin, some up to eight stories high, stood on the site, and some people advocated that they remain as ruins incorporated into a memorial.[41] Ultimately, two of these trident-like pieces of one tower's skin, which were removed from Ground Zero, were brought back as fragments that stood for the vast remains of the destruction that had been piled there (figs. 10.10 and 10.11). The tridents do not stand where they originally did, but rather in the museum's above-ground, glass-enclosed entrance pavilion. They were so large that they had to be installed there before the pavilion was enclosed.[42] This pavilion, distinct from the museum itself, is the work of Snøhetta architects of Oslo. Its irregularly angled forms are visible at a distance walking toward the site, accentuating its aberrance relative to the right-angled buildings nearby, somewhat as Libeskind imagined (fig. 10.5). The tridents (once aluminum-clad, now rusted steel) are beside the stairs and escalators that lead from the museum's ground level entry down to its main lobby below ground. There one sees only the tridents' tops. Looking over the railing, one sees their seven-story length going down to dark lower levels, so they mark both a physical and a psychological transition.

With the memorial and the museum, Ground Zero is transformed from a site of disaster into a focus for tourism, but tourism most often in the sense of pilgrimage. The keynote of sacrality needed to be sustained within the museum below ground, in keeping with the memorial site above. Although the memorial could not be spatially isolated in its urban context, the underground situation of the museum achieves a distinct separation from the diurnal city above, and one that effectively engages with the issue of depth. Designed by architects Davis Brody Bond, the museum's underground space is immense and somber. This cavernous hall occupies what was once the site of the World Trade Center's underground complex, which housed a shopping mall and transport systems.[43] It is now a cathedral-like volume around and between the areas of the two tower footprints. The lighting is mostly low, carefully designed to create a serious aura that inspires sober reflection. Visitors descend from the museum's main lobby at the bottom of its entrance stairs/escalators down a broad ramp that pulls them along by gravity. The ramp recalls the path of the construction ramp that accessed the excavation site.[44] At the end of the ramp, visitors' first sight of the museum interior's full depth and expanse is from a cantilevered mezzanine still high above the bedrock floor (fig. 10.12). This overlooks the displayed section of the west Slurry Wall on one side, and a representation of the west side of the North Tower hovering above ground level on the other side behind new square concrete columns whose monumental height and stately cadence evoke the tower's scale. In this volume, the central artifact is the 36-foot-high "Last Column," as the last of the Twin Towers' steel columns to be dismantled, which became a focus for the community of workers involved in this task. They became a community of witnesses, inscribing on this column graffiti with names of their units, mementoes, and other images of solidarity.

In the museum, the high suspended walls representing the north and south towers are clad in panels of foamed, recycled aluminum, injected with gas under high pressure to create a bubbly, otherworldly surface that appears to glow. The panels' texture alludes to the aluminum in the towers and to its melting in the inferno of the attacks, a theme that resonates with the large fragments of tortured steel displayed in nearby spaces. Instead of being foundational, the high tower walls in the museum appear to float above the viewer as one palimpsestual layer. As with the footprints on the memorial site above ground, the suspended tower walls in the museum are simulacra of the former buildings, though they could be read as artifacts. The perspective on the walls from below activates the viewer's perception of the site's levels as conceptually separable. Directly below the suspended walls along the floor are the lines of shorn-off bases of the steel box columns that mark the foundational perimeter of the towers. These are the true delineation of the footprints.

The main exhibits are in the base areas of the north and south towers. Between them is the central area of arrival in the museum near bedrock level. There on a wall that screens a city repository for unidentified human remains, is a quotation from Virgil's *Aeneid*, in block letters forged out of pitted metal from the ruins: "No day shall erase you from the memory of time." The quotation can refer to the deceased behind the wall, but also more broadly to 9/11 as an event that is to be permanently remembered in the way prescribed by the museum. The repository holds several thousand body

10.12. Davis Brody Bond, architects, National September 11 Memorial & Museum, 2011–14. Interior showing cantilevered mezzanine (upper center) with views of the reconstructed underground west wall of the North Tower, World Trade Center, clad in foamed aluminum (left), the Last Column with initials of worker teams (center), and a segment of the original west Slurry Wall, recessed between new sections of concrete slurry wall with new steel ties (right).

parts from the almost 40 percent of victims not identified.[45] Around the words is the only work of art commissioned for the museum, Spencer Finch's *Trying to Remember the Color of the Sky on That September Morning*. Its 2,983 squares of Fabriano Italian paper—one for every person killed on 9/11 and in 1993—are each painted with a different shade of blue. Their variation conveys both the clarity and the uncertainty of memories of that day.

The South Tower contains the Memorial Exhibition, its core being photographs of the thousands of victims on several walls. The North Tower holds the Historical Exhibition, including sections on sights and sounds of the day 9/11, then events before 9/11 (beginning with the model of the Twin Towers), and, third, a lengthy section on later events that responded to the attacks. Among the displayed artifacts culled from over 10,000 in the museum's collections is a 15-ton composite of four to five tower floors that collapsed into a stack of reinforcing bar, concrete slabs, pulverized dry wall, furniture, carpeting, carbonized bits of paper, and other objects fused by heat and pressure. The once ordered materials are horribly compressed into a mass wherein layers cannot be distinguished. The Office of the Medical Examiner concluded that the composite did not contain human remains, yet its inclusion was controversial because it suggests their entombment.[46] As acknowledgment of how powerful and upsetting encounters with such objects can be, especially for relatives of victims, the lengthy Historical Exhibition has points at which visitors can decide to leave if they feel emotionally unprepared for what lies ahead. The idea of layered experience is one that is both institutionally orchestrated and individually self-edited. As the museum's director, Alice M. Greenwald, says, unlike artifacts housed in museums, "[w]e are, literally, a museum that's housed in an artifact."[47]

As we see in the essays throughout this volume, architectural palimpsests embrace contradictions, or hold unresolved elements in tension. They juxtapose objects, spaces, and periods that have different histories and yet mutually instructive relationships, when placed in proximity to each other, especially in a layered arrangement. If we return to the questions posed near the start of this essay, then we should also ask ourselves about what is omitted from collective memory in Ground Zero's treatment. As several critics of its memorial and museum have noted, its architecture and exhibitions do not engage fully with the aftermath of 9/11 in terms of military and civilian lives lost in conflicts in both Afghanistan and Iraq. There is also scant consideration of the implications of the Patriot Act and similar legislation for the future of civil liberties as the foundations of democracy that the Slurry Wall was to signify.[48] In these and other ways, the site narrates a limited view of events. Ideally it could embrace these additional layers of 9/11's meaning that Ground Zero's architecture and its attendant rhetoric largely pass over in silence. The concept of the palimpsest as an analytical framework thus invites us to consider how the site's commemorative program might encompass a broader understanding in the future.

Notes

I thank the editors of this volume for their vision in organizing the symposium and their perseverance in completing this publication. I thank also Amanda Granek, National September 11 Memorial & Museum; Zoë Siebel, Studio Libeskind, New York City; Maureen McManus, The Port Authority of New York and New Jersey; and especially my wife, Professor Susanne Fusso, Wesleyan University, for her superb editorial guidance.

1 Huyssen 2003.
2 Glanz and Lipton 2003; Goldberger 2004; Stephens 2004; Smith 2006; Sturken 2007; and Greenspan 2013.
3 Okrent 2003.
4 Glanz and Lipton 2003, 40, quoted in Smith 2006, 104. See Olsberg 2014.
5 Quoted in Smith 2006, 103.
6 Page 1999.
7 Kayal and Benson 2002, 50–53; Sorkin and Zukin 2002, 38–39, 122–24, and 131–36; Dunlap 2010; and Dunlap 2012b.
8 Cited in Glanz and Lipton 2002, 38, partly quoted in Smith 2006, 107–08. See Darton 1999, 62–63, 90–92, 130–36; and Glanz and Lipton 2003, 62–87.
9 Smith 2006, 105. See Olsberg 2014.
10 Goldberger 2001, quoted in Smith 2006, 105.
11 Stephens 2002, 124–26, 213; Wyatt 2002, A1, B6; Muschamp 2002, B6.
12 Eisenman, quoted in Jencks 1988, 29.
13 Eisenman 1985, 46.
14 Libeskind 1999; *Jewish Museum* 1999; and Eisenman 2008, 230–54.
15 Libeskind 1990, 29.
16 Libeskind, quoted in Lutyens 2003.
17 Libeskind 2003.
18 Quoted in Deitz 2008, 18.
19 Stephens 2004, 32–35; and Bagli 2011, A19, A21.
20 Childs, quoted in Dunlap 2012a, A19.
21 Childs in the film *Rising: Rebuilding Ground Zero*, which aired on the Discovery and Science channels for 9/11's tenth anniversary.
22 Smith 2006, 106.
23 Gordon 1997.
24 Libeskind 2003.
25 Libeskind, quoted in Trachtenberg 2003, 54.
26 Libeskind 2013, 3–4.
27 "Daniel Libeskind Talks with Doris Erbacher and Peter Paul Kubitz," in *Jewish Museum Berlin* 1999, 17.
28 Libeskind 2013, 4; and Goldberger 2004, 212.
29 Stephens 2004, 36–40; Blais and Rasic 2011; and Greenspan 2013, 117–29.
30 Kimmelman 2014, C1; Gopnik 2014; Clines 2014, A24; and Ulam 2013.
31 Dunlap 2004, B1; Sturken 2004, 317–19; and Sturken 2007, 199–205.
32 Arad, quoted in Dunlap 2004, B1.
33 Arad, e-mail to author, 7 August 2014.
34 Colleen Patterson, National September 11 Memorial & Museum, e-mail to author, 11 August 2014. See Luo 2003, A23.
35 Olga Kaganova, letter, *New Yorker*, 28 July 2014, 5.
36 Libeskind 2013, 4.
37 Bacon 1913, 34.
38 Greenspan 2013, 183–86.
39 Greenspan 2013, 205–19.
40 Smith 2006, 109.
41 de Montebello 2001, A29.
42 Sturken 2015, 478.
43 Sturken 2015, 478.
44 Bevan 2014, 84.
45 Bevan 2014, 88.
46 Sturken 2015, 484.
47 Quoted in Dunlap 2013.
48 Deutsche 2014; and Sturken 2015.

Bibliography

Bacon, Henry. 1913. "Appendix B: Report of the Architect on the Preliminary Design for a Memorial on the Potomac Park Site," in *Lincoln Memorial Commission Report*, U.S. Senate Document, 62nd Cong.; no. 965. Washington, D.C.: Government Printing Office.

Bagli, Charles V. 2011. "After $10 Million, Effort to Coat Base of Trade Center in Glass Is Halted," *New York Times*, 12 May.

Bevan, Robert. 2014. "Criticism," in "Memory Ruins," *Architectural Review* 235, no. 1408, 84–85, 88.

Blais, Allison, and Lynn Rasic. 2011. *A Place of Remembrance; Official Book of the National September 11 Memorial*. Washington, D.C.: National Geographic Society.

Clines, Francis X. 2014. "Seizing the Day at Ground Zero," *New York Times*, 23 July.

Darton, Eric. 1999. *Divided We Stand: A Biography of New York's World Trade Center.* New York: Basic Books.

de Montebello, Philippe. 2001. "The Iconic Power of an Artifact," *New York Times*, 25 September.

Deitz, Paula. 2003. "Is There a Future for Ground Zero," *Architectural Review* 213, no. 1272, 18–19, 21.

Deutsche, Rosalyn. 2014. "The Whole Truth," *Artforum International* 53, no. 1, 139-40, 142.

Dunlap, David W. 2013. "In 9/11 Museum to Open Next Spring, Vastness and Serenity, and Awe and Grief," *New York Times*, 28 June.

—. 2012a. "With a Column of Steel, A Tower Can Reclaim the Sky," *New York Times*, 30 April.

—. 2012b. "An Effort to Save the Remnants of a Dwindling Little Syria," *New York Times*, 2 January.

—. 2010. "When an Arab Enclave Thrived Downtown," *New York Times*, 24 August.

—. 2004. "At 9/11 Memorial, Actual Sizes May Vary," *New York Times*, 12 February.

Eisenman, Peter. 2008. *Ten Canonical Buildings 1950–2000.* New York: Rizzoli.

—. 1985. "OSU Center for the Visual Arts, Columbus, Ohio, 1985," *Architectural Design* 55, no. 1–2, 45–47.

Glanz, James, and Eric Lipton. 2003. *City in the Sky: The Rise and Fall of the World Trade Center.* New York: Times Books.

—. 2002. "The Height of Ambition," *New York Times Magazine*, 8 September, 32–44, 59, 60, 63.

Goldberger, Paul. 2004. *Up from Zero: Politics, Architecture, and the Rebuilding of New York.* New York: Random House.

—. 2001. "Building Plans," *New Yorker* 77, no. 28, 24 September, 76–78.

Gopnik, Adam. 2014. "Stones and Bones," *New Yorker* 90, no. 19, 7 and 14 July, 38–44.

Gordon, David L. A. 1997. *Battery Park City: Politics and Planning on the New York Waterfront.* Amsterdam: Gordon and Breach.

Greenspan, Elizabeth. 2013. *Battle for Ground Zero: Inside the Political Struggle to Rebuild the World Trade Center.* New York: Palgrave MacMillan.

Huyssen, Andreas. 2003. *Present Pasts: Urban Palimpsests and the Politics of Memory.* Stanford: Stanford University Press.

Jencks, Charles. 1988. "Deconstruction: The Pleasures of Absence," *Architectural Design* 58, no. 3–4, 17–31.

Jewish Museum Berlin / Architect Daniel Libeskind. 1999. Berlin: G + B Arts International.

Kayal, Philip, and Kathleen Benson, eds. 2002. *A Community in Many Worlds: Arab Americans in New York City.* New York: Syracuse University Press.

Kimmelman, Michael. 2014. "Finding Space for the Living at a Memorial," *New York Times*, 29 May.

Libeskind, Daniel. 2013. "Ground Zero—The Socio-Political Minefield of Symbolic Architecture," *Amps: Architecture Media Politics Society* 2, no. 2, 1–14.

—. 2003. "Selected Design for the WTC Site as of February 2003; Introduction."
http://www.renewnyc.com/plan_des_dev/wtc_site/new_design_plans/selected_libeskind/default.asp (accessed 30 May 2016).

—. 1999. *Daniel Libeskind: Jewish Museum Berlin; Between the Lines.* Munich: Prestel.

—. 1990. "Between the Lines," *Architectural Design* 60, no. 7–8, 27–29.

Luo, Michael. 2003. "Inside Ground Zero, a Stream of Commuters, and of Tears," *New York Times*, 25 November.

Lutyens, Dominic. 2003. "Ground Hero," *Guardian*, 21 June.

Muschamp, Herbert. 2002. "An Agency's Ideology Is Unsuited to Its Task," *New York Times*, 17 July.

Olsberg, Nicholas. 2014. "Small World, After All," in "Memory Ruins," *Architectural Review* 235, no. 1408, 79–82.

Okrent, Daniel. 2003. *Great Fortune: The Epic of Rockefeller Center.* New York: Viking.

Page, Max. 1999. *The Creative Destruction of Manhattan, 1900–1940.* Chicago: University of Chicago Press.

Smith, Terry. 2006. *The Architecture of Aftermath.* Chicago: University of Chicago Press.

Sorkin, Michael, and Sharon Zukin, eds. 2002. *After the World Trade Center: Rethinking New York City.* New York and London: Routledge.

Stephens, Suzanne. 2002. "Architects without Architecture at Ground Zero; A Commentary," *Architectural Record* 190, no. 1, 124–26, 213.

Stephens, Suzanne, with Ian Luna and Ron Broadhurst. 2004. *Imagining Ground Zero: Official and Unofficial Proposals for the World Trade Center Site.* New York: Rizzoli.

Sturken, Marita. 2015. "The 9/11 Memorial Museum and the Remaking of Ground Zero," *American Quarterly* 67, no. 2, 470–90.

—. 2007. *Tourists of History: Memory, Kitsch, and Consumerism from Oklahoma City to Ground Zero.* Durham: Duke University Press.

—. 2004. "The Aesthetics of Absence: Rebuilding Ground Zero," *American Ethnologist* 31, no. 3, 311–25.

Trachtenberg, Marvin. 2003. "A New Vision for Ground Zero Beyond Mainstream Modernism," *New York Times*, 23 February.

Ulam, Alex. 2013. "World Trade Center Memorial: Hundreds of Swamp White Oaks…" *Topos: European Landscape Magazine* 83, 16–21.

Wyatt, Edward. 2002. "Six Plans for Ground Zero; All Seen as a Starting Point," *New York Times*, 17 July.

Image Credits

Cover: Palazzo Comunale, Bologna. Façade facing south. (Photo: Jeffrey Schiff; cover design: David Schorr)

0.1. Abbey of Saint-Rémi, Reims. Interior view toward the east showing in the foreground the eleventh-century nave walls with their Early Gothic layers and in the background the Early Gothic chevet that replaced the Romanesque sanctuary. (Photo: Clark Maines)

0.2. Abbey of Saint-Rémi, Reims. Detail of the north wall of the nave showing the relationship between the eleventh-century nave wall and its late twelfth-century "layer." (Photo: Clark Maines)

0.3. Two-storeyed pavilion at end of Virupaksha bazaar, Vijayanagara, fifteenth and sixteenth centuries. Showing reuse of eleventh-century Chalukya columns in ground storey. (Photo: Phillip Wagoner)

0.4. Close-up of reused Chalukya column in two-storeyed pavilion at end of Virupaksha bazaar, Vijayanagara. (Photo: Phillip Wagoner)

0.5. Façade of the Fondaco dei Tedeschi, Venice. First constructed in 1228, rebuilt between 1505 and 1508, with later changes. Documented in 2013, before the most recent restoration. (Photo: © Wolfgang Moroder/Wikimedia Commons)

0.6. View of the interior of the Fondaco dei Tedeschi shopping center, Venice. Redesign by OMA, 2016. (Photo: Nadja Aksamija)

0.7. View of the new escalator at the Fondaco dei Tedeschi shopping center, Venice. Redesign by OMA, 2016. (Photo: Nadja Aksamija)

1.1. Deval Masjid, Bodhan, Nizamabad District, Telangana State, India, originally built around 1200, reconstructed in 1323. View from the northeast corner. (Photo: Phillip Wagoner)

1.2. Plan of the monument as reconstructed around 1323. North is to the right. (Drawing: Phillip Wagoner, assisted by Julia Drachman)

1.3. View from the recycled temple *mandapa* to the *qibla* wall, showing the *mihrab* at the center of the wall. (Photo: Phillip Wagoner)

1.4. View of the ruined pulpit in the bay north of the *mihrab* bay, seen from northeast. (Photo: Phillip Wagoner)

1.5. Column from the front of the temple vestibule now marking the central entrance to the prayer hall, showing the roughly dressed side of the shaft which in the temple would have been engaged in the fabric of the wall. (Photo: Phillip Wagoner)

1.6. Floor of the former temple vestibule, showing the ornamental stepping stone, the floor moldings marking the threshold of the doorway to the sanctum, and the base of the *linga* pedestal on the floor of the sanctum. (Photo: Phillip Wagoner)

1.7. Base of the *linga* pedestal on the sanctum floor. (Photo: Phillip Wagoner)

1.8. View from the south of the exterior of the *qibla* wall showing the *mihrab* projection, and the uppermost moldings of the circumambulatory terrace at the base. (Photo: Phillip Wagoner)

1.9. Bay immediately south of the *mihrab* aisle, showing two stones from the top of the temple plinth. (Photo: Phillip Wagoner)

1.10. Plan of temple as constructed around 1200, here conjecturally restored. (Drawing: Phillip Wagoner, assisted by Julia Drachman)

1.11. Interior view of the temple *mandapa*, showing two columns at the north side of the central bay, seen from east. (Photo: Phillip Wagoner)

1.12. Detail of one of the columns of the *mandapa*'s central bay, showing remnants of effaced mythological scene of "Churning of the Milky Ocean." (Photo: Phillip Wagoner)

2.1. Porta Nigra, Trier. View from north. (Photo: Courtesy of Clark Maines)

2.2. Aerial view of the Porta Nigra and Simeonstift. (Photo: © Google Earth)

2.3. Plans of the Porta Nigra: a) Porta Nigra as Roman gate, second or early third century CE; b) plan of the church installed in the Porta Nigra, *c.* 1035–50; c) plan of the church, 1150–1700, with the apse added by Albero of Montreuil. (Plans: Sheila Bonde after Bruno Meyer-Plath, in Gose 1969, vol. 2, figs. 72–77)

2.4. Caspar Merian, *St Simeon in Porta Nigra in Trier*, engraving, 1670. (Photo: Wikimedia Commons)

2.5. Reconstruction plan of the church of Saint Simeon (converting the Porta Nigra) and the Simeonstift in *c.* 1150, recording the platform and terracing shown in the Caspar Merian engraving (fig. 2.4) and discovered in excavations in the 1930s. (Plan: Sheila Bonde after Friedrich Kutzbach, republished in Heyen 2002, 36; and plans in Zahn 1974, 30–31)

2.6. View of the apse from southeast. (Photo: Courtesy of Clark Maines)

2.7. View of the Simeonstift *quadrum*. (Photo: Courtesy of Clark Maines)

2.8. View of the Rococo panels in the west tower. (Photo: Courtesy of Clark Maines)

2.9. Hitler's banner hanging on the front of the Porta Nigra in April 1938. (Photo: Courtesy of Südwestrundfunk | SWR.de)

2.10. Centurion guide at the Porta Nigra. (Photo: Courtesy of Trier Tourismus und Marketing GmbH)

2.11. Karl Marx statues in front of the Porta Nigra, as part of an installation by the artist Ottmar Hörl, May 2013. (Photo: Courtesy of dpa picture alliance/ Alamy Stock Photo)

3.1. *Madrasa* and mausoleum of Sultan al-Nasir Muhammad ibn Qalawun, Cairo, 1295–1303. View of the façade. Documented in 2010. (Photo: Erik Gustafson)

3.2. Area plan of the Bayn al-Qasrayn neighborhood of Cairo: (1) *madrasa* of Sultan al-Malik al-Kamil (1225); (2) mausoleum and *madrasa* of Sultan al-Salih (1243); (3) *madrasa* of Sultan al-Zahir Baybars (1263); (4) Sultan Qalawun mausoleum, *madrasa*, and hospital (1284–85); (5) Sultan al-Nasir mausoleum and *madrasa* (1295–1303); and (6) mausoleum and *madrasa* of Sultan al-Zahir Barquq (1384–68). (Plan: Courtesy of Nicholas Warner)

3.3. Plan of the funerary complex of al-Nasir, Cairo. (Plan: Saeed Arida after Meinecke; © Nasser Rabbat/Aga Khan Program for Islamic Architecture, MIT)

3.4. Funerary complex of al-Nasir, Cairo. Detail of the portal. (Photo: Erik Gustafson)

3.5. Funerary complex of al-Nasir, Cairo. Analysis of material sources in the al-Nasir complex portal: red = Crusader; blue = Mamluk; yellow = possibly Byzantine. (Photo: Erik Gustafson)

3.6. Funerary complex of al-Nasir, Cairo. Detail of portal colonnettes and capitals. (Photo: Erik Gustafson)

3.7. Funerary complex of al-Nasir, Cairo. Detail showing the gap between the façade wall and the right embrasure of the portal. (Photo: Erik Gustafson)

3.8. Axonometric reconstruction of the Great Mosque of al-Zahir Baybars, Cairo, 1267–69. (Drawing: Courtesy of Jonathan Bloom)

3.9. Mausoleum of al-Mansur Qalawun, Cairo, 1284–85. View of the façade. Documented in 2010. (Photo: Erik Gustafson)

3.10. Remains of the *madrasa* of al-Salih Najm al-Din Ayyub (Salihiyya), Cairo, 1243. View of the central portal and one lateral bay. Documented in 2010. (Photo: Erik Gustafson)

3.11. Funerary complex of al-Nasir, Cairo. Detail of the mausoleum *mihrab* wall. (Photo: Erik Gustafson)

3.12. Funerary complex of al-Nasir, Cairo. Detail of the mausoleum's lost dome and squinches. (Photo: Erik Gustafson)

3.13. Mausoleum of al-Salih Najm al-Din Ayyub, Cairo, 1250. Detail of the dome and squinches. (Photo: Erik Gustafson)

4.1. Painted vase (K1523) showing the Hero Twins (prominent, semi-divine figures in Maya mythology) as scribes, Late Classic period (*c.* 600–800 CE). Each twin paints an open screenfold book with jaguar skin covers. (Photo: Justin Kerr and Kerr Associates)

4.2. A page from the Dresden Codex showing vertical and horizontal guides in faint red paint to grid out locations for glyph blocks and figural proportions. (Photo: Courtesty of Sächsische Landesbibliothek – Staats – und Universitätsbibliothek Dresden)

4.3. Multiple levels of replastering and reinscription on the east wall of Structure 10K–2 at Xultun. (Photo: Courtesy of Franco Rossi)

4.4. Tatiana Proskouriakoff, *Acropolis at Piedras Negras, Guatemala* (restored view), watercolor, 1939. (Photo: Courtesy of the Penn Museum)

4.5. Russell Hoover, *Tikal Abandoned* (reconstruction of Tikal after its dynastic collapse), oil painting, 1985. (Photo: Courtesy of the Penn Museum)

4.6. Cutaway illustration showing the buried buildings, especially the intentionally preserved Rosalila, beneath Structure 10L–16 at Copán. (Image: Christopher Klein; © National Geographic Society)

4.7. Lintel 21 from Structure 22 at Yaxchilán, Mexico. The shaded glyph at B7 names Structure 22 as the Four Bat Place constructed and dedicated in 454 CE; the shaded glyph at C6 names the renovated building once again as the Four Bat Place, during a later ceremony in 752 CE. (Drawing: Sarah Newman, after Graham and von Euw 1977, 49).

4.8. A pseudo-color image of folios 110v–105r of the Archimedes Palimpsest, in which an ultraviolet image of both texts and an image showing only the prayers are manipulated to emphasize the contrast of both texts against the parchment. The overwriting is shown in neutral gray tones and the underwriting in red. (Image: http://www.archimedespalimpsest.net. Approved for reproduction by Walters Museum curator Walter Noel under Creative Commons License CC BY 3.0)

5.1. Castello delle Rocche (Castello Estense), Finale Emilia, early fifteenth century. View of the courtyard. Documented in 2006. (Photo: Courtesy of Francesco Ceccarelli)

5.2. Courtyard of the Castello delle Rocche at Finale Emilia after the May 2012 earthquake. (Photo: *Il Castello delle Rocche di Finale Emilia dopo il terremoto*/ www.artribune.com/19 March 2013)

5.3. Giacomo Barozzi da Vignola or Achille Bocchi (attr.), Palazzo Bocchi, Bologna, begun 1545. Detail of the front façade. (Photo: Nadja Aksamija)

5.4. Michelozzo di Bartolomeo, Palazzo Medici-Riccardi, Florence, begun 1444, with later changes. View of the seventeenth-century extension along Via Cavour. Documented *c.* 1890. (Photo: Giacomo Brogi, Archivi Alinari, Florence)

5.5. Filippo Brunelleschi, loggia of the Ospedale degli Innocenti, Florence, begun 1419, with later changes. Documented in 2008. (Photo: © Warburg/ Wikimedia Commons)

5.6. Ipostudio, new brass gates to the Museo degli Innocenti, Florence, 2016. (Photo: Courtesy of Claudia Bucelli)

5.7. Ponte Santa Trinita, Florence. Constructed by Bartolomeo Ammannati in 1567–69, destroyed in 1944, rebuilt (with some original materials) in 1958. (Photo: Nadja Aksamija)

5.8. Rubble of the Campanile di San Marco and the Loggetta in Venice, 1902. (Photo: Musei Civici di Venezia, Archivio fotografico del Museo Fortuny)

5.9. Jacopo Sansovino, Loggetta di San Marco, 1538–45, Venice. Documented before 1874. (Photo: Carlo Naya, Musei Civici di Venezia, Archivio fotografico del Museo Fortuny)

5.10. Detail of the Loggetta showing a reconstituted sculptural relief on the façade. (Photo: Nadja Aksamija)

5.11. Facsimile (with integrated original sculptural elements) of Jacopo Sansovino's Loggetta, Venice, 1912. (Photo: Nadja Aksamija)

5.12. The Institute for Digital Archaeology, scale replica of the Palmyra Arch in Piazza della Signoria, Florence. Documented in April 2017. (Photo: Nadja Aksamija)

5.13. Santa Maria della Spina, Pisa. Erected *c.* 1230; enlarged after 1325; dismantled and rebuilt (on a higher level) in 1871. (Photo: © Carlo Pelagalli/ Wikimedia Commons)

6.1. Political *programmata* covering the eastern half of the south façade of the House of Trebius Valens (*Regio* III.ii.1) as discovered in 1915. (Photo: Courtesy of the Ministero dei Beni e delle Attività Culturali e del Turismo, Soprintendenza di Pompei, Archivio Fotografico C706)

6.2. Plan of the *Praedia* of Julia Felix, *Regio* II.iv.1–12, Pompeii. (Drawing: Christopher Parslow)

6.3. Panel in the Museo Archeologico Nazionale in Naples (MAN 4713) containing *CIL* 4.1136 naming the *Praedia* of Julia Felix along with five other *dipinti* (*CIL* 4.1137–1141), as it appears today. (Photo: Courtesy of the Ministero dei Beni e delle Attività Culturali e del Turismo, Museo Archeologico Nazionale di Napoli)

6.4. Left image: Tracing of the text of *CIL* 4.1142–1143 (MAN NR 834; now lost) as copied by the Bourbon excavators at the time of its discovery in 1756. Right image: Proposed reconstruction. (Drawings: Christopher Parslow)

6.5. Left image: Tracing of the text of *CIL* 4.1153–1154 as copied by the Bourbon excavators at the time of its discovery in 1756. Center image: MAN 4667 (Photo: Courtesy of the Ministero dei Beni e delle Attività Culturali e del Turismo, Soprintendenza di Pompei, Archivio Fotografico D110640). Right image: Tracing based on MAN 4667 and Rosini 1797, plate 12.3. (Drawings: Christopher Parslow)

6.6. Karl Weber, Plan of the *Praedia*, 1757. (Photo: Courtesy of the Ministero dei Beni e delle Attività Culturali e del Turismo, Museo Archeologico Nazionale di Napoli, Archivio Disegni 71)

6.7. North façade of the *Praedia* as it appeared immediately after re-excavation in January 1935. (Photo: Courtesy of the Ministero dei Beni e delle Attività Culturali e del Turismo, Soprintendenza di Pompei, Archivio Fotografico C2098)

6.8. MAN 4713 consisting of *CIL* 4.1136–1141 divided up into nineteen fragments of stucco and remounted together. Composite tracing based on original panel and on Rosini 1797, plate 4. (Drawing: Christopher Parslow)

6.9. MAN 4672 containing *CIL* 4.1145–1150 in eleven fragments of stucco. Based on original and Rosini 1797, plate 10.2. (Drawing: Christopher Parslow)

6.10. North façade of the *Praedia* with segments of wall labeled according to the numerical colocation employed by Karl Weber. (Drawing: Christopher Parslow)

6.11. The provenance of the *programmata* from the central portion of the north façade (*CIL* 4.1136–1150). (Drawing: Christopher Parslow)

6.12. The provenance of the *programmata* from the west end of the north façade (*CIL* 4.1151–1154). (Drawing: Christopher Parslow)

6.13. Left image: MAN 4674 containing *CIL* 1152–1152a. (Photo: Courtesy of the Ministero dei Beni e delle Attività Culturali e del Turismo, Soprintendenza di Pompei, Archivio Fotografico D110638). Right image: Tracing based on Rosini 1797, plate 12.4. (Drawing: Christopher Parslow)

6.14. The *dipinti* on the eastern half of the north facade (*CIL* 4.7576–7583, 7990). (Drawing: Christopher Parslow)

6.15. The *programma* of Orphaeus in support of L. Ceius Secundus revealed under the final coat of stucco on the west façade outside the entrance (*Regio* II.iv.10) to the second floor apartments. (Drawing: Christopher Parslow)

7.1. Priory church of Saint-Pierre-des-Minimes, Compiègne. View of the mutilated west portal. (Photo: Clark Maines)

7.2. Saint-Pierre-des-Minimes, detail of the west portal showing the present state of the tympanum, lintel, and figured archivolt. (Photo: Clark Maines)

7.3. Parish church of Saint-Loup, Bléneau. View of the west portal showing the placement of both Revolutionary cult inscriptions. (Photo: Clark Maines)

7.4. Saint-Loup de Bléneau, detail of the partially effaced inscription "Temple de la Raison." (Photo: Clark Maines)

7.5. Collegiate church of Saint-Thomas de Cantorbéry, Crépy-en-Valois. View of the west façade from the southwest. Documented in 2001. (Photo: Clark Maines)

7.6. Saint-Thomas de Cantorbéry, view of the tympanum of the west portal in 2001. (Photo: Clark Maines)

7.7. Reconstruction drawing of the medieval iconography of the west portal tympanum at Crépy. (Drawing: Clark Maines)

7.8. Reconstruction drawing of the medieval iconography of the west portal tympanum at Crépy with the Revolutionary inscription superimposed on it. (Drawing: Clark Maines)

7.9. Saint-Thomas de Cantorbéry, detail of the lower right portion of the tympanum showing the chisel marks on the mutilated sculpture. (Photo: Clark Maines)

7.10. Parish church of Saint-Pierre, Gonesse. View of the west façade. Documented in 2013. (Photo: Clark Maines)

7.11. Saint-Pierre de Gonesse, view of the west portal in 2013. (Photo: Clark Maines)

7.12. Saint-Pierre de Gonesse, view of the west portal tympanum from below in 2013. (Photo: Clark Maines)

7.13. Saint-Pierre de Gonesse, view of the west portal tympanum in 2013. (Photo: Clark Maines)

7.14. Saint-Pierre de Gonesse, view of the tympanum in 1991. (Photo: Clark Maines)

7.15. Collegiate church of Notre-Dame-en-Vaux, Châlons-en-Champagne. View of the west façade from the southwest. (Photo: Clark Maines)

7.16. Notre-Dame-en-Vaux, detail of the west façade showing the placement of seven symmetrically arranged holes in the spandrel area above the central portal. (Photo: Clark Maines)

7.17. Notre-Dame-en-Vaux, detail of the same spandrel area with a reconstruction of the *drapeau tricolore* and the inscription "Temple de la Raison." (Photo: Clark Maines)

7.18. Priory church of Notre-Dame de Montiers. View of the church from the main road through the village. (Photo: Clark Maines)

7.19. Notre-Dame de de Monthiers, detail of the stair tower on the south side of the choir showing the remains of the painted Revolutionary inscription. (Photo: Clark Maines)

7.20. Satellite view of the center of the old town of Gonesse showing the location of key monuments (in white) and the route of Revolutionary processions (in red). (Photo: © Google Earth)

7.21. Pierre-Antoine Demachy, *Fête de l'Être Suprême*, 1794. (Photo: © Musée Carnavalet, Paris; Wikimedia Commons)

7.22. Anonymous artist, popular print of the *Vue de la Montagne Élevée au Champs de la Réunion* (*Fête de l'Être Suprême*). (Photo: Courtesy of the Bibliothèque nationale de France)

7.23. Notre-Dame-en-Vaux, Châlons-en-Champagne. View of the medieval choir reconstructed as a Temple of Reason. (Photo: Clark Maines)

7.24. Parish church of Saint-Pierre, Nanteuil-le-Haudouin. View of the portal on the south side of the church. (Photo: Clark Maines)

7.25. Saint-Pierre de Nanteuil-le-Haudouin, detail of the lateral portal tympanum showing the remains of a post-Revolutionary inscription. (Photo: Clark Maines)

8.1. Plan of the monuments in the fortress (*gadhi*), Kadwaha, tenth-fifteenth century. (Drawing: Tamara Sears)

8.2. Bijasan Devi temple, Kadwaha, late eighteenth or early nineteenth century. (Photo: Tamara Sears)

8.3. Map of the village of Kadwaha showing the reconstructed contours of the lake. (Map: Tamara Sears)

8.4. View of modern sculpture workshop against the backdrop of the Nahalvar group of temples, Kadwaha, tenth-twenty-first century. (Photo: Tamara Sears)

8.5. Colonial-era *chattri* set in a gap between two houses, Kadwaha, nineteenth century. (Photo: Tamara Sears)

8.6. Map displaying routes of travel through Central India, as described by Ibn Battuta (*c.* 1340s) and Babur (*c.* 1527–28). (Map: Tamara Sears)

8.7. Morayat (or Mulayata) temple group, Kadwaha, tenth-eleventh century. View of fields around the temples from the south. (Photo: Tamara Sears)

8.8. Maps displaying the extent of saturated groundwater around Kadwaha. Left: Physical map (Map data: © Google 2017). Right: Satellite map (Photo: © 2017 Terramatrix via Google 2017). (Map: Tamara Sears, produced using QGIS 2.14.2)

8.9. Monastery and fortress wall, Kadwaha, tenth-fifteenth century. View of exterior from the west. (Photo: Tamara Sears)

8.10. Fortress (*gadhi*), Kadwaha, tenth-fifteenth century. View of the temple, monastery, and fragmentary *qibla* wall of the mosque from the northeast. (Photo: Tamara Sears)

8.11. Fortress (*gadhi*), Kadwaha, tenth-fifteenth century. Digital rubbing of inscriptions on the windowsill of the third-storey room in the monastery. (Photo and drawing: Tamara Sears)

8.12. Fortress (*gadhi*), Kadwaha, tenth-fifteenth century. View of the ruined mosque and temple from the south. (Photo: Tamara Sears)

8.13. Fortress (*gadhi*), Kadwaha, tenth-fifteenth century. View of the recently excavated stepwell. (Photo: Tamara Sears)

8.14. View of the northern town gate, Kadwaha. (Photo: Tamara Sears)

8.15. Toteshvara Mahadeva Temple, Kadwaha, eleventh century. View of an inscription on the pedestal of the icon within the sanctum, *c.* 1523–24. (Photo: Tamara Sears)

8.16. Toteshvara Mahadeva Temple, Kadwaha, eleventh century. View of the landscape from the interior of the temple. (Photo: Tamara Sears)

9.1. Presidential Palace Museum, Kigali. View from the southeast. Documented in 2014. (Photo: Annalisa Bolin)

10.1. Minoru Yamasaki & Associates with Emery Roth & Sons, architects; Leslie Robertson, engineer. World Trade Center, New York City, 1962–77. Aerial view from southwest. (Photo: Courtesy of The Port Authority of New York and New Jersey)

10.2. Little Syria, New York City, *c.* 1890–1940, postcard map with title of the Arab American Museum's 2012 exhibit on the community. The oval shows the site of World Trade Center, between Fulton (north), Liberty (south), Greenwich (east), and

West (west) streets. (Photo: Arab American National Museum; graphic addition: Joseph Siry)

10.3. "Relics of Old New York. At Battery Place. Homes of Greeks and Syrians," *c.* 1930. (Photo: Museum of the City of New York, X2010.12.13)

10.4. Daniel Libeskind, Studio Libeskind, concept sketches for Memory Foundations, Ground Zero master plan, New York City, 2002. (Photo: © Daniel Libeskind, courtesy of Studio Libeskind)

10.5. Daniel Libeskind, Studio Libeskind, winning design, Ground Zero master plan, New York City, December 2002. (Photo: © Joe Poddle, courtesy of Studio Libeskind)

10.6. Ground Zero, master plan revised, showing (left to right): David Childs, and Skidmore, Owings, and Merrill, 1 World Trade Center (formerly Freedom Tower); Bjarke Ingels, BIG, 2 World Trade Center; Sir Richard Rogers, 3 World Trade Center; and Fumihiko Maki, 4 World Trade Center. (Photo: © DBOX, courtesy of Studio Libeskind)

10.7. Michael Arad and Peter Walker, *Reflecting Absence*, Ground Zero Memorial, designed and built 2004–11. View towards northeast showing footprints of North Tower (left) and South Tower (right), and (top center) Snøhetta Architects, National September 11 Memorial & Museum, entrance pavilion, opened 2014. (Photo: Jin Lee, 9/11 Memorial)

10.8. Davis, Brody, Bond, architects; National September 11 Memorial & Museum, 2011–14. Floor plans of (left) exhibition hall at bedrock level showing PATH train tracks within the footprint area of the South Tower and (right) concourse level. (Photo: 9/11 Memorial Museum, Davis Brody Bond, LLP)

10.9. Arad and Walker, Ground Zero Memorial, showing names of victims in "meaningful adjacency." (Photo: Jin Lee, 9/11 Memorial)

10.10. Snøhetta Architects, National September 11 Memorial & Museum, entrance pavilion with "tridents" salvaged from World Trade Center. (Photo: Jin Lee, 9/11 Memorial)

10.11. World Trade Center, view of exterior with steel "tridents" clad in aluminum alloy. (Photo: Courtesy of The Port Authority of New York and New Jersey)

10.12. Davis Brody Bond, architects, National September 11 Memorial & Museum, 2011–14. Interior showing cantilevered mezzanine (upper center) with views of the reconstructed underground west wall of the North Tower, World Trade Center, clad in foamed aluminum (left), the Last Column with initials of worker teams (center), and a segment of the original west Slurry Wall, recessed between new sections of concrete slurry wall with new steel ties (right). (Photo: Jin Lee, 9/11 Memorial)

Contributors

Nadja Aksamija is Associate Professor of Art History at Wesleyan University. Her primary research interests revolve around villa architecture, literature, and ideology during the Counter Reformation, but she has also worked on late-cinquecento emblem books, painted sacred landscapes, landscapes of the *sacri monti*, and cartography, as well as on modern restorations of Renaissance architectural monuments in Venice and Bologna. She has recently co-authored a monograph on the castle of San Martino in Soverzano and co-edited a volume on Gregory XIII's Sala Bologna in the Vatican. She is currently completing a monograph on landscape and reform in the era of Gabriele Paleotti, as well as working on a project on Alfonso Rubbiani and the "discovery" of quattrocento architecture in post-unification Italy. Her work has been supported by numerous grants and fellowships, such as the Getty Postdoctoral Fellowship, the Kress Foundation Collaborative Grant, and the Robert Lehman Fellowship at Harvard's Villa I Tatti in Florence. She received her Ph.D. from Princeton University in 2004.

Annalisa Bolin is a Ph.D. candidate in the Anthropology Department at Stanford University, based at Stanford Archaeology Center. Her research focuses on the Rwandan state's uses of cultural and genocide heritage to build a new post-genocide nation and transform Rwanda's place in the international dynamics of power. Her fieldwork in Rwanda was supported by a Fulbright study/research award, among others, and her dissertation by a Mellon Foundation Fellowship at the Stanford Humanities Center. She received an M.A. in Cultural Heritage Management from the University of York in 2011 and a B.A. in Archaeology and French Studies from Wesleyan University in 2008.

Sheila Bonde is Professor of History of Art and Architecture and Professor of Archaeology at Brown University where she has taught since 1984. She received her B.A. from Cornell University and her M.A. and Ph.D. from Harvard University. She is an active archaeologist, and co-founder and co-director of MonArch (the Wesleyan-Brown Monastic Archaeology Project). That project is presently engaged with the abbeys of Saint-Jean-des-Vignes, Soissons; Notre-Dame d'Ourscamp; the Charterhouse of Bourgfontaine; and the abbey of the Sainte-Trinité de Tiron. Professor Bonde's published work includes a book on fortified churches in Languedoc, co-authored work on Saint-Jean-des-Vignes, and an edited volume on the representation of the past. Her recent work engages with architectural reuse in the Middle Ages, medieval soundscapes, and the architecture of monastic reform. Two forthcoming publications include a co-authored volume on Saint-Jean-des-Vignes and a co-edited volume on digital approaches to medieval studies.

Erik Gustafson received his Ph.D. from the Institute of Fine Arts, New York University in 2012 and his B.A. in Art History from Wesleyan University in 2001. He is Visiting Assistant Professor of Art History at Washington & Lee University. He held a Rome Prize fellowship at the American Academy in Rome from 2007 to 2009. An architectural historian of medieval and Renaissance Europe and the Mediterranean, he is interested in the engagement of historical viewers with architectural space, in the phenomenology of historical religious experience, and in how the constant dialogue between traditions of the past and the needs of the present produced architectural culture. His forthcoming articles examine Franciscan architecture as charismatic space, medieval urbanism and the mendicant orders, and the methodology of Gothic architectural history. He is completing a monograph entitled *Building Franciscanism: Space, Tradition, and Devotion in Medieval Tuscany*.

Clark Maines is Professor of Art History and Archaeology and Kenan Professor of the Humanities at Wesleyan University. His research combines approaches of archaeology, history, and architectural history to the study of medieval and early modern monasticism in Europe. He received his B.A. from Bucknell University and his M.A. and Ph.D. from the Pennsylvania State University. He is co-founder and co-director of MonArch, the Wesleyan-Brown Monastic Archaeology Project that is presently engaged with the abbeys of Saint-Jean-des-Vignes, Notre-Dame d'Ourscamp, the Charterhouse of Bourgfontaine, and the abbey of the Sainte-Trinité de Tiron. He has served as editor of the journal *Gesta* from 2007 to 2009 and has published more than sixty articles, books, and edited volumes, including volumes on the priory of Saint-Loup-de-Naud, the abbey of Saint-Jean-des-Vignes. His recent work includes studies on medieval water management, monastic domain development, and early modern iconoclasm.

Sarah Newman is Assistant Professor of Anthropology at James Madison University. She received her B.A. from Yale University, and her M.A. and Ph.D. from Brown University. Her primary area of research and teaching is Mesoamerican archaeology, with a focus on the ancient Maya. Her work examines changing notions of "waste" and the relationships between humans and animals in Mesoamerica. She has conducted archaeological and zooarchaeological research in Central America since 2006, with a current field project at the site of Topoxté, Guatemala, and is a co-author of *Temple of the Night Sun: A Royal Tomb at El Diablo* (Precolumbia Mesoweb Press, 2015). Her work has been supported by several grants and fellowships, including the U.S. Department of State Fulbright Program, the National Science Foundation, the Dolores Zohrab Liebmann Foundation, the John Carter Brown Library, and, most recently, a Richard Carley Hunt Fellowship from the Wenner-Gren Foundation to support her book, *Talking Trash: Refuse and Ritual in Maya Archaeology*.

Christopher Parslow has been a Professor in the Department of Classical Studies at Wesleyan University since 1991. He holds a Ph.D. in Classical Studies from Duke University and was a Rome Prize Fellow at the American Academy in Rome. His research and teaching is in Roman archaeology, with a specialization in Pompeii. His archival work has focused on the history of the early excavations of the cities buried by the eruption of Vesuvius. His first book, *Rediscovering Antiquity: Karl Weber and the Excavations of Herculaneum, Pompeii and Stabiae* (Cambridge University Press, 1994), was a biography of the Swiss military engineer who had sought to establish a more scientific approach to the earliest excavations and a more context-based method of publishing the finds. His fieldwork in Pompeii, including five seasons of excavations, has concentrated on the ruins of the *Praedia* (properties) of Julia Felix, a complex of baths, shops, and semi-public recreation spaces.

Tamara Sears is Associate Professor of Art History at Rutgers University. Her research focuses on the art and architectural history of South Asia, with a particular focus on the Indian subcontinent. Her first book, *Worldly Gurus and Spiritual Kings: Architecture and Asceticism in Medieval India* (Yale University Press, 2014), received the PROSE award in Architecture and Urban Planning. Her essays have appeared in numerous volumes and journals, including *The Art Bulletin*, *Ars Orientalis*, and *Archives of Asian Art*. She has held faculty positions at Florida State, NYU, and Yale, and she has received grants and fellowships from Fulbright, the J. Paul Getty Foundation, the Society of Architectural Historians, the National Humanities Center, Dumbarton Oaks, and the Clark Art Institute. She is currently working on a new book that examines the relationships between architecture, environmental history, and travel on local, regional, and global scales. She received her B.A. from Wesleyan University in 1996 and Ph.D. from the University of Pennsylvania in 2004.

Joseph Siry is Professor of Art History and Kenan Professor of the Humanities at Wesleyan University, where he won a Binswanger Award for Teaching Excellence in 1994. His books are *Carson Pirie Scott: Louis Sullivan and the Chicago Department Store* (1988); *Unity Temple: Frank Lloyd Wright and Architecture for Liberal Religion* (1996); *The Chicago Auditorium Building: Adler and Sullivan's Architecture and the City* (2002), which won the Society of Architectural Historians' 2003 Alice Davis Hitchcock Award for the most outstanding book by a North American scholar; and *Beth Sholom Synagogue: Frank Lloyd Wright and Modern Religious Architecture* (2012), a finalist for a 2013 National Jewish Book Award. He received the Frank Lloyd Wright Building Conservancy's 2015 Wright Spirit Award for his scholarship. His work was supported by the National Endowment for the Humanities, and the Mellon, Getty, and Graham foundations. He is currently writing a book on air conditioning in American architecture.

Phillip Wagoner is Professor of Art History and Archaeology at Wesleyan University. His research focuses on the cultural history of the Deccan region of South India, primarily in the late medieval and early modern periods. In particular, he is intrigued by historical interactions between the region's established Indic culture and the Persianate culture that arrived when the Delhi Sultanate annexed the region. He has been affiliated with the Vijayanagara research project since 1987, which has led to two published books and numerous articles on topics relating to Vijayanagara. His most recent book, co-authored with Richard M. Eaton, is *Power, Memory, Architecture: Contested Sites on India's Deccan Plateau, 1300–1600* (Oxford University Press, 2014), which won the American Historical Association's John F. Richards Prize and the Association for Asian Studies' Ananda K. Coomaraswamy Prize.